INTRODUCTION

My friend Milt Krims, a World War II bomber pilot, woke up and saw a Japanese soldier in his tent. Even in the dark, Krims could make out the knife in the enemy's hand.

Captain Krims had been going to bed every night with a .45 automatic under the edge of his sleeping bag. He whipped out the .45 and fired eight shots into the face of the Japanese. The enemy fell over dead. Krim studiously looked away from the mess his bullets had made, but had to go outside and be sick anyway.

This wasn't exactly a routine form of killing for a pilot trained to attack at long range, with thousands of feet of air between him and the enemy—but then, Krims was in the Pacific Theater of Operations, where anything could happen, and frequently did.

The War With Japan was bizarre, spectacular, dramatic. Here in the giant amphitheater of the world's largest ocean the greatest sea battles of history were waged—battleships, cruisers, destroyers and PTs locked in night actions, fleets of aircraft carriers fighting to the death in daylight, Japanese kamikazes riding baka bombs on one-way assaults on American ships. Here were man-to-man struggles in the jungle hells of the Pacific islands, where the enemy concealed himself with the craft of the primeval beast, signaled his fellows with bird calls, sniped from trees, and fought to his death in millions of caves from Guadalcanal to Okinawa.

In the following collection of articles about the Pacific-Asian war, from the sinking of the two prize warships of the Royal Navy by skillful Japanese bombers off the coast of Southeast Asia to the searing explosion of the world's first nuclear bomb at Hiroshima, we find the vast sweep of The War With Japan.

Here are many articles done by military men—like Commander E. A. Feldt of the Australian Navy as he tells of the Coastwatchers, our agents (usually former coconut plantation managers) who sent precise radio reports from behind Japanese lines, promptly reporting enemy moves on land, sea and air under the Japs' very noses. Here also are the professional correspondents like Cecil Brown with his sharp eye for detail and his gift for vivid phrase, describing the death of the British behemoths *Prince of Wales* and *Repulse*.

Here are the writings of two eminent American war historians, S. L. A. "Slam" Marshall, telling of the fierce amphibious conquest of Kwajalein atoll, midway in the Pacific and midway, too, in the Pacific struggle; and Admiral Samuel Eliot Morison, the U. S. Navy's foremost chronicler, describing Japan's kamikaze assault, near the war's end: *The Gallant Fight of the Radar Pickets*.

Present is the gripping story of a vital Southwest Pacific mission to Balikpapan, *Long Strike in the Pacific*, told with a master narrator's touch by Elliot Arnold, one of America's noted novelists, working with Donald Hough. And we find the famed account of the Marine assault on Peleliu, one of the bloodiest actions in Corps history, written by George P. Hunt, who was then a lowly company commander in the thick of the fighting.

Colonel Harold Rigelman of General MacArthur's command presents a section of the desperate campaign among the Japanese caves, called *The Caves of Biak*. And there is, from among the ringing sea-chanteys of the naval actions, the torpedoing of the U. S. heavy cruiser, the *Indianapolis*, told with all the painstaking detail of a detective's report on a crime of violence, by an American master of the form, Richard F. Newcomb.

Here also is the fascinating account of the ultra-secret preparation and delivery of the first nuclear bomb, *The Great White Light*, written by an expert on Air Force history, Lieut. Col. Gene Gurney. And against the background of the continent of Asia, Major John Masters, famed for his stories of India, tells a fascinating story of a daring raid behind Japanese lines in *Blackpool Block*; the brilliant British field marshal Sir William Slim writes of the Burma campaign; Kenneth Attiwill tells of *The Fall of Singapore*; and a physician, Dr. Stanley Pavillard, relates the bitter story of the struggle for survival in a Japanese prison camp.

I bid you *bon voyage* on your armchair trip back into the world's most spectacular war.

—Richard Tregaskis
Honolulu, Hawaii
April 10, 1962

COMBAT
THE WAR WITH JAPAN

Edited by DON CONGDON

Introduction by Richard Tregaskis

an original volume

Published by
DELL PUBLISHING CO., INC.
750 Third Avenue
New York 17, New York
Copyright © 1962 by Don Congdon
Dell First Edition ® TM 641409, Dell Publishing Co., Inc.

First printing—September, 1962   Fourth printing—September, 1965
Second printing—December, 1962   Fifth printing—March, 1967
Third printing—October, 1964   Sixth printing—November, 1969
Printed in U.S.A.

Contents

Lightning War in the Far East 7

TRAGEDY IN THE CHINA SEA 9
    by Cecil Brown

Disaster in Malaya 43

THE FALL OF SINGAPORE 46
    by Kenneth Attiwill

Survival Under the Jap 68

BAMBOO DOCTOR 70
    by Dr. Stanley Pavillard

The Heroic Island 92

WAKE ISLAND COMMAND 94
    by Commander W. Scott Cunningham

The Coastwatchers 124

FERDINAND ON HOLLANDIA 127
    by Commander E. A. Feldt

The Secret War 137

RAID ON SINGAPORE 138
    by Brian Connell

Operation Flintlock 171

ACTION AT THE PIGPEN 173
    by Lt. Col. S. L. A. Marshall

MacArthur in the Southwest Pacific 195

THE CAVES OF BIAK 199
    by Colonel Harold Riegelman

Long Strike in the Pacific 217

RAID OF BALIKPAPAN 218
by Captain Elliott Arnold
and Captain Donald Hough

Peleliu 234

CORAL COMES HIGH 236
by Captain George P. Hunt

Burma and the Ledo Road 256

THE NORTHERN FRONT IN BURMA 258
by Field Marshal the Viscount Slim

Behind the Japanese Lines 278

BLACKPOOL BLOCK 279
by Major John Masters

Last Stop Before Japan 309

OKINAWA 311
by Major Frank Hough

Kamikaze 332

THE GALLANT FIGHT OF THE RADAR PICKETS 333
by Admiral S. E. Morison

The Indianapolis 341

ABANDON SHIP 342
by Richard F. Newcomb

Potsdam to Hiroshima 367

THE GREAT WHITE LIGHT 368
by Major Gene Gurney

The Emperor's Role 382

Lightning War in the Far East

In the opening pages of the companion volume *Combat: Pacific Theater* we told the story of the Japanese surprise attack on Pearl Harbor, the success of which was due largely to the vulnerability of U.S. defense.

The British and Dutch had plenty of warning in Asia and the Southwest Pacific, but were just as vulnerable. The British had been at war with Germany for over two years and Italy for a year and a half and were fully mobilized, but the British commanders grossly underestimated the fighting capabilities of the Japanese. For example, they persuaded themselves in face of evidence to the contrary from the war in China that their outdated planes were a match for the Japanese Zero. Indeed, the Far East commanders paid little attention to the lesson resulting from the Atlantic and Mediterranean naval battles: that battleships and heavy cruisers were easy prey to attacks from the air. The *Prince of Wales* and *Repulse* were permitted to sally out in the China Sea without air cover. Worst of all, the British forces fighting on a world front were spread too thin. They were on the offensive in the African desert, raiding the coast of Europe, defending huge shipping convoys from North America, and picketing the Atlantic Ocean against the threat of German submarines and pocket battleships.

Toward the end of summer, 1941, Prime Minister Churchill was urged to build up British naval strength in the Far East. He dispatched as "the first installment" of the Far Eastern Fleet, the *Prince of Wales*, *Repulse* and four destroyers. The aircraft carrier *Indomitable* was to provide air cover but she had to be left behind for repairs, having run aground. Churchill's "general naval policy was to build up under the remote cover of the main American Fleet in the Pacific a British Eastern Fleet based in Singapore, which by the spring of 1942 would comprise seven capital ships of various quality, one first-class aircraft carrier, ten cruisers and 24 destroyers." *

*Winston Churchill, *The Grand Alliance*, pp. 589-590. Church-

The Japanese were well aware of the weaknesses of the Allies. Furthermore, they were daring and as effective as an aggressor can be who is sure of his objectives. They had waged successful war in China since 1937; now in December 1941 they occupied most of the Chinese coast and the offshore islands. As soon as the Germans occupied France and the Netherlands in Europe, the French Vichy government permitted the Japs to build airfields in Indo-China, while the Dutch East Indies were now sitting ducks. From Indo-China it was easy for the Japs to infiltrate across the border to Siam* and there was only token resistance when they invaded on December 8.

Japan's next move was south along the Malay Peninsula to assault Singapore, the British fortress of the Far East, through the back door.

The British had the 9th and 11th British-Indian divisions for the defense of Malaya which, together with some Malayan and Australian brigades, were expected to stand off the Japanese long enough for reinforcements to arrive from India and the Near East. In addition there was a well-worked-out defense plan to thwart possible invasion. On December 8, the Japanese landed forces at Singora and Patani on the southern coast of Siam, the very area where the British expected them, and on December 10th at Kota Bharu on the coast of northern Malaya. Unfortunately, the British command acted so sluggishly that the defense plan was never initiated.

News of the landings reached Singapore on the 8th, 2:30 a.m. That evening Force Z, made up of the *Prince of Wales, Repulse* and four destroyers set sail from Singapore to attack Jap troopships and supporting naval vessels in the Singora area. Admiral Tom Phillips hoped to surprise the landing forces, shoot them up fast and withdraw quickly before the Japs could launch bombing and torpedo attacks from their airfields in Indo-China. He requested fighter cover for the Singora ac-

---

ill says that he and the British cabinet discussed ordering the *Prince of Wales* and *Repulse* out of Singapore "to take refuge in the islands," and/or to join the already crippled American fleet. Bernard Ash in his recently published *Someone Had Blundered* (Doubleday) labels this wishful thinking on Churchill's part, asking how the ships could possibly be maintained among the islands, and further, how they would get to Pearl Harbor through 6,000 miles of Jap-controlled waters.

*Now Thailand.

tion but was told it might not be forthcoming. Indeed, before he was at sea very long, he was signaled on December 9, that there could be no fighter cover. The Japanese had swept the platter clean in northern Malaya.

"The total number of British aircraft based on airfields in northern Malaya was 110. At the end of the first day only 50 were fit for operations. The Japanese had decided superiority with 530 aircraft. . . . The destruction was so swift that when the Commanders-in-Chief of Far East and Eastern Fleet signaled London on December 9 asking urgently for two squadrons of long range bombers and two squadrons of night fighters to maintain British air superiority, British air superiority had already been lost. Air Command were forced to pull back aircraft from five airfields so that by the evening of the 9th—about 36 hours after fighting began—the combined British bomber and fighter force in northern Malaya contained only ten serviceable aircraft. Within another 24 hours—by December 10—all the remaining fighters and most of the remaining bombers had been withdrawn from Malaya into Singapore island to protect the Naval Base." [*]

British Force Z was going into battle naked of air cover. And while the *Prince of Wales* had a full complement of anti-aircraft guns; the *Repulse* was undergunned in this respect.

Cecil Brown, CBS war correspondent then stationed in Singapore, was invited to go along on the ill-fated strike and his eyewitness report follows.

TRAGEDY IN THE CHINA SEA

by Cecil Brown

We went aboard the *Repulse* at 5:15 and almost at once we began moving out . . . at half speed. It was a beautiful evening, that twilight of Monday, December 8th. The bright-red sunset silhouetted the palms on the shore.

[*]Kenneth Attiwell, *Fortress*, p. 35. Doubleday & Co.

9

Within minutes the *Prince of Wales* drew up alongside and passed us. The crews of each ship stood at attention. Captain William Tennant on our bridge waved his white hat. Two men standing on the bridge of the *Prince of Wales* waved their hats. They were Admiral Tom Phillips and Captain Leach.

Lieutenant Halton of the Royal Marines took us on a tour of all parts of the ship. We went up and down masts, into various control towers, into turrets of the 15-inch guns, down into the engine room, and to the top of the mainmast.

When we finished the tour of the ship we went to the officers' mess and were introduced to Commander Denby, the executive officer, a middle-aged but boyishly husky man who was tough and amiable and who introduced us to each of the officers in the wardroom. At that time there must have been fifteen. It was terrifically hot and we were all soaked in perspiration. By then the *Repulse* and the *Prince of Wales* and four destroyers were out in the South China Sea, moving northeast.

We sat around almost all evening discussing rumors. No one actually knew what was going on. We had dinner and then heard BBC at 8:30. The news wasn't good.

The Japs are in possession of South Thailand. Thai resistance has ceased temporarily. Japanese planes bombed Bangkok.

Tuesday, December 9th:
        Gal [1] and I showed up at our action stations on the flag deck at 5:15. We took with us our gas masks, helmets and our anti-flash equipment and lifebelts. The anti-flash equipment is simply a white cloth hood that covers the head and shoulders and leaves exposed only the nose, eyes and mouth. You are supposed to wear it during action to prevent burns from shells bursting on deck. It isn't burns that bother me—it's shrapnel.

Our action station is on the flag deck which is underneath the bridge and is the least protected part of the ship.

---

[1] O. D. Gallagher, war correspondent.—Ed. note.

The flag deck lieutenant is a tough, wiry officer of about twenty-four or twenty-five.

"Is this your action station?" he asked.

"Yes, it is," we said.

"Well, there is one thing about this place. In every action some men on the flag deck get killed."

"That's encouraging," we said.

At about 6:00 a.m. it began to lighten and we found we were about four miles off shore. The *Prince of Wales* was four cable lengths in front. The destroyers flanked us about a mile away. Men all over the ship were sitting and standing by their guns.

At 6:20 an aircraft was reported off the starboard beam, but it kept far away. It might have been a Japanese reconnaissance plane. As dawn came up, lifting the blackness, I felt terribly exposed. One of our catapult aircraft, a Walrus, was put on the track but didn't take off. Gallagher and I were peering into the haze of dawn to see what we could find. He motioned at something.

"You can't tell," he said sardonically, "whether that's an island or five Japanese battleships, ten cruisers, and three aircraft carriers."

"If it's the Japanese fleet," I said, "we won't be interested very long."

The radio is bringing us some news of the attack on Pearl Harbor. It's shocking, but the reaction of the British officers shows how decent these men are. They are amazed by the losses to the American Navy and the heavy attacks on Hawaii, but the general view is:

"Well, the Japanese had the initial advantage of attack. It will take a while to get adjusted."

At 9:45 Lieutenant Halton took us up to the bridge to see Captain Tennant. We hadn't met him before. Halton took me into the captain's sea cabin. This was a room about twelve feet long and five feet wide with glass all across the front. Halton introduced me, and the captain said: "I am very glad to have an American reporter on board."

He gripped my hand hard.

Captain Tennant was dressed in shorts and a shirt with no insignia on the shoulder. His hat was on the shelf. He seemed about fifty years old, with an open, pleasant face, pinkish, smooth skin with wrinkles around the eyes. On the shelf there was a vase of orchids and a picture of his wife.

As he asked me what part of America I came from he paced up and down the cabin, back and forth, peering out of a porthole on each side and the window in front.

"I hope you will excuse me if I move around while I am talking," he said. "The Japs are probably bringing their convoys down over that route. If we are spotted by their aircraft today the Japanese convoy may turn back and they will send two or three battleships and so forth down to meet us."

Captain Tennant was very gay, pleasant, smiling and courteous and seemed confident that we would encounter action.

We told the captain we wondered if the flag deck was the best place to see action.

"Where would you like to be?"

We said we thought we could see more from the after-mast control tower.

"And anyway," I added, "there is a lot of armor protection up there that I would kinda like to have around me."

"Well," the captain said, "I thought the flag deck was better. You can run from one side to the other and watch things from both sides. We'll try that, and if you are not satisfied, perhaps we can put you somewhere else."

"Would you give us an outline of the action after it is over?" Gallagher asked.

"Yes," the captain smiled. "We hope to get some action, and if so I will try to explain it."

It is raining today and it is pretty miserable out. The main 15-inch guns and the secondary armament 4-inch guns are in second degree of readiness. Damage control and supply are at action stations.

At 12:45 a plane was spotted—a tiny dot above the horizon. There was some uncertainty whether it was a Japanese flying boat or a Catalina. Later it was verified as a Catalina and finally it drew closer.

While I was up on the flag deck this afternoon the captain came down and said, "We've a couple of knock-kneed destroyers with us. We've got to oil them. We're going to find a few of your destroyers when we get back to Singapore."

This is the first word that American ships are now operating from Singapore Naval Base.

At 1:20 p.m. a message was blinked from the *Wales* to us. It said: "The Japanese have made an air attack on Kota Bharu which was not followed by landings. Major landing ninety miles north of Singapore. Little is known of enemy naval forces in vicinity. It is believed that *Kongo* is only capital ship likely to be met. There are reported three Japanese heavy cruisers and a number of destroyers likely to be met."

I said to the flag deck officer: "A capital ship, three cruisers and some destroyers? That's the fleet we're going to face, eh? Lieutenant, how about calling a taxi to take me back to Singapore?"

He laughed heartily. "Oh, but they are Japanese. There's nothing to worry about."

Another message just came from the *Wales* giving further details: "An *Akaga*-type, *Kako*-type and *Zintu*-type cruiser have been reported."

I checked up on those. One first-class heavy cruiser and two second-class cruisers.

The *Repulse* has never been in action, the men told me. The closest was off Norway when three German planes dropped eighteen bombs, some pretty close, but the *Repulse* didn't fire a shot.

A notice has just been posted: "All officers and ratings from dawn tomorrow are to be at action stations and are to wear clothing to resist burns from flashes of exploding bombs and shells."

Admiral Tom Phillips, as Commander-in-Chief, just sent this message to the *Repulse* and to the four destroyers:

"The enemy has made several landings on the north coast of Malaya and has made local progress. Our Army is not large and it is hard-pressed in places. Our air forces have had to destroy or abandon one or more airfields.

"Meanwhile, fast transports lie off the coast. This is our opportunity before the enemy can establish itself. We have made a wide circuit to avoid air reconnaissance and hope to surprise the enemy shortly after sunrise tomorrow, Wednesday. We may have the luck to try our mettle against some Japanese cruisers or some destroyers in the Gulf of Siam. We are sure to get some useful practice with high-angle armament, but whatever we meet I want to finish quickly and so get well clear to the eastward before the Japanese can mass too formidable a scale of air attack against us. So, shoot to sink."

I was up on the flag deck at 5:20 this afternoon. For the first time there is a break in the thick, black clouds. Far off in the distance—about four or five miles away, just a speck in the sky—an aircraft was sighted. The word came from a spotter in the defense control tower in the after-mast. The word ran through the ship like fire. I watched the aircraft circling, hardly moving.

"It's a Jap, all right," a lieutenant said as he was thumbing through a book of silhouettes of Japanese aircraft. "That means we have been reported to the enemy."

I saw a number of the gunners and other men rubbing their heads and doing dog steps all over the deck. The signal deck yeoman snorted: "Look at them—all this fuss over one aircraft!"

The *Prince of Wales* has just sent us a signal that a formation of aircraft has been reported. All gun crews hop to their stations, eager to get going. Everyone is very brisk and eager-eyed. That reconnaissance aircraft is still four or five miles away and staying well out of range. What a break that is! Just a few minutes ago there was the first gap in the overcast sky in the entire day and as luck would have it we had to be spotted just at that moment.

The lieutenant commander came by on the flag deck and said to me: "I'm afraid he has spotted us and he may go away before we can get a crack at him."

The general opinion of the flag deck is that the reconnaissance aircraft is a Nakajima Naka 93 seaplane.

I have just been told that in addition to the battleship *Kongo* and the three cruisers and a number of destroyers there are many troopships with the warships. Someone said that there are about thirty. Evidently British reconnaissance has spotted them.

Denby said: "The Admiral has delayed up here in order to get at the *Kongo*. There would be a good moral effect to sinking her."

One of our destroyers is going back tonight. It's the *Tenedos,* an antiquated thing, which is running out of oil.

17:58—Captain Tennant piped over the loudspeaker: "We are now being shadowed by enemy aircraft. We are going to revert to third-degree readiness, but we must be prepared to repel aircraft at a moment's notice."

The gun crews are standing down now.

18:30—We are at dinner listening to the BBC. Heavy fighting is going on in Malaya. The fighting is still confused, but BBC says reinforcements should reach there during the day.

BBC says there is no truth in the Japanese reports that an attack was made on Singapore. The Japs have entered Bangkok.

We sat around in the wardroom. There must have been twelve or fifteen officers discussing the news.

"Those Japs are bloody fools," one of them said. "All these pinpricks at widely separated points is stupid strategy. The Japs should have sent over three hundred planes over Singapore, not eleven."

"Bloody fools!" another snorted.

"Those Japs can't fly," one of the officers said. "They can't see at night and they're not well trained."

"They have rather good ships," one of the officers remarked, "but they can't shoot."

I listened to these remarks about the enemy for some time and then remarked to the officers in the wardroom: "You British are extraordinary people. You always underestimate the enemy. You did it time and again, in Norway and France, in Greece, in Crete. I think it's a mistake to underestimate the enemy. It seems to me the best thing is to figure the enemy is twice as good as you are and twice as smart, and then you make preparations in advance."

There was a moment of shocked silence in the wardroom at this criticism and then someone said in a joking manner to cover up the tension: "Oh, but really, the Japanese are not very good."

Another officer remarked: "Yes, I do think it's wrong to underestimate the enemy."

"Well, there is always the danger certainly," I added, "of underestimating the enemy to the point where you are overconfident."

A number of them chimed in, each in his own way. "We are not overconfident; we just don't think the enemy is much good. They could not beat China for five years and now look what they are doing out here, jumping all over the map instead of meeting at one or two places. They cannot be very smart to be doing that."

21:05—We're sitting in the wardroom again and the voice on the loudspeaker has just said: "Stand by for Captain to speak to you."

In an instant Captain Tennant's cool, even voice came through. "A signal has just been received from the Commander-in-Chief who very much regrets to announce having to abandon the operation. We were shadowed by three planes. We were spotted after dodging them all day. Their troop convoy will now have dispersed. It would be very obvious that if we continued, enemy air concentration would be awaiting us and it would be unwise to continue.

"I know that you all share with us the disappointment in not engaging the enemy at this time, but I am sure that you will agree with the C-in-C's judgment. We are, therefore, going back to Singapore."

In the wardroom there were cries and groans of disappointment and even bitterness. I immediately dashed out of the wardroom into the quarters of the ratings to check their reactions. I went into one sailor's mess and the men were sitting around the long tables. Some of the men had tears in their eyes—two a half years in the war and never a chance to engage an enemy.

"How do you fellows feel about that?"

The remarks I got were: "This always happens to the *Repulse.*"

"It's a bloody shyme."

"We're just an unlucky ship."

Back in the wardroom I stood in the doorway surveying the long faces of the officers sitting in chairs and on divans in front of the fireplace and on the railing around the edge of the fireplace in utter dejection.

Commander Denby and I found a place on a divan and I asked him to explain the type of operation we expected to encounter.

"The essential element of this tip-and-run raid is surprise, and we lost that when that fellow spotted us this afternoon. It amounts to this: we are up against the whole of the Japanese air force with no aircraft protection and no destroyer screen. Well, maybe not the whole Jap force, but at least 50 percent of it."

I slipped up at that moment in not asking what he meant by "no destroyer screen" because we did have four destroyers with us, not much good, but at least destroyers, and one of them was scheduled to be sent back to Singapore that night.

Denby added, "We don't know the extent or nature of the Jap air force or what we would run into. It isn't worth risking two capital ships under the strategic circumstances."

The gunnery officer, a handsome polite Englishman called "Guns" said to me: "How do you feel about turning back?"

"Relieved—and disappointed."

"Well, that's a frank answer," he laughed.

Wednesday, December 10th:

04.00—Awakened after sleeping for about three hours in the steaming cabin. Came up on the flag deck. Pitch dark and I am thirsty as hell. Would like to have tea. No tea on the flag deck, so I went down to the wardroom, but there is no tea there either. It is hellishly hot, so I went back on the flag deck. I see nothing to write in this diary. I can't sleep, I can't rest, and I can't get any tea to drink.

05.05—The call to action stations just sounded. We are still going southward back to Singapore. Instead of hunting the enemy, we are trying to get away from them. Trying to avoid action.

It is a beautiful dawn, the sky is a bright gray, constantly getting lighter. Everyone is on the alert. We expect an attack at any moment.

06.05—The sun is coming up a bright orange.

06.15—"We are changing course," I said to the lieutenant. "Why are we changing course?"

Just as he was about to reply the answer came through the ship's loudspeaker.

"Men, we have just received a message saying the enemy is making a landing at Kuantan. We are going in." That means we intend to shoot up barges and any warships escorting them.

Kuantan is 150 miles north of Singapore on the east coast of Malaya. Gallagher and I remembered it very well as the place where we came down on the water-covered airdrome in our torpedo-carrying bombers. Instead of heading south for Singapore, we are bearing westward for the coast.

06.30—We are putting on cover-alls, anti-flash helmets, and battle helmets. Off to the beam the sky is streaked with gold. All the gun crews are at the action stations. Gallagher and I went down for breakfast of coffee, cold ham, bread and marmalade.

07.20—Back on the flag deck. We are pushing in toward shore very fast. The *Prince of Wales* is ahead; we follow; the destroyers are about a mile or a mile and a half on each side of us. We still have four of them. We can see the shore line and an island far ahead of us.

07.30—The *Wales* just catapulted one of her planes on a reconnaissance. One of the signalers on the flag deck said the reconnaissance pilot had been given instructions not to return to the ship, but to land on the water near the shore after reporting to us on what he found.

07.40—The *Wales* just elevated her 15-inch guns. What a beautiful sight they are! We are speeding in toward shore at about 24 knots. We were watching the Walrus from the *Wales* gain altitude and circle around us once and then disappear out of sight behind two islands shaped like chocolate drops.

"The enemy must be landing behind those mountains," someone on the flag deck said.

But the Walrus reappeared again as a tiny speck in the sky and then flew out of sight once more.

Some of the gunners are putting on asbestos gloves which come up to their elbows and a number of them are wearing goggles. They all look very efficient.

This is a beautiful sight in the brilliant sunlight. I just took a picture of the *Prince of Wales* on the starboard beam. What power there is out here today! The *Wales* is moving with such rhythm, pushing a white wave away from her bow on each side. Every now and then she slaps the water and the spray comes racing over her forward deck.

Our white ensign and hers, too, are rippling out in the breeze.

This is it, I think. This is the way you go in and knock hell out of the enemy.

07.48—We are about eight miles off shore. I can't see anything except green in the foreground, and the mountains rising in the background. I have just taken some more pictures of the gun crews beside their guns.

The communications loudspeaker just announced there is nothing in sight yet; we are going down along the beach.

07.50—The flag officer says, "I think we are too late now. Think they have all gone."

"I wonder," the flag-deck yeoman remarks, "if they have any naval units in there? I don't see a ship anywhere."

One of the youngsters on the flag deck said, "They might be around the bloody corner."

The lieutenant called to the flag-deck yeoman, who was taking signals on the blinker from the *Wales*.

"Is the *Prince of Wales* ready?"

"Yes, they are all ready."

Walrus again came into view.

"That ties it," said the flag-deck lieutenant. "If the Japs were around that Walrus would be down. He can't fight."

08.15—One of the destroyers, I think it was the *Ex-*

press, has just cut across the bow of the *Wales.* The *Express* is going closer into shore.

The land is quite close. I can see many islands.

The destroyer seems very impertinent going in there. I don't understand why we are waiting around here instead of going straight to Singapore as planned.

The reports are that Kuantan Airdrome is being too heavily bombed to get any report from there. I asked an officer what we expected to find in here, but he did not know. It seems quite obvious that the Japs made their landing and then got away.[2]

08.30—We are now going back northward and I understand that we have detached one of the destroyers to go back to Singapore. The one destroyer we sent into shore is going in as close as it can to see what it can find. We are going back northward away from Singapore—the *Prince of Wales,* the *Repulse,* and two destroyers—to see what we can find.

10.10—We steamed northward for about forty-five minutes not far off shore, but we didn't find anything, and we came back and picked up the third destroyer and are moving out to sea.

10.30—I am back on the flag deck again. Fifteen enemy aircraft are reported southeast, but are not in sight. All kinds of signals are being blinked back and forth between the *Wales* and the *Repulse* and between the *Wales* and the three destroyers.

10.40—We are sending off one of our Walrus reconnaissance planes. It goes off the track and just as it does I get a good photograph of it. It dips slightly then climbs up and swings northward. We still have one aircraft left.

10.45—One twin-engined Jap is reported shadowing us. It is the same type that bombed Singapore the first night of the war. It is type 96 Mitsubishi of the Naval Air Service.

The clouds have gone now, and the sky is a robin's-egg blue and the sun is bright yellow. Our ships plow through

---

[2] Actually, the rumor of a Japanese landing was entirely false and cost Force Z precious time.—Ed. Note.

pea-green water, white where the hulls cleave it. Ahead, the *Wales'* 15-inch guns jut, port and starboard, from turrets that bulge like muscles. They seem to quiver, eagerly. The destroyers that flank us are pygmy ships and seem ridiculous and impertinent in such powerful company.

11.04½—The signal yeoman beside me turns away from his spy glass and snaps, "Two masts, one funnel." He jerks it out to one of the signal ratings.

"Report to the bridge. Hop to it." He adds, "We have sighted a ship."

11.06½—The crew of the pom-poms just below us on the starboard is sitting around playing cards, ready for action in an instant. The men on the control towers on the mainmast and after-mast are peering into the sky for enemy aircraft. Men are at the 4-inch high-altitude guns. The men are getting keyed up at the prospect of action. You can almost feel the electricity all over the ship.

Standing on the flag deck, I look down over the decks of the *Repulse*. The guns seem no less eager for combat than the crews themselves.

We're told that Admiral Phillips on the *Wales* has just sent a signal to Singapore asking for aircraft protection.

I haven't had time to shave. I feel bleary and I am terrifically tired. I just took a picture of the gun crew playing cards and another picture of the *Prince of Wales*. Also snapped Gallagher with the flag-deck yeoman.

We are now zigzagging. I only see two destroyers at the moment. The *Prince of Wales* is four cable lengths ahead.

11.07—The communications loudspeaker announces: "Enemy aircraft approaching—action stations!"

I see them: 1-2-3-4-5-6-7-8-9. I would judge them about 12,000 feet, coming straight over the *Repulse*.

11.14—And here they come.

11.15—The guns of the *Prince of Wales* just let go. At the same instant I see the flame belching from the guns of the *Wales,* ours break into a chattering, ear-splitting roar. The nine Japanese aircraft are stretched out across the bright blue, cloudless sky like star sapphires of a necklace.

I've never been so close to so many guns firing at once. The roar of the pom-poms and the hard, sharp crack of the

4-inch high-altitude guns are deafening. The flashes are blinding and suddenly the smell of cordite is strong. I am standing on the port side of the flag deck, in the lee of an air funnel, eight feet from a battery of pom-poms.

I gape open-mouthed at those aircraft coming directly over us, flying so that they will pass from bow to stern over the *Repulse*. The sky is filled with black puffs from our ack-ack. They seem a discordant profanation of that beautiful sky. But the formation of Japanese planes, coming over one behind the other, is undisturbed.

Now they are directly overhead. For the first time I see the bombs coming down, materializing suddenly out of nothingness and streaming toward us like ever-enlarging tear drops. There's a magnetic, hypnotic, limb-freezing fascination in that sight.

It never occurs to me to try to duck or run. Open-mouthed and rooted, I watch the bombs getting larger and larger. Suddenly, ten yards from me, out in the water, a huge geyser springs out of the sea, and over the side, showering water over me and my camera.

I instinctively hunch over, sort of a semi-crouch, and at that same instant there is a dull thud. The whole ship shudders. Pieces of paint fall from the deck over the flag deck.

11.17—"Fire on the boat deck. Fire below!" That just came over the loudspeakers. There are fountains of water all around the ship. Some are near misses. Most of the bombs are hitting the water ten to thirty yards off the port side. Beautiful fountains of thick white at the base and then tapering up into fine spray.

That first bomb was a direct hit. Someone on the flag deck says: "Fire in Marines' mess and hangar."

That bomb struck the catapult deck, penetrated, exploded underneath. The bomb hit twenty yards astern of my position on the flag deck. A number of men (fifty) were killed.

11.21—We got one of the bombers! It is coming down fast, in black smoke. All our guns are still going. I am now near one of the multiple Vickers guns. It is firing 2,000

22

half-inch shells a minute. God what a racket! That bomber smacked into the water about a half mile away.

11.23—The high-level bombers are gone. We are still zigzagging like mad. The *Prince of Wales* seems to be firing, but I can't tell.

I run back to see the damage, but the bomb penetrated the deck armor and only smoke is coming up. Our aircraft is knocked off its track and a red-bearded New Zealand fleet-air-arm pilot is atop the crane attempting to lift the plane to drop it overside, since its gasoline constitutes a menace.

As I pass the gun crews they seem extraordinarily calm, replenishing ammunition, laughing. I hear someone say: "Let's get them all next time."

A gunner remarks: "Bloody good bombing for those blokes."

When I return to the flag deck I note a three-inch hole in the funnel from a bomb-splinter eighteen inches above the spot where I'd been standing. It's obvious my number isn't up yet.

Smoke is still coming up from the catapult deck and strenuous efforts are under way to control the fire. Four stokers come up to the flag deck to get first aid. They're blackened and scorched and their clothes are water-soaked.

They are very calm but wild-eyed and stunned, and their hands are shaking. The skin is hanging from their hands and faces like tissue paper. Someone says: "Make way for these men."

A stoker croaks tremulously, "Water, I want some water."

A glass is placed to the stoker's lips.

11.26—Just heard a report that there are a number of small fires below, owing to near misses.

The men are giving a big cheer. "They got another one," Gallagher shouts in my ear. I look over in the direction he points. There is a splash two or three miles astern. Some of the gunners are not so certain. A pom-pom gunner says: "Maybe he just jettisoned his bombs."

"Like hell he did," I tell him. "They dropped all the bombs they had on us."

11.40—The *Prince of Wales* seems to be hit. She's reduced her speed and signals, "We've a man overboard." A destroyer pushes up to her side. Standing less than 100 feet away, it's as incongruous as a baby running to protect its mamma. The flag-deck lieutenant says: "Those Japs are good, aren't they?"

I say, "Too good to suit me. How badly is the *Wales* hit?"

The lieutenant says, "I don't know. They haven't told us yet."

We are all lighting cigarettes, sucking deeply, and our exhalations are more like sighs. The pause is too brief.

11.45—Distant specks appear. Now they are identifiable. Nine torpedo-carrying bombers, circling four or five thousand yards away at about a half-mile altitude. Circling in a huge sweep, they are swooping lower. Now they are like moths around our flaming guns.

A bugle blows to stand by. A voice over the ship's communications roars: "Stand by for a barrage!"

Instantly every gun aboard the *Repulse* is stuttering and roaring and the whole ship vibrates and the pom-poms are spitting out empties furiously. But the clatter of empty shell cases on the deck is unheard in the slap-slap of A.A. guns, the crack-crack-crack of 4-inch guns. A voice beside me says, "Look at those yellow bastards come!" The *Repulse* is twisting and snaking violently to avoid torpedoes. My only weapons are a fountain pen, a notebook and a camera, so I sidle beside a multiple Vickers gun spewing 2,000 half-inch bullets every minute.

A few feet to my right an eight-barreled pom-pom is coughing incessantly and a half dozen feet away a 4-inch high altitude ack-ack is crashing, its barrel nearly horizontal instead of skyward, to meet the onrushing torpedo bombers.

A cooling liquid is gushing over the guns and the paint blisters on them are as big as tennis balls. Gunners are moving like a movie running too fast. Some are very young and eager and breathless with excitement, their faces streaked with sweat. The white cloth anti-flash helmets covering their heads, cheeks and shoulders are soaked and discolored. Some are wearing life belts and "Mae Wests."

A whole pom-pom swings this way and that, with its seated trigger man, feet braced, riding with it. That is a dizzy job.

The torpedo-carrying bombers are coming in. We are putting up a beautiful barrage, a wall of fire. But the bombers come on, in a long glide, from all angles, not simultaneously but alternately. Some come head-on, some astern and from all positions on both sides of the ship. They level out.

About 300 yards distant from the ship and 100 yards above the water, they drop their torpedoes.

The torpedoes seem small, dropping flat in the water, sending up splashes, then streaking toward us. Those bombers are so close you can almost see the color of the pilot's eyes. The bombers are machine-gunning our decks as they come in.

I've just seen three more torpedoes drop. Another plane just let go a torpedo. Then it banked sharply. The whole side of the bomber is exposed to us. Shells and tracers are ripping into it. It's fascinating to watch.

Tracer bullets from our guns are cross-stitching the sky, just above eye level, with long, thin white lines, slightly curved. For me this whole picture—orange flame belching from the 4-inchers, white tracers from pom-poms and Vickers guns, and gray airplanes astonishingly close, like butterflies pinned on blue cardboard—is a confusing, macabre game.

But this, I realize, is deadly business, too. Three gunners ten feet from me slump over with Japanese machine-gun bullets in them. It's difficult to comprehend sudden death. But they aren't the only casualties in this terrible moment. A torpedo bomber has just dropped a tin fish and banked without gaining altitude. It glides beautifully, parallel with the *Repulse* at a ten-degree angle, and still tracers are plowing into it. It doesn't seem to me the plane is going to crash, until an instant later I see that it isn't going to pull out and is still gliding toward the sea. It strikes the water and immediately bursts into flame. It burns fiercely, a twenty-foot circle of orange on a blue sea.

I run to the starboard side of the flag deck, where another torpedo bomber is coming in. It is difficult to judge distance, but I guess it's no more than 200 yards away when it swerves. I don't see the torpedo. And with good reason. There's a huge hole in the side of the plane. It's aflame, and instantly it seems to buckle. I got a beautiful picture of this one. As though stricken with a cramp, the bomber dives, shapeless, flaming, seaward. It's just a pillar of fire until it hits the water and spreads out into nothingness.

The men on the catapult deck are still trying to get the damaged aircraft over the side. Its gasoline makes it a fire hazard. That red-bearded New Zealand pilot is working atop the crane trying to heave the Walrus over the side. As the Jap torpedo bombers come in to drop their fish and machine-gun our decks, he is firing at them with his pistol.

There are nine bombers in that attack.

11.51½—Captain Tennant is sending a message to the *Wales:* "Have you sustained any damage?"

The answer comes back: "We are out of control. Steering gear is gone."

The decks of the *Repulse* are littered with empty shell cases. Upon the faces of the sailors there's a mixture of incredulity and a sort of sensuous pleasure, but I don't detect fear. There's an ecstatic happiness, but `strangely, I don't see anything approaching hate for the attackers. For the British this is a contest. This facial expression is interpreted by an officer. He turns to me and says: "Plucky blokes, those Japs. That was as beautiful an attack as ever I expect to see."

He'll never see another action. He's at the bottom of the South China Sea.

Our great concern is that the Japs are going to crash-dive the ship. I understand enough about naval warfare to know that the flag deck is a good spot on which to crash-dive. Suddenly it occurs to me how wonderful it would be to be back in Ohio. A voice says: "Here they come again."

12.01—Twelve torpedo bombers launch an attack at all

angles. One even launches a torpedo directly astern, which seems silly, since we are twisting rapidly. Planes coming from port and starboard are headed directly at the bow. I see the *Prince of Wales* being subjected to an attack also, and a bomber is coming toward us from a thousand yards, directly ahead.

I think, "Here comes a crash-dive." The smell of cordite is suffocating. My eyes ache with the blows of shell blasts.

Now I am standing in front of the smokestack. The view is good, and I have just taken some more pictures of the bombers coming in. I hear a rat-tat-tat and whine which seems higher and closer than the crash of other guns. I look around to see where it is coming from and then glance overhead. Two feet above my head, drilled in the smokestack, there is a line of bullet holes. I move away from that position. No sense in magnetizing any more Japanese machine-gun bullets.

It's the same as before—amazingly daring torpedo-bombers are targets for mere moments. They rush headlong into our almost solid wall of shells and bullets and are seemingly unaffected. The water is streaked with tracks of torpedoes. A sudden roar goes up on one side of the ship. It's another bomber down, but I didn't see it.

If it wasn't so awe-inspiring it would be routine: the way planes rush in, drop a tin fish, machine-gun the decks of the *Repulse* and roar away.

During this attack, as during the first wave of bombers, Captain Tennant on the bridge of the Repulse *directly above the flag deck is saying in the coolest, calmest possible voice: "Thirty degrees port. Thirty degrees starboard. Thirty degrees port . . ." zigzagging this 32,000-ton battle cruiser out of the path of those torpedoes.*[3]

12.14—Now all the bombers are gone. Captain Tennant has just ordered this message flashed to Admiral Tom Phillips on the *Wales* up ahead: "We have dodged nineteen torpedoes thus far, thanks to Providence."

[3] Italics denote scenes and remarks which I did not actually witness or hear.

Those who are able light cigarettes. The decks are littered with the debris of battle. There are a number of dead men around the guns, and wounded too. More ammunition is being passed up. Everyone around the guns is soaked in sweat, with blackened faces.

I glance at the notes in this diary. Hastily written. And I've twisted the point of my fountain pen, a green Parker, Martha's pen. I check the pack film in the Plaubel Makina suspended by a strap around my neck. There are four pictures left in the pack, enough, I think. No use taking time to change the pack. I rip open another packet and peel off the tape around the metal container, to be ready for a quick change. My ears ache atrociously and my mouth is cottony. The whole place stinks with cordite. I take off my tin hat. This anti-flash hood is like putting your head in an oven.

A young sailor, about eighteen, is standing there wide-eyed. I grin at him.

"They're sure giving us hell, aren't they?" I ask him. He grins back. I'm as scared as he is.

A few of the sailors are blowing up their lifebelts, I note. I wonder why but only for an instant and forget about it. My lifebelt is stuck up in a small shelf in the roof of the flag deck, too awkward to wear. I feel bulky enough with the cover-alls over the bush-jacket, the camera around my neck, notebook in my left hand and fountain pen in the right hand.

12.19—I see ten bombers approaching. It's impossible to tell whether this will be a high-level or a torpedo attack. They come closer, lower. It's definitely a torpedo attack.

12.20—The communication pipes again, "Stand by for barrage!" and hell breaks loose. A plane is diving straight for the middle of the ship off the port side, 500 yards away, and tracers are rushing to meet it, but it comes on. Now it seems suspended in the air 100 yards above the water, and the torpedo drops.

It is streaking for us. There is a deadly fascination in watching it. The watcher shouts, "Stand by for torpedo." The torpedo strikes the ship about twenty yards astern of my position. It feels as though the ship has crashed into dock. I am thrown four feet across the deck but I keep my feet. Almost immediately, it seems, the ship lists.

The command roars out of the loudspeaker: "Blow up your lifebelts!"

I take down mine from the shelf. It is a blue-serge affair with a rubber bladder inside. I tie one of the cords around my waist and start to bring another cord up around the neck. Just as I start to tie it the command comes: "All possible men to starboard."

But a Japanese plane invalidates that command. Instantly there's another crash to starboard. Incredibly quickly, the *Repulse* is listing to port, and I haven't started to blow up my lifebelt.

I finish tying the cord around my neck. My camera I hang outside the airless lifebelt. Gallagher already has his belt on and is puffing into the rubber tube to inflate it. The effort makes his strong, fair face redder than usual.

The ship is heeled over at a nasty angle. Gallagher says: "You all right, Cec?"

"Yeh, I guess so. No air in my belt though. The hell with it."

"Better blow it. This is it, Cec."

"Yes, Gal. I guess it is. Good going, Kid."

"We'll stick together."

We grin at each other, a weak grin.

Captain Tennant's voice is coming over the ship's loudspeaker, a cool voice: "All hands on deck. Prepare to abandon ship." There is a pause for just an instant, then: "God be with you."

There is no alarm, no confusion, no panic: We on the flag deck move toward a companionway leading to the quarter deck. Abrahams, the Admiralty photographer, Gallagher and I are together. The coolness of everyone is incredible. There is no pushing, but no pausing either. One youngster seems in a great hurry. He tries to edge his way into the line at the top of the companionway to get down faster to the quarter deck.

A young sub-lieutenant taps him on the shoulder and

says quietly: "Now, now, we are all going the same way, too."

The youngster immediately gets hold of himself.

We move swiftly down the fifteen-foot companionway to the quarter deck. Abrahams is carrying his expensive camera like a baby, cradled in his arms. He goes over to a wooden lifebelt locker, about three feet long, carefully opens the lid, gently places his camera inside, and carefully closes the lid.

Beside a pom-pom two men are dead, stretched in grotesque positions of violently won peace. There is blood all around this gun, hot and silent, its base littered with used and never-fired ammunition, too.

I see four sailors carrying Lieutenant Page up the slanting deck of the ship toward the edge. He had been brought up on the deck when the action with the Japanese was joined. He still couldn't walk. Two lifebelts were wrapped around him "in case anything happened." Now he is being lifted to the edge of the ship. The four men heaved, and Page went sailing overboard, so he would have a chance for rescue. Gallagher and Abrahams seem to have disappeared.

I see a lifeboat jammed with seamen and a half dozen officers, still on its davits, still not swung out.

The only way to reach the boat is by a cable. I jump for it and go hand over hand about ten feet, dangling like a monkey by its tail.

I swing myself into a tiny, precarious corner of the lifeboat, first my feet then using my arms as levers on the cable to get all of me inside. I just settle there when someone shouts: "This boat will never get off!"

We all pile out, streaming over the side of the lifeboat, back onto the deck of the *Repulse*. I drop ten feet, hit the slanting, slippery deck, slide about eight feet and crash into a bulkhead. I am dizzy when I pick myself up. Then I fall back on my hands and knees and scramble up the side of the deck, grabbing cables and deck protuberances to reach the edge of the ship.

The *Repulse* is going down.

The torpedo-smashed *Prince of Wales*, still a half to

three-quarters of a mile ahead, is low in the water, half shrouded in smoke, a destroyer by her side.

Japanese bombers are still winging around like vultures, still attacking the *Wales*. A few of those shot down are bright splotches of burning orange on the blue South China Sea.

Men are tossing overboard rafts, lifebelts, benches, pieces of wood, anything that will float. Standing at the edge of the ship, I see one man (Midshipman Peter Gillis, an eighteen-year-old Australian from Sydney) dive from the Air Defense control tower at the top of the main mast. He dives 170 feet and starts to swim away.

Men are jumping into the sea from the four or five defense control towers that segment the main mast like a series of ledges. One man misses his distance, dives, hits the side of the *Repulse*, breaks every bone in his body and crumples into the sea like a sack of wet cement. Another misses his direction and dives from one of the towers straight down the smokestack.

Men are running all along the deck of the ship to get further astern. The ship is lower in the water at the stern and their jump therefore will be shorter. Twelve Royal Marines run back too far, jump into the water and are sucked into the propeller.

The screws of the *Repulse* are still turning. There are five or six hundred heads bobbing in the water. The men are being swept astern because the *Repulse* is still making way and there's a strong tide here, too.

On all sides of me men are flinging themselves over the side. I sit down on the edge of the *Repulse* and take off my shoes. I am very fond of those shoes. A Chinese made them for me just a few days ago in Singapore. They are soft, with a buckle, and they fit well. I carefully place them together and put them down as you do at the foot of your bed before going to sleep.

I have no vision of what is ahead, no concrete thoughts of how to save myself. It is necessarily every man for himself. As I sit there, it suddenly comes to me, the overwhelming, dogmatic conviction. I actually speak the words: "Cecil you are never going to get out of this."

I see one man jump and land directly on another man. I say to myself: "When I jump I don't want to hurt anyone."

Down below is a mess of oil and debris, and I don't want to jump into that either. I feel my mind getting numb. I look across to the *Wales*. Its guns are flashing and the flames are belching through the grayish-black smoke.

My mind cannot absorb what my eyes see. It is impossible to believe that these two beautiful, powerful, invulnerable ships are going down. But they are. There's no doubt of that.

Men are sliding down the hull of the *Repulse*. Extending around the edge of the ship is a three-inch bulge of steel. The men hit that bulge, shoot off into space and into the water. I say to myself: "I don't want to go down that way. That must hurt their backsides something terrible."

About eight feet to my left there is a gaping hole in the side of the *Repulse*. It is about thirty feet across, with the plates twisted and torn. The hull of the *Repulse* has been ripped open as though a giant had torn apart a tin can. I see an officer dive over the side, dive into the hole underneath the line, dive back inside the ship.

I half turn to look back on the crazy-angled deck of the ship. The padre is beside one of the pom-poms, administering the final rites to a gunner dying beside his gun. The padre seems totally unconcerned by the fact that the *Repulse* is going down at any moment.

About forty-two men have made their way through the tangled, destroyed, burning interior of the ship, crept, stumbled and scrambled and have clambered through the inside of the dummy smokestack to the top. They find the wire screen across the top of the stack is fastened on the outside. Someone hears their cries but by then it is too late. The men are trapped.

Midshipman Christopher Bros, from St. Andrews, is in the fifteen-inch transmitting station, at the very bottom of the ship. There are twenty-five men with him in the small room, and the sharp list of the ship is making it difficult to get out. The water is pouring in.

"Fall in, everyone! March. Up you go," Bros orders. The men start streaming out, starting a climb up six decks. One by one they pass out of the room. The water is coming higher. The water comes in faster than twenty-six men can get out. The twenty-sixth man is trapped. Midshipman Kit Bros, tall, slim, Rugby graduate from Scotland gets all his men out. He is the twenty-sixth man.

I slide down the hull of the *Repulse* about five feet. There I brace myself in a porthole, take off my tin hat and white cloth anti-flash hood and place them at my feet in the porthole. I lie on the side of the *Repulse*, watching this incredible scene—men bobbing in the water, black oil spreading over the debris-filled, blue sea, the *Wales* obviously sinking, the sky still filled with aircraft and black puffs of anti-aircraft fire.

I don't want to jump, to leave the relative security of this steel for that mess down below. I have no panic in me, no particular fear, just this numbness. I know I'll have to jump sooner or later. I know I cannot lie here and let the water come over me without fighting back somehow. There's no hurry. To jump into the water will hasten the inevitable.

Captain Tennant on the bridge turns to the navigating officer: "It looks a bit different from this angle, doesn't it, pilot?"

The navigating officer nods, but says nothing. The group of officers on the bridge look at each other, and at the skipper.

"Well, gentlemen," Captain Tennant says quietly, "you had better get out of it now."

"Aren't you coming with us, sir?" two or three eagerly demand simultaneously.

The captain smiles, shakes his head negatively, then says impatiently: "Off you go now. There's not much time." They are all hanging on to something, one leg braced to keep an even keel as the ship heels over more and more.

"But, Captain," the lieutenant commander says, "you

must come with us. You've done all you could for this ship. More than most men could."

Captain Tennant does not budge. The men are getting restive. Almost by prearrangement they all move toward their skipper. They push him forcibly through the narrow doorway and onto the deck. The Repulse *is almost on her beam ends. Captain Tennant will go no farther. The officers and men of the bridge seize Captain Tennant and push him over the side. Then they jump into the sea.*

I seem to be glued to the hull of the *Repulse*. Just my head is loose. I turn it from side to side, watching the last-minute evacuation of the ship. Someone slides down the hull, pauses for a moment at the bulge, stands up and makes a beautiful swan dive. That galvanizes me, and I stand up in the porthole and jump, the camera wildly swinging from its strap around my neck.

The jump is about twenty feet. The water is warm; it is not water, but thick oil. My first action is to look at my stop watch. It is smashed at 12.35, one hour and twenty minutes after the first Japanese bomb crashed into the catapult deck of the *Repulse*.

It doesn't occur to me to swim away from the ship until I see others striking out. Then I realize how difficult it is. The oil soaks into my clothes, weighting them, and I think underwater demons are tugging at me, trying to drag me down. The airless lifebelt, absorbing oil too, tightens and tautens the preserver cords around my neck. I say to myself: "I'm going to choke to death, I'm going to choke to death."

I have a ring on my left hand which Martha bought for me on the Ponte Vecchio in Florence when we were on our honeymoon. It is rather loose on my finger. With oil on my hands, I'm afraid I will lose it. I clench my fist so that it won't slip off.

I start swimming away with the left hand clenched. With my right hand I make one stroke, tug at the cord around my neck in a futile effort to loosen it, then make another stroke to get away from the ship.

That ring helps save my life. Something like it must have

34

helped save the lives of hundreds of men. Your mind fastens itself on silly, unimportant matters, absorbing your thoughts and stifling the natural instinct of man to panic in the face of death.

I see a life preserver eighteen inches long and four inches thick. It is like a long sausage and I tuck it to me. A small piece of wood appears inviting and I take that too. A barrel comes near, but I reject that because the oil prevents my getting a grip on it. All around me men are swimming, men with blood streaking their oil-covered faces.

The oil burns in my eyes as though someone is jabbing hot pokers into the eyes. That oil in the eyes is the worst thing. I've swallowed a bit of oil already, and it's beginning to sicken me.

Fifty feet from the ship, hardly swimming at all now, I see the bow of the *Repulse* swing straight into the air like a church steeple. Its red under plates stand out as stark and as gruesome as the blood on the faces of the men around me. Then the tug and draw of the suction of 32,000 tons of steel sliding to the bottom hits me. Something powerful, almost irresistible, snaps at my feet. It feels as though someone were trying to pull my legs out by the hip sockets. But I am more fortunate than some others. They are closer to the ship. They are sucked back.

When the *Repulse* goes down it sends over a huge wave, a wave of oil. I happen to have my mouth open and I take aboard considerable oil. That makes me terribly sick at the stomach.

As I swim in the water, other men are hanging on to pieces of wood, floating lifebelts and debris. Four or five times I see blood- and oil-covered hands loosen their grip and slide beneath the water.

I do not see Gallagher anywhere. It is difficult to recognize anyone through the oil on his face. About fifteen yards away I see someone struggling and fighting in the water. I finally recognize Sub-Lieutenant Page. There are two men near by. The injured Page is struggling to get out of the two lifebelts wrapped around him, the belts he had on when he was tossed overboard.

"I'm hurt," Page is crying. "I'm hurt. I'm no good any more. You take the belts."

The men can't swim, but Page is insisting and sobbing, peeling out of the belts. "Take them; I'm no good any more."

Page prevails on the two men to accept the belts. They are saved, and Sub-Lieutenant Page slips underneath the water.

Someone calls to me, "Are you all right, War Correspondent?"

"Yes," I say, opening my mouth to say it, and I take aboard more oil. I decide if anyone asks me any more questions I will wave my hand, if I have the strength. I am terribly tired.

A small table, about three feet square, floats by. I grab hold of one leg, but it is too slippery and I know I will lose it. I scramble up on top and lie there for a moment. And then I watch the *Prince of Wales* go down, a big, dark thing sliding into nothingness.

Now the sea seems really deserted, with just men and mess floating on the surface.

As I swim I hear one man yell, "An electric eel just shocked me!"

There are no sharks that I can see, although this area of the South China Sea is usually filled with sharks.

There is a Carley float about three-quarters of a mile away, and a destroyer about two miles distant. I have no intention of trying to reach them. I only want to rest on top of the small table. The conviction that this is my finish is still strong within me. Besides, I want to conserve my strength, want jealously to guard it during the hours before death comes.

I say to myself, "I've gotta remember all this; I gotta remember all this." And the next minute, "What the hell's the use? I will never be able to report this story."

It's so easy to close your eyes, shut out this sight, and fiercely forget what the eyes already have seen.

Strangely enough, I don't think of my wife, my family, or my childhood. I constantly glance around to see if I recognize any of the men, and I am especially watching for Gallagher. I don't see him but I do recognize two or three officers and we smile wanly at each other.

As I lie on the table I pull off my heavy cotton khaki socks. They are soaked and weighted by oil, as heavy as iron. I let the soaked socks slip into the water and feel five pounds lighter. As the warmth of the South China Sea slushes between my toes I think, "That feels wonderful on my feet."

The effort, little as it is, exhausts me. The drag of the camera around my neck and the choking by the life-preserver cord convince me I ought to do something about them. But the water-and-oil-soaked cord of the preserver is knotted and I can't unfasten it. As for the camera, I feel I'd rather drown than throw it away.

I know that I should somehow try to get rid of some of my clothes. The oil makes their weight feel like tons. Tears are pouring out of my eyes from the oil, and I sense tiny salty rivulets running down my oil-covered face.

That oil! It coagulates around each body, around the debris, around the men. One officer in the water shouts, "Spread out a bit, men, and let's get out of this oil." Some of the men do it; others are reluctant to get away from pieces of wood. Others depend on absorbing some strength from men around them. Not only miserable but drowning men love company.

One officer swims by me and says, "Let's make for the raft." I shake my head no, and he swims on.

About ten yards from me I see two youngsters—they must be about eighteen—laughing and joking, and I hear one say, "I'll race you to Singapore." We are fifty miles from shore and one hundred and fifty miles north of the city those youngsters are talking about.

It's the tide, not my efforts, that bring me near the Carley float. The Carley contraptions are rafts, fifteen feet long, ten feet wide, and bounded on all sides by a foot-high bulge. Extending around the bulge is a rope on which men can grab hold.

The raft toward which the tide carries me is jammed. There are men inside, men sitting solid on the bulge at the edge, and every handhold on the rope is occupied. Obviously there is no room for me, so I make no effort whatsoever, letting the tide carry me where it wants. It carries me to that raft.

A Royal Marine sitting on the edge calls to me when I am ten feet away, "Just a bit more, just a bit more." I don't answer, just look at him across that ten-foot chasm.

Gradually I draw nearer. He extends his hand as far as he can and I stretch out my hand. For five minutes our hands are three inches apart, but I don't have the energy to bridge that tiny gap. Once again the tide does it for me. Our hands meet, clasp and I'm yanked toward the raft, leaving the small table which thus far has saved my life.

The twenty-year-old marine, Morris Graney, pushes one of the men sitting on the bulge back inside the raft, on top of another man, to make way for me. Then he pulls me onto the bulge and holds me there.

His first remark is: "My Lord, do you still have your camera?"

"Yes."

"Are you all right?"

I nod.

"Can you sit here?"

I say, "Yes, I am all right."

Actually I'm not, and almost fall face forward into the water. Graney grabs me, takes one of my hands—my right hand, since my left is still clenched to prevent my ring from falling off—and forces it to grasp the lifebelt of a man inside the raft.

"Hang onto him," Graney says.

I hang on.

The raft tosses and heaves with the swell of the sea. Men are bobbing and swimming on all sides near the raft, some trying to reach it, some hoping eventually to get a hand hold on it. We want to reach a destroyer which is stationary about a mile or a mile and a half away. There is one paddle on board, and someone inside, using the paddle, is calling, "Heave ho, heave ho!"

Graney says, "Let's all sing." Not many voices join in his choice, "When Irish Eyes Are Smiling," but the voices that do are cheerful.

Graney wears only shorts and his thick chest is covered with oil. His brown hair hangs over his forehead and into his eyes. I think just the sight of Graney helps many a man. He is almost six feet tall, husky, almost barrel-chested. Above a square jaw he has a slim, delicate mustache and blue, kind, shy eyes. All the time the only one definable emotion expressed in those eyes is amusement. Graney's amusement is enough, though, as the raft tosses. I am deathly sick at the stomach, and dizzy, too, and again almost fall forward, Graney grabs me.

"You stay right here," he says, slapping me on the shoulder.

"I am very tired," I say, "and I want to rest down there."

Graney slaps me across the face, saying, "Now, none of that. You stay right here with me."

"No. Those other men aren't on the raft," I say. "I am tired, and I can rest better in the water."

Graney's hand is digging into my arm and shoulder. It hurts, but somehow I don't protest. I just know it hurts.

"We're watching those other men," Graney says sharply. "They're all right. You stay right here with us."

I'm not convinced, and twist my head around to look inside the raft. It's the wrong time to do that. Men inside are vomiting and glassy-eyed, all of them black with oil. Two men have just died and their bodies are being gently hustled over the side to make room for more men. I feel a twinge of pity at the sight of it, but it seems an eminently practical thing to do.

Six or seven Jap bombers are roaring over again at about 5,000 feet.

"They're coming over to machine-gun us!" someone says.

"Shut up that guff!" Graney growls, because we all feel bad enough as it is.

"If they come over to machine-gun us," a voice suggests, "dive under the water."

I think to myself: "If I have to dive under the water, I'm never coming up again."

They don't swoop down on us and they don't drop bombs. They just go on. It isn't Japanese chivalry or

Bushido. They're just out of bombs and ammunition. With the planes gone and heads turned from the sky to the horizon, we get the impression that the destroyer is getting farther and farther away. In fact, we see one of our destroyers steam away. Someone calls in panic, "They're all going." A reply comes from somewhere inside the raft: "They'll wait for us, don't worry."

As the minutes go on and we seem to be getting no nearer to the destroyer, the morale on the raft begins to slip lower and lower. Graney is one of the first to recognize this. "Keep kicking, keep paddling!" he shouts. "We will soon be there!"

As we drew near the destroyer he said, "All right, now, it's 'Anchors Aweigh'!" And again he starts singing. Almost everyone joins in then, because for the first time we seem to have a chance of rescue.

Rafts and men are converging on the destroyer from all directions. We can already see dripping figures being hauled onto the deck of the ship. Through a megaphone an officer on the bridge is shouting something at us, but we can't make it out.

The oil around the destroyer seems about two feet thick, solid oil. To me it looks like dirty black castor oil. And it tastes the same.

A rope with a loop at the end is tossed thirty feet from the destroyer to us. We miss it. The rope is hauled back and again is hurled. Someone grabs it, but Graney tears it out of his hands and roughly passes the loop over me. "We have an American war correspondent here," he shouts at the destroyer. Then he waves and shouts, "Heave up, heave up!"

He asks solicitously, "Can you hold onto the rope?"

"Of course. Don't worry about me."

And the men on the destroyer pull me off the edge of the Carley float. I sink underneath the oil, and for ten feet while I'm dragged underneath the surface I feel I'm plowing my way through some kind of a solid wall. The pressure pounds at my head like a great rubber hammer.

Then I'm beside the destroyer. A wooden ladder hangs over the side.

A frenzied voice calls, "Hang on, hang on! But hurry!"

I get up the ladder and four men drag me over the taffrail. The deck is burning hot on my bare feet. They strip off my clothes and someone hands me a heavy woolen parka. I put it on, and one of the officers says, "Are you all right?"

"I'm fine," I say. "Who has a camera on board this ship?"

The officer doesn't know, but he calls over another man, saying, "Find this man a camera. There must be one on board."

The rating scoots off, and I stand there while Graney, who has just been brought on board, keeps urging me to sit down and rest.

"There's plenty of time for that," I insist. "I've got to get a camera."

Graney empties the pockets of my cover-alls, bush jacket and shorts, and hands over the precious notebook in which I kept this account of the battle. I open the notebook, and see every page is water-and-oil-soaked but still legible.

About a half dozen men are dead on the deck of the destroyer. Others are being sick from the oil. Some men are laughing and joking.

The hospital of the sick bay is jammed, and some of the dead are being carried out and laid on the deck. Men with blood on their faces are being carried back to the sick bay for attention. Still more survivors are being brought on board, and I snap pictures. I use up all the film. They find me another camera and I use all that film.

The destroyer is the *Electra*, which took 1,100 men out of the hell of Dunkirk to England.

There is no bitterness among these men this afternoon about the absence of aircraft protection, just regret that they've lost their ship. One man is wailing that he'd lost the pictures of his girl friend, his mother, his dad.

After about an hour, three Brewster Buffaloes come roaring over, sweeping ten feet from the ship. The Japs are long gone by now.

In the steaming hot wardroom of the *Electra* forty or fifty officers are drinking tea, most all naked to the waist. The heat is stifling, and as we sit there—I taking notes—

the sweat pours out of us as though we are under a shower.

As the sweat drips from me, I remember how exactly twenty-four hours before I sat in the comfortable wardroom of the *Repulse,* talking with the officers of the battle cruiser, and thinking of the British tendency to underestimate the enemy, to look at them solely through British eyes. "It's better," I said, "to consider your enemy twice as good as you are and twice as smart. Then you won't be surprised."

The British officers, twenty-four hours before had been amiable, cheerful and skeptical. Now in that smelling, sweltering wardroom of the *Electra,* one of the officers of the *Repulse* comes up with a rueful smile on his face and says: "You told us not to underestimate the enemy."

"Yes, I know," I say, "but I take no satisfaction in that now—not even grim satisfaction."

I want to know about Captain Tennant. One man speaks up: "I saw him floating face down in the water."

Down there in the wardroom I am told the sequence of attacks on the *Prince of Wales.*

The attack was similar to our own. High-level bombers and torpedo-carrying bombers. With four torpedoes in the *Wales,* Admiral Phillips said: "Tell the *Express* (which was then alongside the *Wales)* to signal to Singapore for tugs to tow us home."

It was obvious the Admiral hadn't yet made up his mind that the ship was going to sink.

I ask a lieutenant commander from the *Wales* about Admiral Phillips and Captain Leach.

They were last seen standing on the bridge of the *Prince of Wales.*

"The admiral and the captain stood there together," the officer says. "They would not go. As we started away, Captain Leach waved, and called out: 'Good-by. Thank you. Good luck. God bless you.' "

Then the water rose up to meet them, meeting and then covering them.

Disaster in Malaya

As December 1941 wore on, the British-Indian 11th and 9th Divisions fell back before the Japanese thrusts down both west and east coasts of Malaya. The invaders maintained pressure on the front, and at the same time made amphibious landings on the coastal flanks; then their troops sliced inland to harass and roll up the supply lines. The Japanese troops were trained jungle fighters and their tactics were so effective that soon the morale of the Allied troops disintegrated. As in Bataan, the certain knowledge that they were fighting only a delaying action did not enable the Allied troops to put up an effective defense. Unlike Bataan, where the native Filipino troops were invaluable, the Malayans had little stomach for this battle.

As Kenneth Attiwill says: "the jungles, mangrove swamps and thickly treed areas of cultivation present a peculiar and difficult problem. Visibility is limited, the opportunity for ambush lies almost everywhere. There are no fields of fire, tactical features tend to lose significance and roads and tracks become important. All-around protection is essential. Movement, though possible, is severely restricted—yet static defense spells defeat. Movement is easier in rubber plantations, but the interminable lines of evenly spaced trees and the limited view make it difficult for troops to keep direction. Control is difficult, emergencies crop up unexpectedly, and junior commanders' actions assume greater influence. Their errors of tactics, judgment and decision may easily decide an action.

"Brooding above all, adding weakness to morale as well as to military efficiency, lies the jungle itself—a terrifying morass of tangled vegetation, steamy heat, nerve-racking noises and the discomfort of insects; mosquitoes by the myriad, moths, beetles, insects of all kinds, biting, buzzing, irritating and debilitating. Rubber, too, with its gloom, dampness and sound-deadening effect breeds a feeling of isolation. The enemy may be anywhere—everywhere—in front or behind—to left or to right. Noise is difficult to pinpoint; men appear and disappear like wraiths. Rumor begins to spread. In the monsoonal season there is the added handicap of torrential rain, hissing down incessantly upon the greenery, dripping dankly on heads and bodies, humid, sweaty, destructive. . . .

"Within a little more than a month the Japanese had advanced from Siam all the way down the peninsula into northern Johore—and the British were back to their last line of defense outside Singapore Island.

"If there were reasons why the speed tactics and fire power of the enemy should have bewildered and surprised the British commanders, their tactics should now have been plain. Time and again the enemy had surprised the defenders by his ability to move more rapidly over all types of terrain; time and again he had used enveloping tactics rather than the direct onslaught. Yet in Johore the defending commanders chose to try to defend one strongpoint, only to be destroyed piecemeal. Elsewhere, a weak brigade was asked to hold the most likely road for the Japanese advance, while three brigades were allocated to the area they did not assault directly. The result was defeat again and again in Johore, until it became apparent by the last week of January 1942, that a withdrawal into Singapore Island was inevitable.

"That was the pattern—errors by commanders; insufficient or inadequately trained troops; continuous under-estimation of a savage, speedy, highly skilled and highly mobile enemy; spreading confusion and panic. As the 'Great Run' lengthened eyes grew red with sleeplessness, limbs became weary with incessant effort, minds sluggish with exhaustion, nerves frayed, morale and discipline and efficiency constantly diminishing.

"To the troops who did not know the truth about Singapore, the island loomed in their minds like an oasis. In Singapore there would be proper accommodations, proper food; above all, a place to lie down in peace for the one night's sleep they all craved." *

But was Singapore the fortress the troops and, for that matter, the rest of the world had been led to believe? Prime Minister Churchill in a letter to General Ismay on January 16, 1942, more than a month after the invasion of Malaya, was shocked to hear of the island's vulnerability. "I must confess to being staggered by Wavell's telegram of the 16th. . . . It never occurred to me for a moment . . . that the gorge of the

*Fortress, pp. 44-51. Doubleday & Co.

fortress of Singapore, with its splendid moat half a mile to a mile wide, was not entirely fortified against an attack from the northward. What is the use of having an island for a fortress if it is not to be made into a citadel?" *

A few days later in a telegram to General Wavell, Churchill said, in part, "I want to make it absolutely clear that I expect every inch of ground to be defended . . . and no question of surrender to be entertained until after protracted fighting among the ruins of Singapore City." **

But this telegram had little effect upon the authorities in Singapore. Four days later, a Lieutenant-Colonel of the 11th Indian Division who had led a group of sappers from the action on the Siam borders in the retreat to Singapore, reported:

"I was dumbfounded when I sent to the Chief Engineer's office and learned that there was not a trench and not a bit of barbed wire on the whole of the north-east and north-west side of the island. We thought that during our time up-country all these defences would have been installed." ***

When he went to the Ordnance Depot to get barbed wire, he was told, "Half holiday!" The staff had taken the afternoon off to go to the "pictures."

Little was accomplished to strengthen the defenses between the 25th and the night of February 8 when the first Jap landing barges were observed making their way across the Straits of Johore.

"The approach of the enemy should have been the signal for a blaze of searchlights to light them up for the defenders and a savage counter-barrage to blow the enemy out of the water. The searchlights stayed dark and the guns remained silent. Strict instructions had been given to the searchlight crews that they were not to expose beach lights except on the specific instructions of the unit commanders—it was thought that, once exposed, they would inevitably be destroyed—but by the time the assault was launched all the communications had been cut and those lights which had survived the barrage were never exposed. Because calls for the planned defensive artillery fire never reached the batteries the guns did not open up and it was not until

*Winston Churchill, *The Hinge of Fate*, p. 50. Houghton Mifflin Co.
**The Hinge of Fate*, p. 53.
***Fortress*, p. 77. This quote is from a British book.

the S.O.S. light signals sent up by the infantry were seen that any of the guns went into action. In any event, there wasn't enough artillery to cover the whole brigade front; and in some areas—particularly on the front of the 2/18th and 2/19th A.I.F. Battalions—the infantry was left without artillery support. Some gun positions did not see the warning Very light and stayed silent.

"The Australians fought in darkness broken only by gun flashes and the blaze from burning barges, and without the comfort of a counter-barrage from their own artillery. Too widely spaced, and with untrained reinforcements in their ranks, it is not surprising that the Australians could not keep the Japanese off the Island. The enemy was soon ashore—though in places only at the second or third attempt—and they quickly infiltrated the gaps between the Australian positions.

"By one o'clock on the morning of the 9th—only three and a half hours after the invasion had been first sighted—the Australians in the forward areas were withdrawing, under orders, to their battalion perimeters. Groups of men became separated from their comrades in the bewildering darkness. Others lost their way. Many died. The effect of the withdrawals was to dislocate the whole Brigade area, and by ten o'clock on the morning of the 9th—less than twelve hours after the assault had been sighted—the 22nd Australian Brigade, on whose fighting power had rested the defence of the north-western area of the Island, was no longer a cohesive fighting force." *

THE FALL OF SINGAPORE**

by Kenneth Attiwill

From the events of the desperate days of Monday the 9th, Tuesday the 10th, Wednesday the 11th, and Thursday the 12th, there emerges a painful catalogue of error, folly, indecision and indescribable confusion. When the

*Fortress, pp. 172-173.
**Condensed from Fortress, Chapters 11, 12 and 13.

evidence is sifted, it no longer remains a source of pained astonishment that Singapore held out for only seven days. The miracle is that it held out for so long. Indeed, there was a moment on the 11th when the Japanese had split the defense so successfully that their tanks could have driven down the Bukit Timah road into Singapore City with virtually no opposition. They did not do so. They stopped at Bukit Timah to consolidate and had to wait four more days for surrender. No doubt, despite the evidence of tactical weakness they had accumulated during the two m nths since December 8, even the Japanese could not believe that the British defence would be so easily overcome.

The dwindling force of Hurricanes continued in action throughout the hours of daylight on the 9th. Four finished the day by responding to an urgent call for air support and, under cover of smoke from the burning oil tanks, succeeded in driving off bombers which were harassing the troops. But the air position was now hopeless. Only Kallang airfield was usable and with Lt.-Gen. Percival's [1] approval Air Vice-Marshal Pulford withdrew the remnants of the squadron to Sumatra. It was intended to use Kallang only as an advanced landing base; in fact, from that day onward no British aircraft was seen in the sky above Singapore.

In view of the alarming military situation on January 9, when it was known that the Japanese had landed on the Island, the Governor [2] ordered the civil denial scheme to be put into effect. Teams drawn from the Public Works Department, and the Royal Engineers, Excise and Customs Officers, volunteers from the Observer Corps, Chinese and Indians, worked night and day. They were handicapped in their task of smashing plant and machinery by people representing vested interests who did their utmost to pre-

[1] General officer commanding Malaya.—Ed. note.
[2] Sir Shenton Thomas, Governor of Straits Settlements.—Ed. note.

vent the destruction of private property. They lodged appeals with the local authorities. Some companies with head offices in Britain, Australia or India petitioned their home Governments. A few actively intervened to prevent the denial teams getting to work. It was more important to these people—unnamed—that their property should be available for them at some future time, if and when the invader was defeated, than that war potential should be denied to the enemy.

Denial was further hampered by the Governor's orders on the 10th to withdraw all the European Supervisory Staff from the Singapore Harbour Board installations; and again by the unauthorized departure of some officials and key civilians who ran away from Singapore on February 9, 10 and 13. "Nevertheless," says *The War Against Japan*,[3] "with certain exceptions the work was completed by the day of surrender. The exceptions were the installations captured by the enemy before they could be destroyed and those exempted by the Government on the plea of the effect of the denial operations on morale." They were still worrying about morale! The result was that the installations of about forty Chinese firms and the workshops and vehicles of two large motor dealers and their subsidiaries remained intact, and the Japanese received "a welcome present of new vehicles and well-equipped workshops."

Two of the tasks which were accomplished successfully were the destruction of the State money and private stocks of liquor. Mr. Eric Pretty, acting Federal Secretary, burned 5,000,000 Straits dollars in the Treasury—the equivalent of about £600,000. "I never imagined I'd have so much money to burn," he said. Memories of Japanese atrocities in Hong Kong, when their troops got drunk on looted liquor and ran amok, prompted Sir Shenton Thomas's ban on liquor. It came into force at noon on Friday the 13th, but long before then work had begun on the colossal task of destroying every drop of strong drink on the Island.

Gradually the life of Singapore was slowing but still

[3] From *The Loss of Singapore*, Vol. 1. Her Brittanic Majesty's Stationery Office.

Reller's Band played selections at the Adelphi Hotel and people queued for the cinemas. Apologists said it was good for morale, as when the people danced in Brussels on the eve of Waterloo. Raffles Hotel and the clubs and canteens were packed with staff officers who did not know what to do except sit and hope for the best. "All the redtape from all over Malaya was packed into this little Island," said Capt. Charles Corry, Malayan Civil Service Volunteer with 3rd Corps.

Of Singapore in general, Maj. G. Wort, Wiltshire Regiment, wrote: "It seemed that the spirit of holding on and, if necessary, dying at your post had gone out of the make-up of things altogether. Perhaps in some cases it was because no definite orders were issued by the local Government as to policy. In many cases, one got the feeling that the one idea was to get to hell out of it, and the country too, if you could." The streets were daily becoming more dangerous. Fifth Columnists were liable to be anywhere in Singapore now. It was pitch dark by seven o'clock in the evening, and a long night lay ahead with plenty of opportunities for disguised Japanese and pro-Jap quislings to sneak into the city and occupy good sniping positions in the many flats and offices that were now empty. Sniping was a constant danger along the main streets. Ted Fozard and Eric Pretty said that they dodged bullets near the Supreme Court building. There were plenty of windows in multi-storied business houses, tall blocks of flats, hotels and Chinese lodging-houses—though heaven help the pro-Jap if the loyal Chinese got hold of him.

By the morning of Black Friday the Thirteenth, British withdrawal to the perimeter positions was completed; and except in the south-west and north, where the Japanese continued to make gains, the line was more or less stable. It was a false picture, for Singapore's situation was irretrievable. You would not have guessed it, however, from the second issue of the one-page *Straits Times* which appeared that morning. The title had been garnished with the Governor's famous slogan, printed in heavy type:

"Singapore Must Stand; It SHALL Stand." The three columns carried nine news items from which the beleaguered defenders and civilians of Singapore could read that Chiang Kai-shek had seen Mr. Nehru of India, that the United States was planning to raise its Air Force to an ultimate total of two million men, and that Chinese forces had been successful in a small engagement against the Siamese on the Indo-China frontier. It also announced in a half-column story that an air battle had been fought between Japanese and Dutch East Indies forces over the Java Sea. Closer at home, the inhabitants of rural areas were warned that it was an offence to refuse to accept Malayan currency notes; families of Volunteers were told where to find temporary accommodation, potential readers of the sheet were told how to obtain their copies, free; and it was formally announced that from noon it would be an offence to possess intoxicating liquor. The "lead" story, which was headed "Japanese Suffer Huge Casualties in Singapore—R.A. Gunners Stick to Their Posts," contained only five paragraphs—all quotations from British and Australian newspapers. You could not guess that in the streets of Singapore City, black under the pall of oil smoke, the dead lay uncollected and unburied. Administration had broken down. The Army was hard pressed and running short of everything it needed—food, water, petrol, ammunition. Anti-aircraft guns—especially the Bofors on top of buildings—still blazed away at the non-stop procession of enemy planes which dropped their bombs and then returned to Johore to re-load, but they made little impact. Fighters machine-gunned the arterial roads with impunity. Shelling was incessant and no area was spared. Now that the defence line was drawn tight round the City, the whole of Singapore was a legitimate military target.

The City was crowded with armed deserters. An officer patrol rounded up 1,100 of them in the last few days, but there were still too many to be controlled by the Military Police. They skulked through the town, or hid in the basements of concrete buildings, or looted Chinese shops. Col. Chamier saw them going about with their rifles on their shoulders and their shirts stuffed with cigarettes and tinned food. Mr. Dick Mullaly described the municipal building and all the big buildings of Singapore on the seafront as "solid blocks of Australians sitting on the stairs." Some tried to get aboard the boats that were still leaving the stricken Island. There were instances of deserters threatening and even firing their rifles to try to force their way on board. It is impossible to say how many got away. Lionel Wigmore, in *The Japanese Thrust*, a volume of the Australian official war history, reports that Mr. Bowden cabled the Australian Government on February 12 that "a group of Australians and others had boarded a vessel without authority and in it had sailed to the Netherlands East Indies." He also records that on February 14 groups of soldiers, including Australians, were at large in Singapore seeking to escape and that a few, armed with tommy-guns and hand grenades, threatened to open fire on the launch *Osprey* unless they themselves were taken on board. "When the *Osprey* moved out at 11.30 p.m. with thirty-eight on board, rifle shots were fired at it but no one was hit." On Friday the 13th Australian 1st Corps headquarters in Java learned that "a party of 100 reported to be deserters" had arrived from Singapore. On the 14th, one officer and 165 other ranks "presumed to be deserters" were placed under guard in a Dutch prison in Batavia. When questioned, the men said: "Singapore was in a state of confusion, men were unable to contact their units and were ordered by officers whom they did contact to make their way to port and evacuate." In the absence of an official charge or evidence from the master of the vessel that had carried them, or O.C. troops, it was decided that their retention in prison was illegal. They were set free, and fought with Blackforce during the operations in Java.

The War Against Japan describes those troops who left the Island, or tried to, as "most . . . were deserters from administrative units, and men who had recently arrived in Malaya as reinforcements, inadequately trained and disciplined."

By this time, more and more exhausted troops were losing confidence in their leaders and morale was beginning to crack. But the well-trained units still fought stubbornly.

At two o'clock in the afternoon Lt.-Gen. Percival held a conference at Fort Canning. Others present were Lt.-Gen. Heath, Maj.-Gens. Gordon Bennett, Keith Simmons, Beckwith-Smith, and Key, and senior staff officers. They took stock of the situation.

Food was down to seven days' supply of military stocks, though there were still ample civilian supplies. There was sufficient ammunition for the 25-pounders, the Bofors A.A., and the mortars. Petrol was down to one small dump plus the amount still in vehicle tanks, plus the Asiatic Petroleum reserve tanks on Palau Bukum Island. Water was running to waste because breaks in the mains were gaining on repairs. Only low pressure was available at street level, and hospitals were running short. At the docks all civil labour had disappeared, in the town area debris from bombing and shelling remained untouched and the dead lay unburied.

Percival gave orders for the fuel reserve at Palau Bukum to be destroyed—a task which was only partially successful—and discussed the question of a counter-attack. His generals were unanimous that no counter-attack could be launched because the men had been fighting day and night and were approaching complete exhaustion. Gordon Bennett recorded:

"It was unanimously considered that new enemy attacks would succeed and that sooner or later the enemy would reach the streets of the City, which were crowded with battle stragglers. . . . It was decided to send a message to General Wavell urging him to agree to immediate capitulation."

When Wavell's reply arrived shortly afterwards it said uncompromisingly: ". . . Fully appreciate your situation but continued action essential."

The conference also discussed the evacuation of selected personnel from the Island in the final withdrawal of boats. Gordon Bennett said: "Owing to the limitation of shipping, accommodation for only 1,800 from the Army could be arranged. The A.I.F. allotment was 100. It was decided that only those whose capabilities would help our ultimate war effort should be evacuated and also that the proportion of officers to other ranks should be as one is to fifteen."

All that day and throughout the night the chosen few—and some who had not been chosen—made their final preparations. When the men who could not be evacuated heard of it, their morale was not improved.

Altogether about 3,000 people were sent away officially that night—Army nurses, Service officers and technicians, and civilian specialists. Others—the runaways—went furtively. Women and children were pushed on board wherever room could be found. They sailed from Singapore in a miscellaneous fleet of small boats—the last of the gunboats and patrol motor-launches, coastal steamers, tugs, harbour launches, outboard motor-boats, yachts, dinghies, tongkans and sampans. Some were seaworthy and some were not.

Tokyo Radio said that night: "There will be no Dunkirk at Singapore. The British are not going to be allowed to get away with it this time. All ships leaving will be destroyed."

Many were destroyed. Some never got past the minefields and harbour wreckage. Most were attacked by Japanese light naval craft and aircraft in the Banka Strait. None knew when they sailed that the Japanese Fleet now stood between Singapore Island and the haven of the Dutch East Indies. Singapore could not tell them because signals from Sumatra were in code—and the man with the codebook had taken it away with him to Java. Singapore received the messages but could not read them. . . .

Lt. H. Gordon Riches, R.N.V.R. (Malaya) took his 75-foot motor-launch out from Singapore as one of six vessels in tow by a tug. All were sunk at the breakwater except the tug, which took survivors on board and reached Palembang. On the way up the Moesi River they picked up two R.A.F. pilots who were sitting out in trees overhanging the river. They had been shot down.

A group of Army nurses and soldiers from one of the wrecked ships reached Muntock Beach on Banka Island, and surrendered to the Japanese. A party of Jap soldiers marched the men along the beach out of sight; and presently returned, wiping their bayonets. The nurses, who wore the Red Cross emblem, were then ordered to walk into the sea. When they were waist deep in the water, still facing out to sea, the Japanese machine-gunned them. Only one soldier and one nurse survived that outrage.

The *Li Wo*, a former Upper Yangtse river steamer of 707 tons, requisitioned by the Royal Navy for Malayan patrol duty in 1940 and commanded by Lt. T. S. Wilkinson, R.N.R., sailed from Singapore with many passengers in addition to her eight officers and 68 crew. She was attacked repeatedly by aircraft but managed to evade the bombs. On the morning of the 14th she encountered part of the Japanese invasion convoy bound for Sumatra. Although armed with only one old 4-inch gun—for which she had just thirteen shells left—and two machine-guns, Lt. Wilkinson turned the *Li Wo* to attack the Japanese transports and hit one and set it on fire. For an hour and a half she fought against hopeless odds, taking heavy punishment from the escorting Japanese cruiser. When all thirteen shells had been fired, Lt. Wilkinson turned his crippled vessel full steam ahead—and rammed the burning Japanese transport. The cruiser then blew the *Li Wo* out of the water. There were only ten survivors, and the gallant Lt. Wilkinson was not one of them. Years later, when the story at last reached London, Wilkinson was posthumously awarded the Victoria Cross.

Most of the people who left Singapore in the last few days failed to reach freedom. The majority were cast far and wide among the myriad islands south of Singapore and suffered tormenting privations. Some were rescued by fishermen and taken step by step along an escape route which remained open for several weeks. Some were picked up by the enemy and taken back to Singapore, Sumatra or Java. Some were never picked up. Many were never heard of again after they left Singapore.

On Singapore Island the noose tightened remorselessly round the tortured body of the City. In the north and in the south-west the Japanese advanced steadily against a desperate defence. That night—the night of the 13th/14th —the Japanese ran amok in Alexandra British military hospital. The story of that black episode has been preserved in a typescript of unknown authorship which has found its way to the British Imperial War Museum. It states:

"During the morning the water supply was cut off. Shelling and air activity was intense. Bursting shells, mortar bombs, with an occasional shot from our own artillery.

"The enemy were approaching the rear of the hospital from the Ayer Rajah Road. The number of incoming patients had lessened considerably and there was little or no traffic in the wards. During the morning, routine work continued. Japanese troops were seen for the first time at about 13.40 hours, attacking towards the Sisters' quarters.

"Japanese fighting troops were about to enter the Hospital from the rear. Lt. Weston went from the reception room to the rear entrance with a white flag to signify the surrender of the Hospital. The Japanese took no notice of the flag and Lt. Weston was bayoneted to death by the first Japanese to enter the Hospital. The troops now entered the Hospital and ran amok. They were excitable and jumpy, and neither the Red Cross brassards nor the shouting of the word 'hospital' had any effect.

"The following events started at about the same time.

"(a) One party entered the theatre block. At this time operations were being prepared in the corridors between the Sisters' bunks and the main theatre, this area being the best lighted and the most sheltered part of the block. The Japs climbed in through the corridors and at the same time a shot from the window was fired, wounding Pte. Lewis in the arm. About ten Japs came into the corridor and all the R.A.M.C. personnel put up their hands. Capt. Smiley pointed to the Red Cross brassards but the enemy appeared very excited and took no notice. The Japs then motioned them to move along the corridor, which they did, and then for no apparent reason, set upon them with bayonets. Lt. Rogers was bayoneted through the throat twice and died at once. Capt. Parkinson was bayoneted to death as also was Cpl. McHewan and Pte. Lewis. A patient on the operating table was bayoneted to death. He was later identified as Cpl. Holden of the 2nd Loyals. Capt. Smiley was bayoneted but he struck the blade away and it hit his cigarette case which was in his left breast-pocket. He was again lunged at and was wounded in the left groin, the previous thrust having wounded his left forearm. He then pretended to be killed, and pushed Pte. Sutton to the floor calling to the others to be quiet. The Japanese then left the corridor.

"(*b*) Another party of Japs went into the wards and ordered the Medical Officer and those patients who could walk outside the Hospital. In one ward two patients were bayoneted. The Japs then went upstairs and gave similar instructions. These Japs appeared to be more human and motioned the patients on stretchers to stay behind. Patients and personnel numbering about two hundred were taken outside, their hands tied behind them with a slip knot, one length of cord being used for about 4 or 5 persons. Some of the patients could only hobble, others had only one arm, while some were still in plaster and others were obviously very ill.

"Many of the seriously ill showed signs of great distress, one or two collapsed and had to be revived. The party was marched by a circular route to the old quarters, where they were herded into rooms, 50 to 70 persons per room, the sizes of which varied from 9 by 9 to 10 by 12 feet, where they literally jammed in and it took minutes to raise their hands above their heads. Sitting down was out of the question and they were forced to urinate against each other. During the night many died, and all suffered severely from thirst and the suffocating atmosphere. Water was promised but none came. When dawn arrived Japs could be seen with cases of tinned fruit which they kept for themselves. By the evening the shelling was at its maximum and shells were bursting all round. One struck the roof, blowing off doors and windows and injuring some of the prisoners. When this happened, 8 men tried to escape, some were successful but others were hit by machine-gun bullets. Previous to this Japs were leading small parties out of sight where afterwards we heard yells and screams, then a Jap soldier returning and wiping blood from his bayonet which left little doubt as to their fate.

"Except for a few that escaped none of these parties was ever seen again.

"(c) A party of Japs came into the reception room shouting and threatening the staff and patients who had congregated there. Sgt. Sheriff was killed. It was difficult to understand the reason for this barbaric attack on the Hospital. Investigations were carried out to find a possible explanation—rumours had it that a party of Sappers and Miners were digging a trench at the rear of the Hospital and on the approach of the Japs made a run for it. When the Japs passed through the Hospital there were about 40 or 50 herded into the corridor and a guard placed on them. Later the guard went away, and Capt. Barlett went out but could find no trace of the Japs."

Early on the 14th, General Percival was told that a complete failure of the water supply was imminent. Breaks in the water mains caused by bombing and shelling meant that more than half the supply from the reservoirs was being lost. The supply might last forty-eight hours, perhaps for only twenty-four hours. Sir Shenton Thomas warned the G.O.C. of the danger of an epidemic if a large proportion of the population was suddenly deprived of water; but Percival replied that though the shortage was serious it did not make the defence of the city impossible. He intended to go on fighting. Sir Shenton signalled the Colonial Office in London, pointing out that one million people were concentrated within a radius of three miles, with water for only twenty-four hours longer. Percival signalled Wavell in Java, asking, "Would you consider giving me wider discretionary powers?" Wavell replied, "In all places where sufficiency of water exists for troops they must go on fighting. Your gallant stand is serving purpose and must be continued to limit of endurance."

South-west of the city there was further heavy fighting,

but the enemy attacks were beaten off by the 1st Malaya Brigade after bitter hand-to-hand fighting. The Australians were subjected to heavy shelling; and were mortified to observe the Japanese moving west, without being able to shell them. Ammunition was being rationed.

Singapore City was again heavily bombed and shelled. Streets were blocked by the wreckage of smashed buildings, broken telegraph poles and tangled wires. The civil hospitals were crowded with wounded, and the ground floors of many large hotels and buildings were being used to house casualties. The grounds of the Singapore General Hospital were a shambles. Its once smooth, bright green lawns and rich flower-beds were gashed with huge pits dug for the burial of the dead. Bodies were carted out of the hospital and added to the stench, and lime was thrown on top. It was a gruesome business. Inside it was even worse. There were blood and guts and death everywhere. The stench was foul despite the disinfectant. Yet the Matron, Miss Kathleen Stewart, the Sisters and nurses worked on amid the human butchery. Patients, some alive, some dead, were in thousands. They were on the beds, under the beds, between the beds, overflowing out of the wards and filling the corridors. They were even lying on the stairs. Doctors, helped by nurses and orderlies, moved about finding the dead and hauling them out for burial in the loathsome pits outside. Army and civilian doctors had joined forces and worked as a team. The operating theatres were like butchers' yards. Surgeons amputated shattered limbs as fast as they could operate. There was no time for the delicate treatment which might have saved many limbs. The nursing girls stood by and helped. "Those girls were bathed in blood the last few days," said Sqdn. Ldr. Pat Atkins. "Sister Mollie Hill was a very brave girl. She was the head nursing Sister and she worked the clock round. A pretty woman in her late thirties. South African. They were all brave girls. They had no thought for themselves. Completely selfless." Water was short and instruments were sterilized in water that had been used again and again. Towards the end nurses were washing their hands in bottled mineral water.

During the night of the 14th/15th there was little enemy

activity and the general line still held at daybreak on the 15th, despite some gains by the enemy in the west. This was the only crumb of comfort for the defenders as the sun rose on the burning city. Even the ocean seemed to be on fire. The blazing soap factory on Singapore River threw grotesque patterns on the nearby buildings. Out west at Normanton more oil tanks were burning. Alexandra was ablaze. Timber sheds at Kallang shot up huge tongues of flame—one observer said they reached a height of 600 feet. Godowns and warehouses along the waterfront were afire. Paint and oil from anchored lighters spilled and spread on the water, still blazing. Stocks of rubber smouldered and stank.

The Governor watched it from the windows of the Singapore Club. Beside him stood Mr. Pretty. "My chief thought was tremendous relief that my wife and children had gone early on and were safe," said Mr. Pretty. "From where we stood, overlooking the Inner Basin, the whole place seemed to be a blazing inferno. The Governor was very upset. He kept saying 'Isn't this terrible?' or words to that effect."

General Gordon Bennett wrote of Black Sunday the 15th: "Today opened with a hopeless dawn of despair. There is no hope or help on the horizon. The tropical sun is sending its steamy heat on to the dying city which is writhing in its agony.

"The flanks of the Army continue to fall back. The enemy has advanced past Pasir Panjang towards the City. Enemy troop movement along Bukit Timah Road has been shelled by our artillery, as also have enemy troops opposite our own A.I.F. front, but the momentum of the enemy advance goes unchecked."

Early that morning Wavell signalled Percival:
"So long as you are in a position to inflict losses and damage to enemy and your troops are physically capable of doing so, you must fight on. Time gained and damage to enemy are of vital importance at this juncture. When you are fully satisfied that this is no longer possible I give you discretion to cease resistance. Inform me of intentions.

Whatever happens I thank you and all your troops for gallant efforts of last few days."

It was the wider discretion which Percival had requested two days earlier. The decision was now in his hands.

On that same day Wavell sent a long telegram to the Prime Minister in London. Its terms were very different. According to one staff officer, "It was mainly about personalities and it did not pull any punches."

In England, Percival's daughter Margery was celebrating her twelfth birthday.

Lt.-Gen. Percival went to early morning church service at Fort Canning and then called a conference of all senior commanders and key civic officials. The Governor was not present. The G.O.C. told them that the Supreme Commander had granted him the power to capitulate and then they discussed the situation. In Percival's opinion there were two alternatives: to counter-attack in an effort to regain the reservoirs and military food depots captured by the enemy at Bukit Timah, or to surrender. His generals were convinced that a counter-attack was out of the question. The troops were too exhausted and dispirited and had insufficient ammunition and supplies.

Gordon Bennett's diary records: "Silently and sadly we decided to surrender."

At that conference on Black Sunday the 15th, General Percival produced a letter, addressed to him from the Japanese commander, Yamashita. The Japanese had littered Singapore with leaflets; and on February 10 several small wooden boxes had hit the ground. They contained copies of the following:

> Lieut. Gen. Tomoyuki Yamashita
> High Com. Nippon Army
> Feb. 10th 1942

To:—The High Com. of the British Army in Malaya.

Your Excellency,
    I, the High Com. of the Nippon Army based on the

spirit of the Japanese chivalry have the honour of presenting the note to your Excellency advising you to surrender the whole force in Malaya.

Many sincere respects are due to your army which, true to the traditional spirit of Great Britain is bravely defending Singapore, which now stands isolated and unaided.

Many fierce and gallant fights have been fought by your gallant men and Officers, to the honour of British warriorship.

But the developments of the general war situation has already sealed the fate of Singapore and continuation of futile resistance would not only serve to inflict direct harm and injuries to thousands of non-combatants in the City, throwing them into further miseries and horrors of war, but also would not certainly add anything to the honour of your Army.

I expect that your Excellency, accepting my advice, will give up this meaningless and desperate resistance and promptly order the entire front to cease hostilities, and will dispatch at the same time your parliamentaire according to the procedure shown at the end of this advice. If, on the contrary, your Excellency should reject my advice and the present resistance continue, I shall be obliged, though reluctantly, from humanitarian considerations, to order my army to make an annihilating attack on Singapore.

In closing this note of advice I pay again my sincere respects to your Excellency.

Tomoyuki Yamashita.

1. The Parliamentaire should proceed to Bukit Timah Road.
2. The Parliamentaire should bear a white flag and the Union Jack.

On Friday the 13th some more Japanese boxes were airdropped. They contained the following:

I have the honour of presenting to you this Admonition of Peace from the standpoint of the Nippon Samurai Spirit. Nippon Navy, Army and Air Force have conquered the Philippine Islands and Hong Kong and annihilated the British Extreme Oriental Fleet in the Southern Seas. The command of the Pacific Ocean and the Indian Ocean as well as the Aviation power in the Southern and Western Asian Continents is now under the control of the Nippon Forces. India has risen in rebellion. Thai and Malaya have been subjected to Nippon without any remarkable resistance. The war has almost been settled already and Malay is under Nippon Power. Since the 18th Century Singapore has been the starting point of the development of your country and the important juncture of the civilisation of the West and East. Our Army cannot suffer as well as you to see this district burn to ashes by the war. Traditionally when Nippon is at war, when she takes her arms, she is always based upon the loyalty and breaking wrong and helping right and she does not and never aims at the conquest of other nations nor the expansion of her territories.

The War cause, at this time, as you are well aware, originated from this loyalty We want to establish new order and some of the mutual prosperity in the Eastern Orient. You cannot deny at the bottom of your impartial hearts that this is divine will and humanity to give happiness to millions of East Orientals mourning under the exploitation and persecution. Consequently the Nippon Army, based upon this great loyalty, attacks without reserve those who resist them, but not only the innocent people but also the surrendered to them will be treated kindly according to their Samuraism. When I imagined the state of mind of you who have so well done your duty, isolated and without rescuer, and now surrounded by our Armies, how much more could I not sincerely sympathise with you.

This is why I do advise you to make peace and give you a friendly hand to co-operate for the settlement of the Oriental Peace. Many thousands of wives and children of your Officers and Soldiers are heartily waiting in their Native Land to the coming home of their husbands and fathers and many hundreds of thousands of innocent people are also passionately wishing to avoid the calamities of War.

I expect you to consider upon the eternal honour of British Tradition, and you, be persuaded by this Admonition. Upon my word, we won't kill you, but treat you as Officers and Soldiers if you come to us. But if you resist us we will gibe swords.

Singapore   Nippon Army.
13 Feb. 42

The "parliamentaire" set off from Fort Canning. Lt.-Col. Chamier, Commandant, Intelligence Corps, Malaya, saw them go. "I was coming up to Fort Canning and a car came out and passed me at the gates. It was an open car with the hood down. Brig. Newbiggin (Administrative Branch, Malaya Command) was in the car, with Hugh Fraser, the Colonial Secretary, Capt. Wild, the Japanese-speaking interpreter, and another chap.

"Sticking out of the back of the car were two flagpoles. One was a furled Union Jack. The other was a furled white flag."

This first party was sent off to discuss truce terms. Yamashita would not even see them. "Send Percival," he said, and the party returned for the General Officer Commanding.

The British drove to a point near Bukit Timah and there the G.O.C. and his party alighted from their car and marched under Japanese escort to the enemy Headquarters, set up in the Ford Motor Factory. Percival had to carry the white flag in person to Yamashita.

Their conference lasted fifty minutes and the G.O.C. has not revealed—either in his book or his dispatch to Parliament—what took place there. The Japanese were

64

less reticent—it was not painful and humiliating for them. They published the following account of the final conversation:

Yamashita. We have just received your reply. The Japanese Army will consider nothing but unconditional surrender.

Percival. It is 9.15 p.m. Japanese Time, I fear we shall not be able to submit our final reply before midnight.

Y. (loudly) Reply to us only whether our terms are acceptable to you or not. Things have to be done swiftly as we are ready to resume firing in the evening.

P. Won't you please wait until you formally file into Singapore?

Y. It is impossible. In the first place, why not disarm all the British troops here, leaving only about 1,000 armed gendarmes for maintaining peace? In the second place, under no circumstances can we tolerate further British resistance.

P. One of your terms handed to us demanded that we turn over certain representatives of the Chungking régime to you. Their names are not clear to us.

Y. By that we mean that you arrest and turn over to us Ching Kam Ming, one of the Chinese liaison men.

P. I ask that the Nippon Army reciprocate with us in discontinuing attack.

Y. Agreed. What has become of the Nippon citizens in Singapore?

P. They have all been transferred to India. We do not know exactly where. The British troops would like to cease fire at 11.30 p.m.

Y. That is too late. By 11.00 p.m. we shall place part of our Army in Singapore proper.

P. Unless you allow us to 11.30 p.m. I fear that I shall not be able to transmit the order to all my troops.

Y. Then 11.30 will do.

P. Please do not allow the Nippon Army to enter Singapore until tomorrow.

Y. Why not assemble all your arms immediately in the heart of Singapore so that our Army can check them?

P. Why not let us arrange that tomorrow morning?

Y. It is a matter we can arrange as a side issue.

P. Even 11.00 p.m. is a little late for all troops to cease fire. Why not let them cease hostilities in their present positions?

Y. In that case we shall continue firing until 11.30 p.m. I would advise you to order cessation of hostilities immediately.

P. I shall see that they cease firing immediately I return to my H.Q., and that the firing ceases by 11.30 p.m. In the City area the firing will cease immediately and in the distant areas not later than 11.30 p.m.

Y. As proof of your good faith we shall hold the Highest British Commanders and the Governor of the Straits Settlements in custody at our headquarters. (A look of amazement was noticed on General Percival's face.)

P. Cannot the Nippon Army remain in its present position so that we may resume notifications again tomorrow at 7.00 a.m.?

Y. What! I want the hostilities to cease tonight and I want to remind you that the question is strictly a matter of this. If you can discontinue resistance by 11.30 p.m. we shall hold the Highest Commander and the Governor of the Straits Settlements in our custody. If you cannot do this, the Highest Commander and the Governor must come to our H.Q. by 10.00 p.m.

P. We shall discontinue firing by 10.00 p.m. Nippon Time. Had we better remain in our present positions tonight?

Y. Speaking on the whole, see that your troops remain in their positions and assemble tonight, disarmed, at the prescribed places. I approve of the cessation of hostilities at 10.00 p.m. After we have finished firing, all the British troops should disarm themselves save 1,000 men whom we shall permit to carry arms to maintain order. You have agreed to the terms, but you have not yet made yourself clear as to whether you have agreed to unconditional surrender or not.

(General Percival, with bowed head and in a faint voice, gave his consent. It was 7.30 p.m.)

Y. If you have accepted our terms I would like to hear them from your own lips once more.

P. The British troops will cease hostilities not later than 10.00 p.m. Nippon Time.

Y. The British troops shall disarm themselves completely, except 1,000 men whom the Imperial Army will allow to carry arms in order to obtain peace and order. If your troops infringe upon these terms, the Imperial Japanese Army will resume hostilities immediately

P. I agree. I have a request to make. Will the Imperial Army protect the women and children and the British civilians, men, women and children?

Y. We shall see to it. Please sign this truce agreement.

The Commander of the surrendered British Garrison affixed his signature at 7.50 p.m. on the 15th February 1942.

Survival Under the Jap

In victory, the Japanese proved to be arrogant, cruel and merciless to prisoners. At Singapore some were massacred and tortured in the first few hours after the surrender. In the days, weeks and months that followed a more subtle form of killing was practiced. Rations were at a starvation level and very few medical supplies were granted. In consequence, disease caused most of the deaths. Those who lived survived at levels hitherto unimagined by them.

A sense of humor and an ironic appreciation of the vagaries of life helped. One man who had both, as well as the will to survive, was Stanley Pavillard, a young doctor from the Canary Islands, only recently come to Malaya, and a P.O.W. in the Singapore capitulation. He was taken into Siam to help build a railroad from Bangkok to Rangoon for the Japanese. Work parties were sent to jungle camps where they first cut down the jungle growth, then built embankments over which the track would be laid. Dr. Pavillard was Medical Officer for one of three battalions of workers at Camp Wampo.*

On the long marches through the jungles, many prisoners came down with malaria and those who hadn't already contracted dysentery did so now. Dr. Pavillard managed to scrounge medical supplies from the most unlikely places, including the Japs themselves. But the morale of the men was the most serious problem. He says:

"Once a man lost the will to live drugs and treatment were useless. We used every possible subterfuge to keep the men cheerful, even sometimes inventing false news of the progress of the war, and sometimes we succeeded. If a man was past caring about such things it was now and again possible to make successful use of the deeply ingrained habit of military discipline: one could order a man to recover, and even threaten him with court martial if he died. This may seem a little far-fetched, but I have known it to work. I followed the principles of occupational therapy whenever possible, improving men's morale by

*About 1,500 P.O.W.'s.

giving them something to do. We devoted much time and effort to the pursuit and capture of bugs and lice, which we then slipped in vast quantities into the Japanese soldiers' huts. Techniques of the chase varied. One man was an expert on louse catching, having been a P.O.W. in the First World War, and he told me that the thing to do was to place a small piece of cottonwool on my navel when retiring for the night. I thought he was pulling my leg, but I tried it, and sure enough, next morning I found in the cottonwool at least two dozen fat juicy parasites. We gave weekly lectures to the men on hygiene, for the individual's own sake and for the common good: negligence gave dysentery even wider scope. In particular we told men always to dig a hole and fill it up afterwards when they obeyed the call of nature in the jungle. I made use of this form of sanitation myself, since I had caught dysentery and was anxious to scrutinize the signs of its progress day by day more precisely than would have been possible in the confusion of the communal deep latrine. Walking off on one occasion into the jungle for this purpose, I suddenly heard a hissing sound, and saw almost at my feet a large black cobra, already in the striking position: hood fully opened, head swaying from side to side, beady black eyes watching me, forked tongue flickering. I stood there like stone for an instant, and then ran so fast that I forgot my original purpose for two whole days afterwards.

"Daddy Richardson and I built two bamboo platforms in the M.I. room; at night we slept there, in the day we used them as examination couches. The M.I. room had a little door leading into the main hospital ward, behind which we had built a small bamboo hut to serve as a mortuary. We very seldom had any occasion to carry out a post mortem, since when the men died it was usually for very obvious reasons; the mortuary was only made necessary by the fact that the Japs did not always give permission for burial immediately.

"It always surprised me that so many men recovered after operations performed in such primitive conditions on patients in such very poor health. We only operated as a last resort, which meant that those who came under the knife—under the cut-throat razor, rather—were already suffering from malaria, gross malnutrition, and varying degrees of avitaminosis, particularly beri-beri and pellagra. Many of them had acute or chronic bacillary and amoebic dysentery as well, not to mention big tropical ulcers

"Since we never had enough drugs to treat everybody properly, we were constantly being faced with the most appalling decisions. Drugs were withheld as a matter of course until life depended upon their use, but then we had to decide who was to have them. On these occasions I gave preference to married men, especially those with many children, though I often knew that some personal friend of mine would have to die in consequence of this decision. I think I did right: God alone knows how hard it was to decide such a matter. Over and above this, we had to carry the burden and responsibility of easing, so far as we could, the misery and terror of those who were not going to recover. Sometimes we gave them an injection of plain water, making believe it was emetine, or whatever else was needed but not available. In the last stages one had a task like that of comforting a frightened child. I had one man, a sergeant-major in the S.S.V.F., a big burly fellow of tremendous personality and a tower of strength in the Battalion; now he went down with diphtheria, which caused paralysis in his throat, so that whenever he tried to swallow fluid it regurgitated up his nose. Then the nerve type of beri-beri attacked his left foot; I have never seen a man so full of the desire to live, and all I could do was to sit beside him and hold his hand until he calmed down and in the end died quite quietly." *

BAMBOO DOCTOR

by Dr. Stanley Pavillard

As work on the railway progressed, the Japs found it necessary to break us up into three detachments. This meant that I was parted from "D" Battalion: they were sent down to Wampo South, while I and the other doctors had to stay behind in the old camp, travelling backwards and forwards every day to visit our patients.

A new camp had to be built at Wampo South, and then our men got to work on an exceptionally strenuous and even dangerous part of the job. The camp was built on a piece of flat ground quite near the river, on the other side

*Bamboo Doctor, pp. 100, 101, 105, 106. St. Martin's Press.

of which was a high cliff of solid rock. A ledge a quarter of a mile long had to be carved out of this, to carry the railway; working up there, sixty feet above the river, completely exposed to the blazing sun, our men suffered terribly, and many of them collapsed from heat exhaustion. This was the result, not only of the heat, but also of the glare of sunlight reflected from the bare rocks all round; those men who managed to improvise sun glasses out of odd bits of coloured glass managed much better. In the same way, it was possible to make shoes of a sort out of jungle leaves and tree bark, so as to reduce the pain of walking on scorching rock. Even with the aid of such devices, only the strong ones could carry on, working blindly, in a jerky mechanical fashion as if hypnotized or dazed, aware only of the harsh sunlight boring mercilessly through their eye-balls. The body has a natural and automatic heat-regulating mechanism, but this can only be over-taxed so far: for many of the men there came a time when the brain lost control of the situation. Then they would lie there, chest heaving, heart throbbing, face grey and streaming with perspiration. I got these cases into hospital as quickly as I could, but they were suffering very severely from shock and often died quite soon afterwards.

The actual burden of the work was made easier than it might have been, however, by the fact that the Japs provided material and equipment for blasting. The vast explosions which took place could be heard at enormous distances. I remember the first: I was doing my ward rounds at the time, and I had not known that there was going to be any blasting. So when I heard this terrific bang I flung myself flat on the ground at once: everyone else did the same, our reflexes having been thoroughly conditioned during the battle of Singapore. We got up sheepishly, feeling rather fools.

The Japs had a peculiar sense of humour, and very often they used to fire the dynamite charges embedded in the rock without first sounding the warning signal: they did this for the fun of seeing the P.O.W.s run madly for shelter. This amusing game led to many accidents. The first victim was a cook, who was working at the time in the camp, across the river from where the blasting was taking place. A small piece of rock hit him on the forehead between the eyes: Pinky Riley 'phoned for me at once, and when I came I found the man suffering badly from shock. I examined him and I could actually see his brain tissue with small splinters of bone adhering to it. I cleaned the wound very carefully with boiled water and removed the bone fragments, then filled the cavity with three M. and B. 693 tablets crushed to powder, and applied a dressing. Fortunately the brain tissue itself did not appear to be damaged, and after four weeks in hospital the patient had fully recovered and never developed any after-effects.

The next victim was not so lucky: a large piece of rock hit him on the face, damaging the tear duct and leaving a nasty lacerated wound which extended from the inner angle of his left eye to the outer margin of the left lip. I put in eighteen stitches and he recovered all right, but with a mild degree of facial paralysis: careful plastic surgery after the war improved matters somewhat, but he was disfigured for life. We made repeated representations to the Japs about this aspect of their behaviour: they explained to us that it was our men's own fault and that they should get out of the way quicker.

Once a week we had a half-holiday, and the Japs would often enlist our help in large-scale fishing. The river was teeming with fish; a party of P.O.W.s who were able to swim waited by the riverside, and a Jap threw several hand-grenades into the river some two hundred yards up-stream, so as to explode under water. Enormous quantities of stunned fish floated down stream, to be landed by the waiting swimmers, and the Japs always posted several lookouts to make sure that all the fish was brought ashore so that they could pick the best.

Here again one could diddle them: it was just a question of thinking up the right trick. The way to embezzle fish under these circumstances is as follows: you tie a stout wire round your leg, which is of course out of sight while you are wading or swimming, and when a suitable fish comes along you push the loose end of this wire through its gills and allow it to hang there, out of sight and troubling nobody. Then at some convenient moment you can unhook the wire, with several fish on it, from your leg, and fasten it unobtrusively to the underwater roots of a tree by the edge. When the party is over, you can come back and claim your prize.

But the fish in this river were not all beer and skittles: some of them bit. There was one particularly vicious variety, only about two or three inches long but fond of hunting in enormous shoals, and their idea of a joke was to attack us while we were bathing and bite off small bits of our private parts. The scars which resulted were capable of subsequent misinterpretation by insurance doctors or by ever-loving wives, so I gave certificates to the victims making it quite clear that V.D. was not responsible. These certificates were written on any old dirty scrap of paper and read as follows:

To Whom It May Concern
This is to certify that.........................
whilst a P.O.W. in Siam lost a portion of his
Foreskin
———————as a result of a fish bite whilst swimming,
Scrotum
naked, in the river.
                                  Sgd.
                                  Captain: M.O., 1st S.S.V.F.

On 10th April, 1943, I was walking up towards the officers' hut to see Bob Lucas, the Adjutant of "D" Battalion, who was down with malaria, when glancing down a jungle path I was surprised to see a strange party approaching. They were British P.O.W.s escorted by Jap guards and they were carrying heavy packages slung on long bamboo poles. There were eighteen of these packages and I saw with great surprise that they were field medical panniers of the standard army type. It seemed almost unbelievable that the Japs should be sending medical supplies up to Wampo; I watched carefully, wondering what to make of it, while the party reported to the Jap guard room and then unloaded their cargo at the camp rice store, not far from the hospital, placing it carefully under lock and key.

Full of curiosity, I got talking to a member of the party; I gathered that these panniers contained British drugs captured at the fall of Singapore and that they were only going to be left at Wampo for one night. Early next morning the party was to continue its journey, carrying these medical supplies another stage towards their ultimate destination, which was on the frontier between Burma and Siam: they were to be used for the benefit of Jap soldiers fighting the British.

I thought hard. The panniers were not padlocked, but only tied with bits of wire and string. We were running short of medicines, and a move up country was rumoured. The rice store where the panniers had been locked up was only the usual kind of bamboo-and-palm-leaf hut: it had an entrance quite near the hospital, known as the smithy, since a certain amount of ironwork in connection with the railway was done there. Separating the rice store from the smithy was an inner wall or partition, about ten feet high, not reaching to the roof of the hut.

Without telling Daddy Richardson what I was up to I got hold of Pinky Riley and made him keep a sharp lookout near the smithy and let me know if any Japs turned up. Then I scrambled up quite easily over the bamboo partition and into the rice store: the first pannier I opened was full of tins, each tin containing one thousand M. and B. 693 tablets. This was wonderful, as this particular drug was very effective with many tropical diseases. I placed a tin inside my tattered old shorts and tied the pannier up again, and then departed very quickly, with a bulge in front of me that must have made me look at least six months pregnant.

I went back to the hospital and told Daddy Richardson what I had done, and then buried the tin.

This was excellent, but something more substantial was obviously called for, and there was very little time. I went to the officers' hut and explained the situation to Lt.-Col. Lilly, the British Camp Commandant; I pointed out that if we moved up country soon, which seemed very likely as the Wampo stretch of line was nearly completed, our medical situation would be very acute. So I wanted to plan a raid.

Lilly called together the commanding officers of "D" and "F" Battalions, and they weighed the matter up very seriously. Soon they came to the conclusion that my scheme was quite impractical: the Jap Commandant lived practically on top of the rice store, and it was more than likely that extra guards would be laid on to look after these precious supplies. Anyone caught taking part in such a raid would be decapitated at once. The camp administration did not approve and would have nothing to do with the plan.

I went away, feeling well and truly put in my place. But I could not accept this situation for long: and I knew much better than those officers did exactly what a move up country was likely to mean, in medical terms.

So I went to the men's lines and called out four individuals: I explained what I was going to do, and described the dangers and the consequences of being caught. They responded absolutely, without any hesitation at all.

I swore them to secrecy and we worked out every detail of my plan, going over and over again until we had it all by heart. Nobody else was to be told; a few trustworthy men were to be brought along to act as sentries and give a pre-arranged whistle if any Japs appeared, but they were not to be told what was going on.

We planned to start at 9 p.m. sharp. It was obvious that the panniers could not be properly examined in the rice store; each one would have to be lifted over the ten-foot bamboo partition and carried smartly along to the hospital M.I. room twenty-five yards away. There Richardson, Pinky and I would examine the contents of each pannier with a light and take out a suitable quantity of what we needed, but so as to avoid making it obvious that the panniers had been interfered with.

I arranged to go in with the raiding party on their first entry and show them where the panniers were, and then to stay in the M.I. room. I had enlisted four men: two to lift the panniers over the partition, and two to carry them through the smithy and along to the hospital. Pinky was to take the stolen drugs and bury them as we went along.

Eventually the time for action came: we made sure that the coast was clear and that our sentries were alert, and then we went into the smithy and started to climb the bamboo partition, very carefully, very quietly. But just then we distinctly heard the pre-arranged danger signal. We dropped off the partition and crouched in the darkest corners we could find, our hearts pounding: slowly a Jap guard's footsteps marched towards us. Time stopped, agonizingly, and the universe was full of nothing but those footsteps. Furiously, we turned not only our eyes but even our thoughts away from the guard: I had often thought that thought-waves or something similar can betray a man who is trying to hide, and now I made myself imagine that I was falling out of an aeroplane, tumbling and somersaulting, until in my mind's eye I could see only a whirl of earth and sky. This ugly thought was powerful enough to distract my mind and to prevent it from wandering off and attracting the attention of that man just outside.

After what seemed an infinite time of suspense we heard the guard's footsteps receding into the darkness. The all-clear signal was given and soon we were over the partition and at work. I helped the men get the first pannier over and along to the hospital, and soon we had it opened.

And so the work went on, easily and rhythmically: as soon as we had finished extracting a few items from one pannier, another would arrive. It was wonderful and sad to see such a stock of life-saving drugs: sad because of the men now dead for lack of them. We worked with fierce accuracy and speed.

Only one episode, but that an alarming one, interrupted the smooth progress of our work. I put my hand into the last pannier but one to take out a small bottle, and felt a searing pain, as if a red hot poker was being driven into the middle finger of my right hand. I let out a scream of agony, thinking that a snake had bitten me. The pain was unbearable, and within a few seconds I was bathed in a cold perspiration and felt like fainting. I told Richardson and Pinky to look for the snake, since it was important to know what kind it was: I held the hurt finger tight with my left hand, ready to have it slashed open with a razor and dipped in a strong solution of permanganate. But to my relief we found not a snake but a big armour-plated scorpion. My finger throbbed all night and was quite numb for a week afterwards.

Eventually we were told that it was all over: the last of the panniers had been put back exactly as before. I looked at my watch: it was 2 a.m. I thanked the men and commented on the speed with which they had manhandled those heavy panniers over the ten-foot partition. They said, apologetically, that they had opened the door of the rice store from the inside and had brought the panniers out that way, instead of over the partition as they had been told. I nearly had a fit: the front door of the rice store was right opposite the hut of the Jap Commandant in charge of railway construction.

Next morning, with a sigh of relief, I watched the Jap guards and the prisoners carrying the panniers move together out of our camp. Obviously they suspected nothing; I have seldom been so glad to see anybody off the premises. When they had gone I told Lt.-Col. Lilly what I had done, and explained that we now had a year's supply of medicines. The old man replied, "I had a notion you would do it, Pav; as a matter of fact I haven't slept a bloody wink all night."

I arranged that the loot should be left buried for several days in case of unexpected and delayed repercussions, and that it should be shared out equally between "D," "B" and "F" Battalions if all went well.

When I got back to England in October 1945 I submitted a report to the War Office, describing this episode and suggesting that the bravery and devotion of the men concerned should receive official recognition. None was given, and for the record their names are as follows:

No. 5707 C.Q.M.S. Metcalfe, J.M., F.M.S.V.F.
No. 7830 Private Wadsworth, K.T., F.M.S.V.F.
No. 7396 Sergeant Cassidy, T.P., F.M.S.V.F.
No. 13610 Lance-Corporal Miles, E.T., F.M.S.V.F.

I have no doubt that the knowledge that they had put a fast one across the Japanese and had saved the lives of any number of their comrades was then, and still remains, worth more to them than any medal.

Our Wampo stretch of line was almost finished: only part of the work on the cliff face remained to be done. To speed things up the Japs brought in two thousand more P.O.W.s and started what we called the "Speedo Period." Everything had to be done literally at the double. The weekly half-holiday was abolished. The men set off to work before dawn and returned late at night; they had no chance to wash themselves or air their bedding and the number of bugs and lice in action against us increased rapidly. Skin diseases, especially scabies and ringworm, attacked everyone, while malaria, dysentery, and deficiency diseases took full advantage of our exhaustion. Imperial Japanese Army Headquarters had given orders that guards were to bash hell out of the P.O.W.s if they did not work harder.

The worst of the acute and dangerous diseases which we were faced with, apart from cholera, was malignant tertian malaria with its cerebral complications. From this time on we were faced with cases of this sort almost every day. Patients were being brought in with temperatures of 105° to 107°, and unless the proper diagnosis was made and the proper treatment given at once, the patient would sink into delirium and then into a coma, and his temperature would rise to 110°: after this there was no hope of recovery as his brain was literally cooked. The important thing therefore was to keep the temperature down. We took it rectally as soon as the patient arrived in hospital, and if it was 105° or more he would be put on the ground naked, fanned, and soused continually in cold water. Meanwhile, quinine well diluted in saline was slowly injected intravenously. This procedure was not devoid of danger, as it could lead to sudden heart failure, but it was the only life-saving technique we had.

Patients who recovered from severe cerebral malaria had, in general, no recollection of what had happened; but this loss of memory was only temporary, and as a rule recovery was complete.

It was impossible to cope with malaria and its complications properly. At first we never had sufficient quinine; later on, and until our rice-store raid, atebrin had to be kept only for emergencies. Many men refused to take quinine either for prevention or cure: we often found the pills they were supposed to have taken hidden under their rice-sack pillows after they had died. We were always on the move and always at work, and never got a chance to oil the breeding grounds of mosquitoes: the men had no clothing to speak of and certainly no mosquito nets.

Eventually the railway line reached Wampo North. We had been working against our will and in the interests of the Japanese, our enemies; but it was impossible not to feel a certain pride and excitement at the completion of our work. So there we stood one morning, very early, straining our eyes and peering down the line, waiting until eventually the first train to pass over our own railway emerged from the mist and rattled by in a cloud of steam.

Our work at Wampo was done, and the Japs told us that at the end of April 1943 all the men there were to be moved up country. "D" Battalion was the last to leave: our destination was Tonchan South, ten miles to the north of Tarsau. This meant another forced march of about twenty-five miles; as before we had to carry all our kit and cooking utensils. We arrived dead beat after twenty hours.

At first this march followed the railway tracks, and then we left them behind and marched over ground which had been levelled and prepared for them. Further north there were wooden bridges to be crossed: these had been built out of tree trunks, across a number of deep ravines, and it felt very unsafe and alarming to walk across them. They had been built in a crude and clumsy fashion from jungle trees, and the men who built them had taken every opportunity for sabotage: spikes and bolts were put in in the wrong places or left loose, so that when in due course the Japs started to send heavy goods trains over these bridges, many of them collapsed, sometimes causing the locomotive to explode at the bottom of a deep ravine.

When we arrived at Tonchan South we found that the camp already held three thousand P.O.W.s. Another camp had been built to house the labour force which the Japanese had impressed from among the Asian population: there were three thousand of these unfortunate people also, and both the two camps, theirs and ours, occupied less than half a square mile between them. These Chinese, Malays, Indians and Eurasians were in a far worse situation than ours: they had no doctors or medicines and no leaders of any sort, no record was kept of their names and whereabouts, they were fed occasionally when the Japs felt like it, and they were totally ignorant of sanitation. The whole situation was ripe for an epidemic.

I felt very disturbed, but as far as "D" Battalion was concerned, things could have been worse. Before we left Wampo I had lectured the men on cholera precautions, and they had a natural advantage in that their average age was thirty-seven, with eleven years' residence in the Far East. This meant that they were completely acclimatized to a tropical environment, they had a certain sense of responsibility and could be relied on to carry out medical instructions given for their own good, and in most cases they were married and had something to live for. Many other units in Siam were made up chiefly of young men without these advantages, and their survival rate was much lower: a fact which came home to one poignantly when one inspected the rough inscriptions in the various jungle cemeteries.

The Japanese Camp Commandant at Tonchan South was Staff-Sergeant Hiramatsu, a man of few words, tough, rough and brutal: they called him Tiger. But he did have a sense of justice, and the ruthless discipline which he imposed was as bad for the Jap guards as it was for us. We were all afraid of him.

The day after we arrived at Tonchan South he sent for me and for the P.O.W. camp interpreter, who warned me that the Tiger knew English and that I should be careful what I said. Apparently it was beneath the great man's dignity to speak the captives' language or admit that he understood it.

I came into the Tiger's hut and he barked out at me through the interpreter, "You are the new doctor!" I felt like a new boy at school and I nearly answered, "Yes sir"; but I remembered that I was dealing with a bully and I looked him straight in the face and said, "That is so." He looked me up and down and paused and thought a little, and then asked me in a slightly different tone why there was so much sickness amongst us prisoners.

There was plenty to say in reply to that one: I gave him the obvious elementary answers, and pointed out that the conditions we had been living under made sickness inevitable. Men fed on such a poor and defective diet, over-worked to the point of collapse, and compelled to do without proper sanitation were not likely to be pictures of health. I ended up by saying, "I am proud of "D" Battalion: they want to work, and I will keep them fit, but you must help me."

Tiger glared at me for a long time: I could see that he was angry and I wondered if I had gone too far. But eventually he smiled in a cunning way and explained to me that the sickness was caused by our men being lazy, sleeping on the wet ground and without shirts to protect them from mosquito bites. Controlling my temper as well as I could I pointed out the various fallacies in this statement of the situation, and I explained that malaria was a menace even in the best conditions: I had always taken proper precautions in the tropics, but I had still caught malaria.

This made Tiger laugh immoderately, and he advanced what seemed to him a tremendously witty suggestion that if I, a doctor, had caught malaria, it must have been in consequence of taking girls into the jungle at night. I pretended to share his amusement at this brilliant joke and laughed loudly, and the interpreter did so too: the atmosphere relaxed and I realized that Tiger and I understood each other. When he stopped laughing he asked me in a business-like way what I needed to ensure my men's health and ability to work. At once, before he had time to change his mind, I made my terms: 26 ounces of uncooked rice per man every day, one cow or buffalo and six large baskets of mixed vegetables every other day, adequate amounts of tea and sugar, and a half a day's rest every week. This half-holiday was needed very urgently: the men were still sleeping on the ground and had no time to wash what few garments they had. The Tiger thought this over and then agreed, but in a quiet, threatening way: he expected results. I felt very pleased at this diplomatic success, although I had some difficulty at first in making our people believe what I said had happened: it sounded too good to be true. But Staff-Sergeant Hiramatsu was a man of his word.

Three days later he sent for me again: I arrived with the interpreter, very puzzled, and found Tiger lying on the floor under a blanket, obviously in the throes of a malarial attack. He produced an ampoule of quinine, pointed to a saucepan in which a hypodermic needle had been boiled, and told me to give him an intravenous injection.

The situation had its humorous side, and I could not resist turning to the interpreter and saying, "Ask him if he has been taking a girl into the jungle." The interpreter did not have time to translate a word: Tiger roared "Kurrah!" at the top of his voice and grabbed furiously at a sword by his bedside. But he controlled himself and smiled through his shivers and asked me to be less comic and to get on with the injection. I did so, and he was up next day.

We now heard that cholera had broken out at a place called Takanun, which was less than one hundred miles from us up the river. This was very serious news; "D" Battalion had all been inoculated against cholera and I had lectured on the subject, but there were now so many men crowded together in such a small area that an outbreak of cholera could wipe us all out in a matter of days.

Cholera is usually endemic in parts of Siam during the dry season; you catch it by drinking contaminated water from a river or shallow well, or by eating food which has been handled by someone suffering from cholera or carrying it. There have been vast epidemics at various periods of history: Thucydides refers to it in the fifth century B.C., while in modern India there were eight million cholera deaths between 1904 and 1924. I had never seen a case, but I was almost obsessed by the fear of it: the section of my textbook on tropical diseases which dealt with cholera was the only part of that book which escaped being used as cigarette paper.

Now this terrifying thing was at work and near us; I

gave further and more urgent lectures, and insisted that full precautions were to be rigorously observed. Only boiled water was to be used for drinking or for cleaning the teeth, bathing in the river was to stop absolutely, eating utensils were to be dipped in boiling water before use, any food touched by flies or ants was to be thrown away, and each man had to take great care to keep his hands away from his mouth. One additional warning I gave, which was that paper used for making cigarettes should not be licked: the men used any old scrap of dirty paper for this purpose.

In practice these rules could not be enforced as strictly as one would wish, and of course they were wholly ignored in the Asian camp next door.

On the morning of 8th June, 1943, Vincent Bennett, the M.O. of "F" Battalion, sent a message to my tent asking if I could come over at once to see one of his men who was very ill. At the time it was raining heavily, and as I left the partial shelter of my leaky tent the cold rain sloshed over my body and soaked my loin cloth, so that by the time I reached the hospital I felt as if I had a wet nappy on.

The man was lying on bamboo slats looking extremely ill, very pale and with a drawn anxious expression on his waxen face. His nose had a pinched appearance and his eyes were sunken; his finger tips were crinkled like a washerwoman's, his skin was cold and clammy, and his temperature below normal.

I asked him several questions. In a barely audible whisper, he told me that he had been vomiting and passing large quantities of stools like barley water, and that he was now getting excruciating pains in his calf muscles. I told him not to worry, and made various vague and sadly dishonest promises of healing medicines.

Vincent and I walked away and as soon as we were out of ear shot I turned to him and said, "Christ, it's caught up with us, Vincent! There is no doubt, that's cholera!"

"I know, Pav, it's a textbook case." It was a great shock and we felt very bitter: one would think we had suffered enough.

We returned to the hospital and gave the man a shot of morphia, since by this time the cramps in his legs were making him scream out in agony. The cholera poisons make the muscles contract suddenly and so violently that individual muscle fibres actually snap: the pain of it is almost unendurable.

Then Vincent and I went to tell Tiger what had happened. It took him a moment or two to realize the full implications of what we had said: then he started to shout and rave like a lunatic, as if it had been our fault. Eventually he calmed down, and we told him that we must at once clear a small area in the jungle, not far from the camp, to serve as a cholera compound for this case and the others which were bound to occur. This sent Tiger raving again and he screamed that the man had to be sent at once to the Base Hospital at Tarsau. We replied that under no circumstances was the man to leave Tonchan South, as to move him would only spread the disease. Finding his will opposed, Tiger went very red in the face, pulled his sword out and brandished it in front of us screaming, "It is an order of the Imperial Japanese Army that the man be moved to Tarsau!"

I thought that a more conciliatory tone might help, so I said. "It shall be done as you say; since there is a Japanese doctor at Tarsau, why not 'phone him first? If this man goes to Tarsau and spreads the disease there, your doctor will make trouble for all of us." Tiger picked up the telephone with a grunt and started jabbering in Japanese, and after a while he turned to us and said, "Japanese doctor now come—you take man to jungle."

So off we went and arranged for a working party to go and make a clearing in the jungle, a quarter of a mile from the camp. Here we rigged up a tent provided by the Japs; it was full of holes where the canvas had rotted. We put the patient inside, but we could do nothing for him except for an injection of morphia to ease the pain and a drink of water which he immediately vomited.

Before the afternoon was over, we had packed ten more cases inside that small tent; and our first patient had died.

We felt uneasy about burying him, since the ground sloped slightly and rain water might soak through the earth and contaminate the river. So we made an attempt to

84

burn the body, using jungle vegetation to build a funeral pyre: after several attempts we managed to get the green wood alight, but the cremation was not a success, and eventually we had to bury the body in a deep grave only partially charred.

The epidemic which now started did not take me wholly by surprise: I had given the men of "D" Battalion a shot of cholera vaccine before we left Wampo, and I had also worked out plans for making a water distillation plant.

The distilled water was required to form the basis of a saline solution to be administered intravenously. The treatment of cholera is aimed in general at the immediate replacement of body fluids lost by vomiting and diarrhoea, so that the body never becomes dehydrated but remains able to function. I managed to save many lives in this way, pouring anything up to eight or ten pints of my saline solution into the patients' veins every twenty-four hours. But there were various dangerous complications: muscular cramps and, more seriously, complete kidney failure or beri-beri. Both of these very often proved fatal. One curious feature of the epidemic which I noticed was that a man liable to attacks of malaria would find them cured on his recovery from cholera: as if the cholera germs had destroyed their malarial colleagues.

As well as salines, we used M. and B. 693 tablets. If given early enough, before the pernicious vomiting started, this made the disease much milder or enabled the patient to by-pass it altogether.

Even so, we had two hundred cases within two days from our diagnosis of the first. The Japanese flatly refused to give us extra tents, and matters were made worse by the fact that many of the Asians in the camp next door panicked and fled into the jungle. Their only possible route was by the river and its tributaries, and so in a very short time these men contrived to contaminate every available source of water supply. Later on, our working parties found their bodies in the jungle.

The men were now dying at such a rate that I persuaded Tiger to let me have a working party to dig a communal grave. This was granted and we dug a pit, 20 feet long,

10 feet wide, and 20 feet deep; we used jungle vines as ropes, to hoist the earth and the workers out of the pit.

The men were thrown into the pit as soon as they died; and every evening, before leaving the compound, the doctors and orderlies together used to shovel a thin layer of earth over the swollen and distorted bodies.

When a new patient was admitted we placed him on the ground and started to administer intravenous salines at once. This was often difficult, since his veins had usually collapsed as a result of dehydration caused by copious vomiting and diarrhoea. We could not locate a vein with our finger tips: we had to cut the skin in an approximate fashion where we knew there ought to be a vein, and then patiently to dissect the tissues around the vein until it was exposed. The best vein for this purpose was the one on the inner aspect of the foot, just above the ankle bone. Once the vein was located a linen thread was passed under it and it was eased clear of the wound; a hollow bamboo needle was pushed into the vein and tied with the thread, and then connected by means of a rubber tube to the saline bottle. We had two dozen such bottles, glass jam-jars or Japanese beer bottles, and they were all in constant use. The operation was carried out without any local anaesthetic, since none was available; but fortunately the shocked and collapsed condition of the patients was as good as an anaesthetic. The thickened blood inside their veins looked like black treacle and flowed slowly.

One of the worst things about cholera was the painfulness of the muscle cramps; we gave morphia when we could, but there was not nearly enough to go round, and from the compound there arose continually, therefore, a faint desperate moaning which was terrible to hear, punctuated at intervals by appalling shrieks as some unfortunate's muscles snapped.

The compound was hellish in every way. The stench from the burial pit was everywhere. When one approached the pit to use it one saw bubbling millions of maggots. The cholera victims from the Asian camp had no doctors or orderlies to look after them, and the Japanese made no provision at all for them to have food or water. They were just dumped in our camp to lie on the ground in the open until they died or were taken by us into a tent. We did what we could to alleviate their sufferings; when some of our own cholera cases recovered, they volunteered to stay in the compound and help.

We could not keep the bodies too long before burial because of the ants; I usually tried to wait a few hours before burial, just to make sure, and in doubtful cases I cut the man's wrist with a razor blade. Flowing blood would show that he was alive, and could then be stopped by artery forceps.

In describing these days, I may have given an impression of callousness, as though I and the other doctors were past feeling and suffering the situation. In a sense our emotions were anaesthetized: we could not have remained sane otherwise. But then and for a long time afterwards we were liable to find memory reasserting itself at night-time, and to wake up screaming from the black depths of nightmare: this still happens to me from time to time, and once again I see the jungle, the rain, and my friends turning liquid in a pit of flies and maggots.

When I left the compound in the evening, I used to go back to a little tent in the main camp, which I shared with five other officers. On one side of me Bob Lucas slept, and on the other was Captain T. E. Abrams, R.A., known to us all as A.B. He and I were good friends and I shared his blanket.

I remember how he came with me one day to Tonchan main camp; I wanted to get some more rubber and glass tubing for our distillation plant, and he came too, walking the weary twelve miles there and back simply so that I could have someone to talk to. We came to a place where the ground was covered with small brown pebbles such as are used for drives and garden paths in England, and A.B. said to me, "Look, Pav: these pebbles remind me of the path leading to my house. Let's rest here for a bit." We sat down and chatted about our homes, idly picking up these pebbles and flinging them in the jungle, listening to the rustling of the leaves as various birds and reptiles moved away from this bombardment. This episode and these thoughts of home came back to me a few days later, when A.B. woke me up in the middle of the night with agitated whispers. I groped for his hand instinctively: it was cold and clammy, and I could feel the ridges on his finger tips. Very sadly, because I knew what had happened, I said to him, "Tell me, A.B., where have you been shitting?" He answered in a whisper, "Just by the tree outside the tent." I lit a candle: it was four in the morning. By the flickering candle light I could see that his eyes had sunk into their orbits and his skin had become pale and waxy. "Listen, A.B., you are not to worry," I said. "It is a good job we have caught it early—here, take these tablets." But only with great difficulty could he swallow the four M. and B. 693 tablets which I gave him. I woke up the other people in the tent and at frequent intervals we carried poor A.B. outside by the tree where he vomited and passed large watery stools. There was not much more we could do till daybreak. After a while, he started complaining of pain in his calf muscles: I boiled a morphia tablet in a spoon with a little water over a candle flame, sucked the liquid into a syringe, and injected it. This relieved the pain, just for a while.

Dawn came at last. I examined his stools: they had a typical cholera appearance. I organized a carrying party and we took A.B. along to the cholera compound on a stretcher made from two sacks and a couple of bamboo poles. Then before following on, I gave instructions that the tent was to be moved and a fire built where it had stood, and also by the tree, in order to disinfect the ground; already the ants were everywhere, and I strongly suspected them of helping to spread the cholera germ, although I have never seen this in a textbook.

Luckily, several bottles of saline were already sterilized and ready: I warmed them to body temperature and dissected my way down to a vein in A.B.'s right foot. I got several pints of saline into him at once, and more later in the day: his cramps were severe and he had to be given morphia. Sometimes he was delirious; but once he took my hands in a tight grip and said in a barely audible whisper,

"Pav, write to my wife, tell her I love her." Soon afterwards, he sank into a coma and died; it was 5 p.m.

I had not the heart to throw his body into the common pit, since we had lived as brothers, sharing what little we had. So I took a shovel and dug a deep grave by a jungle tree, and his men in the lines afterwards erected a rough wooden cross there with his name inscribed with a red-hot iron.

On 26th June, 1943, Tiger gave me permission to visit Tarsau ten miles away, to see whether I could get some more rubber and glass tubing for our distillation plant. This apparatus worked day and night now, which enabled us to find plenty of saline sterilized and ready for use when we came to the compound in the morning. But the rubber tubing was starting to perish because of the heat.

I went by myself, taking with me a pass in Japanese characters which Tiger had provided in case I should be stopped. He told me to be back by nightfall. I set off in the early morning along a narrow track, carrying a bamboo cane and making a loud noise so as to frighten away snakes and wild animals. Wild life was very plentiful in the Siamese jungle: at night we could hear elephants fooling around quite near the camp, which made the Japanese get nervous and start banging away with their rifles; tigers had been reported and sometimes we smelt them. Large committees of baboons used to hang around our camp quite often, eyeing us in a disapproving way. The last time I had been out on this errand, A.B. had been with me, and now he was dead: it was hard to believe, and very sad.

After walking several hours, I saw a column of men marching towards me. As they approached I began to feel that there was something familiar about the man who was leading the column. "Dr. Livingstone, I presume?"—it was Lt.-Col. Newey, the C.O. of my wartime Battalion, the 1st S.S.V.F. We had parted a year previously at Changi, and here we were meeting by chance in the middle of a Siamese jungle.

The Jap guard in charge of this party allowed me to talk to them for a while. They were mostly Malayan Volunteers, part of an outfit which the Japanese had designated as

"H" Force. They had just come from Singapore; the Japs had told our administration at Changi that they were forming two units, "F" Force and "H" Force, and that all sick men in Changi who were able to walk should be included in these parties, since they were to be sent to a hill station where it was very healthy, with excellent food and first-class hospitals. The camp authorities had no alternative to accepting this lie; in fact, no arrangements had been made to feed these men at all. During the subsequent few weeks we quite often saw parties of these men from "F" Force and "H" Force on their way through Tonchan South: they appeared to be very near starvation, and we gave them what food we could. Now when I told them that they were walking straight into a cholera area, they were completely shattered by the news; they were quite plainly in no state to cope with any epidemic. In fact, the mortality among the men of these two units was extraordinarily high; they had suffered much more than we had.

I left them, and continued my march to Tarsau. The Jap medical officer there gave me the glass and rubber tubing I had come for, and after talking to various friends I set out on my weary and lonely walk home, moving fast, since starvation had made me night-blind and I was afraid of getting lost. The Japs had given me written permission to carry a walking stick at night, and I was to produce this if a Jap guard questioned my being in possession of what they classed as a dangerous weapon. Usually the guards clouted first, before I could produce the document out of my G-string. Even with the stick I was very liable to fall into holes and bump into trees.

This time I was lucky and got back to camp well before sunset. My friends of "H" Force were there trying to find shelter and scrounging around for food, which we provided as well as we could.

That evening when I held my usual sick parade, many of the Malayan Volunteers of "H" Force came along so that I could do something about their blisters and especially their tropical ulcers. These tended to start in consequence of a bamboo scratch or a blistered foot; at the best they were slow to heal, and unless they were treated at once they increased rapidly in size, spreading and eating up the tissues very deeply until even the bone was affected and started to disintegrate. Then secondary infection set in, accompanied by a sickening smell. The doctors of "H" Force had practically no medicines with them; they tried various ways of treating these tropical ulcers such as scraping them clean without any anaesthetic, the patient being held down meanwhile, or the deliberate placing of live maggots in the ulcer so that they would eat it clean. This form of treatment originated during the First World War; severely wounded men who had to lie out on the battle field for several days before they could be rescued often had wounds which were seething with maggots, but incredibly clean and free from any tendency to go gangrenous.

Following this theory, some of the P.O.W. doctors started putting live maggots into ulcers. This form of treatment would probably have been excellent for fit and well-fed men, but I did not approve of it for anyone in our physical and psychological condition: the sight of a bubbling mass of big fat maggots crawling in and out of even the strongest-minded P.O.W.'s ulcer would be enough to send him round the bend.

Instead, I used the "permanent ulcer dressing," as developed during the Spanish Civil War for the treatment of compound fractures. The Spanish doctors used to encase the shattered limb in plaster of paris and leave it to stew for several weeks in its own pus; when the plaster was removed the fracture was seen to be joined and the wound healed. So now with these ulcers: I cleaned them as well as I could and applied a little iodoform or M. and B. 693, and then slapped on elastoplast, covering this with bandages made from old sheets or banana tree bark.

After three weeks the ulcers had vanished completely unless they had been very big, and even then we saw healthy granulation tissue and the process of healing completed itself soon afterwards.

I treated a great many tropical ulcers in this way and no amputations resulted, except in the case of one man who insisted on being evacuated down-river against my advice. If he had done as he was told, he would have kept his leg.

The Heroic Island

One of the most heralded last-stands in modern American military history occurred at Wake Island in December 1941. On this atoll, with its shore line of twenty-one miles, a handful of Marines and construction workers fought off heavy bombing raids and one full-fledged invasion attempt before the Japs managed to get ashore.

Wake was 2,000 miles closer than Pearl Harbor to Japan and considered a part of the U.S. Pacific defense line, a kind of stationary "carrier" from which strikes could be made at the Jap-held Marshall Islands. At the time of the invasion, the island was under the command of W. Scott Cunningham, Commander, U.S.N. He had visited the island twice before. "Aside from the tiny Pan American Airways installations on Peale [island] the atoll in 1940 was virtually the same desolate spot it had been when Mendana de Neyra looked it over, snorted, and departed in the sixteenth century. From time to time there had been talk in Washington about developing Wake's possibilities . . . but its strategic importance had generally been lost on a nation intent on peace. . . . Officially it bore the designation of a bird sanctuary." *

But when Cunningham arrived in November 1941, there were 1,100 civilians hard at work building roads, air strips, and other installations intended primarily for a base to be utilized by amphibious patrol planes; a Marine defense battalion, not up to full strength, was under command of Major James Devereux, and was charged with building the defense installations. Major Devereux had arrived in October bringing three batteries of coastal defense guns, gleaned from retired battleships, and three batteries of anti-aircraft guns. The fire-power of the island consisted of the six batteries, plus eighteen machine-gun emplacements of fifty-caliber, and thirty machine guns of

*W. Scott Cunningham, *Wake Island Command*, p. 26. Little Brown & Co.

thirty-caliber. There was no radar, and it was hard to hear warnings from sirens or whistles because of the unusually loud, booming surf.

Radio broadcasts of the Pearl Harbor attack reached Wake on December 7th; on the 8th, Wake received its first visit from Jap bombers based in the Marshalls. Though the Wake defenders were expecting raids, this first one of thirty-six enemy bombers managed complete surprise; considerable damage was caused.

Commander Cunningham had stationed four planes patrolling over the atoll at 12,000 feet, but the Japs flew in at 2,000 feet out of low cloud formations. Even the roar of the approaching planes was smothered by the noise of the surf.

After the first raid, the defending personnel numbered 379 Marines, seven officers and eighteen enlisted men in the Marine air force to man the planes still in working condition. Out of the approximately 1,100 civilian construction workers, only a few were ready and willing to volunteer for combat duty.

Bombing raids occurred at noon the next two days in succession, but these were met with all the firepower the Wake defenders could muster. Some damage was done, but Cunningham says:

"As the news [two Jap bombers had been downed and perhaps a third was damaged] went round the atoll, morale shot up. We had taken three massive raids in as many days, and we were shaken and hungry and so tired we could fall asleep on our feet, but the situation was looking up. . . . We were learning about war and how to take care of ourselves. . . . We had four planes of our own and a fifth almost ready for action again. . . . We turned to repairs and preparations for the fourth day." *

On December 11th, although no Jap had yet set foot on the island, they announced to the world that their flag flew over Wake. On that day they confidently expected to land their troops; but a surprise awaited them.

*Wake Island Command, p. 82.

WAKE ISLAND COMMAND

by Commander W. Scott Cunningham

The telephone roused me about three o'clock on the morning of the eleventh. I stumbled out into the hallway of the cottage, trying to fight off the stupor of sleep into which I had fallen, and reached for the receiver.

"Cunningham."

"Captain, this is Gunner Hamas at the battalion command post."

I came awake fast. Elmer Greey's head appeared in his doorway and he watched me inquiringly.

"Major Devereux reports ships sighted on the horizon." For all his formality, John Hamas's voice was crackling with excitement. "He requests permission to illuminate with searchlights."

Ships on the horizon! The softening-up process was over, then, and they were moving in for the kill. And what could six old five-inch guns do against the batteries of longer-range weapons they were sure to have?

Our only hope was to ambush them. We must lie silent and dark until they steamed in so close our guns would be effective, and then we must hit them with everything we had.

"No," I said flatly. "Don't use the searchlights. And don't commence firing until further orders."

I slammed down the phone and began dressing. Greey and Keene came into my room to learn the news, and I told them to notify Putnam's command post and any other points they could raise. Then I set off at a run for my truck outside.

It was a perfect tropical night. A half moon was coming up over the ocean and the air was cool and soft. The former bird sanctuary lay peaceful and serene before me as I turned on my blued-out lights and began the ride down the pockmarked coral road to the communications center. Inside, the dimly lighted room hummed with activity. Radio men hung over their equipment; the talker exchanged words in low tones with someone on the telephone; a decoding officer stood by to translate messages arriving or going out.

It had been Wesley Platt, the strong-point commander on Wilkes, who had first got word of the ships from one of his lookouts. And now, as we waited, the alert and the warning to keep the lights dark and the guns silent had gone the rounds. At Peacock Point, at Kuku and Toki, men waited in the dim moonlight for the order to open fire, or dug their foxholes deeper against the shelling that might begin at any moment. At the airstrip, the planes were ready but silent.

So Wake lay, inactive but alert, as the tiny specks on the horizon grew larger.

Three-thirty . . . four o'clock . . .

I was scared, plenty scared, though I tried not to show it. My muscles ached from tension.

Four-thirty . . .

"They're getting closer. An awful lot of 'em."

Five o'clock.

The advance ships in the task force were only about four miles off Peacock Point now.

BOOM!

We could hear it above the surf. The invaders had opened fire.

Still our guns remained silent, our searchlights dark.

A column of Japanese ships moved parallel to Wake's southern shore, advancing from Peacock Point toward Wilkes. Then it turned toward the atoll, moved in closer, turned again, and began steaming back toward Peacock. Other ships advanced toward Wilkes. The guns continued to sound, with increasing frequency.

The telephone talker motioned to me. I grabbed the phone.

"Captain?" It was Hamas again. "Lieutenant McAlister

reports a destroyer, range four-six-hundred, off Kuku Point. Lieutenant Barninger has ships in his sights off Peacock. Major Devereux ordered me to notify you."

I took a deep breath and looked at my watch. It was 6:15. The long silence was over.

"What are we waiting for, John?" I yelled. "Cut loose at them!"

And as Gunner Hamas relayed the order to the batteries around the atoll, I could hear the five-inchers open up.

It was a sweet, wonderful, glorious shoot-up.

Barninger's guns opened up on Peacock and hit a light cruiser on the second salvo. She turned and began to run; the guns scored twice more before she got out of range.

McAlister opened on Wilkes. He had a problem—his fire control equipment was virtually worthless after the bombing of the day before—but that didn't interfere with the work of Battery L. Nothing could bother Battery L this moonlit morning. Battery L was red hot. Three ships were in sight; the guns chose one and let fire. Dead on target! As the crews cheered, it blew up before their eyes and sank.

Another ship; another hit.

Another, perhaps a transport, and another hit.

And yet another, this one a light cruiser from its silhouette, and, by God, another hit!

And now the guns on Peale had their chance to get into the fight. They had been waiting for something to come within range, and the Japs obliged. Three ships slipped on past Wilkes and turned north toward Toki Point, and Kessler's men at Battery B opened up.

They hit the leading ship. The enemy let loose a hail of fire in answer, and the communications lines between the fire control equipment and the guns were shattered. Battery B kept on firing anyhow.

And then, only forty-five minutes after our first gun had sounded, it was all over—at least, so far as the shore batteries were concerned. The task force sent out to take possession of Wake had had enough, and was running for cover.

But it was not all over for the Japs. As the invader retreated out of range behind a heavy smoke screen, Paul Putnam's impatient flyers moved in for their share of the banquet.

They had gone aloft when we opened fire. After discovering, with some amazement, that no planes accompanied the invaders, they had circled beyond range of our own guns and bided their time. Now they struck.

Putnam was up there himself, with Elrod, Freuler and Tharin, and thanks to Freuler's hard work in the brief days of peace, the little Wildcats carried their lethal cargo of bombs that didn't properly fit the bomb racks. It was the first chance they had had to use them, and they made them good.

The Japs threw up all the antiaircraft fire they could, but the Wildcats kept attacking. They bombed and strafed two light cruisers, knocking out the torpedo battery of one and the radio shack of the other. Freuler set a fierce gasoline fire raging on a transport.

As they expended their bombs and machine gun belts, they came roaring back to the airstrip for more, time after time. Two other pilots, Kinney and Hamilton, got their turns. The fleet continued to race for home, and the four little fighters continued to harass them. And it was Hank Elrod, apparently, who scored the greatest victory from the air. He dropped a bomb on a destroyer; minutes later Kinney sent his plane screaming down toward the same ship just in time to see it blow up in his face.

And that was that. The Japs limped away over the horizon and were gone. We had sunk at least two ships and scored hits on maybe half a dozen others. And we had suffered no casualties.

Not until after the war would we know exactly what we had accomplished, or the size of the fleet Japan had sent out to scoop up the remains of Wake's defenders. Rear Admiral Sadamichi Kajioka, commander of the enemy's 6th Destroyer Squadron, had been on that light cruiser Barninger's men hit when the firing opened at Peacock Point; it was the *Yubari*, flagship of a force numbering two other light cruisers, six destroyers, two patrol boats and two medium transports, with a pair of submarines out ahead to run interference.

Rear Admiral Kuninori Marumo had commanded the other two light cruisers, *Tenryu* and *Tatsuta*. There were 450 landing troops in the patrol boats—two old converted destroyers—and a force of garrison troops in the transports.

Despite a heavy sea, they were already beginning to put their troops into small boats when our fire opened. As Admiral Kajioka pulled his battered flagship out of range, the destroyer *Hayate* was sunk by Battery L on Wilkes, which then scored hits on the destroyer *Oite,* one of the transports, and one of Admiral Marumo's light cruisers. It was the destroyer *Yayoi* that had been hit by Kessler's men on Peale, and the destroyer *Kisaragi* that Elrod had sunk from the air.

Having lost two destroyers and at least five hundred men, and with five or six of his remaining ships damaged, Admiral Kajioka withdrew to Kwajalein in the Marshalls. It was, as a Japanese authority would write after the war, "one of the most humiliating defeats our Navy had ever suffered."

And it was more. It was the first authentic victory of the war for our forces. The *Hayate* and *Kisaragi* were the first enemy ships to be sunk by U.S. naval forces since the fighting had begun. The fact that little Wake Island had turned back an invasion fleet would be an incalculable boost to the morale of a nation dazed by the destruction at Pearl Harbor.

We did not know all this on the morning of December 11, but we knew enough to celebrate. And in less than two weeks we would see further proof of the shocking surprise we had given the Japanese. They had been so confident of taking the atoll that they had laid out all their plans for its administration; the copies of an Imperial Rescript issued to us after our capture were dated December 11.

If we had been confident on Wednesday, we were delirious now. At the airstrip, where I went after the shore guns ceased firing, sweating members of the ground crews shouted and pounded one another on the back. Even the loss of two planes—Elrod's fuel line had been cut, and he had to crash-land on the beach, and Freuler nursed his plane back with an engine hopelessly wrecked by enemy flak—could not dampen our spirits. We would wish desperately for those planes in the remaining days of the defense, but now we couldn't be bothered. We had turned back the enemy in force. We had beaten off an invasion. And we had suffered no casualties!

I went down to the defense battalion command post on the southern shore to congratulate Devereux on his men's performance, and then a group of us headed happily for the nearby Marine Officers' Club. There was a little beer left, though the refrigerator was not working, and we felt entitled to a celebration.

It was like a fraternity picnic. War whoops of joy split the air; warm beer was sprayed on late arrivals without regard to rank; already the memories that would last a lifetime—a tragically short lifetime for some—were being recalled, relived, and even embroidered.

Big John Hamas pushed his way through the crowd to the corner where I sat on an empty ammo box, drinking my beer in sleepy, relaxed, triumphant peace.

"Captain," he gloated, "you told us to cut loose at them, and boy, did we cut loose at the sons of bitches!"

I grinned at him happily. He stood there a moment, towering over me, and then he set down his beer can with an air of finality. "Well," he said, "the celebration's over for me . . . sir. Got to round up my civilians and get some more ammunition over to Wilkes." Gunner Hamas was not one to rest too long on his laurels.

I had work of my own to do, the proudest task of my Navy career: report the good news to Pearl Harbor. At that point we were not sure just how many ships, or what kind, we had actually sunk. But we knew beyond doubt that two had gone down—we thought they were a destroyer and a cruiser—and I decided to stick to the positive facts rather than make any claims we couldn't support. I drove back to my command post, dashed off the message, handed it to one of the decoding officers, and looked at my watch.

Only 8:45. I would have sworn the day was half gone already.

Word of our victory brought a response that was all we could have desired, aside from a promise of reinforcements. Back came a commendation from Pearl saying we had performed our duties "in accordance with the highest traditions of the Naval Service."

I read it to Putnam, Devereux and the others as soon as I had a chance, but there was some unavoidable delay. At nine o'clock the Japanese bombers arrived for a fourth raid. And now we had only two planes left to fight them off.

This time there were seventeen of them, coming in from the northeast, and for the first time in four raids I found myself protected by concrete and steel. The unfinished magazine that formed my communications center and command post had its disadvantages—there was no door, for example—but after the plywood at Camp Two, the brush near Camp One, and the foxhole at the airstrip it was a comforting sensation to look up and find a solid roof over my head.

The magazine brought us through the raid without a scratch, though I promised myself we would lay in a supply of sandbags to protect the entrance hereafter, and when I went on my routine post-raid inspection I found the same was true of the entire atoll. No one had been hurt, and on top of that, Lieutenant Davidson in one of the two Wildcats had shot down two more bombers. On this day of victory nothing could stop us.

Gunner Hamas had come as close as anybody to getting killed this time. With a crew of six civilian volunteers he had loaded a truck with shells, powder, detonators and hand grenades for John McAlister's battery on Kuku Point, and they had driven down to the boat landing only minutes before the bombers were sighted. There Kirby Ludwick, the sailor in charge of the boat crews, took the truck aboard one of the launches and set out across the channel.

They had just cleared the landing when the bombers swept in. Hamas and Ludwick looked at each other and agreed without saying a word that they had a job to do. The battery needed the supplies more now than ever. So on across the channel Ludwick guided the boat with its load of explosives, and all hands crossed their fingers and waited for a bomb.

They made it all right—we all led charmed lives that day—and Hamas's crew of civilians abandoned him, with his blessing, to stay on Wilkes and help out wherever McAlister needed them.

Bryghte Godbold's three-inch battery at Toki Point on Peale had attracted a large part of the enemy's fire. Again, no damage had been done, but it was clear Battery D might be wise to take a leaf from Battery E's book and move while there was time. So, late in the afternoon, the job was begun. Two hundred and fifty civilians pitched in to help move the battery almost the entire length of Peale, from Toki Point to a spot near the bridge.

Meanwhile, Pearl Harbor had given me a small assignment for the day: locate a confidential publication relating to direction finders, which had been in the possession of Pan American, and report its destruction. It was easy enough to report *that*. Not only that publication but all others at Pan American's headquarters, and the headquarters itself for that matter, had been destroyed. The Japs had saved me the trouble.

But we had another job to do, along with the usual repairs, and it was one that could wait no longer. Our dead must be cared for.

They had remained in the big refrigerator until now, those who had not been buried where they fell, and I did not dare wait any longer to pay final honor to them and give them as decent a burial as possible.

We did the best we could. A civilian dragline operator scooped out a long trench, and a handful of us stood in reverent silence while the bodies of the dead were laid into it. A firing squad gave a last salute and a bulldozer covered the grave. There was no chaplain on Wake, but one of the contractor's employees, a lay preacher named John O'Neal from Worland, Wyoming, said a short prayer.

I gave orders that in the future our dead would be

buried where they fell or in the closest practical space. There would be no more mass burials—and, I confidently hoped, there would be no need for them.

We had lost twenty-six officers and men of the fighter squadron, two sailors, and three enlisted men of the defense battalion. And how many civilians were dead? Thirty-five, perhaps, or forty or even more, counting those whose bodies had not been found.

It was a sad note on which to end the day. I tried to shake off my feeling of depression, to regain the spirit of victorious confidence we had all shared earlier, to remember the battered task force and the two bombers shot down by Lieutenant Davidson.

And then somebody was running toward me through the dusk, shouting something I could not hear above the surf, and I stopped stiffly and strained my ears to hear.

It was something about Lieutenant Kliewer, and now as the man came closer I could hear.

Kliewer had sunk a Jap sub.

He had found it basking on the surface as he flew the dusk patrol, and he had torn into it with bombs and machine guns. He had gone so low that fragments from the explosions hit his plane, and he had stayed to see the sub disappear below the surface and an oil slick appear where it had been.

Pearl wanted us to conduct unrestricted warfare, did they? Well, we had done it today. Surface ships, bombers, and now a submarine. If they'd just give us enough time we'd lick the whole Japanese Navy by ourselves.

I went back to my cottage thinking the hell with the dangers of a night raid, threw open the window to the soft breezes and the soothing sound of the surf, and slept like a baby.

Nine times during the next eight days the Japs hit us, and not at regular intervals as they had done at first, but spasmodically, at noon or by moonlight, singly or in masses of as many as forty-one bombers in a single raid.

Despite the variations in time and number, despite the

occasional loss of life, despite everything, it grew increasingly monotonous. Nerves remained tense for so long that they grew listless and flabby; the time came when we had to remind ourselves that our lives were the stakes in the tiresome game we were playing. I actually found myself nursing a small-boy resentment against the enemy one day because there was no raid to report to Pearl Harbor.

At the airstrip, work continued daily on the jigsaw task of arranging battered parts into planes that would fly. Two Wildcats were in working order on Friday; on Saturday Lieutenant Kinney's crew was able to get a third into the air, but on that same day a crash-landing brought the score back down to two. Sunday a bomb hit left only one effective; Tuesday we had two again; later in the week, briefly, three planes were flying. By Friday the nineteenth, the count was back down to one.

But aside from skilled work like this, most of the man-hours on the atoll during those eight days were spent in uneasy idleness. There was simply nothing to do the majority of the time but wait. The foxholes were all dug, the shelters covered and reinforced; the time that might have been spent in repairing damaged guns was cut to almost nothing because we had no parts for repairs.

Paul Putnam could not shake off the terrible memory of the destruction that had visited his squadron on that first day. He continued to push himself relentlessly at the airstrip, trying to improve and extend the ground works, and increasingly he grew impatient with Wake's civilians. One day he came to me in an angry frame of mind.

"Captain," he asked, "will you give me authority to use some armed Marines to round up these civilians and make them work? Dammit, they've got to hold up their end."

I turned him down. It was true that many of the civilians had taken to the bush and could not be found except when food was being distributed. And others, after being detailed to working parties, would fade away like old soldiers. There was even a report that one group of civilians had headed for the beach with their suitcases when the Japanese ships approached on the eleventh, determined to be the first to board what they thought were evacuation ships.

But the situation was not as simple as it appeared to Putnam.

For one thing, these men—or the great majority of them—had had no previous military training of any kind. They had not been drilled in that automatic response to discipline which is the first necessity of any fighting force. And they had no government insurance, no hope of veterans' benefits, no prospect of pensions in case of injury. Furthermore, they had been given to understand they would be evacuated, by some means that was never quite spelled out, before Wake was hit by the enemy. Many of them felt cheated and abandoned as the days rolled by and nothing was done about this pledge.

But when all this was considered, the fact remained that a surprisingly high number of them did pitch in and help, faithfully and at personal hazard—far more than Putnam could see from his limited vantage point at the airfield. Already they were stationed all over the atoll in support of the defense battalion's gun crews; they worked at filling sandbags, moving guns, delivering food and ammunition, operating heavy equipment to scoop out personnel shelters. At the airstrip itself they had accomplished much since the war began, bulldozing the surrounding area, making bunkers for the airplanes, helping to mine the landing strip, putting the radio station underground, assisting with personnel dugouts. And their group had suffered the highest number of casualties on the atoll.

Meanwhile, we had begun to get messages from Pearl that indicated thought was being given to the problem of reinforcements. On the twelfth the office of the Pacific Commander in Chief, Admiral Kimmel, asked for a confidential report on the status of aviation matériel for maintaining planes. I replied that, while we could operate two squadrons under the physical setup, maintenance work was limited to the salvaging of spare parts from the wrecked planes. The same day we were asked for, and gave, a report on the ammunition situation, which was still reasonably good.

A silence followed these reports, and on Sunday the fourteenth I made a few requests of my own, listing some of the many supplies we so urgently needed. At the end of the list I added the one thing that, at the outset, we had needed most of all:

"One radar."

On Monday I gave a general report on the effects of the raids to date, and added a request for 300,000 sandbags. We had plenty of coral sand, but by now the crews of civilians and Marines were having to put it in empty ammunition boxes for want of bags.

Still no word came from Pearl on what we could expect. We waited hopefully, and then on Wednesday we received a message whose unconscious irony was overwhelming:

HIGHLY DESIRABLE CONTINUE CHANNEL DREDGING. ADVISE FEASIBILITY UNDER PRESENT CONDITIONS WITH EXISTING EQUIPMENT. GIVE ESTIMATED DATE COMPLETION. . . .

I suppose I must have blown my top. I did not answer for almost twenty-four hours, except for a message reporting yet another raid—the twelfth since the war had begun —and when I did, it was with some heat. Friday morning, we enjoyed nearly forty-eight hours of peace, the longest stretch of relief during Wake's defense.

It was about midway in this week that we first heard a strange and, in some ways, exasperating story from the home front. There were a number of short-wave radios on the atoll, private property of civilians and servicemen alike, and occasionally one of them brought us a creditably clear portion of a broadcast from America.

We had heard with pride that President Roosevelt himself had hailed Wake's resistance effort, and we had tried to discount as propaganda for enemy consumption the gloomy reports that relief for Wake could not be expected. But now we heard something that set our teeth on edge.

When Pearl Harbor asked the defenders of Wake if there was anything that could be done for them, the story went, an answer came back:

"Yes. Send us more Japs."

If there was anything we didn't need at Wake it was more Japs. I had sent no such message, and since the release of dispatches was at all times under my direct control, I dismissed the story as a reporter's dream, as did most of the others on the atoll who heard it.

Not until years later, in fact, did I learn through Bucky Henshaw, one of the decoding officers, how the story began. Bucky got it from his fellow-decoder, Bernard Lauff, when they met in Honolulu after the war, and so far as I know this is the first time the details have ever been published.

Part of the decoders' job was to "pad" messages with nonsense at the beginning and end as a device to throw off enemy code-breakers. Such padding was either entirely meaningless or, on occasion, something involving a private joke between Henshaw and Lauff on the one hand and their opposite numbers at Pearl Harbor on the other; it was not expected that the padding would be filed with the text of the message.

On the morning we turned back the invasion fleet, Lauff said, he had done the padding on my message. He had begun it:

> SEND US STOP NOW IS THE TIME FOR ALL GOOD MEN TO COME TO THE AID OF THEIR PARTY STOP CUNNINGHAM MORE JAPS. . . .

So what the world took as a gesture of defiant heroism from Wake Island was actually nothing of the kind and was never intended to be.

The battle continued, and each day we grew weaker. We had been returning shot for shot, and by now an impressive number of enemy planes lay under the waters off Wake along with the two ships we had sunk, but still they came back with more. Twenty-seven bombers were in the Friday raid.

The list of parts and supplies I had requested from Pearl was an indication of the gravity of our matériel needs. We were short on everything, from recoil fluid to range finders, from firing pins to height finders, in addition to the tremendous shortages with which we had begun—and by now I could have sent another list just as long as the first. Our personnel losses had been cut to almost nothing, but it was the machines of war rather than the men who served them that would finally settle the issue of Wake.

We went into our second Saturday of the war sleepy, lean, weary, confident of our ability to hold out unless the Japs threw still bigger blows at us, but wondering more and more whether Pearl had in truth written us off as beyond reach of relief.

And then, at 7:10 on that rainy Saturday morning, an electrifying message arrived from Midway:

DEPARTED MIDWAY FOR WAKE ONE PREP SAIL PREP.

A Navy patrol bomber was headed our way. At last we could hope to learn when, or whether, relief might arrive.

The PBY arrived about 3:30. I went down to the remains of the Pan American installation to meet it and took the pilots, Ensigns Murphy and Ady, to my command post. As we bounced along in my pickup truck past bomb craters and the wreckage of Camp Two, their eyes opened wide in surprise. Like some of the dispatch-writers back at Pearl, it appeared, they had not realized the extent of the damage the Japanese had done us.

The orders they brought—and about which they of course knew nothing—contained good news. We were to prepare to receive another fighter plane squadron. Ground troop reinforcements and needed matériel were on the way. All but about 350 civilians were to be evacuated; the remainder, selected by specified trades, would remain to work on construction projects. Pearl Harbor had still not abandoned its conviction that the ship channel across Wilkes must be completed.

Many questions were left unanswered; even the estimated date of arrival of the promised help was not indicated. But it was enough to send our spirits soaring. With reinforcements, with supplies to repair our guns, with more planes to take the air over Wake, we would be strong again. And there should be plenty of time; after the ignominious retreat of the Japanese invasion fleet less than ten days before, I felt it would be many days or even weeks before another landing attempt was made.

I passed the news on to Keene, Devereux, Putnam, Greey and Teters, and as it filtered down through the ranks the atmosphere of Wake took another turn for the better. Teters got busy drawing up rosters of men who would remain; talk of what we would do to the enemy when our reinforcements arrived was indulged in freely by all hands; letters and reports were hastily written to send back to Pearl on the PBY when it left the next morning.

In the report I wrote for Admiral Bloch, I tried again to make the picture of destruction clear, and praised the work of the fighter squadron and the defense battalion.

"Our escape from more serious damage," I wrote, "may be attributed to the effectiveness of AA fire and the heroic actions of the fighter pilots, who have never failed to push home attacks against heavy fire. The performance of these pilots is deserving of all praise. They have attacked air and surface targets alike with equal abandon. That none has been shot down is a miracle. Their planes (two now remain) are full of bullet holes. Two forced landings, fortunately without injury to pilots, have occurred with loss of planes."

As a matter of fact, relief was miles closer than I dreamed as I wrote my letter, though I was not to learn just how close it was until after the war was over.

As early as the second day of the war, Admiral Kimmel, the Pacific Commander in Chief at Pearl, had begun planning our relief. And he had planned on a grand scale, hoping not only to succor Wake but to score a major naval victory that would punish the enemy for the destruction at Pearl.

It was to involve three Pacific Fleet carrier forces. Admiral Bull Halsey, with a group built around the *Enterprise*, would move out beyond Johnston Island, covering Pearl and standing by to support the main action if necessary. Admiral Wilson Brown and a task force built around the *Lexington* would head for the Marshalls for a raid to keep the enemy busy to the south of us. And Admiral Frank Jack Fletcher, with a force built around the *Saratoga,* would dash to Wake with a new fighter squadron, ground reinforcements, ammunition and equipment. With three task forces on the prowl, the chance to engage and defeat an enemy naval force would be bright.

There had been the inevitable delays. The *Saratoga,* bearing the fighter planes, had been off San Diego when the war began. With an escort of three destroyers she began racing for Pearl, but it was the morning of December 15 before she arrived. Meanwhile, the other units of Admiral Fletcher's force had been made ready. The *Tangier,* with ground reinforcements, and the oiler *Neches,* escorted by a division of destroyers, left by order of Admiral Kimmel on the same day the *Saratoga* arrived for refueling. By the next day, the big carrier had set out to catch up with them, accompanied by three cruisers and a destroyer squadron. On the seventeenth, they overhauled *Tangier* and *Neches,* released their destroyer escort, and continued toward Wake.

Meanwhile, Admiral Brown's task force had left Pearl on the fourteenth on its bombing mission to the Marshalls, and Admiral Halsey's group sailed shortly after the *Saratoga* had departed.

It had been a slow start, but there was still time. My messages from Wake, which Admiral Fletcher was reading, indicated the need for urgency. Throughout his task force, men worked in a fever of activity to get ready for what they knew might be an opposed landing at Wake. Planes and guns were checked; the radar that was headed for us at last was explained by experts to the men who would use it; plans for lightering men and equipment ashore off Wake's south shore were studied and re-studied.

But now a complication arose. The oiler *Neches* could travel at a top speed of less than 13 knots, as opposed to the 34 knots which the *Saratoga,* as well as the cruisers and destroyers, could make. Admiral Fletcher set the pace of his task force to match that of the *Neches.*

Even at this speed, they made progress. The seas were

109

calm and there was no sight of the enemy. When the PBY arrived on Wake, relief was already well on the way. By Sunday, when the PBY departed, the task force was less than 700 miles away.

Ensigns Murphy and Ady and their crew took off at seven Sunday morning for their return trip, sped on their way by the optimistic thanks of all of us. Besides the letters and reports we had written, they took with them Major Bayler, the Marine specialist who had been waiting for transportation off the atoll since before the war began. But the unfortunate Mr. Hevenor of the Budget Bureau, who had missed the last Clipper, was left again. This time a routine regulation stood in his way: there was no parachute available for him.

We waved good-by to the big plane and went back to our posts with high spirits. And then, less than two hours afterward, a new move by the Japs staggered us.

Twenty-nine dive bombers accompanied by eighteen fighters—obviously from aircraft carriers—roared down on Wake.

If enemy carriers were within striking distance, our plight was far more critical than we had dreamed. Nothing but the greatest speed could bring us relief now. I reported this new development in a dispatch to Pearl marked *Urgent*.

It was during this first carrier-plane raid that Major Putnam added further luster to the brilliant reputation he had acquired during the defense of Wake. At the time the planes came over, he was in a dugout a few hundred yards from my command post, conferring with Commander Keene and Dan Teters. It was immediately apparent that the planes were from a carrier, and Paul Putnam wasted no time. He grabbed a phone, called me, and asked permission to drive to the airstrip, take off in one of our two surviving planes, and go out to look for the carriers themselves.

An attempt to reach the airstrip while the raid was in progress would be hazardous in the extreme, but Putnam was eager to try it and I knew that if he could locate the enemy ships the information could be of incalculable value to Pearl Harbor. I told him to go ahead and to be careful.

He got into a truck and began the ride of perhaps a mile to the airstrip while the planes roared overhead. Twice along the way he was strafed by enemy fighters and had to leave his truck and take cover. But neither he nor the truck was hit, and he did get to the field, where he took off and made a long search for the carriers. That he was unable to locate them in no way dimmed the heroism of his exploit.

At noon we were hit again, this time by land-based bombers, and destruction to the remnants of our fighting equipment was considerable. The obliteration of Camp Two was completed, Peale took another shellacking, and Battery D on the islet was badly hit. One bomb here took the life of Sergeant John Wright, who thus became the fourth casualty of the defense battalion. Four others were wounded.

And now our defensive position was critical indeed. Battery D's director was a complete loss; Battery F had never had one. The only director on the atoll now was at Battery E inside the head of the wishbone on Wake Island. And Battery E had no height finder.

Assisted by a work crew of 125 civilians, Captain Godbold accordingly sent a portion of his battery down to Battery E so we could have one antiaircraft unit at full strength. One gun, the height finder, and a power plant made the move; Godbold's three remaining guns were moved once more, northward from their second position, to be used on the beach against surface targets.

I went to sleep on my sandbag pillow that night hoping the promised relief would arrive in time. Enemy carriers were in the area and we had only one effective antiaircraft battery now to use against the swift fighter planes we had seen that day for the first time.

Monday began on a hopeful note with a message from CINCPAC asking the condition of our runways. But that was the only bright spot in the day. Shortly after noon we had our second attack by a combination of land and car-

111

rier-based planes. They came in greater force than ever and they looked even newer and more deadly than the day before.

Against their overwhelming numbers, Captain Freuler and Lieutenant Davidson tore in to do what they could with our two tattered Wildcats. Freuler shot down two or perhaps three of the fighters, but his plane was damaged by the explosion of one of his victims and he was barely able to nurse it back to a crash-landing that destroyed it. Freuler himself, hit twice by machine gun bullets, went to the hospital.

Lieutenant Davidson did not return.

So ended the glorious record of the Marine flyers, at least so far as flying operations were concerned. Paul Putnam and I went to the hospital later to see Freuler and tell him the sad news about Carl Davidson. Putnam, who was filled with a grim pride in the record his men had made, pretended to be angry with Freuler.

"What do you mean," he demanded, "mixing with those Jap fighters when we told you to stick to the bombers?"

Freuler grinned wearily. We left him then, and Putnam walked back to the airstrip, collected his few remaining able-bodied men and the dozen or so faithful civilians who had refused his orders to take cover in the bush. Together they all went to Devereux's command post and reported for duty as infantry.

I would have been even more uneasy than I was as I settled down to rest that night if I had known what was going on in the waters northeast of Wake occupied by the task force sent for our relief.

Grimly determined to keep the oiler *Neches* with him— though his ships had adequate fuel and he could have doubled his speed if he had chosen—Admiral Fletcher had actually lost ground during the day.

By noon of Sunday the twenty-first he had known we were under attack by carrier planes and therefore in serious trouble, but he neither increased his speed nor refueled. The earlier he accomplished the refueling, the earlier he could get rid of the *Neches,* but still he waited.

He waited until the morning of the twenty-second—and then, as if to emphasize his poor judgment, the weather changed from favorable for refueling to unfavorable. Heavy seas hampered the operation, and the wind direction forced the ships to steam in a direction that actually increased their distance from Wake. During the entire day only four destroyers were fueled, leaving four more for the next day.

By eight o'clock on the night of the twenty-first, postwar studies were to show, the *Saratoga* was only 600 miles from Wake. At a speed of 25 knots, she could have been close enough by noon of the twenty-second to launch planes. But by eight the next morning, the carrier was still 515 miles from us. And twelve hours later she was no closer.

Meanwhile, Admiral Kimmel had been succeeded at Pearl on December 17 by Admiral W. S. Pye, serving in a caretaker capacity until the arrival of Admiral Chester Nimitz. On the twentieth Admiral Brown's task force, whose mission was to make a diversionary attack in the Marshalls, was directed to turn northward to support the relief expedition. When Admiral Pye reported this to Washington he was told in reply that Wake was considered a liability, and he was authorized to evacuate it rather than reinforce it if he thought best.

The situation was confusing, but there is no indication that Admiral Pye made it less so. On December 22, Wake time, he first ordered Fletcher to send the *Saratoga* ahead to launch her planes; then he countermanded the order and directed that the *Tangier* go ahead to evacuate the garrison. As I went to sleep that night, neither plan had been put into action.[1]

Shortly after midnight on the twenty-second I received a call reporting flashes of light to the north. I climbed onto

[1] I am indebted to Samuel Eliot Morison's *The Rising Sun in the Pacific* (Little, Brown and Company, 1950) for information on which this brief look at the relief expedition's unhappy record is based. Neither I nor the American public back home knew the details until long after the war was over.—W. S. C.

the top of my concrete igloo and studied the display, which was evidently at a considerable distance from the atoll. The lights would blaze up, then sink slowly like parachute flares from star shells. With several others I watched this display for some time, wondering what it meant. We had seen other unexplained displays of lights and rockets offshore at night from time to time. No definite conclusion as to their meaning was ever reached. In the light of later information it has been theorized that enemy ships who had got off course were firing somewhere at what they thought was Wake Island, but the mystery has never been completely cleared up.

I went back inside my command post and was about to try for a little more sleep when the first blow fell.

Watchers reported barges and landing boats had been sighted near the beach on the south shore of Wake and Wilkes.

This night we had no moon to help us see the enemy, as we had had on the morning of the eleventh. The night was intensely dark; visibility was limited to only a few yards at best. And this time the enemy had profited from its earlier mistake of firing as it approached. The ships had crept in, silent and unseen, until they were ready for the invasion.

At first, conflicting reports pouring into my CP indicated there might be some possibility of error. There were no landings, only the mysterious lights; there were landings; ships were approaching but no boats had attempted to come ashore.

But gradually the truth began to emerge. A Japanese fleet was in the immediate vicinity. Two old destroyer-transports had run in so close in the dark that the five-inch guns on Peacock and Kuku points could not fire on them. Landing craft had definitely been sighted.

At 1:45, after the report of the lights, I had messaged to Pearl Harbor: GUNFIRE BETWEEN SHIPS TO NORTHEAST ISLAND. The message was directed to Admiral Bloch's headquarters. Now, at 2:50, I could no longer hope we were experiencing another false alarm. Guns had begun to flash in the darkness offshore. I sent a second message, this one directed to the Pacific Commander in Chief:

ISLAND UNDER GUNFIRE. APPARENTLY LANDING.

The enemy had arrived, and this time surely they would be coming in greater force and with greater determination than before. Fighter planes could be expected at any moment. Casting about for some hope of help, I remembered Pilly Lent and the *Triton*.

I yelled to the radio operator to send a message in plain English—it was no time now to concern ourselves with codes—directing the *Triton,* if it received us, to attack enemy ships to the south.

At 3:19 a chilling reply came. It was not from the *Triton,* but from Admiral Pye's headquarters.

NO FRIENDLY VESSELS SHOULD BE IN YOUR IMMEDIATE VICINITY TODAY, it said. KEEP ME INFORMED.

Reading it, I did not know how bitter the whole truth was—that the *Triton* had been recalled earlier to keep it out of the way of the relief expedition, which had now been called off—but I knew enough.

We were on our own.

The mishandling and final recall of a relief expedition that almost without doubt could have saved Wake from the enemy, and scored a great naval victory in the process, was one of the darkest marks on the Navy's entire war record.

If Admiral Fletcher had been endowed with some of the energy exhibited by the Japanese invaders in the closing days of December, 1941, he could have arrived ahead of them and forestalled their landing. And he could have delivered a smashing blow to the Japanese Navy—for, if after contacting the enemy he had decided they were too much for his task force to handle alone, there was another task force under Admiral Brown, built around the *Lexington*, within supporting distance. And still a third, Admiral Halsey's, was close enough to join the action if a real battle developed.

It is true our battleships in Pearl Harbor had been hard hit on December 7. Otherwise, though, we had escaped with remarkably little damage. Our carriers were untouched, our cruiser, destroyer and submarine strength was very little reduced, our fuel supplies and workshops at Pearl were intact. We even had some of our shore-based airplanes left.

But there is no question that the attack had also hit us hard in another area—our morale. The pendulum had swung from contempt of the Nipponese to an exaggerated fear of their capabilities. It seems fair to say that neither Admiral Pye nor Admiral Fletcher really wanted a battle, unless they could be certain of superiority of forces. And while the odds were all in favor of this superiority, the desire for certainty held them back.

An American victory would have been a glorious Christmas present for the American people. And here was the opportunity. The Japanese were within reach, and our officers and men should have been smarting with rage over Pearl Harbor and anxious for revenge. And they were; in the *Saratoga* and elsewhere in the task force, it developed when the facts were finally revealed, there was general dismay and even mutinous feeling when Fletcher received and carried out his order to retire while we on Wake were actively engaged with the enemy.

Both in the progress of Admiral Fletcher's task force and in the orders from Pearl that culminated in the withdrawal, our Navy failed, in short, to make the most of a great opportunity to fight back.

All I knew of this in the stormy pre-dawn darkness of December 23, as the Japanese began to swarm ashore on Wake, was that help was not coming—and that even such help as we might otherwise have counted on from the *Triton* had been withdrawn. We were alone against the enemy.

116

So the battle began, in an atmosphere of desperate confusion from which only one clear factor emerged—the overwhelming numerical superiority of the invaders.

This time, the postwar records would show, the Japanese were taking no chance on another humiliating defeat. Rear Admiral Kajioka, who had been given a chance to redeem himself, had a vastly stronger force for his second try. The two destroyers we had sunk had been replaced. A third had been added. Three other ships, a minelayer, a seaplane tender and a transport, beefed up the original force. More landing troops were aboard, some two thousand according to best estimates. And in addition to all this, two other impressive forces had been assigned as support—four heavy cruisers with accompanying destroyers from Truk under command of Rear Admiral A. Goto, and two aircraft carriers, two cruisers, and still more destroyers under Rear Admiral Hiroaki Abe, detached from the fleet that had struck Pearl Harbor. This latter force had more than 100 planes, the first of which had struck us on Sunday.

Wake's geography, and the multiple landings of the invaders, made it inevitable that almost from the first we would be cut up into relatively ineffective pockets of defense. And the early breakdown of communications completed the isolation of our various fighting units.

The telephone system was so laid out that all defense positions fed into Devereux's command post. Peale Island, Keene and Teters's dugout, and perhaps one or two other positions on the north portion of Wake were on a common line with me to the battalion switchboard, and I could talk directly with them. But I was not in direct touch with any of the stations on the south part of Wake, or with Wilkes Island, and had to depend on Devereux for information regarding all the positions that actually were engaged with the enemy. The telephone wires were all above ground. As the Japanese landed and crossed them, they cut them. Soon after the first enemy troops got ashore all communications with Wilkes were severed, and the various strong points along Wake's south shore were isolated shortly thereafter. Only the northern portion of the network remained effective. I was able to direct portions of the defenders on Peale to reinforce the troops on Wake, but from the opening phase of the battle most of the other units were forced to act on their own.

It is worth noting that communications almost never turn out to be fully effective under the stress of battle. Conditions change with lightning speed, mistaken observation results in faulty information, orders become inapplicable to the situation before there is time to carry them out. Accounts of battles frequently suggest that the commander has moved each of his formations around like men on a chess board, but this is seldom the way it happens. After the fighting begins, most decisions are made by subordinate commanders on the spot.

For battles don't go according to plan. There is always confusion, whatever the advance preparation may have been. And there was confusion in plenty on Wake. Little groups of defenders came under enemy attack and fought back without a chance of co-ordinating their actions with any over-all plan. Both our own troops and the Japanese were at times firing toward friends as well as foes. From my command post, trying vainly to establish what was going on over the entire atoll, I could see tracer bullets flying in all directions, and there is no doubt some of the reports I had to assess were based on mistaken assumptions as to who was firing the bullets. Further, the cut-off groups naturally tended to believe they were about the only ones left, and what few reports we did get from them reflected such views.

So it was that the picture which eventually emerged of the last defense of Wake could only be pieced together after it was all over and the various unit commanders told their stories. At the time neither Devereux nor I had, or could have had, more than a dim and often totally false idea of what was happening.

The invaders grounded two destroyer transports off the south shore of Wake and sent troops ashore from both. Two barges unloaded onto the beach at Wilkes. Two other landing craft put men ashore on Wake just east of the channel entrance. Other troops, as best can be determined, landed on Wake's inner shore from rubber boats that entered the shallow lagoon from the northwest.

As these landings began, the bulk of the active defense on Wake fell to mobile forces comprised of Marines, sailors and civilians, for a major portion of the defense battalion's strength was immobilized at the three-inch and five-inch guns. The area from Camp One eastward toward the airstrip was defended by Lieutenant Poindexter and the defense battalion's mobile reserve, augmented by Boatswain's Mate Barnes and fifteen sailors, and a considerable number of civilians. Each end of the airstrip was guarded by machine-gun crews. Near the airstrip's western end, Lieutenant Kliewer of the fighter squadron took a stand with three others at the generator which was wired to set off the mines along the strip. The three-inch gun on the beach south of the airstrip was manned by Lieutenant Hanna and another Marine and three civilians. A defensive line was formed around the gun by Major Putnam, other surviving members of the fighter squadron, and a dozen civilians.

These were the hot spots on Wake as the fighting began.

Hanna and his crew at the three-inch gun poured fifteen rounds into one of the destroyer transports within minutes after it was grounded, and then began firing at the other, but the invasion troops were already swarming ashore. As they advanced on the gun position, Putnam's little defense line fought back, giving ground stubbornly until at last it formed virtually a circle around the gun. Some Japanese remained to contest the position while others proceeded past the pocket and into the brush.

At Camp One, landing craft approaching the channel were fired on by machine guns. When they grounded on the reef offshore, Poindexter, Barnes and others began throwing hand grenades. Barnes scored one direct hit just as the troops began to disembark, but it was not enough to stop them. They began to pour ashore as the Camp One defenders grouped and fought back.

Devereux had done his best to maintain contact with his units, but it was fast becoming impossible. Within half an hour after the first landing, telephone communication had been lost with Camp One, Lieutenant Hanna and the defensive line under Major Putnam, and Battery A on Peacock Point. And reports from Wilkes were becoming more and more fragmentary. We knew only that a considerable force had landed there and was being resisted. Later, contact was lost altogether.

From Peale, the only area where no landings had been made, Lieutenant Kessler reported by telephone that he could use one of his five-inch guns on a destroyer off Wake. I told him to go ahead. I also authorized Captain Godbold to send some of his men down to join the fighting. It could have been a mistake if troops were about to land there too, but we had a real crisis on Wake that took precedence over a possible one on Peale. Accordingly, a truckload of men under Corporal Leon Graves came roaring down the north-south road and were directed to go in support of Major Putnam's group. But in the confusion they never made it; eventually they wound up in a defensive line set up at Major Devereux's command post.

In the midst of everything else, a ludicrous problem arose for me to deal with. A civilian cook came boiling into my command post, drunk as a lord from that evil concoction known as "swipes" about which I had been warned before the war began. He wanted to go out and tackle the Japs single-handed. It was quite a while before we could get him quietly disposed of.

Meanwhile the enemy was moving deeper into the island from its beachheads, and beginning to spread out through the brush. Lewis's Battery E, inside the head of the wishbone, had been firing in answer to the steady shelling we were receiving from the cruisers offshore; now his position came under fire from invasion troops. And down at the point of the wishbone, mortar fire began to fall on the five-inch gun positions of Lieutenant Barninger's Battery A.

At the machine-gun setup on the eastern end of the airstrip, Corporal Winford J. McAnally was in command of a force of six Marines and three civilians. An hour before dawn he reported the enemy was beginning to attack strongly up the north-south road—evidence either that the invasion of our south shore had been successful or that the Japs were landing at yet another spot.

By now I knew beyond doubt that the enemy had landed at three places and perhaps more. As yet no planes had arrived, but we could expect them by dawn. The off-shore shelling continued without letup.

Admiral Pye had asked me to keep him informed. I decided it was time to do so. At five o'clock I messaged:

ENEMY ON ISLAND. ISSUE IN DOUBT.

This message, interpreted as a final gesture of defiance, was to provoke great comment back in America when it appeared in the accounts of Wake's defense, but as a matter of fact no bravado was intended. At the moment I began to write the dispatch, a phrase I had read sixteen years before came into my mind. It was from Anatole France's *Revolt of the Angels*. He was describing the assault made upon the heavenly ramparts by the legions of Satan. "For three days," he wrote, "the issue was in doubt."

Why I should have recalled those words at such a time I do not know, but they seemed appropriate and even hopeful. In France's story, the victory had gone to the side of the angels. And while I knew we were outnumbered and outgunned, I was still unable even to consider the prospect of defeat. It would be more than an hour before the notion actually sank into my mind that we might not, somehow, make out.

In one sector our forces were indeed making out, and would shortly do far better than that. That was on Wilkes.

A force of one hundred Japanese had landed there to wipe out the defenders—Captain Platt, with seventy Marines and a number of sailors and civilians. The enemy had captured Gunner McKinstry's three-inch gun emplacements but had been blocked from expanding their beachhead. Even as I sent my dispatch, Captain Platt was reorganizing his forces for a counterattack that, before seven o'clock, would virtually wipe out the invaders, killing at least 94 and ending all immediate threat to Wilkes.

121

It was a substantial setback to the enemy, but I did not know of it until after the surrender. Among the various reports I received was one at dawn that Wilkes had fallen.

This word came from observers on Peale, who were about a mile away from Wilkes across the lagoon. When daylight came they could see Japanese flags displayed at many places on Wilkes, and concluded that the islet had capitulated. As I had no reason to question the report, the assumed loss of Wilkes was one of the considerations I had to take into account in sizing up the situation.

But brilliantly as Wesley Platt had conducted his operation, still Wilkes was only a small fraction of the total defense, and even the truth about conditions there could not have altered the final outcome. On the big islet, Wake, were concentrated most of the defenses and the defenders, and on Wake the situation was steadily deteriorating. Each group of defenders was pinned down while the enemy enjoyed wide freedom of movement.

As the build-up of enemy strength increased the pressure northward, chiefly against the machine-gun position held by Corporal McAnally, Devereux ordered Major Potter to set up a final defensive line south of his command post. But the unrelenting pressure continued. And as dawn came, the carrier-based planes swarmed over us like angry hornets.

Devereux and I had been in regular contact throughout the battle, and each time he reported to me he described the situation in darker terms. My own word to him that no relief could be expected made the picture even worse. At 6:30, when it appeared that his was the only position not yet overwhelmed, he reported enemy pressure there was getting heavy and gave the opinion that he would not be able to hold out much longer.

I knew the time had come to consider the question that only a few hours ago had been unthinkable. Accordingly, I asked for his opinion. Would I be justified in surrendering, in order to prevent further and useless loss of life?

Devereux evaded a direct answer. He said he felt the decision was solely up to the commanding officer. I was well aware of that, of course, but I was not willing to act without reviewing the situation as fully as possible.

We talked a while longer. He asked if I knew that Wilkes had fallen. I said that I did. At last I took a deep breath and told him if he felt he could hold out no longer, I authorized him to surrender.

I hung up the phone and sent a final dispatch to the Commander in Chief, reporting two destroyers grounded on the beach and the enemy fleet moving in. Then I had all codes, ciphers and secret orders destroyed, and ordered the communicators to haul down our transmitter antenna. It would be too easy for the Japanese dive bombers to spot. Besides, I had no more messages to send.

Devereux called me again about 7:30 and asked whether I had reached the Japanese commander by radio. I told him I had not. He repeated his statement that he could not hold out much longer, and I repeated mine that he was authorized to surrender. He said he was not sure of his ability to contact the enemy, and asked me to try. I promised to see what I could do.

But before I could do anything, it was all over. Devereux rigged a white flag, left his command post, and moved south down the road toward the enemy, giving our troops the cease-fire order as he reached them. I became aware that the surrender had begun when someone reported that bed sheets could be seen flying above the civilian hospital near Devereux's command post.

I looked around me at the men in my command post and could think of nothing to say. In a sort of a daze I walked out of the unfinished magazine, tossed my .45 pistol into a nearby latrine, got into my truck, and drove away.

I went, not south to the enemy, but north to the cottage I had occupied in the early days of the defense. It was battered and badly damaged but, moving mechanically through the debris, I took off the dirty old khakis I had been living in night and day, shaved and washed my face, and put on a clean blue uniform. Then I got back into the truck, drove down the road, and surrendered.

The Coastwatchers

Ferdinand was the code name of a highly effective intelligence group of several hundred men (planters, missionaries, government officials and the like) working under the supervision of the Australian Navy who reported Jap movements in the tropical islands in the Southwest Pacific. Its network kept under surveillance an area of more than half a million square miles. Their story, as E. A. Feldt, their Commander, describes it is one of "damp, dimly lighted jungle camps, of hidden treetop lookouts; of silent submarines landing a few intrepid men on hostile beaches in the dead of night; of American airmen mysteriously rescued from enemy-held islands surrounded by enemy-dominated seas; and how Allied coastwatchers managed, in strange and devious ways, not only to exist under the noses of the Japanese, but also to radio vital military information.

"The story of its origin goes back to 1919 and to the problem of protecting Australia's long, undefended coast line. The island continent, its population of seven million largely concentrated in its southeast corner, presents large areas where, in wartime, an enemy might operate without hindrance and, in fact, without anyone's being aware of it. Pondering this problem after the last war, the Navy hit on a scheme of appointing selected civilians in the coastal areas as coastwatchers. Frugality was the governing factor in the design of the system, for the Navy had little money in peacetime. The coastwatchers were unpaid, and it was not possible for the Navy to supply them with radio equipment." *

Eventually administrative personnel in Papua, New Guinea, and the Solomon Islands, along with planters, were added to the organization. In September 1939, Commander Feldt was sent out to visit those members living in the islands who had teleradios. He visited men in New Guinea, New Britain, the Solomons, and elsewhere, enrolling more tele-

*E. A. Feldt, *The Coastwatchers*, p. 7. Oxford University Press.

radio operators, teaching them code, what to report, etc. Back in Australia, he persuaded the government to increase the number of coastwatchers operating teleradios, and by August 1940 the additional sets had been placed. As Commander Feldt says, "the instrument had one serious disadvantage, it was difficult to carry—requiring 12 to 16 porters" to move it any distance.

"When, a month after Pearl Harbor, the hurricane of war struck at the Northeast Area, it worked havoc with our island intelligence chain. Here and there, parts of the chain were left freakishly intact; in other places it was destroyed or its links dislocated.

"There was, for instance, C. C. Jervis, planter and retired Navy telegraphist on Nissan Island, who watched an enemy ship move toward the lagoon entrance of his low, undefended atoll; he calmly coded and sent a report of its presence, and was never heard of again.

"There was J. Daymond, assistant district officer at Gasmata, a noisome, marshy native prison island off the south coast of New Britain, who warned Port Moresby of its first air raid, giving the town ample time to prepare, and then was betrayed, unwittingly, by his countrymen: the news was broadcast in Australia that enemy aircraft had been sighted over Gasmata, direct information to the Japanese that we had a reporting station at that point. Promptly the enemy bombed and gunned Gasmata station. For the nonce. Daymond and his staff were saved, having wisely moved with their teleradio across to the mainland. Unsatisfied, the Japanese landed a force at Gasmata two weeks after the fall of Rabaul. According to the story that percolated through, they asked the first native they saw where the *kiap* was, and were led, in innocent simplicity, to Daymond and his assistant, who had returned to the island. A third member of the staff radioed the bare facts of their capture, and that was the last heard from him, too. We did not even receive an acknowledgment of our reply to his desperate message.

"There was, on the other hand, L. G. Vial, a young assistant district officer evacuated by the Air Force from Rabaul, who was swiftly commissioned an Air Force Pilot Officer, supplied within a week with teleradio, codes, food, and instruction, and flown to Salamaua on the New Guinea coast a few days before the Japanese moved in. Hidden in the hills above Salamaua airfield, for six months, in his quiet unhurried voice, he reported aircraft on the way, their types, numbers, course, and height. His was the voice most listened for at Port Moresby, and at last a correspondent dubbed him 'the Golden Voice,' a title which embarrassed him considerably. At the end of his watch, he was awarded the American Distinguished Service Cross.

"There was D. G. N. Chambers on Emirau Island, north of Kavieng, who made a remarkable escape by launch, passing enemy-held Rabaul at night. Next morning, driven ashore by an enemy destroyer, his launch wrecked, he managed to find a party of other refugees and to make his escape with them. His experience was typical of a number of the watchers who were forced to flee their posts but who survived to serve *Ferdinand* another day.

"There were W. L. Tupling on Ningo and J. H. McColl on Wuvulu, small coral islands in the Admiralty Group, 250 miles northwest of Rabaul. When the radio station at Rabaul was silenced, they tried desperately to raise Port Moresby on their teleradios, but distance and the intervening mountain ranges were too much. So, uninstructed, they remained at their lonely posts to warn a small detachment of Commandos in the islands of approaching ships, to help in destroying everything of use to the Japanese, and finally to aid in evacuating the soldiers. At last one of their signals was picked up, they were instructed to evacuate, and in a plantation launch they made their way, like Chambers, to safety and to future service." *

By 1944, as the war moved closer to Japan, the coastwatchers were no longer needed for intelligence information. It is the belief of Commander Feldt that "Had *Ferdinand* not existed, Japan would still have been defeated but victory would have come later and at a higher cost of life. . . . Without the coastwatchers, the U.S. Navy would surely have faced still stronger enemy forces when it advanced through the Central Pacific." **

The selection that follows tells the story of one of the coastwatchers in the last days of their epic fight.

*The Coastwatchers, pp. 20, 21.
**The Coastwatchers, p. 236.

FERDINAND ON HOLLANDIA

by Commander E. A. Feldt

The Allied forces, after taking the Admiralty Islands, decided to land at Aitape far to the west on the New Guinea border and at Hollandia in Dutch New Guinea, thereby neutralizing the Japanese at Madang, Hansa Bay, and Wewak. Headquarters wanted on-the-spot information of Japanese strength and positions in this area.

Under the Allied Intelligence Bureau system, the Dutch should have been delegated to provide information from Hollandia. But the Dutch had so few people that they could not provide a party. Stavermann and his group, who had attempted to reach Hollandia in the first part of 1943, had been killed before they even crossed the border. In fact, the Dutch had no one in their scant forces who had ever even been to Hollandia.

So it was decided that *Ferdinand* should provide a party, to which the Dutch would add an Indonesian sergeant as interpreter. And at *Ferdinand* headquarters, it was decided that here was a job for "Blue" Harris.

Harris had been pestering *Ferdinand* for a real job. He had assisted in the New Britain evacuation, then had sat on the Rai Coast for about eight months, bickering with the other idling watchers there while he waited for the war to come his way. At Talasea and Witu he had escaped the enemy in the nick of time. He had landed for two nights and two days at Finschafen and had stared into the eyes of a Japanese there, but nothing more had come of it. He had been scheduled to land in the Admiralty Islands, but the attack had taken place without any preliminary reconnaissance, and his job had been cancelled. To "Blue," this just didn't add up to enough.

The Hollandia job was just what he wanted. It meant a landing on an enemy-held coast, among natives who were an unknown quantity and whose reactions and thoughts would be difficult to judge.

With the meager information already at our disposal, he prepared as carefully for the job as he could. He painstakingly studied every chart and air photograph available. His team was already made up—the one he had prepared for the Admiralty Islands work. It consisted of Lieutenant R. B. Webber, Sergeant R. J. Cream, and Privates J. I. Bunning, G. Shortis, and P. C. Jeune, all of the Australian Army; Julius McNicol, able seaman in the Australian Navy; and Sergeants Yali, Mas, and Buka and Private Mariba of the New Guinea native police. Webber had been a soldier in the Admiralty Islands when the Japanese had occupied them, and McNicol, Yali, and Mas had all been with Harris on the Rai Coast and at Talasea. To this party, Sergeant Launcelot, the Indonesian interpreter, was added.

The party planned to land from a submarine thirty miles west of Hollandia, then push inland to the mountains, without any contact with local natives if possible. To ensure communication, a party under Captain C. J. Millar, who had been with Bridge in New Guinea, was landed by plane in the Idenburg River, a hundred miles south of Hollandia, where the enemy had not penetrated. If base stations could not receive Harris' signals, owing to the distance, Millar was to relay them on. Harris was to remain ashore for fourteen days and to be picked up at the end of that period by submarine.

The party embarked in the U.S. Submarine *Dace* on 18 March 1944. Four days later the submarine was off Cape Tanamerah, the landing point selected. A day was spent examining the shore through the periscope, and a site chosen, but as the submarine surfaced after dark and approached the shore, a powerful light was sighted just where the party was to have landed. So the submarine held off, and next day, after further examination, a small beach on the open coast was decided upon, even though there were several native huts near by.

With true *Ferdinand* caution, Harris decided to land with

128

a reconnaisance party before committing the entire coast-watcher group. With him he took Webber, Shortis, Mas, and Launcelot, arms, a walkie-talkie and a flashlight. Code signals were arranged—"Groggo" to indicate that all was well and the remainder of the party was to be sent ashore; "Washout" to indicate that the remainder should stay aboard the sub, which was anchored more than a mile offshore.

The reconnaissance party set off in the rubber boat on the dark, calm sea. Suddenly, before it knew what had happened, it was in trouble. The low ground swell, innocuous in deep water, bunched itself into heavy breakers at the edge of the reef. The reef had not been observed through the periscope, and the rubber boat was against it and tossed by the breakers before the men realized it was there. They tried to shoot across, but the boat struck on the reef and Harris and Shortis, with some of the equipment, were washed overboard. They and the other three struggled to shore, about a hundred yards away, dragging the swamped boat with them. As they reached the sand, tense and shaken, a fire flared up in a near-by hut.

Any attempt at concealment was useless, and a bold front seemed the best move. Harris, Launcelot, and Mas walked to the hut, while Webber and Shortis unpacked the soaked and battered walkie-talkie, to find it completely ruined.

The natives in the hut, questioned by Harris through Launcelot, said that the nearest Japanese were two and a half miles away to the westward. They appeared friendly; on the surface there was no reason for Harris to be suspicious of them, but he was not satisfied. Years of dealing with New Guinea natives had given him an instinct more to be relied on than reason.

On the strength of his hunch, he ordered the signal "Washout" to be given. Webber flashed the signal with a light, and then sent a further signal asking that the submarine return the following night. No acknowledgment was received from the submarine, so Webber climbed to higher ground to repeat.

From the slight eminence, he was startled to see the other two boats with the remainder of the party just outside the breakers. He watched them repeat the process of overturning and of wading ashore, dragging what equipment they could. On board the submarine, it seemed, some flashes of light not sent by Harris' group had been seen. Imagination had filled in the gaps to make "Groggo," the signal that all was well. Only Sergeant Cream, who had had an attack of malaria, had remained aboard.

A worried and sleepless coastwatcher party awaited the dawn. Harris reflected that if the natives were unfriendly they would report the party in any case. If they were friendly, or in doubt, a show of trust might hold them to him. To his own party he put on a show of confidence. With the morning, he said, they could strike inland and try to reach the Idenburg River.

Dawn showed that the eleven in the party had twelve firearms among them, of which four were submachine guns, two carbines, and the rest pistols and revolvers. A box of hand grenades, some medical kits, the codes and maps, and about one week's rations had been saved.

There had been four natives in the hut. In the morning they were joined by another, who appeared to have some authority over the others, and who agreed that one of the youths in the hut should guide the party clear of the occupied area.

Hiding their rubber boats as best they could, the party packed up and moved off. They crossed the jungle that fringed the beach, continued inland, and finally made camp in a creek bed. At this point their guide left them, explaining that he would seek a better camp site. When he did not return, the coastwatchers feared he had gone to betray them.

Actually, their landing had been reported to the Japanese as soon as they left the beach. The natives in the hut had waited only until they were out of reach of reprisals from the party. Harris had been right when he signaled "Washout."

Next morning, with still no sign of the guide, the party left its camp in the creek bed and followed a path leading through the jungle. It led them up a spur to an open patch of kunai, and they halted at its edge before going into the open. Harris had given his carbine to Yali—perhaps to raise confidence, perhaps because he felt there was trouble ahead and he would give Yali the best chance while he, the leader, took the worst.

As they paused, voices were heard behind them and Webber, dropping his pack, started back to investigate. Dimly he saw a line of Japanese moving forward in the jungle, and he ran to warn Harris, who, meantime, was hurrying the party across the open patch to the shelter of the jungle on the other side. Yali, Mas, Buka, and Mariba were leading, and they had just reached the far jungle when firing broke out. At the same moment, Webber ran into the open and dropped to earth. McNicol bore to the left and reached the jungle. Harris, Bunning, Shortis, and Launcelot struck to the right under heavy fire, while Jeune, who was last in line, lay still near Webber.

Machine guns and mortars joined in the firing. The position was surrounded and the Japanese were moving in on the open patch. Mariba, wounded, fell after the first burst of fire. Harris, Bunning, and Shortis, still in the open, kept up an accurate fire, drawing the enemy on themselves. McNicol crawled to the edge of the jungle, at a place where there was no firing, and beckoned Harris to come to him. Harris, wounded in the left shoulder and with his pistol in his right hand, waved McNicol away toward the south.

Sadly, McNicol moved off, seeing that he could do no more for his leader. His movement was seen by the enemy soldiers, two of whom turned to fire at him. Firing in return, he escaped. Then, coming upon two dead Japanese, killed by their own mortar fire, he took the rifle of one. While searching the bodies for cartridges, he heard more Japanese approaching and had to retreat.

Yali and Buka remained hidden on the edge of the jungle, not knowing in which direction to move, while Mas slipped off toward McNicol. Launcelot, uninjured, reached the edge of the jungle, a few yards from Harris, who was still in the open. Jeune crept over to join Webber and the two remained concealed.

The Japanese attack converged on Harris, Bunning, and Shortis. The final phases can only be reconstructed from captured Japanese reports, but these are clear enough. The three men kept up the action for four hours, until at last Bunning and Shortis lay dead and Harris, wounded in three places, faced the enemy alone with an empty pistol. Then they rushed him.

"Blue" Harris faced his captors unflinchingly. The Japanese dragged him to a tree in the open and propped him against it. They questioned him about the party, about the ship that had landed it, about future attacks and movements. But Harris faced them with dumb contempt. He knew his wounds were mortal and that he need fear nothing from their threats or even worry that any weakness of the flesh might betray him. His lips remained closed and his eyes defied them until, exasperated, they bayoneted him and, all of their questions unanswered, gave him the release of death that he desired.

Launcelot lay hidden for four days in the one spot, hardly moving, while the Japanese searched within a few yards of him. He had two tins of emergency rations of which he ate a small portion, and licked the rain drops from leaves. When at last the enemy seemed to have left, he set off for the beach, keeping to the jungle. A few days later he met a friendly native who fed him and hid him until our forces landed a month later. When he saw the convoy, he paddled out in a canoe and was taken to General Eichelberger, to whom he told his story. Launcelot, at this time, believed himself to be the only survivor.

But five others, also, had managed somehow to live through the massacre.

Webber and Jeune had crawled into the jungle, where they remained until dusk the next day. Then, taking stock, they found they had an Owen gun, a pistol, two knives, one tin of emergency rations, five bouillon cubes, some medicines, and a compass. They set out through the jungle, heading first east, then south.

After five days they realized they had no hope of reaching the Idenburg and that their only chance lay in keeping to deep gullies and trying to survive until our forces landed. Seven foodless days later they found two small caves where they hid for another fourteen days, with only the raw hearts of palm tops as food.

By this time very weak, they heard the air raids and, on 21 April the bombardment that heralded the attack. Next morning they set out for the beach, and late that afternoon found natives who gave them a hot meal of taro and sweet potatoes, the first real food they had had for four weeks, and sheltered them for the night. Next morning they again set off, guided by two natives. But Jeune was so weak that he could hardly walk, so the natives, by signs, suggested that he be left in a hut while Webber searched for an American patrol. Webber gave his Owen gun to a native to carry, while he supported Jeune, but kept his revolver. Webber tells in his own words what happened next.

When we reached within ten or fifteen feet of the hut, a Jap rushed out and charged us, armed with a sword. I called a warning to Jeune of the presence of the Japanese, released him, and turned to take my gun from the native. I was sure there would be more Japs in the area. The natives were already running.

Jeune, somehow, while my back was turned, was closest to the Jap, therefore was attacked first. He fended off a sabre blow and hung on to the blade.

Overestimating my strength, I tried to knock the Jap out with punches to the face and throat rather than use my pistol for fear of bringing more on to the scene. After a struggle, during which the Jap nearly got possession of my pistol, I shot him by forcing the barrel into his stomach, thereby hoping to deaden the sound. This struggle required the combined strength of both Jeune and myself. Jeune told me later he forced his two fingers into the Jap's nostrils and the remaining fingers and hand into his mouth. This caused partial suffocation, thus enabling me to use my pistol effectively. Then, to prevent any outcry he might make, Jeune stabbed him through the heart with his sabre.

As it turned out, he was alone and I could have used my pistol earlier than I did without jeopardizing our safety.

Jeune had suffered cuts on the ear, neck, forearm, and hand, and was still further weakened by the struggle. The two remained hidden awhile, then continued for the beach, Webber scouting ahead and supporting himself on the sabre, while Jeune staggered along, using a long stick for the same purpose. Frequent halts were necessary, but late in the afternoon they met up with American soldiers and were taken to a battalion hospital. Both were evacuated and both recovered, although Jeune's health was permanently affected.

McNicol, who had met up with Mas briefly during the heat of the attack, had lost track of all the members of the party. Late in the afternoon of the day of the ambush, he heard firing near the beach and made his way toward it. He saw about fifteen Japanese, but could not make out at what they were firing, so he hid and worked his way back toward the scene of the ambush. Next day he searched for survivors and, finding none, set out for the mountains, following Harris' last orders to him.

Next day he met Mas again, and for thirty-two days the two men lived in the jungle with hardly any food. When they heard the bombardment and reasoned that it must be the landing, Mas was so weak and ill that McNicol set off alone for the beach. He reached an American medical unit and was promptly put in a hospital. All the while, his voice a whisper from a skull, his large eyes pleading, he begged that they go after Mas.

A patrol was sent out almost immediately, but failed to find him. Later another search was made, but with no success.

Yali and Buka had fallen to the ground during the ambush, when Mariba was shot beside them. Buka was unarmed, but Yali fired in the direction of a machine gun that was spitting bullets at Harris. Several of the Japanese wheeled and advanced on them. Yali fired, then he and Buka escaped into the jungle.

The two searched for two days, but could not find any other members of the party, so they struck out for Mandated New Guinea. So far as they knew, the nearest friendly forces were at Saidor, more than 400 miles away, but they faced the journey fearlessly. This is Yali's story:

> We had many narrow escapes while walking to Vanimo. As we had no food or matches and could not cook any of the food we stole from native gardens, we grew weaker.
>
> When near Vanimo, Buka became ill and weak. One day we were walking near the beach and heard a launch engine near by. I decided to investigate as I thought it might be American soldiers.
>
> I left Buka in the bush as he was too weak to come down with me, and then walked down to the beach. Upon arrival at the beach, I ran into some Japanese soldiers who saw me and shouted out to me, asking if I were an Australian policeboy. I then ran into the bush and kept away from the area where Buka was, as I did not want the Japs to follow me back to him.
>
> Later, I returned to the spot where I had left Buka but could find no sign of him. I searched the vicinity for two days and then decided that he had been captured by the Japs.
>
> I then decided to push on to Aitape, and after arriving at Vanimo, I received help from the natives and here learned of the American landing at Aitape. I arrived at Aitape where I contacted the Angau officer in charge.

So reported Yali to Lieutenant Ben Hall, planter and labor-recruiter, a man not likely to be sentimental about a native. Hall added to the report that Yali's story "does not relate fully the courage and determination displayed by this man in his return to the Allied lines, a journey of a hundred and twenty miles."

Mariba, he who had been the first wounded by the ambushing Japanese, turned up, incredibly, eight months later. He had been captured and held prisoner, but had escaped and made his way back to our lines. His return gave us some faint hope for Mas and Buka.

Throughout the world there have been foolish arguments on racial virtues. There are those who contend that mixed races inherit the worst traits of both parents, and there are others who hold that complete mixture of races, once stabilized, is best. Others say that all men are creatures of their environment and training. Coastwatchers wouldn't know the erudite points of such matters. They only know that the half-caste Julius McNicol and the full-bred native Yali can have a place in any party where courage and resource are the qualifications.

Among the coastwatchers, the disaster to the Hollandia party spread a gloom which no other casualties had caused. "Blue" Harris was the most striking personality among a bunch of notable individualists, a man whose vitality was such that his death was, at first, unbelievable. Harris, Shortis, Bunning, Mas, Buka—all had been lost; hearing it, men muttered the meaningless blasphemies and obscenities which had replaced prayer in their vocabularies.

The Secret War

In any war there are men who are unwilling to wait for the main offensive operations to be organized; they are restless under the mass training methods necessary to develop a major fighting force. Such men often work out schemes for raids on the enemy, usually at great risk to themselves, which are fashioned to strike a telling blow at an enemy strong point. This sort of raid not only causes damage but, if publicized, earns psychological advantages for the raiders and their country.

During the early part of the Pacific war, raids were necessarily long-range operations to make contact with the enemy and were launched from ships, submarines or aircraft.

Captain Ivan Lyon, who had escaped from Singapore, was such a man as described above. He had a burning passion to get back at the Japs because he had been compelled to leave his wife and child in Singapore when that city fell. After a long struggle with Allied Command officers, he got their approval for a raid on the shipping in Singapore.

In such operations all members of the raid were carefully chosen and then rigorously trained. "Jaywick," as the operation was known, would be carried out by three canoes, each manned by two commandos, launched as close to Singapore as safety permitted. After toughening their bodies, and mastering the art of handling the canoes, the members of Jaywick practiced working with a new explosive—the limpet mine.

"The limpets, which looked like rectangular chunks of rusty iron, measured 11 x 8 x 3 inches. They weighed fourteen pounds loaded and contained a powerful horseshoe magnet and ten pounds of P.E. (plastic explosive), which was enough to blow a hole about five feet square in the plates of a ship. Limpets had two holes at the top. The instantaneous fuse and time pencil, which could be set for explosion any time up to six hours, went into one hole. One end of a five-foot wooden pole, like a broomstick, fitted into the other.

"The technique of fixing limpets was simple. As a two-man Folboat came alongside a ship at night, the bowman clamped a small magnetic 'holdfast,' with a line attached to it, to the ship's side, and held the 'anchored' canoe steady. The other canoeman, his limpet fused and timed, then fitted his 'broomstick' into the other hole and lowered the limpet into the water between canoe and ship, getting it as deep as possible before carefully easing it onto the ship's plates. Limpets could be fixed without noise, but if carelessly applied, they gripped too quickly and clanged against the plates, a sound that could easily be heard inside the ship and lead to discovery. Once the limpet was applied, the canoeman worked the stick out of the hole, the bowman released the holdfast, and the canoe was paddled or allowed to drift to the next limpet position." *

By August 1943, Captain Lyon's group was ready. An old Japanese fishing boat, the *Krait*, was especially fitted out to take them through the Jap-infested waters to Singapore, but first they had to sail from Cairns on the northeast coast across the top of Australia to Exmouth Gulf on the west coast. From here they would pick up new canoes and make final ready. On September 2, 1943, the *Krait* set sail for Singapore.

RAID ON SINGAPORE

by Brian Connell

At half past five they cast off, with everything ship-shape and ready for sea. Exactly one minute later, the shaft extension piece on the engine broke. Paddy McDowell's imprecations shook the engine room more than the broken shaft, but even his loving care could not achieve the impossible. *Krait* was immobilised and had to anchor. It looked as if the whole expedition would have to be called off. Only a long tow down to Fremantle and a week in

*Ronald McKie, *The Heroes*, p. 31. Harcourt, Brace & Co.

the dockyards would put the damage right and by that time their time-table would start to overlap the monsoon. Lyon and Davidson were drafting the unpleasant wireless messages telling of their plight when, three hours later, the *U.S.S. Chanticleer,* the submarine-repair ship, entered the bay. This was too good to be true. Lyon had himself rowed across in the dinghy, and in no time *Chanticleer* sent a motorboat to tow *Krait* alongside. The broken shaft was taken out and by the following morning brazed together again, although the American mechanics insisted that it was only a temporary job and might perhaps get them back to Fremantle for a proper replacement.

Lyon, who had come to trust Paddy McDowell completely, asked him what he thought. "I think it will hold," the tough old Scot replied imperturbably—and that with 4,000 miles ahead of them in enemy waters and no spare. Lyon did not hesitate. At two o'clock in the afternoon of September 2 they put to sea—and three hours later nearly foundered.

As they cleared North West Cape, the full force of the wind hit them. With a wicked tide-rip running, *Krait* was beam on to the Force 7 westerly seas. They knew she could roll, but this was outside all their previous experience. Badly overloaded, she lurched drunkenly from side to side, with great green seas pouring inboard and crashing on the afterdeck. The wheelhouse looked like the conning tower of a submarine, completely awash. The hatches to the cabin and the engine room were battened down, but the men off watch in the cramped space under the awning had to hang on for their lives to the nearest stanchion, often waist-deep in swirling water.

It seemed as if one particularly large wave had finally put them under. Nothing of *Krait* was visible forward of the wheelhouse. She trembled, shuddered, almost on her beam ends, and then, just as it seemed as if they were going down, slowly shook herself free. Lyon himself was at the helm and slowly, with the help of Carse, managed to fight *Krait* round to port, head on to the murderous sea. For the faithful Morris, clinging desperately to the rails by the engine house, it was the worst moment of the whole voyage. The tough Welsh miner had really thought that his last moment had come.

Within an hour they were out of the coastal tide-rip and in relatively calmer water. Course was once more set to the north.

The third day out, with only a gentle swell, white cloud flecks in the blue sky and a warm breeze presaging the hot days that lay ahead, Lyon called the crew together under the awning: "It's time you knew where we are really going," he told them. "It is not Surabaya, it's Singapore. I am sorry I couldn't tell you before, but we had to keep it completely dark for security reasons."

Singapore—more than a thousand miles inside the new Japanese empire—was a very different proposition from Surabaya, just round the corner once they were through the Lombok Straits, but the men were absolutely exhilarated at the prospect.

Later that day they started blackening themselves with the skin dye they had brought with them. It was a sticky, evil-smelling mixture, thinned with spirit. It stuck to everything better than it did to their own bodies. They had to leave white rings round their eyes because of the spirit and another white patch round their private parts, although the native sarongs they donned put that right. Sweat, water, and oil brought it off again, and however often they applied the dye, they never presented anything better than a curiously mottled appearance. It might serve to confuse the Japanese and natives from a distance, but, close to, the blue eyes of most of the party would give them away.

If challenged, the plan was for Jones, Berryman, and Huston, the three darkest of them, to run on to the foredeck, gesticulating innocently and pointing at the Japanese flag they were going to hoist at the stern. None of the others would bear close scrutiny. McDowell looked like a stringy fakir, Carse vaguely Burmese, and Lyon might pass under a cursory glance for a Malay—except for those green eyes. But Poppa Falls was definitely ginger and Young quite fair and if they put the dye in their hair it stood up as if electrified, with patches of the original colour showing through where the scalp sweated. The only real defence was somehow to dodge all shipping.

Carse, his logbook looking more like a Scotland Yard fingerprint record with its black smudges, thought little of the experiment: "It proved a rank failure," he wrote, "more black everywhere than on the person after an hour or two. The crew now resemble blackamoors. A more desperate looking crowd I have never seen. The sea remains calm and glory be praised the scattered clouds of this morning are becoming more and more numerous, showing every indication of poor to bad visibility for the day of days, or rather night of nights."

He was thinking four days ahead to the dangerous passage of the closely guarded straits between the islands of Lombok and Bali, the gantlet *Krait* would have to run to break through into the South China Sea. The following day, the sixth, with the sky clouding up nicely, they hauled down their blue ensign and hoisted in its place the poached egg of Japan. The flag they had brought with them was far too clean and new for its purpose, so they scuffed it round the deck with their feet until it looked sufficiently grubby and weather-beaten. Paddy McDowell also switched his engine over to the silencer and the powerful chug-chug-chug of the exhaust died away to a reassuring purr. It cut a little off their speed and they never reached seven knots again.

With the look-outs' eyes peeled for enemy aircraft, they held course to the north. The Admiralty pilot book for the eastern archipelago informed them that at this time of year weather conditions would be hazy, with visibility down to 6,000 yards, but to their consternation the weather during the seventh was as bright, clear, and sunny as a spring day. The eighth dawned the same, and, to add to their troubles, the engine started coughing on a faulty feed pipe, but this was repaired during the morning.

They were now well within range of Japanese air patrols, and they knew there was a large air base at Den Pasar on Bali. Shortly after midday they sighted the mountain peaks of Lombok and Bali to the north. They needed night for the dash through the straits between them, so they throttled down to four knots and even spent a couple of hours going back on their tracks to gain time. After they had turned again in the late afternoon they passed within twenty feet of a large floating log, surrounded by a school of huge sharks which seemed to be trying to bite it. It was not a pleasant sight and considerably doused their spirits. It was not only Japanese air and naval patrol craft they had to fear.

By dusk, the massive island volcanoes, Gunong Agoeng, 10,000 feet on Bali, and Gunong Rindjani, 12,000 feet on Lombok, seemed to fill half the sky. Nusa Besar Island, in the middle of the entrance to the straits, was about fourteen miles distant. As the light faded, a powerful searchlight started to sweep from the high land on the south-eastern corner of Bali off their port bow.

Lyon and Davidson were in the wheelhouse with Ted Carse. "What do you think, Don? Can we make it?" Lyon asked. Davidson gave a slight shrug of his shoulders. Carse had been watching the sweep of the light intently. "If we keep well over to the Lombok side," he said, "the flash should pass over the top of our mast. We are so low in the water that I think we shall be below their horizon." Paddy McDowell was told to subject his faulty bearing to maximum revolutions, a glorious six and a half knots, and, heading slightly to the north-east, *Krait* started to force the fifty-mile passage.

Misled again by the pilot book, they had underestimated the southerly tidal set in the narrows. Once a day the whole of the Java Sea tries to pour through this narrow funnel into the Indian Ocean, and they had caught this tremendous rip at its height. By 9 o'clock they were barely abeam of Nusa Besar Island. An hour later, as a fixed steady light became visible on its highest point, probably an observation post, they were barely a mile further ahead. At eleven o'clock they had actually lost ground and were back in the same position as they had been two hours earlier. The tide was running faster than the straining diesel could push the overloaded craft.

Between midnight and four in the morning they made about six miles. They had passed innumerable flickering lights, some of which might be bush-clearing fires, but several of which looked like the headlights of motor cars. They had assumed Nusa Besar to be uninhabited—it had been, under the Dutch—but there was so much activity that they were thankful they had not carried out their original intention of lying up under its lee during the day and attempting the passage on the second night.

With every man on look-out, they peered into the darkness. Tired eyes can play curious tricks. Once, Lyon, who seemed to have a cat's vision at night, thought he saw a cruiser closing them, with three masts and a huge bow wave. After a few tense minutes, with arms at the ready, the bow wave resolved itself into a tide-rip and the masts into three tall trees on the top of a distant hill. Another naval patrol craft seen through their night-glasses turned out to be a sailing junk, beating laboriously against the current.

Although *Krait* was taking several minutes to thump through the worst of the tide-rips, the force of the current was now slackening, and Carse was reasonably sanguine about their being safely clear by the morning.

Their hopes were rudely shattered. As dawn broke they were still in the northern narrows, with Nusa Besar just visible astern. Daybreak was so spectacular that for a moment they forgot their danger. As the sun struck the top of the towering volcano, Gunong Agoeng, on Bali and the morning mists started to roll down the sides, the light caught the prismatic colours on the pinnacles and outcrops, cascading down, like a torch shone on mosaic. As the clouds cleared, the coast was left clear with perfect visibility. To the east, on the Lombok side, a merciful haze persisted, which should shield them from being sighted from Ampenan, the only known Japanese base in the area.

Apart from sighting a few coastal sailing *prahus*, no alarm was raised. At ten in the morning Carse wrote in his log: "Fixed position 8° 5′ South, 115° 55′ East. Thank Christ we are through the Strait, steering for Sekala, 68 miles distant. After a clear early morning the haze now at 1020 is increasing, although the island of Bali is still clearly visible. Lombok is almost totally obscured. . . . This war is certainly hard on the nervous system."

If all went well the next part of their journey should be

144

less eventful. Keeping to the east of the Kangean Islands, north of the Lombok Straits, the plan was to turn north-west, skirting the coast of Borneo, and then strike across to the Lingga Archipelago, the most southerly group of the maze of islands extended up to Singapore.

On the tenth, the day after they had cleared Lombok, Ted Carse's log was much more cheerful and discursive: "The morale of the crew is excellent. Corporal Crilly is doing a marvellous job in making all meals tasty in spite of bad weather and worse conditions. . . . By dark tonight we will be across the main shipping routes from Surabaya and Batavia to Balik Papan, Timor and all ports using the Macassar Strait. Our look-outs are particularly keen and so far have always sighted any objects long before we could possibly be seen by them. We have ample supplies of everything needed except water, which is rationed to three cups of tea a day and a water bottle every three days. Most of them seem to have no difficulty in this but I have been praying for a good shower of rain ever since the days have become hot. In latitude 5° South, with the sun only 5° North, its heat as close to the water as we are is terrific. The decks become too hot to stand on in bare feet. To counteract this, our freeboard is so little that with even a calm sea our waist is continually awash."

By the fourteenth they were standing away from Borneo on the last lap of their sea journey. That evening Carse made another of his revealing log entries: "A heavy cloud bank surmounted by mare's tails is rising astern. It might presage a fairly heavy blow. No rain so far. I can visualise a small nudist colony when it does come and bad luck for the man at the wheel. Summing up this afternoon, I decided we had seven more really dangerous days with the ship. Namely, to-day and tomorrow, dropping and picking up operatives, two days for this passage on return and, last but not least, THE STRAIT. If we survive the next two days the operation should be carried out successfully and then for our return journey. All the ship's company are in the best of health and spirits and are thoroughly enjoying the trip. So far we have experienced the most wonderful weather. Right from Cairns we had a following wind and sea (these are

145

the conditions in which the ship behaves best) and no really bad weather. But the last three days we have seen no flying fish at all. This seems rather remarkable in these waters. One solitary turtle was seen to-day and countless jellyfish."

The next day they sighted a junk on a converging course and *Krait's* labouring engine was unable to shake her off. "The fact that we can't leave a junk behind, although she is beating slightly to windward, is causing quite a little merriment," Carse commented. The two ships remained within sight of each other most of the day, but as the wind shifted during the afternoon, *Krait* started to draw ahead, without any sign of suspicious activity on the junk. Just to make sure, everyone had rubbed on another coat of their foul-smelling, sticky dye and Carse's logbook was covered again with his smudged fingerprints. There was also a more worrying note: "My eyes have been giving trouble lately," he wrote. "I can't read the sextant now by artificial light and this will mean working by sun and dead reckoning. Sun sights at present are rather unsatisfactory. Probably with a fortnight's rest away from this constant glare, they will improve sufficiently for the run home. I sincerely hope so."

They were now within a hundred miles of their target. Arms were inspected, their camouflage renewed, and every man, except for look-outs, told to remain under the awning with the minimum of movement.

At ten o'clock of the morning of September 16 they saw their first aircraft, apparently heading north for Singapore on a steady course, and then two sailing ships coming down the Strait towards them. One was a European-type yacht, probably captured at the fall of Singapore, but they both ignored *Krait* and, to everyone's delight, a cloud bank started building up from Sumatra, reducing visibility drastically and threatening a violent storm. The heavy black cloud formations came boiling up from the west, blotting out the sky. Lyon, Davidson, and Morris had seen this phenomenon before. It heralded a dreaded "Sumatra," a violent cyclonic storm which has wise seamen running for harbour. *Krait* had weather conditions as bad when clearing

Exmouth Gulf and if they could hold course they might be able to get through the Strait without detection.

Suddenly Davidson gave the order for action stations, each man taking up his Sten or Bren gun and going to his loophole post under the awning. Not 400 yards ahead, a 10,000-ton freighter emerged from the murk on their port side and cut across their bows. They reduced speed immediately, but the ship held on course and gave no evidence of having sighted them. Minutes later the storm struck and everything was blotted out. The wind hit *Krait* as if she had collided head on with a solid rock. The sea was lashed inboard, lifting spindrift twenty or thirty feet high. Then came the torrential rain lasting nearly three quarters of an hour.

The more inexperienced members of the crew had been warned what to expect, and once the first shock was over, busied themselves carrying a large sail forward to catch the precious fresh water. Hanging on grimly to rails and stanchions, they ferried every container they possessed past the wheelhouse to fill up the water tanks. Drenched, shouting, and happy, revelling in their first bath for a fortnight, the tension of half an hour earlier was completely forgotten.

The storm cleared as quickly as it had come, and they found that they were through the Strait and already north of Pompong Island, the first Lyon had decided to reconnoitre as their rear base for the pick-up and get-away. They were now in the almost land-girt sea, some 60 miles from east to west and 150 miles from north to south, which lies between the coast of Sumatra and the convex sweep of the islands of the Rhio and Lingga archipelagoes. To the north, within a score of miles of Singapore, the islands curve round towards Sumatra to form a natural barrier, with only half a dozen narrow channels between them. *Krait* had avoided the wide and well-guarded Singapore Straits, which lead into the port from the east, but was safely within the inner barrier to the south. Her outward task was largely done. Almost any of the islands in the northern part of this inland sea were within canoe range of their target.

They run very much to a pattern. Humps of dark-green

jungle, heavy with ficus palm and knotted undergrowth, vibrate in the heat haze, with mud flats and mangrove swamp on the shore, interspersed with rocky outcrops and small sandy beaches. Most of the inhabitants live in fishing villages, either built on stilts along the shoreline or clustered on some rare stretch of level land with a clearing for their primitive agriculture behind. Except for the occasional plantation, everything else is jungle, teeming with animal life. If they chose their hides carefully, the canoe teams were unlikely to be discovered even by the occasional hunter. The villagers are nearly all fishermen, their means of communication the *kolek* and the *prahu*. To these men *Krait* would be an object of no interest, provided her movements were not suspicious. But the canoes—that was another matter. They were unlike anything to be found in these waters and the merest sight of one of them would cause a buzz of *kampong* gossip.

Reducing speed, *Krait* turned south and slowly ran past Pompong Island. There seemed far too many native huts and fishing stakes along the shores for comfort and as they stood in to round a point they had another bad scare. Carse suddenly sighted a long straight mast with crosstrees about a mile and a half away, its structure unmistakably that of a naval patrol craft. Clamping on full speed and swinging the helm over, he turned through 180 degrees and sent little Berryman, with his keen eyes, scurrying up *Krait's* own mast to report.

The look-out soon had reassuring news. Only the mast was visible sticking out of the water and it must belong to a wreck.

Krait then stood over to the eastwards to see if Bengku Island offered any better shelter, but they found it surrounded by a seemingly impassable reef. They launched the dinghy to take soundings, and Davidson was just about to cast off when they heard the sound of an aircraft. It was coming in so low that for a moment they could not see it. With quick presence of mind, Lyon snatched up one of the conical coolie straw hats they were carrying on board, tossed it down to Davidson, quickly donned one himself, and as the plane roared over at not more than a hundred feet, looked up at it and waved in the most natural manner in the world. He could actually see the Japanese pilot looking down at them. He gave no sign of surprise, continued straight on, and was soon out of sight. It had been a bad moment. Lyon blew out his cheeks in relief and blessed the foresight which had made him have everyone blacken themselves with the dye as soon as the storm was over. Curious as they looked, it obviously worked.

Bengku proved useless, and towards evening they moved back to Pompong, where they had spotted one sheltered and uninhabited bay. They christened it Fisherman's Bay and dropped anchor for the night. The four officers held a conference. In spite of the scares of the day, Lyon had made up his mind that patrol activity was limited and that the best thing for *Krait* to do was to cruise gently northwards and then strike west to Pulau Durian, to arrive at dusk the following day.

"I don't know how the day is going to end," Carse was writing in his log, voicing the feelings of them all. "We have been zig-zagging and zig-zagging all day long from one deserted spot to another, only to find that we are approaching a worse one. Out of the frying pan into the fire would be appropriate, but it does the system no good. We have been looking for a place to anchor but the population is against us. As long as we keep moving, no matter how aimlessly, we don't seem to excite suspicion, but I don't think we could do it for long. We are within about 30 odd miles of Singapore and still getting closer by means of a staggered course, waiting and praying for dark. No lovers ever longed for darkness as we do, although it will probably show us the lights of Singapore. One thing about it is that we should be able to pick up all searchlights and observation post positions guarding the city."

Lyon had always hoped that *Krait* would be able to lie up in some deep cove, camouflaged with branches against the shore, to await the return of the attack party. This plan had now been abandoned. No suitable cover had been found, and in the eighteen months since he was last in these waters, the Japanese had clearly organised extensive patrol activity. He would have to take the risk of sending *Krait* on an innocent-appearing run to Borneo, returning for the rendezvous. She was safer in the uninhabited sea lanes, off the main shipping routes, than in this congested litter of islands.

At four o'clock in the afternoon they passed along the small island of Panjang. A dark-green hump of hill and jungle, it appeared entirely uninhabited and offered several good beaches and sandy coves. Lyon made up his mind at once. This would be the base for the canoes, but they dare not land and reconnoitre in daylight, still within view of the observation post on Galang Baru, so they carried on northwards towards the Bulan Strait approach to Singapore to waste the three remaining hours of daylight.

It would be half past seven before it was dark enough for them to turn about. As the tropical night fell, a diffused glow seemed to fill the northern sky, even individual specks of light appeared. Lyon grabbed Davidson by the elbow. "There she is, Donald," he said. They were looking at the reflection of the lights of Singapore, twinkling a mere twenty-two miles ahead. They called the rest of the crew up into the bows. There was no mistaking the elation in Lyon's usually calm voice as he told them what they were looking at. The tension suddenly seemed to lift. The voyage was half over, they were safe, and they now knew the full extent of what was required of them. Slapping each other on the back, pointing, wrestling, panting in their excitement, it was several minutes before they took up their stations again.

Lyon whispered an order and Carse turned *Krait* round for her run back to Panjang. They started to get out the rest of the attack stores on the forward deck. Lyon, Davidson, and Page watched their every move to make sure that there was no last-minute confusion, while Carse's bad eyes peered ahead to con their position.

"As we turned, we noticed a searchlight coming from the Galang Baru O.P.," he wrote later in his log. "Then a violent rain squall accompanied by heavy, gusty winds struck us, obscuring everything. Suddenly out of the darkness ahead, our fishing *pagar* showed a lovely bright light. As we were at that time surrounded by reefs, with a strong ebb tide and no vision, it appeared God sent. If we return from this trip I am thinking of setting up a monument to their glory."

They arrived off Panjang at ten o'clock and anchored, but the sea was too rough and the wind too high to risk landing. At midnight the weather showed no signs of abating, so they weighed anchor to see if they could find a lee shore on the opposite side of the island. No sooner had they got under way than the wind dropped. They moved inshore again and Davidson and Jones paddled to the beach in the dinghy to reconnoitre. Within half an hour Jones was back, to say that the beach was perfect for the purpose.

The crew had practised transporting the canoes and loading the stores so often that they could do it blindfolded. Quickly Lyon ran through the final check: arms, knives, charts, binoculars, rations and water for a month, protective clothing, and, last but not least, the mines and spares that went with them. *Krait's* freeboard was so low that loading the dinghy presented no difficulty. Paddy McDowell came up from the engine room, and Young from his wireless set, to see them off. It was now half past four in the morning. Morris shouldered his way forward and leant over to shake Lyon by the hand: "The very best of luck, sir, and may we be seeing you again soon," he said. "Thank you, Morris, I hope so indeed," replied Lyon to his oldest companion.

Light-hearted as it all was, those left on *Krait* had the nagging thought that they might be seeing their six companions for the last time. The pick-up was to be at Pompong after dusk on October 1. If anything went wrong, *Krait* was not to wait beyond the rendezvous date, but to return to Exmouth Gulf without the operatives. There was no point in risking the whole party, and Lyon was confident that if the six of them survived they would be able to capture a junk and find their own way home.

For the six men of the attack teams, the parting from

Krait had been an even greater wrench. Although the vital stage of the expedition lay ahead of them, they felt very lonely, deposited a thousand miles inside the enemy lines, faced by a fortnight abandoned to their own slender resources. Lyon was worried as he stood on the sandy beach and watched *Krait's* familiar, ridiculous outline fade into the night—worried about Carse's eyes being able to stand up to the strain of the pin-point navigation which must bring them back to Pompong at the end of the month, worried about *Krait's* ability to give an account of herself now that her firepower had been reduced by half, worried that the only other two men with real knowledge of local lore and jungle survival, Davidson and Page, were standing beside him and that there was no one left aboard to hold the youngsters together should anything go wrong.

His other five companions gave him no qualms. They were fighting fit in spite of the fatigues of the voyage and the unbearable strain of the last forty-eight hours. Davidson, with his inexhaustible energy and inventiveness, tough as oak; Page, intelligent, resourceful, and utterly reliable; Falls, the young Greek god, powerful, tireless, ever alert; Jones, with his power-packed, thickset body and ready smile; and Huston, the "Baby" of the party, dogged, endlessly willing and making up in will power and determination for his lack of years. If they could not get to Singapore and back, then no one could.

For the moment they felt safe enough. In his quick reconnaissance from the dinghy into the jungle earlier in the night, Davidson had found nothing to indicate that this part of Panjang was in any way frequented. The folboats and the stores had been dragged up into the undergrowth and all was quiet, the breathless hush which even in the tropics precedes the dawn. Around and above them the huge ficus trees were whispering in the light airs. Beyond the horse-shoe of rocks that hemmed in their little haven, the treetops were etched in sharp profile against the glittering slate grey of the night sky, with the clouds slowly building up for the morning overcast.

It was an idyllic, peaceful scene. After the sour smell of diesel oil, hot tar, and timbers and the lingering fish stench from *Krait's* ancient bilges, the jungle scents were almost overpowering in their sweetness. Ground lilies and a flowering tree with white midnight blossoms made the air round them almost tangible. They breathed it deeply, gathering strength for the trial that lay ahead.

There was nothing further they could do that night. Their muscles ached from the unloading and their brains were tired. Ducking back into the bush a few yards under cover, each of them burrowed out a hip hole under his groundsheet, wrapped himself in a blanket, and to the soothing rustle of the jungle insects was on the instant asleep.

The respite only lasted three hours, but was infinitely refreshing. As they sat round their first breakfast of emergency rations they held a council of war. The drop had been carried out ahead of schedule and they could afford to take the next two days resting, getting their land legs—each of them still swayed on solid ground with the inbuilt movement of *Krait*—building up their dump, and sorting out their stores. Davidson, the best silent tracker, moved off into the jungle to see how safe their hide-out was. Huston, sent down with a rake to remove all traces of their landing, was soon back with the encouraging report that the tide had obliterated everything up to the high-water mark and that a legion of bustling little land crabs had made his work quite unnecessary.

Davidson was equally reassuring. There was a native fishing village about a quarter of a mile away on the other side of the spit of land, but no sign of any tracks leading in their direction.

The forty-eight hours that followed were the best of the whole trip. They lazed around, wallowed in the fresh water, scrubbing off the filth of the voyage and enjoying the unspeakable luxury of cleaning their teeth in something other than pure brine. There was the occasional scare. For a tense half hour the shrilling of birds up the hill made them think that some native was after all making his way over from the village, but the noises in the undergrowth resolved themselves into a troop of monkeys, who surveyed the party with chirpy curiosity and then gradually leapfrogged away again. During the evening, they heard the disturbing plop-plop of a diesel. Clearly there was a patrol boat making an irregular inspection of the area. They heard it again on the second night, but at a different time, and it was obviously an inquisitive adversary of whom they would have to beware.

The evening of September 20 found them in magnificent trim. The stores and equipment for the three folboats were checked and rechecked—food and water for at least eight days, charts and the Admiralty register of enemy shipping, arms greased and ammunition inspected for mildew, and, above all, the precious limpet mines themselves. Here Page was the expert. The rods down which they were slid to be clipped on the side of ships with their magnets were cleaned and oiled until they ran like silk. The detonators, the hinges for the magnets, every working part was inspected.

They represented the last stage in the long haul across from Sydney and nothing could be allowed to impede their successful functioning. Three sets of them went into each canoe, together with the magnetic hold-fast which enabled them to hold steady in the tide as the canoe came alongside its target and each successive mine was fixed. Everything was in order and they were replaced inside their watertight containers. Then came the boats themselves. Every bamboo strut, every inch of the rubberised canvas, was run over by keen eyes and probing fingers for the slightest snag or flaw. The waist bands which fastened round the operators and prevented a single drop of water reaching the inside of the boat were checked for the slightest puncture; so were their hoods and protective clothing. Everything had survived the pitching and tossing of *Krait's* hot hold without a mark. They were ready to go.

Fully loaded, with its two operatives, the seaman in front and the officer to correct the course and speed behind, each canoe weighed some 800 pounds. They were low and sluggish in the water, but to ensure success they could not carry less. Once the mines and half the rations had gone, it would be a very different matter and even tired paddlers should be able to make them bounce back on the return journey.

After a last survey of the hide, with Page giving the natural camouflage a few final touches, the canoes were launched.

For their final hide and attack base, Lyon had selected Pulau Dongas, a small island lying just off the north coast of Batam and due south-east of Singapore, just behind Pulau Sambu. Paddling evenly now, with the west-east tide, they reached it just after midnight on the 22nd. Lyon had remembered it from his pre-war sailing days as entirely uninhabited, with an all-important supply of fresh water. There was an extensive swamp on the south side and a sandy spit at its northern head which should provide an excellent landing place. So indeed it proved to be. The canoes ran past its jungle-covered hump, and Davidson, in his usual role of scout, went in ahead. He returned full of enthusiasm. The sand beach ran in under mangroves, providing perfect cover and a much more extensive and comfortable hide even than on Bulat. The canoes were hauled up, with some difficulty as the tide was low, and, with one of their number, as always, on watch, the other five collapsed into sleep.

They had touched the limit of human endurance. In the three days since leaving Panjang none of them had had more than half a dozen hours' sleep. Lyon was the worst hit. For him the physical strain was compounded by the responsibility and concentration of leadership. This was the testing time for his plan. Davidson was a superb foil, but only Lyon could supply the detailed, instinctive knowledge of the terrain, the snap decision on tactics, choice and change of hide, and, with his knowledge of the Malay language, any hint from the overheard conversation of fishermen and villagers that their plan needed to be modified. He had lost weight and was looking gaunt and hollow-cheeked. Reading his mood, his companions redoubled their efforts, taking the minor details off the shoulders of the one man on whom everything depended.

They could afford to spend the next day resting. A detailed search of the island revealed not a single sign of human habitation or movement. Their sole companions were a colony of large black- and yellow-striped sea iguanas and a couple of small crocodiles. While the others remained in the hide to check their canoes and equipment, Lyon and Davidson climbed to the highest point of the island to begin their watch on the Roads and work out their plan of attack.

Once a suitable observation point had been chosen, constant watch was kept by the six men in turn, plotting the position of the various ships at anchor and endeavouring to identify them with the help of the Admiralty Register they had brought with them. This went on for forty-eight hours.

"The Dongas observation post was opposite and eight miles distant from Kallang," Lyon noted in his report. "In conditions of good visibility it was possible to see into Keppel Harbour. A night watch was kept until 2300 hours on September 23, revealing no signs of any defensive activity. There was no black-out in Singapore and the lights of cars driving down Beach Road could be clearly seen. No harbour or navigation lights were burning and all shipping was stationary.

"The following day we were well rested and maintained a keen watch, during which we carefully scrutinised both shore and shipping. There was no change to be seen in the general outline of the city. A row of five to seven tall wireless masts have been constructed on the site of the former Paya Lebar station and there is a single mast on the roof of the Cathay Building. On the southernmost point of St. John's Island there is now a small signal station. At Sambu, three miles from our observation post, all visible oil tanks were still as left by the Dutch. There was tremendous activity on the western side of the island. The hammering of plates and drone of engines by day and night suggested either ship repair or building.

"In the harbour and Roads of Singapore there was considerable movement of shipping. At no time was there less than 100,000 tons at the same time."

That afternoon they plotted their targets, identifying and noting for the intelligence files back in Melbourne every ship they could see. The tankers they would ignore. It was the one type of vessel against which the limpet mine was least effective. Their main target was merchant ships. Three limpets laid along the side against the main holds would blow a hole four or five feet in diameter and the ship must inevitably sink. Davidson and Falls, in the No. 2 canoe, were to take the group of ships lying in the Singapore Roads proper, to the east of Keppel Harbour. Of the other two, Page was to concentrate on the ships lying alongside the wharves on the island of Pulau Bukum, to the south-west of Singapore, and Lyon was to deal with the other group of ships lying in the examination anchorage between Bukum and the main island.

With the precious mines checked and double-checked again, they launched the canoes for the attack about eight o'clock at night. Everyone knew his role and there was no need for long farewells. Each man gripped the others' hand, they wished each other good luck and started off in company in their usual arrowhead formation. Readily accessible, each man carried a small rubber pellet filled with lethal cyanide. If any of them should be caught one bite brought instant death. If the attack failed, the Japanese would at least be denied the triumph of exhibiting their captives— and the crew of *Krait* would be safe.

They skirted warily past the glare of Sambu and, to their relief, as the night advanced, the lights of Singapore started to dim. Halfway to the target area, a searchlight was suddenly switched on from some high point, probably the top of the Cathay Building, swung slowly round, and then came to rest on the three folboats for a full half minute. They flicked their canoes bow on and sat transfixed. Then it continued its sweep and was as suddenly switched off. They expected every searchlight in the harbour to open up, but nothing happened. At moments of such heightened danger, every fear is justified, but it really seemed as if they had not been spotted.

They resumed their course, only to find that the increasing force of the tide started to take its toll. They turned the bows of the canoes further east to meet it, but they were barely making headway. They had now been paddling for more than three hours. Practised canoe operatives can continue for much longer without excessive fatigue, but it was becoming clear that they were rooted in mid-channel and time was running out on them. They were nowhere near any ships yet and, even in the most favourable conditions, they would have to allow at least an hour for the actual attack. At all costs they must be back in their hide by daybreak. By one o'clock in the morning the attempt had become hopeless. At Lyon's careful hail, the three canoes drew together and the bitter decision was taken to break off the attack and run for safety. They would have to try from a point further west two nights later.

The tide was an equal enemy on the return journey. It carried them well to the east of Dongas and when it started to slacken they decided to race for the hide individually. Davidson and Falls, Page and Jones, the two stronger couples, reached the mangrove swamp in time, but there was no sign of Lyon and Huston. Wrestling with their lopsided canoe, they had lost contact.

The strain was beginning to tell on Lyon by now. All the planning, all the responsibility, and most of the worry had been his and the physical effort was starting to wrack his frail frame. He might have done better to change partners with Davidson, as Poppa Falls could paddle for two all day, but this was not Lyon's way. The make-up of the crews had long since been determined and it was essential to have a pair of fast paddlers for emergencies and spying out the land ahead.

Lyon and Huston were safe. They had battled on until they could hardly see from exhaustion and had mistaken their bearings. They landed on the wrong side of Dongas just as dawn was breaking and spent an unhappy, sleepless day in pouring rain, hiding in an outcrop of boulders.

At seven o'clock that evening, having recovered sufficiently to discover where they were, they paddled round the point to rejoin the main party, to be greeted with cries of relief. "Lieutenant Davidson had anticipated our arrival and organised a much needed hot meal," Lyon was to report tersely but gratefully. "He had also made plans for an immediate change to an alternative hide, whence an attack could be launched the following night of the 26th/27th, under favourable conditions. His prompt action on this occasion contributed greatly to the success of the expedition."

The new base, which both Lyon and Davidson had noted from their observation post on the previous day, was the island of Subar, lying due west from them on the other side of the Bulan Strait. As soon as Lyon and Huston had rested a little they set off, with Davidson and Falls in the slow folboat, and managed to beat the tide, which ran less strongly along the northern coast of Batam, quite comfortably. Subar had no beach and no water but was mercifully uninhabited. Dawn caught them still manhandling stores and canoes over the boulders, but they managed to hide everything under bushes and behind rocks and this time slept the whole morning.

By the afternoon they were sufficiently recovered to climb up for another look at their target. There had been little change in the moored ships and they had a much better view, straight into the examination anchorage, than had been possible from Dongas. The target areas were not changed, but the plan was altered to permit Davidson and Falls to take off separately, due north, to Keppel Harbour, while the other two canoes headed in a more north-westerly direction for Pulau Bukum. That evening, the twenty-sixth, found them faced by the sixth night of eight hours' paddling out of the last seven. They were still in relatively good shape, although their legs were suffering from a curiously rubbery feeling that came from long hours spent in an unnatural position in a canoe. But they had the spur of the actual attack to keep them going.

This time the final farewells were real. They were now two days behind schedule. Some check would have to be made on the results of the attack and, although Davidson was the expedition's photographer, he and Falls, as the strongest pair, in their original boat, were to ride the easterly set of the tide on their return journey and make their way down the Rhio Strait to the east of Batam Island, doubling back thence to Panjang and then making a bee-line for Pompong to hold *Krait*. The others should be able to make Dongas again from the examination anchorage and after confirming the effects of the raid, would rejoin the rendezvous down the Bulan Strait, the way they had come.

"Cheerio, Ivan, best of luck," said Donald Davidson, looking a little worriedly at Lyon's hollow-cheeked face, with the sleepless shadows under his eyes and the short stubble of his beard.

"The same to you, Donald. And thank you for everything. See you back at Pompong."

The others were more light-hearted, but their hand-grips were not less fervent. They manhandled their slate-grey canoes over the rocks, checked the fastenings on their skin-tight black vests and hoods, climbed in to the narrow circular opening which sealed the inside of their folboats from the sea, and with a last salute of their paddles set off.

The more northerly course made possible by the change of base had made things very much easier. Davidson and Falls were across the Straits in a couple of hours, and although they kept a wary eye on a searchlight which opened up on Blakang Mati Island off to port, encountered no serious difficulties. The two men had developed a warm understanding and chatted easily, with Davidson pointing out the main buildings and sights of Singapore to his fascinated companion. It hardly seemed possible that they could be passing unobserved right across the inner harbour of this Japanese bastion. As they drew closer in, they muffled their voices until Davidson pointed out the unmistakable triad pylons of the Keppel Harbour boom ahead of them.

Just as they altered course slightly, Falls spotted a set of navigation lights moving out at them from the night. They proved to be on a large steam tug turning into the same channel. It headed straight for them until it seemed impossible that they should not be either sighted or run down. Then, at the last moment, it turned towards Blakang Mati and they were left safe but badly shaken.

As soon as they had regained their composure they forged ahead again and to their surprise found the Tanjong Pagar end of the boom opened. The temptation was too strong for Davidson. Two days earlier, from Dongas, two large freighters had been sighted tied up alongside the wharves. If these could be sunk, they would block the entire dock for months. Unhesitatingly, Davidson turned hard aport right into Keppel Harbour. It was a mad gamble to take, as the harbour was little more than five hundred yards wide, but the tug had not succeeded in spotting them from a mere fifty yards away and Davidson was so confident of the efficacy of their camouflage that he ploughed straight in. They paddled the whole length of the wharves, but their targets had gone. The vessels in the Empire Docks behind were too brightly illuminated and too small to justify the risk involved.

As they turned and made their way out again they found two small freighters against the east wharf, but considered that they were not worthy of their attention, compared with the large ships lying out in the Roads which were their original targets. Apart from the busy unloading going on in the Empire Docks under the arc lights, there was little sign of movement in the main harbour. Davidson could scarcely credit that the Japanese had become so lax in their security, but then, as he considered ruefully, perhaps they had very little to worry about—apart from enemy folboats loaded with limpet mines. But they had obviously not thought of that.

Out through the boom again they continued due east towards the shipping in the Roads. Here it was merely a question of taking their choice. The look-outs must have been unbelievably slack, as the operation went like clockwork. They might just as well have been attacking abandoned hulks in Sydney Harbour. Swinging at their anchors, the bows of all the ships were pointed towards Singapore in the current and, as the canoe drifted down the port side of each, they were nicely in the shadow from the lights of Singapore. The tide was running at about half a knot, perfect for their purpose.

Firm-fingered, they went through the drill. Out with the hold-fast and, as Davidson steadied the canoe, Falls set the fuse, slipped a mine down on its placing stick, and snapped the magnets against the hull well under water. It was as easy as that. Release the hold-fast, drift down the length of cordtex to the side of the next hold, and plant another mine. Three times and that was the ration. Slowly and silently they drifted down to the next victim, which they had identified as the *Taisyo Maru,* which they had seen from Dongas. Ignoring a 10,000-ton tanker, they carefully chose three substantial cargo vessels of at least 6,000 tons' displacement. The third one had arc lights burning on deck, illuminating the surrounding water, but so confident were they now that nothing could deter them. As they worked, they could hear the chiming clock on Singapore's Victoria Hall counting out the quarter hours.

By half past one it was all over. The placing stick and hold-fast were dropped silently over the side. The mines were timed to blow at five o'clock. They had less than three hours in which to cross the Straits again and find a hide on the north shore of Batam Island. Confident, triumphant, swinging easily on their paddles, they set off to the southeast.

Eight miles to the west of them, the two other canoes had remained in company to within a mile of Pulau Bukum. The time was nine o'clock, just as Davidson and Falls were slipping into Keppel Harbour. Page and Jones continued straight on to the Pulau Bukum wharves, and Lyon and Huston turned a little north to the examination anchorage. They had both had an even easier passage than the third canoe, apart from the sweep of the searchlight on Blakang Mati which had bothered Davidson and Falls.

Page and Jones found that the wharves were brightly lit, with sentries on guard at the ships' gangways. They paddled the whole length of the docks, keeping fairly well out to sea, but only saw one suitable target, an old freighter of the *Tone Maru* class. A large tanker was too heavily laden to make any attack worth while, and the third vessel, a small freighter, had a barge alongside on which a number of dockers appeared to be working under arc lights against a background of what looked like cauldrons of steam. They both watched curiously this odd spectacle for some time but could not make up their minds what the men were doing.

They drifted down to the *Tone Maru*-class freighter and slipped down their first three limpets. They could hear the Japanese crew and workmen chatting away, completely unaware of the destruction which was in store for them. Number 3 canoe then made off again to the north towards the examination anchorage. Their second target was reasonably easy to identify, with its three sets of goal-post masts. They had marked it from the Admiralty list on Subar as the *Nasusan Maru*. This whole group of ships was blacked out and, as the lights of Singapore round the corner of the mainland to the east were greatly dimmed, they had some difficulty in finding their third target, an older 6,000-ton freighter. However, the tide carried them right down to it and they bumped the bow quite heavily as its dark mass emerged from the night. There can have been no look-outs on duty at all, as they heard no movement, fixed their mines without the least interruption, and immediately set off, in their turn, south-east, to the original Dongas hide.

Lyon and Huston had the most alarming experience. They were due to attack the more northerly group of ships, lying right up against Singapore Island itself. On the way they passed the *Nasusan Maru* with its three goal-post masts, but recognising that this "belonged to Page," carried on to the north.

The lights of Singapore were now hidden behind a spit of land and the two men found it completely impossible to distinguish the outlines of their targets against the background of hills. They paddled to and fro, losing a lot of time, until finally, in desperation, Lyon decided to return to the examination anchorage proper. All the ships there were blacked out, but two large tankers they had noted earlier were showing their obligatory red riding light, and rather than waste further time, he decided to attack one of these.

They had fixed one limpet on the propeller shaft and were just lowering a second, beside the engine room, when Lyon saw Huston looking upwards. He glanced up himself, and there, not ten feet above their heads, a man was watching them intently out of a porthole.

He made no sign or sound and, with an inspired reflex action, Lyon gestured impatiently to his partner to get on with the work.

There is no rational explanation for the man's complete inactivity. Whether he thought they were starving

Malays picking off barnacles for the family pot there is no way of telling. He continued to watch them earnestly as they fixed the last limpet and then, with Lyon willing Huston to remain calm, withdrew his head and lighted the lamp in his cabin as they pushed off. If he lived to tell the tale, he must have been a very surprised man three hours later. "He'll soon be dead," Lyon whispered to his partner with relish.

Nevertheless, he had upset their plans and they could not risk dallying in the anchorage any longer. For all they knew the alarm would be raised at any moment. Grim with anxiety at the thought that the whole purpose of the expedition was about to be wrecked by a general alarm, they bent their backs to their paddles and fairly skimmed the swell in a straight line for Dongas.

Both western canoes reached the island safely within a few minutes of each other shortly before five o'clock. Hauling up their folboats into the mangrove hide, Page had just given Lyon an excited account of their successful attack and Lyon was just telling the other two of the extraordinary incident with the tanker when the first booming explosion was heard. It came from over on the Keppel Harbour side and was their first indication that Davidson too had been successful. Listening intently, they counted two, three, from the Keppel Harbour direction and another four from their own area. So Davidson had successfully laid all his limpets, and unless he had had as unpleasant an experience as Lyon, must be on his way to safety.

The thunder of the explosions reverberated round the Straits and echoed back from the surrounding hills. No flashes were to be seen as the charges were all well under water. This was fantastic. They danced up and down, slapping each other on the back, whispering hoarsely and incoherently with delight, their rigid discipline not letting them down even in this moment of triumph.

The eastern sky was beginning to lighten. Within minutes of the last explosion every ship's siren in the Roads started to howl and a quarter of an hour later Singapore and Sambu Island were suddenly blacked out.

Leaving Page and Jones to see to the safety of the boats, Lyon and Huston fought their way up through the trees in the direction of the observation post. By the time they had panted and clawed their way up the hill there was just enough light for them to find their vantage point.

As dawn came up, they could see that most of the ships in the anchorage had got under way and were starting to cruise aimlessly up and down. This made it very difficult to determine what had been sunk and what had not. One ship was definitely half submerged, with her bows sticking up out of the water, over in the examination anchorage, and the big tanker, the *Sinkoku Maru,* which had given Lyon and Huston such a fright, was burning fiercely and belching out thick black smoke which covered the whole area. This left five to be accounted for and, for the time being, they had to be entered as "certainly damaged, probably sunk."

The sirens and commotion continued most of the morning. At a quarter past six a flight of twin-engined aircraft took off from Kallang airfield and roared westwards towards the Malacca Strait. They returned about two hours later and, after putting down again briefly at Kallang, took off individually and started to scour the southern approaches. One of them passed right over the Dongas hide and could be clearly identified as a twin-engined medium bomber.

By this time Page had joined the other two, leaving Jones to watch, bringing a welcome sackful of rations. They were too excited and intent on the activity in the Roads to eat very much, but nibbled absent-mindedly and thankfully at a few bars of chocolate.

At half past two another flight of nine medium bombers took off from Kallang and headed north. These they did not see return. The harbour area was patrolled throughout the day by Zero fighters and miscellaneous light aircraft, but the whole weight of the search was clearly concentrated to the north-west, the Japanese having assumed, quite reasonably, that the attack must have been launched down the Malacca Straits. Apart from the few perfunctory patrols to the south in the forenoon, no special flights were made in that direction again, an excellent omen for the party's escape.

A mass of small motor sampans and other various craft started to congregate in the two roadsteads where the ships had been sunk, but it was very difficult to determine through the glasses whether they were engaged in salvage work or not. No ban seemed to have been placed on the movement of shipping. Native craft continued to move across the Straits all day, while the flights of civil aircraft in and out of Kallang appeared to follow the normal pattern of the previous four days of observation.

Innumerable patrol craft and launches criss-crossed the harbour throughout the day without any apparent purpose becoming discernible in their movements. Ships continued to arrive from the north-west and appeared to pass into the inner Keppel Harbour and, as the day advanced, most of those which had been out in the Roads either joined them or steamed off towards the north.

The Japanese were completely baffled and infuriated to the point of frenzy, as much by the loss of "face" as by their shipping sunk. They turned savagely on the Allied prisoners in their hands in their search for suspects and scapegoats. One British civilian under sentence for supposed espionage activities was interrogated, beaten, starved, and tortured when he failed to admit authorship of the sabotage raid. The internees in Changi gaol suffered a murderous period. Malays and Chinese were arrested in their hundreds on suspicion of possible complicity. For months, Singapore was subjected to a wave of terror which included the infamous "Double Tenth" massacre on October 10. For this the perpetrators paid with their heads when the Allied war crimes tribunals reckoned with them after Japan had surrendered.

The high command in Singapore never did learn how the attack had been organised or from whence it came. The confidential report which was dispatched in due course to Tokyo, and extracted from the files after the war was over by the Allies, read in part: "Singapore shipping espionage has been carried out by natives under European instructions. . . . An enemy espionage affair developed early in the morning of 27th September 1943 at Singapore. It was commanded by Europeans hiding in the neighbourhood of Palai in Johore. It was carried out by Malayan criminals through a Malayan village chief and the party was composed of ten or more persons, all of them Malayans. As a result of the raid, seven ships were sunk by bombs due to a clever plan."

Although it took weeks for the information to filter through, confirmation of the success of the operation slowly found its way through the Chinese guerrillas in Malaya to Chungking and thence to London and Washington. There was no doubt about it. All seven ships had been sunk, a total of nearly 38,000 tons, hundreds of miles within the Japanese perimeter. Surely it is one of the most astonishing exploits of the whole war.

For the "Jaywick" party on the spot, the most encouraging reaction came from the Malay villagers themselves. Three hundred yards south of Dongas was the village of Patam on the northern coast of Batam Island. Soon after it was light, Lyon and Huston heard so much shouting and noise coming from this direction that they swung round and focused their glasses on the village. The Malays could be seen running up and down, slapping each other on the back in high glee, imitating the noises of the explosions and raising both hands upwards and outwards in illustration of their effect. It must have been the first time that they had heard such reverberations since the fall of Singapore and it could only mean one thing. The Allies had struck back. Scores of *koleks* started pulling out from points along the shore and paddling into the Straits to see the fire and the pall of smoke hanging over the harbour.

One such *kolek* caught Davidson and Falls unawares. They had made their way across the harbour unscathed, but the tide had started to turn against them and they were still about six miles short of Pulo Nongsa, a little island off the north-east tip of Batam, which they had hoped to use as their hide, when the imminence of dawn obliged them to duck for cover immediately. They found an adequate hide behind a strip of beach under some rocks and dropped off to sleep. Half an hour later they were awakened by the explosions. They were by now some fifteen miles from Singapore, and although they ran down to the beach, could see very little of the commotion in the haze.

They, too, counted clearly up to seven and wondered why the other two canoes had only accounted for four ships between them. Did it mean that someone had run into trouble? The fact that there had been any explosions at all seemed to rule that out. They considered every combination of possibilities but realised they would have to wait four days until they met at Pompong before finding out the truth.

It was while they were standing there that the native canoe came round the point and caught them in full view. It was their first bad security lapse and entirely their own fault. In their excitement they had forgotten all the prescribed precautions, and if the natives had been hostile, might have had to pay dearly for it.

The sight of two bearded white men with their hands on their pistols was altogether too much for the simple villagers. It did not require much deduction for them to associate these two interlopers with the uproar in the Roads. Spinning round in their *kolek,* they paddled back like furies round the point again.

The question now was what to do. Should they risk a day passage to a new hide and probably run into further trouble or should they assume that the obviously terrified Malays would consider discretion the better part of valour and take no direct action? Their hide was in a fairly desolate part of Batam Island and it was extremely unlikely that there would be telephones or any such modern devices by which to report their presence to the garrison. The nearest centre of consequence was probably several hours' paddling away, so Davidson and Falls decided to stick it out. They spent an uneasy day at the alert among the boulders and, as night fell again, thankfully launched their folboat and started on their "forced march" south.

Hugging the eastern shore of Batam down the five-mile-wide Rhio Strait, they reached Tanjongsaoe Island, in the centre of the Strait, after nine and a half hours' steady paddling. The shore was uncomfortably congested with fishing huts and *pagars*, but they managed to find a service-able hide.

The next night, that of September 28–29, they weaved through the maze of islands, keeping to the north of Pulau Lepang and Pulau Anak Mati, and then squeezing down the narrow channel between Pulau Rempang and Pulau Setoko until they reached the southern entrance of the Bulan Strait, a dozen miles from Panjang.

In relatively open water again, they were paddling on their last lap past the point of Tanjong Klinking when they heard again the threatening plop-plop of the diesel patrol boat which had harried them round Panjang. Edging into the shallows to avoid pursuit, they watched the launch pass within fifty yards. They could see the glow of light in the wheelhouse and could hear the crew talking. It passed on beyond the point, missing them again. Keeping close to the shore for the last five miles, they pulled safely into Otter Bay about four o'clock in the morning. The dump was intact, but there was no sign of the other canoes. At the end of their tether, they lay down to sleep.

The other canoes had still not joined them by the evening of the twenty-ninth, so, leaving a note describing their experiences and movements with the stores, where they knew it would be found, they pressed on. It was thirty miles to Pompong and they intended to stage halfway on the island of Abang Besar, on the far side of Dempu Strait. It meant passing dangerously near to the observation post and searchlight on Galang Baru, but this particular problem was solved by an even worse hazard.

The sky was already full of scurrying clouds when they set off. They could see the great black pall of a "Sumatra" building up, and just as they were about to draw abeam of Galang Baru it hit them. The wind, waves, and spin-drift had been bad enough in *Krait*. In a tiny cockle-shell canoe in the open sea it was terrifying. The only thing they could do was to turn the folboat's bows into the wind and sea, close their eyes against the battering rain and flying spume, and judge their direction by the force of the hurri-cane on their cheeks.

The hermetically sealed canoe rode the mountainous seas like a porpoise, sliding up and down the immense waves without once threatening to overturn. The battle lasted two hours, when the storm dropped as suddenly as it had come. They just made Abang Besar before daylight, slept off their leaden tiredness during the day, and by one o'clock in the morning of October 1 had the canoe safely hidden under the trees in Fisherman's Bay on Pompong.

They spent the day drying out, resting, and sorting the new supply of rations they had picked up at Panjang. If all had gone well, *Krait* was to pick them up that evening.

From dusk onwards they kept uneasy watch. The hours ticked slowly past as their hopes sank. By midnight *Krait* was well overdue. There was no sign of the other canoe crews and the iron-nerved Davidson was just about to settle down on his groundsheet for a few hours' sleep, leaving Falls to continue the watch, when his sharp-eyed companion shook him awake again. "There's something moving in over there, sir," he whispered. "Can't hear a thing though."

With hope clutching fiercely through their infinite weariness, they tried to focus on this shadow within a shadow. It drifted nearer and suddenly there was no doubt. That long, low shape with the deckhouse covering the whole stern could only be *Krait*. She had come back and they were safe.[1]

---

[1] The other two crews made the rendezvous October 1st and the *Krait* got back safely to Australia on October 19. They had been away 48 days, traveling more than 4,000 miles to Singapore and back.—Ed. note.

Operation Flintlock

After the Coral Sea battle and the defeat of the Japanese carrier forces before Midway in May and June of 1942, the U.S. took the initiative in the Pacific, never to lose it. Soon after the Japs had invaded Guadalcanal, U.S. Marines landed and pushed them off, but only after a bitter battle. From here on, our tactics followed a pattern: soften up the next group of enemy-held islands with air strikes; bombard enemy installations from offshore naval ships; then assault the beaches with the Marines and, when help was needed, the infantry. Thus, in the Central Pacific, the strategy of "island-hopping" developed; it was destined to keep the Japanese off balance throughout the rest of the war.

Some people called it "going up the ladder" to Japan, for the islands stretched out in the direction of Japan like a spider's web. New Georgia, Bougainville, and New Britain were overrun, effectively neutralizing Jap naval and air attacks on General MacArthur's campaign in New Guinea. Then the Navy swung northeast and assaulted Tarawa in the Gilbert Islands in the first move to outflank Truk, Jap naval stronghold in the Carolines. After fierce fighting* the Gilberts were secured; air fields were rebuilt and supplies landed to provide a base for the continuing flanking movement around the Carolines.

The Marshall Islands were the next objective. As the operation took shape, air strikes were made on all the important islands in the Marshall group to keep the Japs guessing where the main blow would fall. Their planes and air strips were destroyed, eliminating Japanese air reconnaissance so that our attacking force achieved complete surprise.

Kwajalein atoll, largest island atoll in the world, was selected as the target. Our reconnaissance had discovered the Japs at work building a strip long enough to handle bombers. Two assaults were to be launched within the atoll itself: at Roi-Namur, the northern tip of the

*See *Combat: Pacific Theater* for the story of Tarawa.

atoll, and forty miles to the southeast, Kwajalein Island, which supplied the name of the atoll.

The northern attack force consisted of the 4th Marine Division and 15th Marine Defense Battalion; the southern attack force was all Army—the 7th Infantry Division, plus 3rd and 4th Defense Battalions. The 7th Infantry Division had seen action in the capture of Attu in the Aleutians; the 4th Marine Division was new to combat, although they had undergone intensive training in Hawaii for the assault.

The Marines went ashore at Roi-Namur on February 1, 1944, meeting fierce resistance, but they succeeded in overwhelming the smaller forces and the island was declared secured on February 2.

Simultaneously, the infantry landed on Kwajalein. According to Captain Frank Hough, "the nearest island to the northwest, Enubuj, was seized with no great difficulty on the 31st of January, but Ebeye, the only island within practicable artillery range of the opposite end of Kwajalein, was so strongly held that its seizure was postponed until more troops could be made available."*

Meanwhile, because of the narrow front on Kwajalein, only two battalions were able to "operate abreast in contrast to four in line on Roi-Namur . . . [and] since the distance traversed was considerably greater, the securing of Kwajalein Island required somewhat more time."* It was not declared secured until February 4.

"In the meanwhile, the 17th Infantry had opened the assault on the smaller strongly held island of Ebeye, directly north of the Eastern end of Kwajalein, abetted by naval and air support, plus artillery from the main island. The 1st Battalion landed on February 3 on the southern end and drove northward over badly battered terrain, against stubborn resistance." *

A close-up view of part of that action follows.

*Capt. Frank Hough, *The Island War*, p. 199.

172

ACTION AT THE PIGPEN*

by Lt. Col. S. L. A. Marshall

The 1st Battalion, 17th Infantry, passed the day of February 2 (D plus 2 day) on Ennylobegan Island, cleaning equipment, sunbathing, and hunting for souvenirs. The quest for souvenirs brought grief to two men, one of them a staff sergeant named Deini. In fooling with a Jap pistol, he shot a comrade in the stomach. It seemed as if the man would probably die.

Meanwhile the battalion commander, Lieutenant Colonel Albert V. Hartl, had received orders: The 1st Battalion would attack Ebeye Island the next morning. It was certain not to be a snap assignment like Ennylobegan Island. Ebeye, the third island north of Kwajalein Island on the eastern side of the atoll, held a Jap seaplane base. It was known to be strongly garrisoned.

So Hartl thought the case of Sergeant Deini over and figured that having lost one man, he couldn't afford to lose two. He called Deini and he said to him: "I'm not going to do anything about you. That man may die. In any case, we can't use him this time. That's your fault. You can square it by doing enough fighting for two men." Deini, who is a stevedore on the San Francisco docks in normal times, took it pretty grimly. He said he would do his best.

The mile-long, 250-yard wide target island was battered throughout that day by naval gunfire and air strikes. In the afternoon, Hartl's executive officer, Major Maynard E. Weaver, reconnoitered it first from the deck of a destroyer and then from a naval observation plane. He was over the island for two hours. Most of the buildings seemed to have

*From *Island Victory* published by The Infantry Journal 1945.

been leveled by the bombardment, but Weaver noticed that there were heavy concrete structures and fire trenches still in good condition at the north end of the island on the ocean side. Since the landing was to be made at the south end on the lagoon side, it seemed probable that the American right wing would carry the heaviest burden during the attack.

Hartl's battalion went ashore at 0930 on February 3 (D plus 3 day) after a preparatory hour-long bombardment by cruisers and destroyers. The Ebeye Island plan called for an even distribution of force across the island, with both flanks evenly weighted with arms and personnel. As it worked out, however, the enemy was by no means evenly distributed. Weaver had seen from the air that the heaviest buildings were on the ocean side of the island, where Company A was to operate.

That seemed significant; on Kwajalein Island, where the fighting was still in progress, the heaviest fighting occurred always where the enemy could make most use of his walls and cellars. But on Ebeye Island there were no pillboxes, fire trenches or underground works of any kind in between the shattered buildings. Thus there was little reason for Japanese to cling to the built-up area as it had no special strength. It seems probable that a large-scale redistribution of the garrison took place as a result of fire concentrations on the outer side of the island, and that they chose to defend most heavily on the lagoon side because it provided better ground cover. Company C carried the fight on the first day. One platoon did most of the fighting for the company.

The landing was unopposed. The 3d Platoon, which was to be in support position for the company during the advance up the island, landed in the first wave with the engineer detachment. It had come ashore in Alligators. Two of them stopped on the reef instead of going to the beach, and the men had to wade ashore through waist-deep water. One man fell into a shell hole and lost his BAR in the water. Private First Class Angelo Ciccotti stepped into another shell hole with the SCR-536 and drowned it out. The platoon pivoted on its left, while the right made the swing around, keeping contact with the platoon from Company A.

LVTs[1] kept their machine guns going from 300 yards out until they hit the beaches. Buffalos blazed away at the foliage line. The scene grew deathly quiet as the line formed and its right swung around the southern tip of the island. It came up even. The line then went ahead a few yards and halted. The 3d Platoon had completed its initial task.

The 1st and 2d Platoons, which had followed the 3d in by just a few minutes, halted and took cover at the beach only long enough to get their bearings. Then they came on through the 3d Platoon—the 1st on the right, the 2d on the left. For about 100 yards, the line stalked quietly through the underbrush, the men picking their way around uprooted trees and piles of debris.

The Buffalos had gone on up the beach, ahead of the left. Perhaps twenty minutes after the advance started, they broke the stillness by volleying inland, some distance ahead of the American line. Whether or not this fire did any damage to the enemy, it had one effect on our own forces. It made so much noise that when the first enemy fire crackled above our infantry line, the men did not sense it as a body. There was no sudden, sharp hail of bullets. By squads and by little groups, they heard the warning zing-zing-zing overhead or saw something rip through the foliage above them. This noise was doing them no harm, but by squads and by little groups they flattened as they heard the danger mount. It was a characteristic action, typical of the manner in which infantry so often loses momentum in attacking through brush-covered country. The faults that produce such stagnation are partly tactical and partly rooted in human nature.

That was true of Company C on this particular day. When the men went to earth, they could not see one another. No man knew where the next man lay on his right and left. To each man came a sense of loneliness. Yet the desire to cling close to the protecting earth was stronger than the desire to move and find one's fellows. It was not instilled in the squad and platoon leaders that their first duty on going

[1] Landing vehicle, tracked.

to earth was to check the whereabouts of their men so that group unity would develop group action. There was no SOP on this point. So they, too, waited until some grew tired of waiting and began calling to their men. Others stayed prone, doing nothing, "waiting for something to happen."

It also seems to be true of the infantry soldier that his feeling of insecurity rises according to the rate of fire which is coming against him, even when the fire is general and inaccurate. His confidence lifts with the lifting or ceasing of the fire. But let him then advance into the area from which the fire has come, and it will require, unless the fire picks up again, all of the driving diligence of his superiors to make him be wary and thorough. He can quickly convince himself that all is secure. Many of the infantry studies from the Pacific confirm this point. Company C was to prove it over and over on this particular day.

A few yards beyond where the center of the line first felt the fire passing overhead, there was a deep and wide storage bay running toward the lagoon from the left side of the road. It looked like a tank ditch. To the right of the road, some yards on beyond, was a second bay. A large enemy blockhouse and an air-raid shelter were on the far side of it. This was the source of the enemy fire though our men did not recognize it as such at the time.

The 1st Platoon was on the right of the road. Some of them saw the storage bay on the right of the road and figured that if they could get up to it, they would have a good **breastwork**. But automatic fire lowered and closed in on them and they had to take refuge in a shell crater. The two light machine guns were then brought up and fire was put on the bay. One squad bounded ahead to the bay and fired on the shelter. From the bay it moved off to the right of the shelter, took cover behind some palm stumps, and resumed fire.

The second squad was still some distance back and doing no good there. Sergeant Richard Maples went back to rally it and was hit by a bullet while talking to Lieutenant Isadore I. Feinstein. The squad came on up to the bay. As the **men jumped** down into it, heavy automatic fire poured in on them from the left rear. They had to hug the back walls of the bay to get away from it, thereby exposing themselves to the fire of the enemy. One gunner had the presence of mind to put his panel on a rifle and wave it high in the air. The fire stopped. The men believed then that the fire had come from one of our own Buffalos on the lagoon shore.

The company line was already sagging backward, bow-shaped. The 1st Platoon was moving on the right. Its men were checked periodically by bursts of enemy fire and the forward movement was sustained through forward rushes by three or four men at a time. There was no real pressure against them, but the circumstances of fire and cover were such that they no longer worked in close co-operation one with the other.

Along the lagoon, a half-squad advancing up the beach had also speeded ahead with no interruption to its progress. This sector of the beach was clear; there were no Japs using the first fringe of cover inshore. So the half-squad went on and outdistanced the men on its right. The other half became echeloned [2] toward the rear as enemy machine-gun fire, coming from the blockhouse on the right of the road, developed against the right flank of the platoon. They went to earth man by man just inside the treeline. It was a fateful pause, for there the Jap artillery found them. Technical Sergeant Walter Feil and Sergeant Carl Swanson were hard hit. The wounded were soon carried out, but the shock of the artillery fire coupled with the effect of the machine-gun fire kept them pinned to the ground. They stayed there doing nothing.

These things contributed to the stretching of the line. The center was still well behind, retarded by automatic fire which was ranging across both sides of the road. Technical Sergeant Manford B. Lauderdale, Staff Sergeant John I. Inseth, and Private First Class Clay Vanwinkle, with a BAR, worked up under this fire, trying to get to the left-hand storage bay. They saw three Japs running from the forward shelter—the first enemy soldiers seen by the company.

[2] Bent or stepped back.

Sergeant Seth Stear yelled: "There they go. Get 'em, Rip!" But before Vanwinkle could fire the BAR, the Japs ducked into the bush. The group then threw grenades in their direction.

Over on the far right, Private Percy Johnson, the contact man with Company A, saw four Japs standing in a clearing about seventy-five yards ahead, and slightly left. He yelled to Lieutenant Erwin Desmonde, his platoon leader: "Come here! I see Japs."

Lieutenant Desmonde looked through his field glasses and exclaimed: "By God, they are Japs!" They fired and so did Private First Class Ballard T. Cogar with his BAR. The four went down—the first men hit by the company.

The reports of contact with the enemy by the 1st and 2d Platoons reached Lieutenant Charles E. Murphy at the company CP within seconds of each other. Lieutenant George E. Linebaugh, who commanded Company C, then took the extra precaution of ordering a Buffalo to advance up the left flank, take station, and stay in readiness to fire at any enemy force coming down the beach. He was worried about the half-squad on the extreme left which was up by itself and in position to be cut off. The Buffalo went forward, stopped thirty-five yards short of the men on the extreme left and began an indiscriminate fire inland which fell among the men who had been checked by the artillery. Sergeant Manuel Mendez yelled: "Cut out that goddam fire!" The Buffalo heard him and drew off.

As the stretching of the line continued owing to the advance of the right, men from the center pulled off in that direction and a gap appeared. Sergeant Gilbert Montenegro and his squad moved up automatically into this breach from the support, and, reaching the storage bay to the left of the road, found themselves in the front line. It was a good spot from which to get a clear view of the ground ahead. Montenegro saw that the automatic fire which had been harassing the center came from the blockhouse to the right of the road. The squad stayed there for a few minutes doing nothing about it. Then the tanks came up.

They had been ashore quite a while but did not move up into the action until Linebaugh phoned Murphy to send them along—two tanks on each side of the road so that two tanks would arrive in each platoon sector. The pair that came up on the left found the ground difficult and veered to the road. On the right, one tank got stuck in soft ground just short of the front line and the other didn't want to come along until its mate was free. Montenegro went to one of the tanks on the left and told the crew over the telephone that he wanted the tank to advance against the shelter to right of the road.

The tankers replied that they were taking orders only from the battalion commander. Lieutenant Charles E. Elliott, Jr., tried it and got the same reply. The tanks remained in place while there was hot argument back and forth as to whose authority the tanks were moving under. This added to the heat of a day already made oppressive by large fires which were throwing a choking smoke over the whole area. The tanks then told the battalion commander that they couldn't proceed because they were being fired upon.

Colonel Hartl replied: "The infantry is even farther forward and it's receiving fire." About forty minutes were lost during this futile interlude. Co-operation flagged because the men in the fire fight thought they had the authority to assign targets to the tank crews and the tankers had understood otherwise.

During the argument, Privates First Class Gerald D. Draughn and Edward Hodge, who were handling the bazooka, were ordered by Lieutenant Elliott to move up to an advanced position on the right of the road and fire at the shelter beyond the blockhouse. Covered by Private First Class Emmett Mull with a BAR, who came along behind them, they moved sixty yards out in front of the company, having to go that far before the bazooka could bear on the shelter door. Draughn couldn't see his first rocket because the discharge blew sand back in his eyes. But he thought it was a dud. The second hit fair on the entrance. He was ready to fire a third when he saw two Japs charging him from out the shelter. He yelled: "Get 'em, Hodge!" and Hodge shot one man with his M1. The other had already gone down. Private First Class Jack Winn, from the storage bay, had winged him with a snap shot. The third rocket was fired into the target. By that time the other men of the squad had come up to the two men and they stayed there under cover.

The deadlock between tanks and infantry was ended by a direct order from Battalion. One tank moved forward to attack the blockhouse. It had been told by the Infantry commander to engage with its artillery but it opened the attack with machine guns. The slugs had no effect. At fifty-yard range, the tank then shelled the entrance with its 75mm. gun. The infantry went along with the tank, and with this forward surge, the company line again became fairly straight.

The 2d Platoon's 1st Squad came under automatic fire while moving up the right side of the road toward the blockhouse. Two men were hit. Others in the squad saw Japs taking cover near a burned truck which lay ahead.

Then two more men were hit. These things happened just like that—one, two, three—a matter of split seconds. The survivors figured the fire had come from the Japs hidden around the truck and they grenaded the ground all about it. The fire ceased. They thought the grenades might have done it. But what had happened was that a Jap machine gun far over on our left was firing across the front into our right. The half-squad moving along the beach put the blocks to the machine gun and its crew and could see that it had been working against the men moving up to the block-house.

Private First Class Wilbert Jackson had taken cover where he had a good view of the shelter which had been attacked by the bazooka. He saw a Jap rifleman come out of the rear entrance and shot him with his BAR.

The tank, having blasted the entrance, started on toward the blockhouse. Four Japs rushed it from the doorway as it got even with their position. One threw a grenade in the tracks. It bounced from the tank and the four Japs were cut down by fire from all along the 1st Platoon's position.

Such were the incidents developing from the first brush with the enemy, the defeat of his forward positions and the restoration of some mobility to the company. From the rear the 60mm. mortars had barraged the area of the enemy shelters within a few minutes after the line stopped moving. The fire was at 400-yard range, and it was ranging about 200 yards over, on the right of the road. At least one burst was seen by the men of the 1st Platoon to hit Japs crouching in a foxhole. That was the only firing done by the company's light mortars. When the 2d Platoon came in check, it asked Lieutenant Linebaugh to have 81mm. fire put down just ahead of its lines. He refused. He figured that the left was so badly strung out at the time that any fire which could be put down safely would also be ineffective insofar as the enemy immediately engaged was concerned.

One BAR man, Private First Class James H. Gatlin, had carried on a one-man mop-up campaign during the first phase of the fighting, working over every debris pile at a close range with his weapon. He had been thoughtfully regarding one pile of palm and broken foliage when he saw it move. He fired into it, then lifted the branches and found two dead Japs, their wounds oozing blood. He then went on, firing into other piles, holding the BAR over sideways so that instead of climbing it went forward, and then turning it over and sweeping it back across again.[3] In one other pile he collected three dead Japs after giving it a burst of fire.

As the platoon had come forward it had received a few rounds of sniper fire. When this happened, one or two men began firing at the tops of the few palms that were still standing. This was contagious. More men fired at the tree tops, meanwhile paying little regard to the rubble piles and broken foliage through which they passed. If no fire came from such a spot, they assumed it was safe. It was only when our men began to drop from rifle fire well back of their lines, and the spraying of the tree tops yielded noth-

---

[3] When fired automatically the BAR tends to rise at the muzzle. This is controllable when the firer is shooting prone, but not in firing while standing. Private Gatlin, by turning his BAR half over as he fired it, obtained a horizontal movement of the gun and distribution of his fire along the ground, instead of a vertical distribution.

ing, that our men learned to prowl everything they came to, either by dosing it with rifle fire or tossing a grenade into it. The BAR proved an excellent weapon for this kind of work.

The 1st Platoon, having freed itself with the aid of the tanks, couldn't understand why the 2d Platoon wasn't going ahead. Neither could Company A, which had been moving along easily on the ocean side of the island. The advancing line was supposed to keep roughly straight. The units on the right, although no great distance from the men who had been checked on the lagoon side, were as remote from them in sympathy and in situation as if they had been on another island.

Derisive calls drifted over from the right flank. "You can't win a war sitting on your ass." That galled the men on the left even more than the invidious comparisons made by the battalion staff over the telephone. "If Company A is able to get forward, why can't the left flank of Company C go ahead?" The 2d Platoon had no ready answer to any of these critics. Engaged as it was, it had no way of knowing that it was carrying the big load for the battalion and that the other outfits were comparatively unengaged. The command in the rear couldn't get this view of the situation.

On the other flank, things were going ahead so leisurely that when water in the canteens began to run low, the men had time to cut up coconuts which littered the ground when the artillery ceased mauling the trees. That flank moved ahead by slow, easy stages to avoid getting too far beyond the 2d Platoon's position. Its experiences were in ironic contrast to what had been going on on the left.

The blockhouse by the road was well-battered when the tank ceased firing upon it. There were several gaping holes by the doorway, through which a dead Jap lay sprawled. One of the men from 1st Platoon tossed a couple of grenades inside and then the line passed on. Before the support got up to it, Staff Sergeant Otis Lasswell, Jr., saw a man from Company D shoot a second Jap as he stuck his head out the door. This made Lasswell wonder if anyone had cleaned out the shelter. He asked Lieutenant Daniel A. Blue if anything had been done to follow up the work of the tank. Blue didn't know. A bulldozer was then brought up to seal the entrance. The driver looked the place over, said: "It's too hot for me," and turned back toward the rear.

Lasswell went after a flame thrower. The flame was shot into all three entrances. The operator then climbed on top of the shelter and shot the flame through a six-inch vent on the roof. "There's no one in there now," he said to Lasswell when he got down. Lasswell agreed. They started to walk away.

Five Japs came out of the shelter with their hands up. One had been hit by a shell and died shortly after. Another had a slight burn on the arm. The other three hadn't been touched.

While they were collecting the Japs, a kitten walked out of the shelter. The troops played with it long enough to discover that it was shell-shocked. When put in any position, it would stay just that way and blink at them. Lieutenant Desmonde left them playing with the kitten and trying to stand it on its head. He went on over to the left to see what was holding up the 2d Platoon. He wanted to get his own 1st Platoon forward and he figured maybe the units on the other end of the line needed a little prodding.

The 1st Platoon's 2d and 3d Squads had moved up to the shelter on the right. During the approach, a couple of Japs were seen sitting in the doorway. They ducked back inside. But these Japs having disappeared, the men took no immediate steps to finish them. They stretched out on the ground around the shelter, resting and waiting for the company's left to get in motion. Half an hour passed. Private First Class Elmer Powell leaned against one end of the shelter, eating a candy bar. At the other end of it, a Jap machine gun fired periodic wild bursts toward Company A. The 1st Platoon's men saw the Jap was just wasting ammunition so they let him have his fun. On the ocean side of the shelter, around the corner from Powell, was another low entryway. A second Jap popped out of it, carrying a machine gun. He stumbled on the steps and the gun went off, alerting the Americans near by.

Private First Class Hjalmar Pederson lay in a shell hole opposite the entrance. Without raising his voice, he said to the man next to him: "My Got, de're cooming oudt." His second shot crumpled the Jap. Powell dropped his candy bar and leaped for the nearest cover, ten yards off. Private Cogar threw a grenade. It dropped fair into the far opening and exploded right under the Jap who had been shooting toward Company A. There was quiet for a minute or two. Then five distinct explosions were heard inside the shelter.

The men figured that that number of Japs had blown themselves up. Under the sudden excitement, their mood changed instantly from extreme carelessness to pronounced caution. They stood at a respectful distance and heaved ten grenades at the doorway. Then they improvised a satchel charge by wiring six blocks of TNT together with a detonator and tossed it in the door. It exploded with a loud report and blew dirt and timber from the building. Right after that the platoon advanced to a position beyond the shelter. Sergeant Romaine Kitcheon, spotter for the mortars, took up a post behind some sand-filled oil drums which protected the entrance to the shelter. He heard a noise, looked up, saw a Jap emerging and shot him through the head.

As the day wore on past noon, the battle lost its sweat for the men of 1st Platoon. The fires still blazed about the island but a strong wind from the eastward was whipping the smoke to the lagoon side. The men saw no sign of the enemy. They were through shooting for the day. They idled behind the palm stumps and in small shell craters and if they snoozed now and then in the strong sunlight, the enemy took no action to rouse them from their slumber. They knew that the left must be having some trouble because they could hear the rattle of automatic fire and snort of grenades exploding on that flank. But that was someone else's fight and the sounds signified little more to them than did the distant rumble of the artillery breaking over Kwajalein Island where the battle of the 32d and 184th Infantry was wearing into its third day. That one hundred yards of mangled palm forest which separated the two platoons made all the difference and their imaginations could not bridge the distance. It was as well so. They could do nothing to help the 2d Platoon and rest is good for weary feet wherever it is to be had. They marked time and they enjoyed the afternoon.

A stray chicken wandered into the 1st Platoon area. Three of the men ran it down. Then came a pig—a 150-pound pig, one of the farm boys present estimated. The pig seemed unconcerned but was straying back from somewhere up in the battle area. Lieutenant Feinstein had found a grass rope among some Jap stores and was carrying it around for a souvenir. He suggested to Kitcheon that they capture the pig, in lieu of anything better to capture. "And I will tie it by the neck," Feinstein said.

"It won't work," said Kitcheon. "You can't hold pigs that way." But he and Private First Class Raymond Cochran ran the pig down. Cochran caught it by the hind leg. The pig squealed and dragged him along the ground and everyone yelled. He and Kitcheon then roped it around the hind legs. In a few minutes it broke away and ran grunting toward the rear. The men kidded Kitcheon. They wondered where the pig had come from. The men of the 2d Platoon could have told them.

While the 2d Platoon had stayed pinned to the ground in the hour-long lapse which followed its buffeting by the artillery, two medium tanks stood steady in the ground occupied by the support squad. They took no part in the action. The platoon leader tried to talk with the crews. But they didn't respond to the telephone and they wouldn't open up when he hammered on the armor. The foot soldiers saw all this and the reaction upon their own spirits was characteristic.

The records of the Central Pacific operation show consistently that whenever tanks and infantry are supposed to be working in close combination and the tanks won't move, the infantry is always reluctant to go forward. The presence of immobilized tanks is a discouragement. They can stall the movement of an infantry that on its own might be quite willing. The 2d Platoon got hung on this rock. Motion was at last restored when on direct order from Colonel Hartl over the radio, the tanks came on up into the ground held by the assault line.

The scattered groups of the platoon responded immediately, and without orders. As the tanks came through, they got up from their cover and moved toward the enemy, even though a wild, harassing fire from rifles and automatic weapons continued to break over the front. Twenty-five yards farther along one tank threw a track on a coconut log and went out of the action. The other tank kept going. It stayed buttoned up and there was no communication. The tank would lurch forward fifteen or twenty yards, the infantry going along with it or a little behind it. Then the tank would stop; the crew wanted to be sure that the infantry was still with them. The infantry would flow on around the sides of it. When the tank again saw the infantry on ahead, it would come through and take the lead for another score of yards.

It was a crazy, jerky advance, continued like a game of leapfrog. But it was appropriate to the situation. For the moment, both arms needed the assurance which came from the presence of the other. As for the infantry movement, some of the men moved ahead at a walking gait with weapons at high port and others moved from cover to cover by short rushes. They advanced, not on orders, but according to their own initiative. If the first man in a group spurted for cover, the others in the group did the same. If two or three in another group started walking out, the whole group moved out the same way. Gradually the rest of the line moved up abreast of the half-squad which had held the advanced position on the beach.

They advanced perhaps 125 yards when the squad moving just within the line of cover along the shoulder of the beach saw a Jap caliber .50 air-cooled gun off to its left about twenty feet. The gun was pointed in the direction of the morning landings and is presumed to be the weapon which hit three men in the headquarters group when they came in on a later wave. The tank had passed on beyond the gun after firing a machine-gun burst down into the pit.

Sergeant Roger Horning crawled up to within about ten feet of the gun and fired one round from his M1 into the magazine. The gun blew up. Some of his men covered him as he crawled up to the pit and looked in. He was face to face with a live Jap who blinked at him; they were so close that they could have bumped heads. It "scared the living hell" out of Horning. He flopped back into a shell hole just at the edge of the pit, a grenade in his right hand and a rifle in his left. As he recoiled, he threw the grenade. It came right back to him, rolling down the sand and settling at his feet.

He looked at it and kept on looking at it; he didn't think either of touching it or moving away from it. His thought and his body were paralyzed. The grenade was a dud. Seconds passed and he realized that the grenade wasn't going to explode. He jumped up and ran back to the squad, yelling for grenades. There were none at hand. He ran farther back, yelling for a flame thrower. Someone signalled him that the flame thrower was out of order.

Returning to the pit, he found that Sergeant Robert Genung had come up with an improvised satchel charge. Horning threw it at the pit, but he was excited and the cast was wild. The charge exploded across the surface, spinning the ground around. The two BAR men who had been covering Horning walked up to the pit, firing as they went. As they reached the edge, one BAR ran out of ammunition and the other jammed. They scurried back to make the necessary readjustments.

"This time," said Horning, "one of you fire during the advance and the other hold fire until you reach the pit." That was what they did. As they pumped lead into the pit, they saw one Jap fall but they could not see what was beyond him.

The spider holes began just beyond this gun position. The beach proper, which had been unoccupied during the first stage of the advance, had been organized from this point on with small pits just large enough to hold one man and in such juxtaposition to holes on beyond it that the occupant could move in either direction to quick cover. The holes had been covered with tin sheeting, palm fronds or other camouflage material, and could not be seen from a ten-foot distance. Amid these nests of small and rude individual positions were a number of redoubts built solidly of logs and bulwarked with oil drums or iron sheeting, so that along the beach the enemy ground was much like a crude trench system organized in depth. Flanking the lagoon, railroad iron had been cabled to the coconut trees to repel tanks or other vehicles coming ashore. The 2d Platoon was approaching the area generally from the flank, but the detailed defenses of the ground were such that there was menace in every direction.

As Horning crawled on beyond the flank of the machine-gun pit, he saw a layer of palm fronds on the ground twenty yards to the fore. Quite suddenly the palms moved, as if from pressure below, and he knew there was a Jap there. He told Lieutenant Elliott what he had seen, and Elliott ordered him to go forward and prowl the spot.

He crawled on, five, six yards, then he yelled back to Elliott: "I won't go on until I'm sure there's no one in that pit." Elliott threw three grenades in the pit. Horning heard them explode and he crawled on. He got up to the fronds and under the edges he saw a black pit and something moving within. He pulled the pins of two grenades and rolled them over the edge. Both exploded. The Jap inside the hole took death sitting down.

Private First Class Robert Everett had crawled up to Horning while he was working. He then crawled on around the hole. Horning, preoccupied with the grenades, didn't see Everett rise up and stand with his back to another patch of fronds just beyond the first hole. When his gaze rose, there was just time to yell: "Watch it!" A Jap from out of the second hole was making a flying tackle at Everett's knees. Everett spun out of it, and as he twisted, he jammed the muzzle of his BAR against the Jap's head and pulled the trigger. They went down together, but only Everett got up.

That was the way it went. The holes were everywhere. Each one had to be searched from close up. Every spot where a man might be hiding had to be stabbed out. So greatly was the beach littered with broken foliage that it was like looking through a haystack for a few poisoned needles.

Before the 1st and 3d Squads gave over this kind of duty for the day, two men had been killed and eight wounded by fire from the spider holes. The attention of all hands had to be focused on the foreground. The fire which cut the men down came from the spider holes farther up the line. It was the kind of bitter going that made it necessary for the junior leaders to prod their men constantly. The leader of the 3d Squad had been trying to get his men forward against the fire. Private First Class John Treager got up, rushed forward about ten yards, hit the dirt, fired a few shots with his BAR and crumpled with a bullet in his head.

Somewhat farther along, a bayonet was seen sticking up through a patch of fronds. The Jap crouched within it hadn't room to draw in the whole length of the weapon. Private First Class Edward Fiske fired his BAR at the hole; the dried fronds caught fire from the tracers. At that point Fiske ran out of ammunition.

Private First Class Julian Guterrez then took up the fire with his M1. He stood directly above the hole and fired down into it. Then the hole exploded; the Jap inside had turned a grenade on himself. A man's shattered arm came flying out of the hole and hit Guterrez on the shoulder, splattering blood all over his face and clothing. The arm bounced off and fell to the side. As Guterrez looked at it, fascinated and horror-stricken, he saw another bayonet rising out of a patch of fronds just beyond the outstretched and still-quivering fingers. He yelled to a man behind him. The man relayed a grenade and Guterrez pitched it with all of his might into the patch of fronds. It erupted a shower of palm leaves and blood and flesh.

Guterrez reeled over toward the lagoon to cleanse himself of the blood. Before he could reach the water, in sight of all the other men, he vomited all over the beach. Minutes passed before he could gather himself together again.

By this time 2d Platoon, officers and men, had lost all sense of time. They had come along for several hours, clearing the frond coverings from the spider holes with their bayonets, where they did not first blast them after detecting some sign of the enemy. They were dog tired. Their losses had been fairly heavy. Yet oddly enough, most of them thought it was late morning though the day had worn into late afternoon. Lieutenant Linebaugh had given battalion headquarters a report on casualties. He then talked to Lieutenant Elliott about a relief. Elliott went around to his men and told them to halt in place until the 3d Platoon came through.

Lieutenant Blue told his men to drop packs and gas masks and the 3d moved up, two squads on the line. Each squad had two scouts out front, the leading scout moving about fifteen to twenty yards ahead of the platoon and the second splitting the distance back to the line. No tanks went forward with the men; it wasn't the kind of fight in which tanks could do much good. However, the situation was quiet for the moment. When the 3d reached the front, the men of the 2d were sitting around tight-mouthed. There was no fire.

The platoon advanced at a walk in squad column and kept going. As they passed the 2d, Genung said to Blue: "Tell your men that they must watch out for the spider holes. They must search every one of them." Lieutenant Blue then saw for the first time what 2d Platoon had been up against. As far as he could see up the beach, there was a reticulation of the palm frond patches which meant danger to his men. He passed the word to them: "Go at every patch with fire first and then with your bayonet." He kept telling them that that was what they must do.

They moved on twenty-five, thirty, forty yards. There was no enemy fire. The men searched the first few lines of holes diligently, ripping the fronds off with their bayonets. They found nothing. Lieutenant Blue noticed that they had already begun to ease up, hitting a hole and then skipping a hole. They went on another twenty-five yards. The man ahead of Blue stepped across a frond patch and kept on moving.

Blue yelled: "Godammit, what are you doing—stepping across a hole you're supposed to search. There may be a Jap in there." A Jap rifle lay across the hole. From underneath, a hand reached up for it before Blue could close the distance. Blue saw the hand; saw, also, that five of his men were beyond it. He took the chance and fired at the hand. The bullet split the hand at the knuckles. The Jap had started to rise, but Blue's rifle was so close that the blast

190

knocked him back again and the helmet flew from his head. Blue fired two slugs into the back of the Jap's head.

"Start looking into every hole or we'll all be killed," Blue shouted to his men.

It was then that Staff Sergeant Pete Deini, who had accidentally shot a man on Ennylobegan Island, came to the fight. Deini had been walking along like the others, but had been doing a lot of thinking. He knew there was something wrong with the platoon. He could feel it. He knew the men were afraid. He felt fear in himself. But he wondered how he could feel it in the others. Then he got it. The sergeants had clammed up. The men were accustomed to hearing them bark. When they didn't, the men knew the sergeants were fearful, and they could not rally their own confidence.

He found what to him was the obvious answer: Somebody had to talk it up and keep talking it up; it wasn't enough simply to act or to bark an order after things had gone wrong. He saw his duty and throughout the rest of the afternoon he spark-plugged the whole operation. Moving from group to group, he showed them how the thing had to be done, and he talked as he worked. When he saw men hesitate in front of a spider hole, he went through them, ripped the fronds away, and used the bayonet, if the bayonet was needed.

As he worked, he talked without ceasing: "Come on. You can do the same thing. Watch me. There are more of them. Keep busy. Keep moving. Keep your eyes open." Then he moved on to another hole. It was Lieutenant Blue's estimate that Deini in person cleared out at least fifty per cent of the positions covered by the platoon and that the thoroughness of the other men was due almost wholly to him. The other men acknowledged it, only they said their lieutenant shot too low when he credited Deini with only half of the work. The man does not talk well. He has an impediment in his speech. But his was the clearest voice sounded by a junior leader during the invasion of Kwajalein Atoll.

Spider holes in large number still confronted the left of the platoon when the right came up to an obstacle of a different kind. Between the road and the shoulder of the beach the ground fell away into a deep swale which had been cleared for about seventy-five feet in both directions. Within the swale was a shelter for pigs. Vines grew all around and over it and tin sheeting had blown down around the sides so that it was impossible to see clearly what lay within. Forward of this penned area was another small structure—a shed or feed house—lying close to the road.

The left flank, moving along the beach, was about abreast of the pen but had not yet seen it, when Private First Class Vern Howell, the front scout of the right-hand squad, came alongside it. He stepped up to the nearest corner and the second scout, Private Clifford Hahn, caught up with him. Howell was puzzled. It was his first time in the lines.

"What is the front line like?" he asked Hahn.

"You're it," said Hahn. "Didn't you know it?"

"But what do you do?"

Hahn replied: "You just keep going until you see someone shooting at you. And you keep looking all around."

Howell kept going. The squad had come on up even with him and the two scouts continued on, Howell some feet ahead. He paused for a minute and squatted at the forward corner of the inclosure. Then he began to straighten up. As he came half-erect, fire from the pen and the little building riddled him. Then men of the squad saw his body jerk, but he did not fall. He sagged over against the side of the inclosure.

There was no recoil in the platoon. They knew where the fire had come from. They weren't sure whether Howell was dead. But the sight of him standing there galvanized them. The squad from the beach moved up to the left side of the inclosure. The right squad pressed up against the rear. They could not lie prone and fire. To bear upon the pen at all, they had to stand erect and shoot down into it. But they gave it everything they had—BAR and rifle fire, grenades and finally satchel charges.

Private First Class Edwin Jeffers, a BAR man, ran up to within reaching distance of where Howell stood, put his BAR on the hole through which the Jap volley had poured, and kept on firing until he was called back by his platoon

192

leader, who figured that Jeffers would get it if he stayed there. The fire was still hot. A first-aid man got up to the men who were firing along the rear of the pen. Howell was pointed out to him. The men figured if he could stand he must still be alive.

"Do you think I can get up there?" the aid man asked Sergeant Lasswell.

"That's up to you," Lasswell answered. "I can't tell you to go."

He asked another man and got the same answer.

The aid man didn't say anything. He took one more look forward and then ran toward Howell. That was too much for Private First Class Jeffers. He couldn't stand the idea of the man going out alone, and he too went running forward to cover the aid man with his BAR. They reached Howell. The aid man took hold of his shoulder. The figure fell over, and from the manner of the fall, the men of the squad knew he was dead. Jeffers and the aid man tore back for cover.

The fight went on. Lasswell, looking through the rails of the pen saw a wounded Jap lifting a rifle. He fired three slugs into him. At each hit, the Jap shook all over but kept crawling toward Lasswell, pulling himself with his elbows. Lasswell gave him four more bullets and the man died.

Deini had grenaded the pen from the right and had heard men scream as the grenades went off. He then ran around to the left of the pen. Sergeant Steinkamp saw a Jap moving toward the rails on the left and killed him with his first bullet. A rifle poked up through the vines in the center. Deini saw it, realized that it was pointed straight at him, ducked instantly.

Private First Class Nick E. Eloff was standing right behind Deini and the bullet hit him in the wrist. Deini saw that he couldn't get the Jap marksman from that side, and he whipped back to the right where there was a good opening. He shot the Jap with his rifle. Then he ran out of ammunition, reached for more and found that a Jap grenade had cut away his ammunition belt and half of one trouser. He had felt the burst but hadn't believed it was that close. He called for a satchel charge, and he heaved it far over the rail at the spot where he had seen the grenade thrower's hand come up from above the timber. There was a terrific explosion which shook down the building inside the pen. Private First Class Thomas Burrescia brought up his flame thrower on the beach side and tried to reach the mass of wreckage with it. But the wind was too strong and the flame blew back on our men.

All of this time battalion headquarters was prodding the company commander to get the platoon forward, and he in turn was prodding Lieutenant Blue. He was told to leave the pigpen to Company B which would do the mop-up job, and to get on with the advance. But Blue figured that the commanders were much too remote from his situation to judge of it. As the pen grew quiet and it appeared that the Jap detachment which had driven the pigs out of their cover was pretty well liquidated, he still did not wish to leave the safety of his rear in Company B's hands. He couldn't see the support force and wanted to be sure.

So the 1st Squad moved around the pigpen by way of the beach and took position in front of the pen. The support squad came up to the line on the left and the platoon continued forward. A medium tank came along a few minutes later and after the covering squad had moved out of muzzle-blast range, the tank fired three rounds of 75 HE into the pen. Still, a live Jap was caught crawling from the pen on the following morning.

Spider holes confronted the left of the line for another 150 yards. Deini again led the way through them, working four times as hard as any other and talking to the men all of the time. They reached another Jap air-raid shelter then. A medium tank was sent against it. The tank was still pumping 75 shells into it when Company B came through and Lieutenant Blue's men fell back to the mop-up position.

As for the soldier Deini had accidentally wounded by a bullet from a Jap pistol on Ennylobegan Island, the Medical Corps managed to save him to fight in other battles.

MacArthur in the Southwest Pacific

While the Navy "island-hopped," General MacArthur, Allied Commander in the Southwest Pacific, drove up the northeastern coast of New Guinea, on his way back to the Philippines. He had a dirty job. His supply lines were halfway round the world, and his priority for ships and supplies was generally second to the Navy's.

MacArthur developed his own style of island-hopping. Army assault units of American and Australian troops were put ashore up the coast to surround and wipe out Jap strong points; in this manner, Salamaua, Finschhaven, and Lae were taken, and then, by-passing the big Jap stronghold at Wewak, Aitape and Hollandia were assaulted.

Walter Karig says, "Although several airfields had been acquired with the Hollandia occupation, none could be used by the Army's heavy bombers which had to use the strips near Lae or those in the Admiralties, 440 miles to the east. It was of strategic urgency to obtain heavy bomber fields closer to the operating area.* There was nothing suitable short of Biak, where the Japanese had three excellent strips along the south coast." **

On the morning of May 27, 1944, Major General Horace Fuller's 41st Division hit the beaches. There they would find a garrison of 10,000 Japs and when the island was taken, the last major target in New Guinea would be secured. But Biak was not an easy nut to crack. The terrain, as General Eichelberger describes it, "was scarred and pitted by the accidents of Nature's past, and some of the cliffs and limestone terraces along its southern shore seemed as barren as the mountains of the moon.

"[There were] caves with the dimensions of a narrow dark hallway, caves as deep and large as five-story tenement buildings and with as many levels of connecting galleries, caves with weird stalactite and

*For the campaign in the Philippines.
**The End of an Empire, pp. 204-205. Rinehart & Co.

stalagmite formations reminiscent of the Carlsbad Caves of New Mexico. It is also an island of subterranean streams, and scarce (and evil-tasting) surface water. Soldiers fought for the precious water-holes, and more than one American died as he crawled forward in the night to replenish his water-bottle.

"It was plain that Biak could not belong to us before we had captured the caves. The first riddle—no one had solved it before 1 Corps arrived—was to find the main caves. Where were they? Where were the entrances and exits? Aerial photographs were of no help in locating them. Our maps told us nothing."*

The following selection about the caves of Biak is written by Colonel Harold Riegelman, Chemical Officer to the Corps Commander, General Eichelberger. As such, one of Col. Riegelman's duties in chemical warfare was, if called for, to direct the use of the flame thrower. The experience with this weapon in the early days of the war was disappointing, to say the least. He tells of one such experience during the attack on Buna in New Guinea:

"On December 8, early morning, Lieutenant Emory of E Company reconnoitered, crawling slowly through the kunai grass and circling toward the breastworks. Corporal Giglio of the Engineers, one of the flame thrower operators, followed close behind. They reached the breastworks. Giglio could not see the grass-screened gun embrasure. Emory removed his helmet, raised it on the muzzle of his carbine ever so little above the crest of the breastworks. A spate of fire bent the grasses in front of the bunker but the helmet was just outside the arc. Giglio thus located the embrasure. The two returned to E Company lines.

"The sun was high and cooking when Giglio moved again on hands and knees through the steaming kunai. His 60 pound fuel tank covered with burlap weighed heavily on his back. The flame gun and hose snagged the base of the tall grass. Sweat poured over his face and body. The alternate operator followed to take on where Giglio left off if Giglio was hit. Then came Emory, Sergeant Niese of the Division's Chemical Section laden with grenades and a wrench for the flame thrower, and four riflemen.

"At the same time, three automatic riflemen circled through the kunai toward the left flank of the bunker. They hoped to get to its

*From *Jungle Road to Tokyo* by Lt. Gen. R. L. Eichelberger. Viking Press.

rear and fire into it to divert the occupants and the snipers from the flame thrower party.

"Emory's team reached the breastworks without drawing a shot. Giglio slid along the shallow trench to its far end. He was not hot now. He was cold as ice. The three automatic riflemen on the opposite flank opened diverting fire as planned. Giglio left the trench. He crawled eight yards. He started his ignition and pressed the fuel release. A searing flame billowed toward the bunker. Something wrong with the pressure. The burst rolled only fifteen yards—seven yards short. The four riflemen charged from behind the breastworks. One was hit in the shoulder and dragged himself back to cover. The other three were pinned to the ground. Giglio crouched low and moved forward. He repeatedly released bursts, which were shorter and shorter as the pressure grew weaker. Yard by yard he drew closer to the bunker. Yard by yard the range of his weapon faded. Giglio knew he was licked. But he was so close to the gun port. He could see it plainly enough. Too plainly. A magnet that drew him onward. If only the goddamned gun would work! He was only fifteen yards away now. A set up. A perfect set up. If only the goddamned gun.

"Emory was desperate. He ordered the alternate operator to stay under cover. What else to do? The flame gun was no damn good. The whole business was a flop. The goddamned.... Blackness. Niese ordered the men back. Giglio was motionless. The wounded rifleman had stemmed the trickle from his shoulder. The lieutenant was dead. The sniper had got him between the eyes. Somehow the wounded and the well crawled back to our lines. Two of the automatic riflemen did not return.

"And there was Giglio. The sun was low when his eyes fluttered open, and consciousness emerged from the black depths. The lead which had crashed through the top of his helmet had knocked him out cold, but left him untouched. He lay quiet in the short twilight. His head throbbed. His mouth was very dry. As darkness fell he slowly, very, very slowly disengaged the straps which supported the fuel tank. He inched back almost imperceptibly to the shallow trench, to the breastworks, through the kunai. As he approached his lines he whispered hoarsely, "I'm Giglio. Don't shoot. I'm Giglio."

"There was indeed plenty wrong with these weapons. There was the low pressure in the nitrogen, hydrogen, and fuel cylinders. Many cylinders had pin holes through which gas was lost. Batteries for the ignition were not protected against New Guinea heat and humidity. The permeating moisture corroded the ignition system.

"The pin holes had to be welded. The flame throwers were rebuilt and thoroughly waterproofed so that they could be fired after twenty hours immersion in water. These things were not done in the States. They were done by our 10th Chemical Maintenance Company in Brisbane.

"The weapon was still not entirely dependable. Four times out of five it would perform. That was a lot better than at Buna. But there was still the question of tactical employment. That remained to be worked out.

"Also I learned that the Japs had flame throwers, better indeed than the model with which we were then equipped. But the Japs had not used their flame throwers. This fact gave point to reports of the almost pathological dread of fire by the Japanese. I had heard that from early childhood they are warned against fire and forbidden to use it under any circumstances likely to endanger the flimsy houses in which they lived. Evidently the lesson was well learned and was carried into battle to such a degree that they even dreaded to use their own very efficient flame throwers. It was, of course, possible that the development of the weapon was not accompanied by development of techniques to use it. But that would not prevent unsuccessful attempts to use it, resulting in the death of the operator—a cost these Japs did not used their flame throwers. This fact gave point to reports of the reported to me.

"All men fear fire. But there are degrees of fear. And if as I began to believe, the Japanese fear was beyond normal, certainly the possibilities of using flame with minimum risk to our own personnel were well worth exploring." *

Flame throwers were used on Biak against the caves but, according to General Eichelberger, with only limited success. Other means were necessary, and as usual it was at the risk of soldiers' lives. Colonel Riegelman arrived on the island about the middle of June at the time General Fuller was being relieved of command because of "not sufficient progress."

*Colonel Harold Riegelman, *Caves of Biak*, pp. 67, 68, 69. Dial Press.

THE CAVES OF BIAK

by Colonel Harold Riegelman

In the afternoon came the call from Sixth Army Headquarters, now bivouacked on the east shore of Humboldt Bay. General Eichelberger hurried over by jeep and boat. General Krueger ordered him and his staff to take over the "Hurricane" Task Force at Biak. Krueger said that despite the communiqués and press stories to the contrary, things were not going well. Severe fighting, incredibly rough terrain, and heat and scarcity of water were rapidly wearing down the 162nd, part of the 163rd, and the 186th Regiments of the 41st Infantry Division which made up the bulk of the task force. Krueger was not satisfied with the contradictory reports he had received. The airdromes had not yet been secured although it was nearly three weeks after the landing. Eichelberger and his Corps were to relieve General Horace H. Fuller and his staff as the Task Force Command, but Fuller was to remain as Division Commander. Eichelberger was to take with him, in addition to his own headquarters, the 34th Regimental Combat Team of the 24th Infantry Division.

On the evening of June 15 we were aboard LST 459 anchored in Humboldt Bay. We were to proceed west to Wakde, pick up a destroyer and two more LSTs, and then move on to Biak. Our small convoy carried Corps headquarters, Corps artillery, and the 34th Regimental Combat Team.

We left Hollandia in early afternoon of June 16 and made rendezvous with the rest of the convoy off Wakde. The sunny skies till mid-morning of the second day out gave way to rain and blessed overcast, screening our approach from air observation.

All I knew about Biak was that it was an island, a degree

south of the Equator, one of the Schouten group lying north of Geelvink Bay toward the western end of New Guinea. Biak was roughly triangular in shape. The south shore ran about 40 miles east-west; its west shore slightly shorter, ran north-south; its hypotenuse north-east with a shoreline of some 50 miles. Biak was 300 miles from Hollandia, less than 1,000 miles from the Philippines, and within fighter-plane range of that poisonous dot in the ocean, Palau, from which most of our air troubles were stemming. The northern portion was mountainous with ridges up to 2,000 feet. The altitude dropped toward the south but the country was broken throughout, except for the area of the three landing fields—Mokmer, Borokoe, and Sorido—on the flat, low, southern coastal fringe of Biak. There could be no assault on the Philippines from New Guinea unless Biak were secured on the east of the sea lane and Halmehara on the west.

I remembered now with gratitude that we had stripped everything at Hollandia in order to outfit the "Hurricane" Task Force for its mission. As of May 27, when it stormed Biak, it had no lack of munitions and supplies. I was troubled about General Fuller—a splendid officer, aggressive, resourceful, and worshipped by his Division. This must have been a terrific blow to him. Krueger was ruthless when it came to relieving commanders who did not deliver on Krueger's schedule.

Early morning of the third day, Sunday, June 19, we landed dry shod at the jetty and were transported along a soupy coral road westward to the half-evacuated headquarters of the 41st Division.

Lieutenant Colonel Frank Arthur's Division chemical section had just left its quarters in the skeleton of a former native church, its roof half off, its timber supports leaning drunkenly toward the road, as though it were a toothless, decrepit face leering out from under a thatched fringe. I directed Sergeant Harriman to set up a command post tent next to the church and pray that, if fall it must, it would collapse forward or backward and not sidewise. While our truck was on the way, I hurried off to General Fuller's tent.

I felt as though I were making a condolence call. Fuller's

face did not weaken the illusion. It showed the deepest distress. In repose, it was alert, sinewy, mobile. Direct grey eyes, tanned, taut skin. Now the lips were tight, the lines deep, the eyes moist.

"We're all sorry, General."

"I know. But what's done is done. I'm leaving the Division."

"General, don't do that. The Division idolizes you."

"No, Harold, I've been kicked out as Task Force Commander and the Division can't have the confidence in me it must have in its leader. . . . From the beginning I begged and pleaded for one more regiment. I know what this operation needs. With one more regiment we'd have had the airdromes in operation a week ago. Now, they send in another regiment—but not to me."

The grey eyes filled and a tear streaked the weathered cheek. Anger, frustration, humiliation.

He left the tent, mounted a jeep, and rode away from the Division he'd brought to Australia more than two years before, trained to razor edge at Rockhampton, commanded brilliantly from Buna to Hollandia, and landed at hot, cave-infested, waterless, stubborn Biak—with a smaller force than the mission required.

Now my section was set up. My bedding roll was taken over to my tent. All through the morning there had been intermittent small arms and mortar fire over the hill to the north. Our howitzers were growling west of us.

After noon mess, I was off to visit Frank Arthur at the new Division headquarters near the Mokmer drome. As my jeep moved west I began to appreciate Fuller's difficulties. The densely jungled strip between the road and the shore widened. Beyond the shore line the reef extended some 200 yards the length of the south shore and was now exposed by the low tide. On the land side of the road the brow of the high ridge came closer and rose higher. The jungle disappeared and revealed a steep slope of rotten coral rising eighty feet to the base of a sheer eighty-foot coral cliff. Near the base of the cliff a gallery was deeply etched; some twenty feet above this there was another gallery. We passed this stretch, crossed a polluted stream which emerged from under the cliff. From this point the high cliff mass pushed the road out to the very shore line. This was the former village of Parai. Just past the abandoned hovels, the road was forced into the shallow sea, soon emerging as the hill mass fell back and swung in a wide arc behind Mokmer drome, which was commanded from the north by these receding heights.

This was the almost fatal route of the 162nd Infantry. It landed at Bosnek on May 27 against light opposition. The Japs took to high ground, held their fire except for occasional sniping, and did not use their planes. By that night the regiment had slogged eight miles up the coastal road and well past the narrow defile beyond Parai. There had been no fire from the cliff galleries as the regiment passed below, and came to a point less than a quarter mile from Mokmer Airdome. One battalion was further advanced than the rest. The troops moved too fast for their artillery and had none in support. Desultory sniping continued through the night.

At dawn the Jap trap was sprung. Artillery, machine gun, rifle fire, and mortars plastered our troops. The forward battalion was cut off by an invisible, deadly wall of steel and lead. Tanks bore down on that isolated force but for some mysterious reason failed to follow up their advantage.

Our destroyers came in close and, while not effective in causing casualties among the cave-protected Japs, discouraged an attack which might well have annihilated the regiment. The destroyers themselves took some punishment from Jap six-inch shells. The forward battalion managed at length to rejoin the main body, and this fell back under the protection of the cliffs where they overhung the sea west of Parai.

That noon a rescue party of amphibious engineers arrived with ten "buffaloes." These wriggled across the reef bearing ammunition and medical supplies. They delivered their precious cargoes and departed loaded with wounded. By some miracle the barrage of artillery and mortar fire laid upon the sea-going vehicles took no toll of them, their cargo, or their crews.

That night the 162nd was sealed off by the Japs at Parai and the cliff galleries which were no longer silent above the coastal road. At dawn the Japs attacked again and again and yet again. Seven of their tanks were destroyed by five of our Shermans. All attacks were repulsed with heavy losses on both sides. The night of the 28th, the fleet of buffaloes under cover of darkness evacuated the 162nd with its equipment. A bad licking. A near disaster which could have been a major calamity had the regiment fought less valiantly or the Japs followed up their early advantages more aggressively.

Nevertheless, here was Mokmer drome—ours, though not yet sufficiently secure from enemy fire for use by our planes. This feat had been accomplished by the 186th Infantry Regiment, reinforced by the 163rd when that Regiment was later brought in from Wakde. The 162nd had effectively demonstrated that the coastal road was an unprofitable approach to the drome. The 186th worked its way northward up the slopes of Bosnek and then westward through the broken rocky ground behind the heights overlooking the sea. This land was waterless save for one water hole which the Yanks won, lost, and won again. Water, ammunition, and supplies had to be man-packed. Every inch of the way was contested. Japs magically appeared and disappeared into their caves. They laid ambush after ambush. Much of the fighting was with pistols, knives, and bare fists. Jap artillery and mortars fired and were withdrawn into caves. The heat was unbearable. But the invaders were persistent and, at long last, overran Mokmer drome and held the nearest ridge to the north. But the Japs still controlled the higher ridges further north and northwest. Patrols reached Borokoe and Sorido, but these objectives had not yet been occupied in force. General Eichelberger had reorganized his forces, reconnoitered the contested areas, and was ready to move hard and fast.

I found Arthur in his shelter near the sea, somewhat leaner than at Hollandia and equally serious. Arthur was always serious unless something struck him as particularly funny. That brought a swift, brief guffaw, after which Arthur was serious again. It was quite evident that nothing struck him as being particularly funny just then. He was manifestly glad to see me and I was certainly glad to see him. He was worried.

"How are things going, Frank?"

"Not too well, sir. These damned caves. If we could only use some of the Jap gas. We've captured a lot of it, mostly poison smoke candles. Just the thing for these caves."

"How about the flame throwers?"

"Fairly good. No good against the deep ones. The day after we landed we took heavy fire from a beach cave. We organized a flame thrower assault party. The riflemen deployed across the beach and neutralized the cave entrance while the flame-thrower operator advanced under cover of the embankment until he was within 20 feet of the cave entrance. Then he let go, obliquely into the entrance, and moved directly in front for a final burst. The flame flushed four Japs, all of whom were killed by the riflemen in the party.

"A number of beach caves got that treatment from the 186th Infantry. Right after the final burst, high explosives were thrust into the cave and detonated.

"We've used flame throwers against them in the hills, usually without sufficient reconnaissance and usually with too few flame throwers. There have been good exceptions. We found Japs dead in caves, their clothes burning. Some were dead with no marks on them, nothing to indicate the cause of death. Still others rush out, often with clothing aflame, and are picked off by rifles. And some few commit hara-kiri. Our tactical theory has proved itself. Where there have been failures it is because the doctrine has not been well applied. . . . We could use more flame throwers if we had them. The Jap planes have been nightly visitors at our old headquarters where you are. We spent a good part of the dark hours in the ground."

"I gathered as much. Damn near room for a battalion in the holes you dug at Headquarters."

"You'll be glad we dug 'em."

Arthur's Sergeant Roe called me to one side to say that

the Lieutenant Colonel was a bit sensitive on this subject. As Roe put it: "You see, sir, down Bosnek way we got strafed or bombed very frequent. The Lieutenant Colonel, he used to jump into an open ditch. And well, there was a latrine on one side of the ditch, a garbage dump on the other side. And well, a Nip bomber came over one night and dropped two eggs. Not in the ditch, sir. There was one in the garbage dump and most of the garbage landed on the Lieutenant Colonel. But you could still see who he was. The other landed in the latrine on the other side of his ditch. And after that you couldn't see the Lieutenant Colonel, sir. And for a long time you wouldn't want to see him. But, by Jesus, you could smell him a hell of a long way off."

We talked about our arrival and Fuller's departure. Arthur resented the replacement, but his resentment was directed at Sixth Army. I assumed this feeling was general. I hoped it was. It would not have helped this operation if it were directed against us.

I saw the disabled Jap tanks, inspected a nearby mortar platoon, talked to the men, noted their drawn, bearded faces and eyes, red from lack of sleep. They did not complain. "I guess they think we must be pretty good, sir, to have our company, just one company, support the whole goddam task force."

Evening mess at Corps. Long tables. General Eichelberger with his four Gs, Chief of Staff, and aides at one side of the tent. Chiefs of sections at the next table. There was a buzz of conversation.

Above it, Eichelberger's voice:

"How about it, Chemical Officer? What do you do with those caves?"

"We got a lot of Jap gas that isn't being used, sir."

That was a pretty weak topper for the General's little joke. The buzz of conversation stopped a moment and then resumed. Much to my relief the joke was dropped.

I picked my way gingerly toward my section tent. I felt superfluous. Arthur was the best division chemical officer in the Southwest Pacific. There was really nothing. . . . Good God! Maybe Eichelberger *wasn't* joking! I stopped dead in my tracks and hurried back through the maze of tent ropes and mantrap air shelters. The General was on his way to his tent. I overtook him at the flap.

"Sir, it just came to me that you might not have been joking when you popped the caves at me."

He looked at me gravely.

"Harold, I was never more serious in all my life."

"Very good, sir. That's all I wanted to know. Good night, sir."

"Good night. And be careful. I don't want to have to get a new chemical officer."

"Thanks! My sentiments exactly, sir."

The air alert wailed. A single Jap plane swooped over headquarters. There were bursts of strafing fire down the road toward Bosnek. It was over almost before the alarm ceased. And I was back in my C.P. tent and planning for the morrow.

Three days later, Wednesday, the 21st, I was ready to report to the General.

In the areas investigated Sergeant Harriman had always been with me along with two or three other enlisted men armed with grenades and carbines. On two patrols Arthur had joined us. We had uncovered a number of beach caves east of Bosnek. We took turns crawling into each cave; where possible, one man went directly behind and covered with a carbine the one whose turn it was to enter first. When in doubt whether the cave had been abandoned, we tossed in a grenade or two before entry. That would sterilize the caves, which were not large. I measured each cave, sketched it in plan and elevation, and indicated its field of fire and tactical use.

There were beach caves just west of Parai. Each was examined. I was climbing up the face of the cliff above the entrance of one of these caverns when my hand, groping for a hold on a narrow shelf, disturbed a smooth, round object. As I pulled myself up, a skull grinned at me from among a small pile of human bones. I had evidently uncovered the corpus delicti of an ancient crime.

With Arthur I crossed Mokmer drome by jeep to the first rise beyond. Our objective was one of the outlets of the

West Caves. These were still held in force by the enemy. The First Battalion of the 162nd Infantry had invested them. But the main and secondary entrances could not be approached without drawing fire.

We dismounted short of the rise and followed a rocky trail over the ridge into a hollow, up a steep incline to higher ground beyond. We stepped warily now for, while we claimed the ground as ours, the fact was still in dispute. Over to our right the smoke of battle rose from what appeared to be a wide crater. Rifle and machine-gun fire were intermittent. Occasionally a Jap "knee mortar" coughed and we looked skyward for the small black projectile which could be ducked if seasonably seen. We circled to the left and crawled forward through the brush to the edge of a hole a full sixty feet deep and 120 feet across, the sides perpendicular, the bottom strewn with broken rocks. We peered cautiously over the edge. In the opposite wall was a cave portal twenty feet high, the view within obstructed by large stalactites. This, Arthur explained, was the "funnel" or west "entrance" of the West Caves.

"We believe there is," he explained, "some sort of gallery with side chambers running about 300 feet easterly to another open fault or sump about twenty feet deep and seventy-five feet across. The main entrance is in the wall of that sump. And the sides of the sump are not so sheer as this. In fact, there is a trail from the cave entrance along one side of the sump leading to normal ground level. There are a couple of machine-gun emplacements on that side and on the opposite side of the sump. A hornet's nest if ever there was one. We call that the south sump. A narrow neck of ground separates this from the north sump, which is wider than the south sump and deeper. At the northwest corner of the north sump there is another entrance. I know all these connect because we lowered a half dozen 4.2 inch mortar shells filled with FS (sulphuric fumes) smoke into this funnel just inside the cave and detonated them electrically. We saw smoke rise from the north and south sumps. Also from several fissures between here and the south sump. We dumped several hundred gallons of gasoline into those fissures and then dropped phosphorus bombs through them.

The gasoline caught fire and set off a lot of ammunition within the cave net. You can still hear it popping."

I could. Deep in the cavern a sound as though of children's firecrackers in a neighbor's basement.

"We know there's a lot of Japs in there, but we don't know how many. We think they are very unhappy."

It was after Wednesday evening mess. I was putting the finishing touches on my recommendations for reduction of cave defenses, when a message arrived from Clovis Byers. "Dawn attack on the West Caves tomorrow." I told Perrini to stop typing. There might be changes in the text tomorrow. I went to bed.

Dawn, Thursday. Lieutenant Colonel Henry Antell, Cornell '17, lately of the *New York Times,* presently assistant G-1, was with me. He had asked me the night before to take him along. Sergeant Harriman drove the jeep. Before sun-up we were at the headquarters of the First Battalion, 162nd Infantry. The battalion commander, Major Benson, was waiting. He showed me his dispositions on the field map. The south sump of the West Caves was the main objective. The first platoon of Company C was in position there with two tanks. The rest of the company was engaged in neutralizing and sealing off egress from the north sump. The two other companies of the battalion were held in reserve, available as needed.

We started from battalion headquarters, Benson leading. I followed. Antell and Harriman, each with carbines, and three riflemen walked single-file through sparse woods. We passed over a flat area, odor of the dead heavy in the still, cool air, and worked our way into a fold below the south sump. The pop of the Jap knee mortars divided our attention between the treacherous, rocky footing and the sky. Off to the right a single bark of one of our own sixty-millimeter mortars evidently registering. There were occasional rifle shots and short bursts of machine gun fire. We crouched low as we moved ahead.

We reached a point below the sump and crawled up the steep embankment. Smoke haze hung over the cratèr. Two light tanks were maneuvering on the rim. They opened up with a succession of salvos from their seventy-fives. A splintered tree stump was near one of the tanks. I wriggled on to the ridge behind the stump. The opposite side of the sump was a vertical wall. In this wall, the main entrance to the West Caves. Thick stalactites hung from the upper lip of the ten-foot mouth, giant tusks which extended to the lower lip and melted into it. Behind these columns the roof of the mouth and the floor sloped back and down into blackness. The seventy-fives made no impression upon the coral. I worked my way around the rim of the sump. Bodies of dead Japs were about. Not all the dead were Japs. Ahead was an American sergeant lying on his back, his young, thoughtful face placid, his black hair tousled, his body relaxed in last repose.

The sun was up. The seventy-fives were still firing. It was late in the morning. There had been no progress. The Japs were sitting it out, deep within their caverns. An idea had begun to come to life. It might be a wild one, but it could hardly be worse than what we were doing. I talked with Benson. He thought it worth trying and sent a request to the engineers. The plan was not complicated. It was apparent that the cave was impervious to all calibres we could bring to bear. Its entrance defied demolition. But if a large enough charge of TNT were exploded at the entrance, perhaps the concussion would stun if not kill the defenders. In either case we could get in and destroy them.

Across the sump at a point just above the cave entrance a party of engineers arrived with a quarter-ton trailer. They set up a winch and lowered 850 pounds of TNT with wires attached. It was now just past noon. I suggested to Benson that he pull his troops back a hundred yards and bring the tanks to lower ground. These orders were issued. We lay on our stomachs a safe distance from the sump. Firing had ceased in the area. Silence, so still one felt it. I had no idea what 850 pounds of TNT would do. I only knew it was a lot of TNT, a great deal more than I had ever seen used. A crack-brained idea. I wondered if we were far enough back. My speculations were cut short by an ear-splitting roar. A cloud of dust and smoke rose out of the sump, high in the air. The thud of falling rocks. A few landed about us. We came sharply to a squat in order to bring as much of us as possible under the protection of our steel helmets. The platoon and the tanks were ordered back into position.

Benson and I proceeded to the sump. The coral columns screening the mouth had disappeared. They lay in broken pieces on the lower lip of the entrance. But then another problem occurred to me. I presumed that gases had been generated by the explosion, which might endanger an assault party. If this were true I had no idea how long it would take these gases to dissipate.

There seemed but one solution. It was as distasteful to me as it was obvious. I walked down the trail cut into the north side of the sump. Benson and Antell followed. Harriman trailed above and behind, his carbine ready for any movement within the cave. There was none. I advanced into the gaping mouth and peered down into the blackness. The blackness stared back. After a moment, I could see dim outlines of prostrate forms. Foul odors drifted up from the hole. But whether these were poisonous or the backdraft of decomposing flesh, I did not know. I suggested to Benson that he wait a minute or two and then send his men in to bayonet every Jap whether breathing or still. I had my battered folding camera in a leather case attached to my web belt. I took a closeup picture of the toothless yawning mouth.

My work seemed finished here, and I felt I could now complete my report. Antell, Harriman, and I left. We passed half-crouched around the rim of the north sump. Beyond was a large shell crater. Our guide explained that a party of seven Japs had collected there early that morning to eat breakfast preparatory to a sortie on some unknown mission. The crew of a sixty-millimeter mortar spotted them and fired a single shot, the shot we had heard on our way from battalion headquarters. It landed precisely in the center of the Jap patrol, and there were the seven bodies radiating from the point of impact symbolically like the rays of the rising sun.

My report was ready that evening, complete with sketches. Sergeant Sliger took it to the Chief of Staff.

"The techniques of reduction of cave nets are frontal and vertical attack, envelopment, isolation, siege, and assault.

The means include all ground fires capable of being laid on the target using high explosive and white phosphorous shell and grenades, air bombardment, strafing, flame throwers, gasoline demolition charges, and smoke. Tanks are employed to precede infantry, firing cannon and machine guns at point blank range.

"Clusters of FS-filled 4.2-inch chemical mortar shell are defused, No. six detonators being substituted, lowered in front of windward cave openings of cave nets and fired electrically. In addition to the harassing effect of FS in confined spaces, the drift of the smoke rising in plumes from remote openings reveals their precise location and they are promptly invested, thereby cutting off supply and escape without unnecessary risk of reconnaissance." I also recommended the introduction of HC smoke pots into windward entrances. This smoke is harmless in the open, but is lethal in enclosed spaces. Neither of these smokes was classified as a poison gas.

"When demolition proves impracticable due to the hardness of the coral rock, charges of TNT ranging up to 850 pounds are exploded at a cave entrance with telling concussion effect that kills or incapacitates the occupants. But this requires prompt assault by infantry shooting or bayoneting all bodies alive or dead."

There was further detail concerning concussion charges and a suggested ratio of these to the size of the cave net; also a note on the desirability of simultaneous detonation at several entrances to the same net. This section of the report also covered charges placed in holes drilled in the ground above caves to disrupt subsurface communications and lighting, produce casualties, and destroy stores.

I stressed the importance of thorough ground and air reconnaissance before any assault and the removal of screening foliage by searching high explosive and white phosphorous fires including rockets and bazookas. The report noted that otherwise bombardment and strafing had little physical effect except to pin the enemy within the cave and obstruct and limit his field of fire.

I discussed the portable flame thrower and how it should be used in attacking shallow caves to avoid back-blast; the use of mechanized flame throwers against cliff galleries. And gasoline poured into windward or depressed entrances and ignited by grenades to exhaust oxygen, harass the defenders, and explode their ammunition.

I skeptically retained a suggestion which occurred earlier in my investigations and had become less and less attractive: the employment of well-trained war dogs to carry time charges into caves. We had several of these dogs with us in Biak. They were invaluable in alerting our patrols against ambush.

Meanwhile G-1, with the help of prisoners taken during the day, had pieced together events which preceded the previous day's attack.

The commanding officer of some 10,000 troops defending Biak was Colonel Kuzume. The West Caves were his last stand. These accommodated 900 men, were equipped with electric light, radio, and fresh water and well supplied with food and ammunition. By Wednesday, June 21, the force was reduced to about 235 men. Colonel Kuzume assembled these in the large chamber between the south sump and the funnel. The officers, who occupied the more elaborately improved connecting cave which opened into the north sump, were present. Colonel Kuzume stated that further organized defense was useless. He suggested that the remnant of his command still in the West Caves could remain and continue to resist or make a banzai suicide attack or escape into mountains in the northern part of the island with the possibility of ultimate rescue. Then he burnt all his documents, placed the regimental colors upon the pyre, and, as these were reduced to ashes, disemboweled himself in traditional fashion. At the end of that night, while the moon was high, 109 of his officers and men elected the banzai attack and were wiped out. This left 125 in the caves when the First Battalion attacked next day. A number of these were wounded and others were in bad physical and mental condition as a result of the harassing technique preceding the attack.

Kuzume's tactics were plain enough and were well suited to the cave-pocked terrain. His men were in detachments of varying sizes depending upon the size of the caves and cave

212

nets to which they were anchored. They broke out of these shelters for surprise attacks and then returned to their warrens. Their mortars and artillery were kept under coral cover when not in use. These tactics were harassing and costly to us. But they suffered from a weakness which indicated that they might later prove fatal to the Japs. They precluded the massing of a co-ordinated, effective striking force and invited isolation and piecemeal destruction. Judging from the evidence of plentiful stores along the coast, the caves were abundantly supplied with food, equipment, ordnance, and ammunition. Also, with radio communications. So the key to securing the airdromes was the reduction of the caves within striking distance of the coast. With these cleaned out the main fighting force could be destroyed, and the southern coastal strip which was all that was tactically usable on the Island would be safe, save perhaps for occasional and decreasingly effective raids by diminishing numbers of wasting remnants unable or unwilling to chance the forbidding areas to the north.

Night. A message to report to Clovis Byers' tent.

The floor of Clovis' tent was three feet below the surrounding ground. Two feet more of sand bags fairly secured the interior from air bomb fragments and sniping. The flaps and sides were sealed to black out the lantern light within. General Eichelberger was seated at Clovis' field table. Clovis, the four Gs, and the Artillery Officer were seated in a horseshoe facing the General. All were grave. I sensed some sort of disagreement and this was confirmed by the General's first question: "How much Jap gas do you have?"

"Plenty, sir. We have taken great quantities, mostly poison smoke."

"Could this be used against the remaining caves?"

"Yes, sir."

"With what effect?"

"It would reduce them in half the time, with possibly one-third fewer casualties to us."

"Harold, there is a disagreement between me and my staff. I believe we should use that gas. My staff differs. I shall follow your judgment."

"Sir, in my opinion the staff is right. And I believe you'd be relieved in twenty-four hours after you used gas. In the end that would cost us more in time and casualties than if we keep on as we are."

"Thank you. That is all."

I returned to my tent and went to bed. I never thought I should see the day when I would oppose the use of gas against the Jap, especially his own gas. Yet I could not think I had been wrong in this.

On the fifth day after the attack on the West Caves I returned to inspect the north sump and was not surprised to hear that the West Caves were no longer a threat, but was shocked to learn that our troops had not yet occupied the cave net. It was clear that if I was over-cautious in respect to the accumulation of lethal gases from the explosion, Major Benson went me one better and held his men out long enough for a small number of the defenders to recover from the effect of the concussion. These were sufficient to keep one rifle company in the cave area for five days. I had been the first and last American in the net in that period. The lesson was clear. The gases from the explosion dissipated within a few minutes. I had expected that, having gone in and come out myself without drawing fire, on the heels of the first day's attack, patrols would quickly follow. But they did not. A twenty-minute delay spoiled that opportunity. Since then a half-dozen Japs had been shot from time to time attempting to escape from their fateful tomb.

At long last a patrol was about to undertake the mopping up of the main cave net. Meanwhile, I wished to explore the north sump. All was silent there. No Jap had shown himself in that sump for several days. I organized a small party and prepared to enter. The north sump was almost forty paces across and forty feet deep. A small cave opened off one side. I placed an enlisted man there with orders to shoot if there was any movement within which did not identify itself as of our party, and I proceeded to the larger entrance across the sump. Within the mouth I followed an incline ending somewhat below the floor of the sump, at a cavern which appeared to have been used as a kitchen. One side of the cavern showed a drop of ten feet to a shelf. I disposed of the party so that the first men down were covered from the kitchen and these in turn covered the next group to descend. From the shelf we peered into a large pit, the floor of which, twenty feet below, was covered with wood planks. A ladder led to that level. Down it a grizzled, bearded enlisted man climbed with pistol and flashlight, searching out the dark crannies with his beam as he paused from rung to rung, our own carbines and pistols cocked to nail any sign of life. Once down, he became the security detail, and we rapidly followed. The chamber in which we found ourselves was large, dark, unbearably hot, fetid, and swarming with flies. All of us were dripping perspiration. A third of the area of about 500 square feet was occupied by a palm-thatched hut, evidently an officers' billet. Another third was covered by a tarpaulin for junior officers or, more likely, orderlies. The center, where the ladder was located, was open.

I found in the hut a treasure house of equipment, sketches, and diaries. I carefully bundled the sketches and diaries for G-2. Among the sketches I found a map of the West Caves and was relieved to note that it conformed closely to the sketch appended to my report, save for two additional chambers in the main net. The map showed a passage connecting the officers' cave with the net, as expected.

I found the passage at the point indicated by the map. It was barely wide enough for one man to squeeze through. I worked my way along this damp, foul corridor, feeling for a precarious footing on the slimy, jagged rock floor, until a breath of cooler air warned me that I was about to enter the main net. I went no further. If our patrols had entered as planned, a movement on my part in the dark might well end a promising career. I returned. The party climbed up and out of the pit.

The patrols had in fact entered the south sump cave mouth and had finished their round of the net. A hellish tour. More than a hundred bodies in various stages of decomposition. One live Jap who was promptly shot. The stench was weighted to suffocation with filth, death, and corruption. And this ended the story of the West Caves—

longer by five days than it needed have been. But fruitful in result and in the clue it had given to the reduction of similar nets. The one mistake which postponed the end would not be repeated. It was not a costly mistake, for the explosion permanently paralyzed the striking power of the defenders, and they caused no further casualties among our troops. Yet these same troops might have been more usefully employed elsewhere.

We left Biak to return to Lake Sentani on June 29, less than a fortnight after Corps arrived. Mokmer, Boridoe, Sorido were all secure and in use. There were still some caves to be cleaned out, notably the East Caves in the pocket above Ibdi near Parai. But these were isolated and did not retard the development of the airdrome.

Long Strike in the Pacific

In early September, 1944, General George C. Kenney, Commander of the Allied Air Forces in the Southwest Pacific met General MacArthur at Hollandia. He proposed a series of attacks on the Japanese oil refineries at Balikpapan (Borneo). Most of the aviation fuel used by the Japanese air forces was produced at Balikpapan; if the refineries were destroyed, the enemy would suffer fuel shortages to an extent that many of their planes might be grounded.

General MacArthur was scheduled to invade the Philippines only weeks away and gave the plan of attack his approval. The missions were to be flown just as soon as the bomber strips could be readied on newly won Biak and Noemfoor.

On September 30th, October 3rd and 5th, B-24 Liberator bombers blasted the refineries with 1,000-pound bombs. The Japanese rushed reinforcements from their air fields in the Philippines but General Kenney, informed of the move, drew on all available bombers in the area to increase his strength.

On October 10th, 106 Liberators, escorted by P-38s picked up along the way, had "one of the toughest fights of the war" to quote General Kenney. But this strike, plus another on the 14th, put the Balikpapan refineries out of commission for the rest of the war.

The preparations for the first raid were unusual because the round trip of 2,500 miles to Balikpapan taxed the flying capacity of the B-24 to the utmost. Until the B-29s with their longer range began to operate from Saipan this was the longest strike of the war. It could be said to be the most daring.

RAID ON BALIKPAPAN*

by Captain Elliott Arnold
and Captain Donald Hough

On a blistering hot day in September, 1944, a few officers were called together at the headquarters of the Far East Air Forces in the Southwest Pacific and were told to make plans for a bombing mission: the target was to be the Dutch oil refinery at Balikpapan on the east coast of Borneo.

The officers went to a map. They put their fingers on the island of Noemfoor, in the Netherlands East Indies, from which the B-24s would take off. They found Balikpapan. They measured. It made a round trip of twenty-five hundred miles.

Now the heavy bombers in the Southwest Pacific were not unused to flying big distances. Planes in groups of twos and threes had flown that far in the early days, and once some thirteen B-24s made a round trip of about that same length.

But there was one vital factor in the distance involved in this new mission that none of the earlier strikes had encountered: there were to be no less than seventy-two airplanes involved, and for the bulk of the run they had to fly in formation for protection in attacking the most heavily guarded target in the Southwest Pacific.

And airplanes flying in formation have to jockey endlessly to keep their positions—and in this slipping back and forth burn up gasoline.

For size of attack and for the mission involved there was only one other place in the world they could look for comparison: at the bombing of the Ploesti oil refinery in

*From *Big Distance*. Duell, Sloane and Pearce, 1945.

Rumania on August 1, 1943. That didn't help much. That added up to a little over two thousand miles, and that was considered a milestone in long distance B-24 bombing at the time.

This mission, as it was outlined to the officers on that summer afternoon, would take the formation from Noemfoor—which was the closest we could get our Liberators to Balikpapan at that time—across the northeast tip of New Guinea, across the Ceram Sea, past the Soela Islands, across Molukka Sea, across the Celebes, and finally across the Makassar Strait to the target. The planes would be in the air for more than sixteen hours.

Stretched across the face of Europe it would be the approximate equivalent of bombing Leningrad from London and return.

And the trip would have to be made without fighter protection, because no fighters could fly the distances from the bases we then had available. And from the moment the big four-engined bombers left their bases they would be in enemy-controlled territory every inch of the way. It was known there were many enemy bases en route, all of them operational, many of them with clusters of fighter planes. And it also was known that Balikpapan itself was defended by the newest and deadliest of the Japanese anti-aircraft guns.

For a target they had a dilly. Balikpapan, with its two main plants and its paraffin works, was Japan's largest refinery in the Netherlands East Indies, with a capacity of four million barrels of crude oil. It was estimated that Balikpapan, discovered originally by American oil men and developed with their skill, was supplying Japan with thirty-five per cent of her war fuel requirements.

The men got down to work.

The order specified that each plane was to carry three thousand pounds of bombs and full ammunition for the gunners to protect themselves. Best striking time would be just after eight o'clock in the morning, when atmospheric conditions should be most helpful. That meant a night take-off.

The seventy-two airplanes were to be flown by two groups

of the Thirteenth Air Force and one group of the Fifth Air Force, and men from all three groups co-operated in laying down the plans.

In view of the distances to be flown in formation, the planners decided to forget most of the flight characteristics of a B-24 over long distances, and to pretend they were starting out with a brand new airplane. The problems of loading each plane would be so utterly different from anything attempted before that for all practical purposes the Liberator might well have been a new type aircraft.

The first thing the men did was to get out all the data on weights and balances and figure out just what the airplane would weigh when fully loaded and gassed for the trip. The figure added up to the total of almost seventy thousand pounds. Now the B-24 was originally designed to carry a maximum gross of forty-eight thousand pounds, and with the knowledge gained over the years, normal overloading was up to sixty thousand pounds. And that was for "normal" missions—the fifteen- and eighteen-hundred-mile strikes.

They went over the ship inch by inch and threw out what they thought could be spared. Little things—bomb hoists, extra bomb shackles, radio frequency tuning meters, tool kits, personal equipment. They finally got down to rock bottom: sixty-eight thousand five hundred pounds. They were more than four tons over normal overloading and they could lighten the plane no more.

Somebody remembered the Truk and Yap missions of which the boys still spoke dreamily as long missions, long and heavily loaded missions. They looked up figures. Each plane would weigh over a ton more than any plane that had bombed Truk and Yap.

Gasoline was the next problem. The exact amount of fuel used in these missions is a secret, but it can be revealed that more than seven hundred gallons of gasoline above the normal load was needed for each plane. A gallon of gasoline weighs six pounds.

To get the most mileage from the gas it was necessary to put the center of gravity at a place where the ship would fly the easiest. The factory-determined center of gravity, with normal gasoline load, was useless under these new conditions with the additional weight distributions. To add to that problem was the fact that an instrument night take-off and instrument flying for the first few hours of the trip would be necessary.

Still working on the theory that as far as all previous specifications went they were going to handle what would be tantamount to a new airplane, the airmen next called in the civilian factory representatives from Consolidated, the builders of the B-24, and conferred with them. Every scrap of information from the factory now was carefully studied with the representatives on hand.

The center of gravity decided upon could not be constant, because, as the airplane burned up its gasoline, as the gunners fired their ammunition, the load would lighten and the weight would become redistributed. Especially as the gas tanks in the different parts of the ship emptied.

Individual airplanes were loaded as they would be for the mission and flown in test runs. It was found necessary after exhaustive experiments that a special series of directions be contrived, taking into consideration each hour of flight and the changing conditions attendant on each hour. Instead, for instance, of each man wearing from the start his parachute, his emergency ration belt, his medicine kit, flak suit, helmet—even his canteen—a special and definite place in the ship was chosen to place these things. Even the men themselves were redistributed in the airplane, away from their normal stations.

Then the factory representatives were called upon again, together with the most experienced pilots in the theater, along with engineering personnel, to figure out the best power settings to get maximum mileage. Flying an airplane is not a mechanical job—some pilots get much more mileage out of their gasoline than others because of their more expert handling of the controls and for this mission no such latitude could be permitted because the gasoline leeway was too critical to permit it.

The speed of the airplane was set at one hundred and fifty miles an hour and the planners figured out a theoretical chart of power settings to get maximum range. Taken into consideration were the take-off, conditions of climb, cruising, approach to target, breakaway, descent and cruise home, and for each hour of the trip a chart of changing settings was set up to allow for the changing weight of the plane as the heavy gasoline was consumed.

These weight-distribution and power-setting charts were printed for each pilot who was to take part in the mission.

Some odd things were discovered. For instance, flaps normally are used to slow up an airplane. With the load carried, however, it was found that for the first couple of hours of flight five degrees of flaps increased the air speed three miles an hour. This fact was noted.

With a working plan to go by, the men outfitted six airplanes and loaded them as the new specifications called for. Six average crews were chosen—men who were not distinguished either for their excellence or their lack of skill. A flight plan was drawn up which would duplicate the projected Balikpapan mission in mileage and route— except that it was flown over territory that was either friendly or neutral. The planes were sent out, with a daylight take-off, to test the theories.

The airmen who planned the show sweated out that mission. It would tell them whether they had been right or wrong, whether the show was feasible or not. The mission would have to be undertaken in any case, but this test flight would indicate whether there was going to be an inevitable bail-out or a chance for home.

The planners were exhausted. They had received word of the Balikpapan mission-to-be just nine days before the day designated for the strike. During that time some of the planes were changing from one base to another—from one island to another—in the general strategic shifting of air bases in the Southwest Pacific. Only the flight echelon had moved to its new base, forward, and the water echelon was still behind. Not all the equipment had arrived. The men had to plan for and work on the Balikpapan show in the midst of this move, a move which always entails a great amount of confusion and difficulty.

The six planes returned to base. All of them had made the flight successfully. They had carried the extra heavy loads of gasoline. In the planning, each plane was allowed a surplus of four hundred gallons. So close was the planning that the plane which returned furthest off schedule had burned just seventy-five gallons more than estimated. The closest of the six planes was just two gallons off estimate.

The airmen breathed easier. The mission, at least on logistics, was feasible.

Then the navigators sat down to plan the route. There were high mountains in New Guinea and they couldn't fly the planes straight across. They decided that the planes would take off individually, just after midnight, fly individually all night, and then rendezvous at daybreak at a selected assembly point. Formation flying at night was ruled out—it would tire the men too much and burn up too much gas.

Rendezvous was pinpointed over the middle of the Celebes. Daybreak was the hour. Celebes was entirely enemy-held and the rendezvous was within forty miles of a Jap airdrome known to be operational.

The rendezvous was about ten hundred and thirty-five miles from the point of take-off. It was about two hundred and twenty miles from the target. The first twelve planes were given just twenty-four minutes to assemble at rendezvous and start out in formation to the target. The sections that followed were given similarly rigid schedules. That meant that individual navigators had to navigate for almost one thousand miles at night and reach a given point within twenty-four minutes of each other.

It was arranged that the leader of the first section, Colonel Thomas C. Musgrave, Jr., would circle the assembly point, fire a red flare, flash an Aldis lamp, and that would be a signal for the others to gather for the remainder of the trip to the target. For formation over the target a javelin step-down was selected. This called for three-plane elements, each element slightly lower than the one in front of it.

The formation made for a beautiful bomb run, keeping the pattern tight and neat, but it was more dangerous than other kinds would have been as far as protection against enemy fighters was concerned In that formation, planes cannot give each other maximum protection.

The weather officer, nicknamed Thunderhead in honor of the stuff he usually reported, was called in for a preview of the weather to be expected. He went into a huddle and emerged with the following prediction: a series of high towering cumulus—the dreaded cloud monuments that airmen fear and avoid. These would continue through the night. There would also be thunderstorms. However, over a ten-year range, the weather, it was estimated, would be better that time than at any other time in the year, and from the weather angle also, the mission was feasible.

The men who would have to fly the mission were getting so they winced every time they heard the word "feasible." It sounded so damned weak. . . .

Last-minute preparations were perfected. One of the groups was based elsewhere than on Noemfoor. The planes from that group were to collect on the Noemfoor strip with the others and all would take off from there. Each plane had to be airborne exactly sixty seconds after the one ahead of it. While planes were taking off, the ones which preceded them would be en route to rendezvous. Delays in take-off would add up at the end of the night flight and if the schedule were not maintained, planes would have to circle pointlessly over rendezvous, burning precious gasoline. With seventy-two planes taking off from the same strip, if there were an average delay of only thirty seconds a plane that would add up perhaps to a delay of more than a half an hour over assembly point.

Crash trucks, derricks, bulldozers, all were brought down to the strip. So heavily were the planes overloaded it was feared that one or more might crack up on the night take-off. Orders were issued that if a plane cracked up it was to be hauled off the strip immediately so as not to delay the others. Planes that got into trouble after take-off had to keep in the air until the last plane got away before landing again. Ambulances were stationed near the field. Medics went to the line to wait for emergencies.

At two o'clock on the afternoon of September 29th the first briefing of all aerial engineers was undertaken. Then the pilots and co-pilots were called in. The printed long-range distribution and weight charts were explained. The

224

reasons for every item of change in them were analyzed. This was not the usual "poop" which might be conveniently disregarded once the airplanes were aloft. A parachute *had* to be moved from here to there at exactly this time—this had to be shifted there and a man must move from this point to that point. This all had to be done, or a gallon of gasoline, ten gallons, maybe more, would be wasted. The tiniest deviation from the charts might mean the difference between a safe return and a bail-out over enemy-held territory.

The engineers were given refresher courses in transferring fuel. The ordinary wing and wing-tip tanks were to be augmented by bomb-bay tanks holding several hundred gallons each and tests had disclosed that a few of the airplanes flew nose heavy, at a slight angle; it was thought there might be some difficulty in transferring gasoline with the planes pitched at that angle.

At seven-thirty that evening the main briefing took place. Everybody who was going on the mission was told officially for the first time what the target would be. There had been a lot of rumors but this was the first official announcement. The men opened their eyes slightly, sighed, some of them, and said nothing.

They were told exactly what lighting facilities would be available for take-off. In the event the Nips came over to strafe and bomb during take-off the enemy was to be ignored as far as possible and take-off to proceed on schedule. Planes were to circle in a definite pattern before relanding if they developed mechanical trouble. If the mechanical trouble was so serious the planes couldn't stay aloft until the last plane took off, the pilot was to run his faulty ship over the water, bail out with his crew and let the ship crash. Nothing, nothing at all, must interfere with the mission. There was only one strip for this particular show and top priority for all movement on it was for planes taking off.

The men were told that from the moment they were airborne they would be over enemy territory one hundred per cent of the way. They were given dictionaries of native words in case of forced landings.

The first plane was ordered to take off at 0030—just thirty minutes after midnight on the morning of September 30, 1944.

Meanwhile the strip itself had been readied for the show. Palm trees at the far end of the strip had been cut down, tops had been removed, so the weighted planes would have plenty of clearance. A field hospital was taken down and moved away from the end of the strip. Final instructions were given: twenty minutes before each individual time of take-off the planes were to start engines, crews check for combat readiness, and then the pilots to taxi into position.

It was a beautiful night. There was a moon. The palm trees were silhouetted against the light sky. You could see clearly and plainly. The men liked the moon. They would have it only for a few hours but what there was of it was welcome. There was tension in the air. Rumors spread. From all over Noemfoor—or at least from the portion of it that we owned—men gathered. The linemen, looking over their airplanes, patting them, stroking them gently. Other flying men. The ground personnel. Men from other branches of the service. They were all there looking at the long line of airplanes. Most of the airplanes were unpainted, shining silver in the moonlight. Some still had the old camouflage.

Then at the right moment the first airplane rolled up to the head of the strip and the motors roared until the island itself seemed to quiver and then the giant lumbering craft moved on down the strip and gathered speed and then was airborne and climbing slowly. The mission was started.

The first twenty-four airplanes were airborne in exactly twenty-four minutes. Despite the load there was no accident. The last plane of the seventy-two got off safely. There was a long-drawn sigh from the men on the ground. So far so good. Then, a little later, two airplanes returned with mechanical failures. They climbed out of the planes almost in tears. Seventy airplanes were off on the show.

In the air it was a long night. Frequently the navigators figured when they had crossed their tiny points of land by the towering cumulus clouds which usually stack up over land. The navigators sweated. The men moved like clockwork inside the planes deftly moving things from place to place—often a matter only of inches—as the charts required.

Dawn broke over the Celebes. It was one of those incredibly beautiful mornings that occur only in the tropics, thousands of feet in the air. The morning was purple and red and the clouds tinted with pastels; then the sun rose above the clouds. The men blinked their eyes. With the first light they were crossing the Celebes, on schedule.

The first section of twelve planes was collected at rendezvous point within thirteen minutes. The navigators had flown nine hundred miles in the dark and had reached their pinpoint within thirteen minutes of each other. It was the kind of navigating that brought lumps to the throats of pilots and men scattered throughout the ships.

Then suddenly Musgrave, in the lead ship, found he had unexpected company. Two Jap twin-engined airplanes began to parallel the formation, just out of gun range. The men knew why they were there and why they made no attempt to attack the bombers. They were flying along, radioing course and speed and altitude for the Jap antiaircraft at Balikpapan.

The Americans watched them bemused. There was nothing they could do.

A Jap airdrome, Mangar, was to be used as a checkpoint. It was an ironic thing to choose as a checkpoint but there was nothing else. The field was just thirty miles north of the target. Shortly after the turn on Mangar the lead plane was to be turned over to its bombardier to fly over the target for the bomb run. The other planes were to follow in formation. When the formation got to Mangar it ran into unexpected weather.

The clouds were closed in ten-tenths below them. That means total coverage. The clouds were packed together until they looked like the top of a soap bucket. You couldn't see anything through them. The planes flew the prescribed course to the target. So far the enemy had made no attempt to stop them. The element of surprise had been more successful than anyone had dared to hope.

But then, just before the formation got five miles from the target, when it was already settled into the long bomb run, into the climax of the mission, into the job for which the airplanes were made and the men trained, the Jap fighters came up in droves, like specks of hailstorm, and hit them.

It was an attack that dry military parlance calls determined and sustained. The men call it eager. The Nips were eager beyond anything that anyone had ever before experienced. They came to within twenty-five feet of the big bombers, blazing away with all their guns. They flew into and through the formation. They got above the bombers and went into an almost vertical dive, every gun shooting as they came down. It seemed as though they had been sent up with orders to stop the raid, to turn it away, at all costs. Balikpapan was vital to the Jap war and the Japs knew it.

The planes plodded on. The gunners were shooting away. A Jap plane here and there went down. Finally, the planes came to the target area itself and to the bullets and cannon shells of the enemy airplanes now were added the shells from the anti-aircraft on the ground. The flak was thick and heavy and the Jap fighters ignored it and kept attacking through it. That in itself was unusual. It is more normal for fighters to break away when their flak takes over, but the Nips disregarded their own ground fire and pressed in.

Then came a heart-break. When the bombers finally arrived over the target itself, it was almost completely covered with clouds.

Musgrave saw a small hole in the clouds and through it a portion of the target. The Nip was throwing up shells from his new 120-mm ack-ack guns and each time a shell exploded it crashed open with a terrific noise and if it came close enough the concussion rocked the ships back and forth. The air was filled with phosphorus bombs, incendiaries.

The easy thing to do was to drop the bombs in the general target area. The hole had closed in but the men knew roughly where the target was and could have dropped their bombs, sure of hitting something, then got the hell away. That would have been the easy thing to do.

But the men had been briefed on pinpoint targets within the refinery, on the small vital nuclei which would put the whole thing out of business for a while. The mission had been planned too laboriously, the trip had been too long and too hard to sacrifice accuracy and deadliness at the last minute.

Musgrave ordered the bombardier to hold his bombs. He swung the formation in a great arc to the east. He would try to come in at a new angle. It didn't matter if the new attempt gave the Nip fighters a field day, if it gave the ack-ack just that much more time to try to shoot them down.

A few minutes later the formation approached from a new angle. The planes and flak had followed it all the way. Following Musgrave, the formation circled for forty-five minutes until they could see exactly what they had been told to bomb, and then, and only then, did Musgrave give the word and the bombs were released.

Later reconnaissance pictures showed that the bombing had done just what it was supposed to do. In that mission—and in the three that were to follow in short order—almost half of the Balikpapan refinery was destroyed and the remainder was put out of action for more than six months.

Their bombs away, the planes turned and started for home. The Jap fighters were remorseless. They attacked for one solid hour without let-up. Now that the bomb run was over the bombers could devote themselves entirely to scrapping with the enemy fighters. The boys shot down seven of the Nip planes and counted nine probables. We lost two Liberators, and many others were damaged. Some were damaged so badly they had to make forced landings en route, but when the mission was ended only one crew and half of another crew were missing. The rest were rescued.

The furious Nips swarmed all around. The stories some of the men told when they returned have become sagas among our flying men in the Southwest Pacific. The planes had been over the target, in all, for more than an hour. Time over target, normally, is counted in minutes. . . .

Over the target a lead ship of one of the elements got it and nose-dived into Balikpapan town before anyone could bail out. First Lieutenant Oliver L. Adair, pilot of another ship, pulled into the lead to take the missing ship's position. At the same time Adair's ship was hit in an inboard engine and the wing and tail and fuselage were hit. Oil spurted over the red hot cylinders and started to burn. Flames were blazing in a fifty-foot tail behind the airplane. Despite this, Adair shoved up the power on his three remaining engines and moved into the lead.

His right-waist gunner, Staff Sergeant Charles F. Held, had his gun shot out of his hands. The mount was destroyed and the ring site knocked off and the back end of the gun broken apart. He rigged up his parachute for a cushion. He held the loose gun against the chute pack and grabbed the hot barrel with his other hand and fired bursts at the attackers.

"I couldn't aim, but my tracers were coming close enough so the Nip knew the gun was still working."

He could only fire a few bursts at a time. The recoil would jolt him back against the other side of the plane and when he returned home finally his chest was black and blue, covered with bruises from the pounding and the hand that held the barrel of the gun was burned through the glove that he wore.

Everybody on that ship prayed. Once the boys heard the co-pilot, Second Lieutenant Raphael F. Baird, try to wisecrack in his throat mike to cheer up the men, and then give up the attempt, and instead, whisper, "Oh, my God, let me get out of here, please God, let me get out of here. . . ."

The top-turret man, Staff Sergeant Wilbur L. Bowen, said later, "Half the time I was praying hard enough to save half the people in the United States. And half the time I was cursing hard enough to put a good bishop in hell. When I saw three planes coming in at once with their wing edges sparkling I just prayed they wouldn't hit us. And then when one of my guns jammed I would pound on the magazine and cuss in the worst way I know how."

On the way home they had to chop out the ball turret and the top turret to lighten weight. Working with axes and a machete they chopped the top turret into small pieces and threw it out. Then they worked for three hours on the ball turret. They got nearly everything out but some braces and armor which the ax wouldn't cut. One of the men pulled his automatic pistol and shot away the rivets that held the metal together.

The main gas tanks were full of small leaks. The men stopped them up with bits of candle, rags, a pencil, a broken screwdriver. There were holes in the hydraulic brake line they couldn't see.

The pilot figured he could make a normal landing. He ordered seven of the crew on the flight deck. The ship went in to land on Morotai. It settled for a perfect landing. The brakes held long enough to slow the ship down to eighty-five miles an hour and then the left brake broke its line and the right brake locked and the ship jerked to one side toward a bank.

It ploughed through palm trees. One stump flew into the bomb bay and hit Held in the leg. One of the props on the ship cut through a parked truck as the driver raced for cover. The nose wheel buckled and flew back into the bomb bay to hit Held in the other leg.

Twelve seconds after the ship had buried its nose in a sand bank every man was out of the ship. Held got out of the top escape hatch, hit the top of the ship, and did a complete flip-over into the dirt.

And from a latrine in the path of the bomber a first sergeant ran out—his trousers still below his knees. . . .

One of the waist gunners in another ship began to pass out ammunition to the other gunners and had to leave his own gun abandoned. Staff Sergeant John W. Clarry, the other waist gunner, began to fire both guns simultaneously, standing in the middle of the airplane, his arms outstretched.

"I saw one coming in at the right and I fired until he went out of sight," he said later. "Then out of the corner of my eye I saw an attacker coming in from the left. I fired at him and then they were coming in fast and thick from both sides. I started to fire both guns at once. Of course I couldn't do any aiming but I managed to turn a couple away with my tracers. The guns were shaking me to pieces. I could hardly hold on to them with one hand. For a while I could fire with one gun for a second and then turn and fire the other. I never was so busy in my life."

Flak tore apart one of the big airplanes, ripping the belly from nose to tail. The first burst crashed through the bombsight and sent powdered glass spraying into the eyes of the bombardier, Second Lieutenant Gordon G. Schimke. This was before the bomb run, and Schimke knew he still had a job to do. He was almost unconscious from shock and the pain was excruciating, but he felt his way back, temporarily blinded, and salvoed his bombs. Other men on the ship were knocked unconscious from the concussion.

Two engines went out. The electric system was shattered. The fuel lines were cut so fuel could not be transferred. Shells burst into the bomb bay and metal fragments tore into the flak suits the men were wearing. The rudder and the tail assembly were riddled and the pilot, First Lieutenant Richard G. Egelston, had to trim the ship to hard right rudder to keep it going straight.

They couldn't keep on. The pilot ordered the men to bail out. Another B-24 stayed close to help in whatever way it could. Then a Navy flying boat hove in sight. The co-pilot of the B-24, Second Lieutenant Ralph L. Krueger, saw it. Everyone bailed out except the pilot and co-pilot. With Egelston still fighting the controls, Krueger crawled through the ship to make sure every man was out. Then pilot and co-pilot bailed out together.

Within two hours the flying boat had gathered every man out of the sea. The boat made six attempts to get off the choppy waters before it could get itself airborne. Then finally aloft again, all the men looked at the ball gunner from the B-24, Staff Sergeant Richard B. Page, who was accounted a very calm man ordinarily. While descending in his chute he had been seen to uncork his canteen and drink a long swig of water.

"I suddenly felt thirsty," he explained simply.

The flying boat proceeded to base. The troubles were not yet over. The ship came in during an alert. Trigger-happy ack-ack gunners fired several salvos at it before it was recognized.

Did you ever hear how the infantry, sometimes after a bitter fight, after the long march back, straightens out its ranks, gets into parade order, its ranks depleted but the heads of the remaining men high and proud?

Well, on the way back Musgrave found four ships near him. They all seemed to have the same idea. They closed into perfect formation.

On the ground at Noemfoor men were sweating out the mission. There were thousands of them packed among the palm trees. Pilots from a nearby night-fighter squadron were there. They said the bomber boys had sweated them out time and time again and now they were there to help sweat out the bomber boys.

And then the planes came in. The first five planes in their perfect formation. Riddled with holes. Parts of the tails and wings and turrets gone. But in perfect formation.

Captain William J. Stuart, Jr., Operations Officer for one of the groups, burst into tears as he recognized his own ships. He stood there rigid, the tears pouring down his face.

"I'm not ashamed of it," he said. "God damn it, I'm not ashamed of it."

Peleliu

General MacArthur was now in position to invade the Philippines, but first he had to secure final approval from the Joint Chiefs of Staff, and priority for naval support for the landing operation. Admirals King and Nimitz were promoting a different strategy that would by-pass the Philippines, or at most occupy Mindanao in the Philippines for its airfields. While these two points of view, among others, were debated in the councils of the JCS, there was concurrence on the necessity for the invasion of the Palau Islands, on the southern flank of Truk, the Jap naval base. The airfields on Peleliu and the bomber strip on Anguar were deemed necessary for the invasion of the Philippines.

At the last minute Admiral Halsey suggested to Admiral Nimitz that the Palaus be by-passed; in the first days of September 1944 he had led carrier strikes on Yap, the Palaus, and Mindanao, and met almost no opposition from enemy planes. He deduced that the Jap air forces in these areas could be written off as a threat to the Philippines invasion, particularly if his carriers were attached to MacArthur for air support.

S. E. Morison says, "Admiral Nimitz did not accept this suggestion. He felt Peleliu and the Kossal Passage (to the north) were needed as staging points for Leyte." * Furthermore, the Peleliu expedition was only two sailing days away from their scheduled D-Day.

This force was III Amphibious Corps, commanded by Major General Roy S. Geiger. The assault troops for Peleliu were the 1st Marine Division, under Major General William H. Rupertus. The 81st Infantry Division, under Major General Paul J. Mueller, had as its main target the island of Anguar, although they were to stand by to help with Peleliu if needed.

"Naval bombardment blew off most of the scrubby jungle growth

---

*S. E. Morison, *Leyte*, p. 33. Little Brown & Co. Copyright 1958 by Samuel Eliot Morison.

behind the airstrip and beaches [on Peleliu] revealing numerous caves; but few gave them a thought. Admiral Oldendorf was so pleased with the results of his three-day bombardment that on the evening of 14 September, over voice radio to Admiral Fort, he made a very unfortunate remark: 'We have run out of targets.' And General Rupertus rashly predicted to news correspondents that Peleliu would be secured within four days." *

The men gathered in the troopships hoped the brass were right. The bombardment of Kwajalein had so stunned the Japs that the landing waves had a comparatively easy time in the early hours of the invasion. But such was not to be at Peleliu. Even after the first waves were in, there was still havoc on the beaches; Captain Frank Hough describes the scene:

"These later waves crossed the reef amid the debris of those which had preceded them: wreckage of gear and vehicles, bodies bobbing sluggishly in the shallow water or draped grotesquely across protruding coral heads. Shells still fell among them, and some were hit. Ashore, they found the beach and a stretch extending up to a hundred yards inland heavily mined. . . . They found pillboxes dug into the raw coral, roofed with coral chunks set in, and piled on . . . blending in so well with the natural terrain that a man had to walk practically up to the narrow firing apertures before recognizing them for what they were. They saw a few Japanese dead, some of them wearing gas masks, for reasons best known to themselves; but they saw a lot more dead Marines." **

At the extreme left of the assault beaches, the 3rd Battalion 1st Marines hit a coral ridge, 30 feet high, which was filled with spider trenches and pillboxes, and which enfiladed their part of the 3,000-yard landing beach. The story of this action follows.

*Leyte, p. 35.
**Hough, The Island War, p. 293. J. B. Lippincott.

CORAL COMES HIGH

by Captain George P. Hunt

After running as hard as I could for about seventy-five yards I slid into a shell hole out of breath, my lips and tongue as dry as sandpaper. Black vapor and the pungent odor of gunpowder which was seeping from the earth helped to clog my throat. Sweat was running off the end of my nose. I rolled a swig of water around in my mouth. Looking behind I saw that Kelly and Blackburn, my runners, and the radio operator and Stramel were in the hole with me. Schmittou was just over the edge of the hole flattened behind a bush. A bullet snapped into the dirt right next to me. I heard vicious rattlings of shots and earth-shaking bursts of mortar shells which fell in a relentless pattern, closer and closer, to the right, to the left, straddling our position. Shrapnel whistled and plunked into the trees.

I could not see my platoons, but I thought I heard the sound of their firing on my right and left.

"Corpsman up here!" Schmittou was calling. "Burton's hit." Delbarter, big, muscular, crawled out of the hole.

"Hello, control, this is five; hello, control, this is five. Do you hear me? Over." That was the radio; Sellers calling. He should be about fifty yards down the beach.

"Send up stretchers. We're getting casualties," I told him.

"Comin' right up," his drawl blurred over the air.

I was trying to get in with my platoons on the radio; I had to know how they were doing. "Hello, one, hello, two, hello, three: This is control. Do you hear me? Over," the radio operator droned on. No word.

Colonel Ross from Regiment jumped into the hole. Good God! What was he doing here? He must have landed too far to the left.

"What outfit is this?"

"K Company. Like a cigarette?" I offered him one.

"No thanks. I've got to be moving. Take care of my radio operator; he's been hit."

"No, he's dead, Colonel," said Delbarter.

"Oh," he paused: "Good luck." He scrambled out of the hole.

I heard a scuffling behind me. Blackburn was wounded in the arm. His young face turned very white, and his lips curled up with the pain. I got Sellers on the radio again.

"Where in hell are the stretchers?"

"I sent 'em up fifteen minutes ago. They should be there by now. There's Japs all around us back here."

A few minutes later Dempsey and Hooker appeared with a stretcher. They laid Burton on it and carried him off. A mortar shell struck just then, very near. I saw Dempsey standing up, raising a hand which was dripping with blood. He pointed to his fingers.

"Two of 'em gone," he shouted, and damned if he wasn't smiling!

The radio operator was still calling the platoons. Still no answer. The uncertainty became agonizing. I heard the heavy throbbing of big stuff, the unmistakable persistence of Jap machine guns from the vicinity of the Point. I saw flame and smoke rising from our beach, heard the sizzling of burning Alligators, and the mortars were pounding about us with more intensity. The Jap fire was building up.

Suddenly I heard the call I had been waiting for. It came slurred and crackling at first, then clear as a bell.

"Hello, control, this is one, hello, control, this is one, do you hear me? Over."

"Yeah, Willis, I hear you, what's the dope?"

"Hello, old man, I'm up just behind the third platoon. Estey and Koval were hit. They've had a hell of a lot of casualties and need stretcher bearers badly. I'm seein' what I can do up here."

"Do you have contact with the second on your right?"

"No, nothing in there but Japs."

"Well, push through and take the Point," I told him, "I'm coming right up."

"OK, OK," he answered, "that's what I figured."

I called Major McNulty at Battalion on the radio. "We're pretty well shot up and there's a gap between my two assault platoons. I'm throwing the first platoon in to take the Point. The goddam naval gunfire didn't faze the Japs! We need stretcher bearers!"

"All right, Bub, I'll have L Company fill in the gap. I'll send up everybody I can spare with stretchers."

But there was still no word from the second platoon.

Kelly, whom I had sent up to find Estey and the third platoon, returned with a bullet hole through his shin. Pantingly he told me:

"Jese, there are K Company guys dead and wounded lyin' all around. Mr. Estey got it twice in the arm. He's lyin' in a hole and looks pretty bad. They're askin' for you. They got shot up when they were goin' up the beach toward that Point. Yeah, and they think Koval's dead, and McNeel, and Webber took over. I got hit up here about ten yards." Just then a bullet clipped off the radio antenna.

The decision was made now; I had committed my whole company.

I told the radioman to follow me, rolled out of the hole and, running from tree to tree, headed toward the Point.

The human wreckage I saw was a grim and tragic sight. First it was bewildering; then it made me hot with anger; but finally my feelings cooled to accepting a gruesome inevitable fact. There was Gasser, whose face, always pale, was as white as the sand on which he lay. Shrapnel had shattered his rifle and a piece had penetrated his neck. It was an effort for him to grin, but he did. I saw Culjak, very tall and dark, with a bloody bandage around his arm. Kneeling in a hole in the sand I asked him what had happened to him. He was in the second platoon.

"I was on the left with Bandy and Dolan trying to keep contact with the third platoon. But I got separated from my outfit. I don't know what happened to them. Then I ran into a Jap and killed him with a grenade, but he got me in the arm."

I saw McMatt lying on his side with a small hole in his stomach which oozed purple blood. Someone had taken off his clothes. Slowly he turned his head toward me, and

I saw that his blue eyes were glassy. He opened his mouth, and his white lips formed a word, but no sound came forth. Exhausted by the effort he let his head slump back, and blood was drooling from his mouth. The corpsman who was squatting next to him shook his head.

These were only three of the wounded and dying which littered the edge of the coconut grove from where we had landed to the Point. As I ran up the beach I saw them lying nearly shoulder to shoulder; some of them mine; others from outfits which landed immediately behind us. I saw a ghastly mixture of bandages, bloody and mutilated skin; men gritting their teeth, resigned to their wounds; men groaning and writhing in their agonies; men outstretched or twisted or grotesquely transfixed in the attitudes of death; men with their entrails exposed or whole chunks of body ripped out of them. There was Graham, snuffed out a hero, lying with four dead Japs around him; and Windsor, flat on his face, with his head riddled by bullets and his arms pointed toward a pillbox where five Japs slumped over a machine gun; and Sharp, curled up on his side, still holding his automatic rifle which pointed to a huddle of dead Japs thirty yards away. His aim had been good. Stieferman was alive, his face and body peppered by shrapnel. His words came slowly and raspingly.

"Hello, Captain. Sorry I had to get it like this, but I saw those three Japs, and as soon as I threw a grenade at 'em I got one in return. It cut me up a little bit, but I got all three of them. I know I did."

I saw McNeel, his eyes turned up in death, a yellow pallor on his rugged face. He was lying directly in front of a forty millimeter gun lodged in a pillbox of reinforced concrete. The gun was scarred and wrenched from its base. Inside dead Japs sprawled on top of each other. An open, half-empty canteen and a Tommy gun lay next to McNeel's head.

No wonder the Japs had done such damage. The Point, rising thirty feet above the water's edge, was of solid, jagged coral, a rocky mass of sharp pinnacles, deep crevasses, tremendous boulders. Pillboxes, reinforced with steel and concrete, had been dug or blasted in the base of the perpendicular drop to the beach. Others, with coral and concrete piled six feet on top were constructed above, and spider holes were blasted around them for protecting infantry. It surpassed by far anything we had conceived of when we studied the aerial photographs.

Willis had moved swiftly and had already assaulted the Point; the sound of sporadic firing came from the other side. Jap dead fringed the base of the rise to the Point and filled up the niches and holes in the coral. They were big healthy men, and had new equipment. I climbed up the rocks and saw Willis' muscular, bowlegged figure.

"Good going, Will," I congratulated him, "you've done a wonderful job."

"It wasn't me, it was these men," he answered, waving his arm in a wide sweeping gesture.

"We've got to hold this place now," I said, "how many men do you have left?"

"About thirty, all that's left of my platoon and Estey's. What happened to the second? There's nobody on our right."

"I don't know," I answered, "I think they've had a hell of a rough time. It looks like we're isolated up here."

The men were in a line behind boulders forming a circular, all-around defense of the Point. They were resting, occasionally rising up to shoot at a stray Jap. Otherwise it was quiet, except for the steady thumping of mortar shells on the beach and the reef behind us, and the distant chattering of machine guns far off to our right. The immediate silence seemed ominous. Standing on the rocks I looked back and could see gray files of troops moving inland from the beach, through the debris of the coconut grove. They would push on the right and overrun the airfield. I wondered how the fight was progressing over there, but there was no way of knowing now. The entire beach was swarming with tractors, men evacuating wounded and unloading supplies, aid stations which had been hurriedly set up to meet the sudden rush of casualties. The sands were black with milling men.

"What a target!" I exclaimed to Willis. "No wonder the Japs are raising so much hell!"

It was ten-thirty. I called Major McNulty on the radio and told him that the Point was secured.

"That's fine," he answered, "what supplies do you need?"

"We need water, grenades, ammunition and barbed wire, and as many reinforcements as you can scrape together. I've only got about thirty men up here. We must have machine guns! Mine were nearly all shot up when they landed."

"OK, Bub," he answered, "I'll get the stuff up to you as soon as I can by tractor along the reef. Be on the lookout for L Company moving into the gap on the right. They will make contact with you."

There was nothing to do but wait, rest and strengthen our line. The men had already started to build foxholes of rocks and fallen logs. The clouds had broken overhead, and the sun was relentlessly beating down on us, reflecting from the coral rocks with doubled intensity. As the men worked the sweat drenched their clothes and skin. In the bay the warships were firing far inland, and even where we were we could feel the concussion. The Point seemed almost unscarred by the terrific bombardment we had seen before the landing. I was amazed that the pillboxes had weathered it untouched. Few trees had grown in the coral, and what ones were there were short and crooked and gnarled. Our shelling had reduced most of them to jagged stumps. We had paid dearly for the Point, but there was compensation in the fact that we had counted 110 dead Japs and that we now held a very strategic position. There was no possible way of knowing how many out of my entire company had been killed or wounded. I knew there were a lot, nearly two-thirds I estimated, figuring that the second platoon over on the right had suffered as heavily as the first and third. Stramel radioed that most of my machine-gun platoon had been mowed down on the beach and there were no more than eight men left and all the guns had been knocked out. Hanson radioed me that the mortar section was still intact down the beach where Sellers was, but there was no wire communication available to the Point. We would have to rely on the radio to direct mortar fire, but the batteries were fading fast and would probably be entirely dead by nightfall. Sellers was dangerously straddled by Jap mortars.

I walked along the line and met Webber and Hahn. What was left of their third platoon was in position on the line, and the three of us had time to sit down on the baked rocks for a few minutes and have a sweaty cigarette. We were dripping with perspiration, and our wet fingers soaked and spoiled our smokes before we really had time to enjoy them. They were anxious to talk about the fight. Hahn's gray eyes were bright with excitement, and a half grin crooked the thin line of his mouth. He pointed to a rise in the coral behind me. "Right there," he said, "Humplik and I walked right into three Japs who were setting up a heavy machine gun. We came barging around these big boulders like two damn fools and were on top of them before we knew it. They looked up at us and started jabbering excitedly and reaching for hand grenades. Luckily I had one in my hand which I threw just in time. It went off in the middle of them and killed two. The other one took off at a dead run after tossing a grenade at us, and Humplik drilled him. The grenade hit directly between us. It was a dud. We set the Jap gun on the line, up there by those high rocks."

"I saw it," I said. "Have you got plenty of ammunition for it?"

"Sure, there's stacks of it in some of these pillboxes."

Jap mortars began to drop shells on the beach, close to our lines. We ducked behind the rocks and waited for them to pound in our positions. But fortunately they stopped just below the Point and started back down the shore line in a rapid series of explosions.

"God!" exclaimed Webber, "that's murder for all those people crowded together on that beach!"

"Yeah," added Hahn, "and they could certainly raise hell with us if they dropped a concentration in here."

"You know, Captain," said Webber, changing the subject, "I wonder what the Japs thought when we hit the beach. We were all striped up with camouflage paint and poured out of the tractors hollering like a bunch of Indians and charging at the Japs full speed. Several guys were shouting 'Gung Ho!' but most of them had their own war cry. We ran smack into the Japs as they were running out of their pillboxes to their spider holes."

"Damn right," I said, "if you hadn't moved in so fast we would never have had the momentum to take this Point." Webber flicked away his cigarette and leaned forward with his elbows on his knees. He was as unruffled as though he were riding in a streetcar. "And you should have seen Rowe," he went on, grinning broadly, showing straight teeth. "He has these white workman's gloves, and every once in a while as he moved up with his BAR under his arm, which is almost as big as he is, he would stop right in the middle of all the shooting, pull off his gloves, take a nail file from his pocket and file his nails. Then he would twirl his mustache. And Lindsey Jones was just as funny. When the Japs were all around us below the Point, Lindsey sat in a bush picking them off, sayin' all the time in his southern accent, 'Mah, mah, theah suah a' lot of Japs around heah.' "

"The Japs didn't seem to bother him much," commented Hahn, smiling. Sweat rolling down Hahn's face left streaks in the camouflage paint and the gray coral dirt smudged across the top of his cheeks. He took off his helmet and rubbed the perspiration from the back of his neck.

"Nothing can bother that guy," replied Webber, "he's as rugged as an ox. When Carter was hit, Lindsey went over to help him. He was putting a bandage on Carter's chest when he saw a Jap sneakin' up on him. He waved his arm at the Jap and yelled at him, 'Git away from heah, you Jap, can't you see I'm fixin' a man?' The Jap got behind a tree and all Lindsey could see of him was the edge of his helmet sticking out on either side of the tree. So Lindsey put aside the bandage, took up his BAR and fired a shot which went right through the tree and into the Jap's head."

I told Hahn and Webber what I knew of our situation and to keep a sharp lookout for L Company which was to close the gap on our right, then continued along the line which in total length could not have been over a hundred yards. I saw Sovik, Willis' platoon sergeant, who told me about a Jap who wanted to surrender and come into our lines just after we had seized the Point. His words tumbled out quickly.

"The Jap had his pack on and was carrying his weapon, so we shot him, just to be on the safe side, and damned if he didn't blow up. He must have been loaded down with dynamite and grenades."

"Yeah," drawled Lees, who had come up while Sovik was talking and whose sallow, hardened face bore a casual expression, "they're tricky little bastards. You've got to watch 'em. There are lots of 'em running around out there with our helmets on."

The men were asking for water; their canteens were dry. There were only a few grenades left and what ammunition each man had in his belt. We looked expectantly toward the beach for the Alligator which would bring us supplies, and to our right for signs of L Company moving up.

I was sitting behind a white boulder trying to enjoy a cigarette. I felt as though I was in an oven, and the rocks were hot to the touch. My thoughts wandered to the dead men lying on the slope of the Point. So many lives had been snuffed out so quickly that it seemed impossible and incredible. Once again I thought of a fantastic dream with no logic, only a pattern of grotesque, lugubrious shapes and a background of tuneless music and uncontrolled rhythms.

The explosion of a mortar shell startled me— Then more—they were dropping in our midst. Shrapnel whined through the rocks, ricocheting and clipping the tree stumps. I heard a voice say very calmly, "Looks like I'm hit." A chunk of steel smashed into the rocks on my left, throwing chips of stone. Again the voice, "Yes, I'm hit all right; in the leg. Feels like the bone's broken." The barrage stopped. There was silence, and I waited for the cry "Corpsman!" None came. One more round fell on the edge of the cliff. I looked around; yes, it was Duncan who was wounded in the leg, and he was as cool as ice. His face had turned as gray as the rocks around him. They carried him to the water's edge to wait for the tractor. If the Japs continued those concentrations soon there would be none of us left. But perhaps they did not know—

Then I saw Sergeant Bandy of the second platoon scrambling over the rocks toward me. He had lost contact in the area of the gap and had just found our positions. I was certainly glad to see him. "What happened to the second platoon?" I asked him. He waited until he got his breath back before answering, and he wiped the sweat out of his eyes with the sleeve of his jacket. About a hundred and fifty yards in from the beach most of the second platoon had been caught in a tank trap and on trying to assault out of it had been terribly shot up. The trap was nearly fifteen yards wide, ten feet deep and extended parallel to the shore line for several hundred yards. It was a mammoth trench with sloping sides of loose coral sand, hidden in the torn and uprooted underbrush of the coconut grove. It was raked by machine guns from the sides and from the precipitous coral ridge to its front where pillboxes had been blasted in the rock. Woodyard was dead and Macek, his platoon sergeant, had been hit in the arm as soon as they had landed. Good God! I called Sellers on the radio and told him the information.

"We just got the same word down here," he said. "We're going to try to evacuate what's left of the second platoon as soon as we can. Battalion is bringing up tanks."

Dusk was approaching fast. The tractor with the supplies had just arrived, and we had to work quickly unloading it so that it could get back to the beach before night. Case after case of hand grenades and ammunition, cans of water which tasted of oil and had grown hot under the sun, rolls of barbed wire, crates of "C" rations, we piled on the coral ledge at the foot of the cliff and by chain gang lugged it up the rocks to the top of the rise where it was distributed to the men. The crew of the tractor gave us two of their machine guns which strengthened our scanty line considerably. Parties moved out in front of the positions to lay the barbed wire. Snipers harassed them, and a bullet lodged in the heart of a redheaded kid with freckles who had just been talking to me. "Gosh, Captain," he had said, "I never expected it to be as rough as this. If I live through it, I sure hope I never see another one like it." He had walked away with a broad smile on his grimy face. The tractor left and rolled down the reef. Mortar shells began to drop near it, following it all the way back but miraculously never scoring a hit.

Sniper fire had increased, popping from every direction outside of our perimeter. Occasionally a mortar shell would burst dangerously near. Two squads of L Company's machine-gun platoon had worked their way up to us during the afternoon, but no troops had appeared on our right where the gap was. Haggerty with his eighty-one millimeter mortar observation group had joined us, but he had no communication with his guns two thousand yards behind us. So he and his four men reinforced our line, manning a machine gun. Over his carrot-red hair he was wearing a blue baseball cap.

My radio was on its last legs. I had heard Sellers say that they had successfully evacuated what was left of the second platoon from the tank trap under the cover of tanks and that an estimated 150 Japs had moved in the gap. Then the radio faded out. I called him loudly for more information, but there was no answer.

It was almost dark. I was talking over our situation with Willis when Monk Meyer and Dolan appeared over the edge of the cliff from battalion headquarters. They had stolen through the coconut grove behind us and said it was lousy with Japs. Battalion had established a provisional line about two hundred yards back after the second platoon had been withdrawn from the tank trap.

"You're isolated up here," he said, looking at me, "and surrounded by Japanese."

"Yes, I know that," I replied. "Nobody has made contact with us."

"A Company and L Company have been trying to all afternoon. They had the hell shot out of 'em attempting to move into the gap which must be over two hundred yards wide," he said; then after a pause: "Do you think you can hold out?"

246

"Sure we can. Looks like we'll have to."

"Well, I must get going now. I think I'll swim back outside the reef. Take it easy and good luck." He disappeared over the rocks, and we sat silently for a few moments absorbing his information. I heard the water lapping against the rocks at the foot of the cliff. The evening was quiet and breathless.

"Anyway," said Willis, suddenly, "there's one thing to be said for our situation. We'll be able to kill some more of the bastards!"

As blackness crept up and completely enveloped us, we were subdued to an eerie silence. Even the clicking sounds of a small stone falling from the rough surface of a rock, probably brushed off by the sweep of a man's elbow, seemed a harsh disturbance. Though there was no moon, the sky, massed by thick and voluminous clouds, was just light enough to reveal the weird and grotesque silhouettes of knotted trees and stumps. The jagged, pinnacled rocks rose like witches' fingers, and the bald, cracked humps of boulders, appearing indiscriminately and catching the merest reflection of light, seemed like tremendous human pates which had been brutally clubbed to submissiveness. Surrounding us were the woods which had become dark and impenetrable in the night.

When one lies in a hole peering intently into the black, listening, smelling, hearing only the sound of one's breathing, waiting, expecting, the stillness may become appalling, dead objects may rise slowly and live, the motionless may move, sounds of leaves stirred by the breeze may become the sneaking movements of human feet, a friend may be an enemy, an enemy a friend, until, unless controlled by toughness of mind, one's imagination may become haunted by the unseen and the unheard. One may panic under this strain, jump up, screaming hoarsely and firing his weapon blindly all around him until shot dead by his friends because he is endangering their lives and might have already shot one of them. One may suddenly see incredible sights in the trees such as a shining yellow airplane, hung there, swarming with Japs and belching fire and bullets, and whisper what he sees to his buddy who then gets a friend and carries the raving one off the line. Another may be merely nervous and fire shots at nothing, giving away his position to Japanese scouts who are silently watching from the underbrush. Still another, feeling no alertness and allowing himself to be overcome with fatigue and being a slouch of a man, may fall asleep and meet a dreadful end on the point of an enemy bayonet. That man betrays himself as well as his friends.

I wanted to catch some sleep during the early hours of darkness as the Japs would probably attack later on. I lay down on the ground which was strewn with stones and stiff, prickling growth and found myself wedged between two rocks. I raised up and tried to rake the stones out from under me with my fingers but found that most of them were firmly embedded. In spite of the fact that I was extremely tired, the immediate concern of trying to twist my body into a position which would ease the prodding of the stones kept me awake. Alternately, each of my legs would go to sleep, requiring a painful shift to wake them up, and periodically the small of my right foot would develop a cramp. My body finally became used to these discomforts, and I was able to lie still, drifting into that drowsy state of mind when thoughts of the past flow swiftly and easily.

I dimly heard the occasional crack of a grenade being thrown, then the explosion, and the shrapnel humming through the air—a few Japs sneaking around in front of our lines—that's the way to keep 'em off, use grenades— good—the men knew their stuff—don't fire your rifles and machine guns until you can hear the Japs distinctly and know that they are attacking—don't let 'em know where our guns are located—wait until they hang up on our barbed wire—goddam these crabs. I thought I felt a slight breeze relieving the closeness of the night. It was a shame about Woody—I wonder if he knew he'd get it—no, I was just reading into him—it was strange that he should have instructed Stramel back in the states when he was a corporal and Stramel only a private then—the two were certainly glad to see each other—and now—well, I hope Stramel's OK. And I had heard a rumor along the line that Schmittou had been stuck with a bayonet—couldn't believe it—not Schmittou who was pretty good with his Tommy gun. Another explosion and whine—hope that one got a couple of 'em—I had seen Bennett very solemnly sitting in a shell hole looking at a picture while bullets were clipping the brush around him.

"What are you doin'?" I asked him.

"Lookin' at my wife's picture, wonderin' if I'll ever see her again."

The crack of a rifle made me rise up, fully awake. There was long silence. I listened very intently but heard no sound. I screwed my helmet around on my head and lay back once more on the bed of stones. I looked at my watch; the luminous dial showed eleven thirty-five. I noticed that here and there the clouds had broken and stars were blinking through the openings.

LaCoy was calling Sellers softly over the radio, hoping that it would work in a possible change of atmosphere. But all that the batteries could pick up was martial music. It was the second time the Japanese had jammed the air, the first having occurred in the morning when Sellers was trying to call the second platoon. A woman had broken in, jabbering incessantly, drowning out his call. He bellowed through the mouthpiece.

"F— you, you bitch! Git off the air!"

The woman continued to jabber.

LaCoy remarked to me several weeks after we left Peleliu that during battle when he found himself stationery for any length of time he frequently felt a warning from nowhere to move. He always obeyed that feeling. In one instance he was sitting behind a rock on the Point and suddenly felt this urge. No sooner had he jumped to another spot when a bullet snapped into the rock exactly where his back had been resting. I have experienced the same thing several times. I was on the Point in a hole among the rocks, and for no reason at all other than a quick hunch I moved thirty yards away to another one. Immediately a mortar shell burst about five feet from where I had left. The shrapnel flew alarmingly near to my new position but did not touch me.

Premonition of danger is a definite thing. When all your senses are alert you can feel its approach. On patrol through jungle trails where you are liable to meet Japs head-on, where they wait in ambush, where they bivouac, you can feel when they are near. A sharp, prickling sensation runs up your back, you slow down your patrol and approach with infinite caution and silence. It is similar to that feeling when you are sure that someone is looking at you but you cannot see him. Something happened to Hahn on the Point which is like it. He came up to two friends who were resting by a Jap pillbox. He sat down to talk with them when he suddenly felt himself alerted by this premonitive feeling. He stood up quietly and approached the exit of the pillbox. Inside he saw five Japs dressing wounds on their legs. He sprayed them with his Tommy gun.

Hand grenades were bursting in rapid succession. The explosions were muffled in the woods where there were gullies and small miscellaneous ridges. Then much louder bursts—approaching our lines—closer—and I heard the cry "Corpsman!" Jap mortars, big stuff, were pounding in the middle of us. Shrapnel was clinking across the rocks. We could only hold and take it, and there was nothing to fire at but the impenetrable black of the woods. The Japs were probably trying to soften us up for the attack. If we could live through the barrage we would be waiting for them. Wham, Wham, Wham, awful thumping along our lines.

"I'll be damned!" Jarvi was muttering, "that one got me in the thigh." He put on a bandage.

"Cut me in the arm too," Sovik was swearing, "it's hot as hell."

The fury increased. Flares swished up from the rear. Sellers was shooting blind—I followed the cometlike streaks through the sky, and as they passed over my head I prayed they wouldn't break over our own positions and light us up like a Christmas tree. But they burst into flaming sparks well in front of us, flooding the woods with orange light— good work, Bull!—he had hit the range on the button.

"There they are. I see 'em, I see 'em!"

"Well, plug the bastards, don't look at 'em!"

A machine gun fired a burst, another one—it opened up with a vibrating roar, BARs and rifles and grenades chattered in a wild medley.

Then it was dark. White muzzle flashes spit into the black. The noise increased as the Japs answered and their bullets spattered on the rocks and ricocheted in every direction and their mortar shells thundered into the coral, raising a stink of gunpowder. Sellers was shooting more flares. They would keep the Japs down. The roar of the fight gathered new strength. Our tracers cut flaming trails through the woods, and then suddenly the Jap mortar shells stopped falling; were they closing in for the assault? And as quickly our fire ceased on the left, on the right; in the center it continued for a moment. There was utter silence. The smell of powder smoke hung over the rocks.

The woods were grim and ominous, and sometimes we could hear faint scuffling in the rocks and the underbrush. Flares revealed nothing. We fired short bursts and threw grenades at the sounds. Except for that and the pleading, sometimes angry cry, "Corpsman!" the night remained quiet.

At the first sign of daylight the Japanese suddenly renewed their activities with such intensity that an assault seemed almost certain, and we soon understood the sounds that we had heard during the night. Snipers swarmed in the trees and bushes all around us, and from a long dip in the ground about thirty yards in front of us came barrage after barrage of grenades and mortars. We could see the Japs bob up quickly, catch the fling of their arms as they hurled. Below in the rocks we presented excellent targets for the Japs in the treetops. Almost before I knew it we were engaged in a blistering fire, fighting with our backs to the ocean.

A larger gun opened up, and the shells spread pink smoke as well as shrapnel. We were spraying the trees. The fight became a vicious melee of countless explosions, whining bullets, shrapnel whirring overhead or clinking off the rocks, hoarse shouts, shrill-screaming Japanese. Faces were gray with coral dirt and the smeared remains of the camouflage paint. Hibbard ran by to pick up a BAR from a man who had slumped over with a bullet in his chest. I caught a glimpse of his face—chalked with dust, blue eyes almost turned black, dark circles under them, creases around his mouth. Knight was smiling—dark, roughly chiseled, Indian face—Hunter standing over Kuld's body just for a moment, strangely meditative, I remember—Kuld, big and red-headed and freckled, as calm in death as he had been in life with blood at the corners of his mouth—Beazley, his side ripped open by a grenade—our trousers torn by the sharp coral—water supply low, our lips and tongues parched.

"Hello, five, this is control. Hello, five, this is control. Do you hear me, over?" LaCoy was trying to get Sellers. If he did I would holler for reinforcements—they could bring them up by tractor. We needed them—badly—no answer —the air was as dead as a morgue. Then Haggerty was volunteering; his red hair had turned sandy with dust—eyes like black needle-heads.

"Yes, Hag," I shouted, "go ahead. Get through. Bring some more people up here—anybody, I don't give a damn. Hurry and take care of yourself!"

"I'll bring 'em up!" he yelled, and climbed down the rocks to the beach.

Casualties were mounting fast. They ran past me down to the shelter of the beach shelf, holding bloody arms, with red dripping down their legs, cursing their luck and the Japs. Some were carried down on sagging stretchers. I smelled the powder vapor, acrid, choking, could see it swirling white—sweat in my eyes, stinging—jacket was wet on my back—rock chips spattering at my feet. Jap stuff kept coming—Jesus! why didn't they assault?—then we could knock them down like tenpins. They were dodging in and around the rocks in front of us—closer now—wiry little bastards—bandy-legged. I saw Hunter standing up throwing a grenade. As his arm swung forward he ducked and bullets crackled on the rocks over him. He stood up with his rifle at his shoulder and fired three shots. Suddenly he whirled around, his rifle flew up, and his helmet was rolling on the rocks. I saw blood streaming down his face.

"Hell of a lot of 'em out there," he was saying. "I got that mortar with my last grenade, but I missed the bastard that hit me. Just a graze on the head; I was lucky." He ran down below the cliff. I saw Willis and Lees next to me, crouching behind a rock.

"The line's getting awful thin," Willis observed, "looks like we'll have to draw in and tighten up."

"But that'll mean pulling back about twenty yards, and the Japs will move in on us covered by these boulders. We would be worse off then than we are now."

"Yeah, once they get in among these rocks here we're through." A Jap grenade struck a boulder, rolled and clinked down to within three yards of us.

"Another dud," Lees remarked casually, "we've been getting a lot of 'em."

Roderick, white as a ghost, jumped behind the rock with a shrapnel hole in his back which pumped up blood in spurts. "Take it easy," Lees told him, "turn around and I'll fix you up." He placed a bandage on the wound tying it firmly across the shoulders. The blood seeped through the bandage. Willis was shouting: "We must get these wounded boys out of here! Where in hell is the tractor?"

More and heavier stuff throwing pink vapor—the din was increasing—I was wondering if we'd get out of this alive—we were surrounded—we must hold the Point—even if we—

I looked down the beach. There were no troops coming our way, no tractor. Mortar shells were crashing on the sand and the reef just below the cliff, spreading shrapnel dangerously near to the wounded men who were lying there.

"Get in closer to the rocks!" I bellowed.

Over on the right McComas was gazing intently at a rocky rise about a hundred yards in front of him. His eyes were coal black and his muscular body was alertly straining forward. I remembered his immobility, strangely noticeable in the turmoil of the fight. A grenade was fixed on his rifle which rested lightly in his hands. With a catlike movement he suddenly disappeared from my view behind the boulders.

I heard Webber's voice, calm—Boston accent—saw his face, hawk-nosed and gray-eyed and smiling through dirt smears.

"McComas just knocked out the big mortar that's been hittin' us so hard. I think we've nearly cleaned 'em out on the right; there's a slew of dead Japs out there on the rocks."

I saw Devlin on the left standing upright on the line throwing grenade after grenade. His jacket was unbuttoned and flying out with his motions.

"There he goes!" he yelled, pointing with a long arm towards the woods. Hoffman, his face smudged with dirt and powder grime, stood up beside him, and his BAR vibrating and spitting flashes. Then other men stood up on the rocks. Then more, in the center, on the right, firing faster, hurling barrages of grenades that hammered a resounding note of finality. I saw the backs of running Japanese.

I turned around and there was Haggerty coming toward me with his rolling gait and his baseball cap low over his eyes. He pushed the visor back. An unlighted cigarette was hanging from the left corner of his mouth, "I've got some men, extras from other outfits I found on the beach, and we laid a phone wire along the reef from Battalion."

"Good work, Red. Get 'em on the line. The Japs are falling back."

Fifteen men were piling out of the Alligator onto the coral edge, and our wounded were taking their places. Stacked on the beach were cans of water and more grenades and bandages and sulfa drugs and morphine and stretchers. I picked up the phone and rang Battalion, but heard no rasping sound. The wire had snapped already.

Now, just after the Japs had pulled back, the line was quiet except for the occasional crack of a rifle. Powder smoke clung low on the rocks and curled in and out among the niches. The men were watchful, haggard; some had stubble under their chins, many had shed their jackets and were trying to cool themselves. The dirt mixed with sweat had ground into the skin, and several had scorching red rashes under their arms. Dark circles were prominent under their eyes which were bloodshot. They were talking in low, calm tones. I heard no bravado, no complaining, no hysterics, no irritable arguments. Every face seemed older than it should have been, more hard-bitten.

Rowe was sitting on top of a rock with his knees crossed. He wore his helmet cocked on the right side of his head as though it were a Stetson. He fingered his thin mustache musingly as he watched the woods and the rocks in front of him where dead Japs lay in brown heaps.

"Hello, Rowe," I accosted him, "how have you been doing?"

"Pretty well, Captain, pretty well," his voice was razor-edged, "except that I'm wonderin' how O'Brien is—whether he kicked off or not. A-a-a-ah," he spat, "when you see your buddy stiff on the deck with foam droolin' out of his mouth, his eyes poppin' out and his hands clutchin' at the air you feel like you could kill every livin' son of a bitch of a Jap from here to Tokyo. I got a few of those bastards out there but that's not enough. I wouldn't stake a hundred of 'em against Obie. Yeah, Captain, and it all starts you wondering —whether—well, that's war I guess."

Through every mind ran the same thoughts; we had lost too many good men; how long could it keep up? The Jap had laid off for a while, but he would hit us again; we were still out on a limb; would we get relief so we could sleep? would we die?—so what—and we were bitter mad at the Japs. We hated them, and we would kill them and keep killing them or we would be killed. If it hadn't been for him we would never have been on this goddam island in the middle of no place with all these rocks, the blasted heat and no water or chow.

Burma and the Ledo Road

The Japanese had moved into lower Burma early in 1942, pushing the British-Indian 17th Division ahead of them as they advanced on Rangoon. In March, they drove the last British troops out of Rangoon, and scattered the Chinese divisions Chiang Kai-Shek had sent in to help. The retreating British were joined by remnants of the Chinese who were led by American General "Vinegar Joe" Stilwell. Still, the onrushing Japanese never gave them time to organize for a concerted front. By the end of May, what was left of Burma Corps had retreated across the Burmese border into India.

General Slim, commanding the Burma Corps, described the last days of the retreat: "Ploughing their way up slopes, over a track inches deep in slippery mud, soaked to the skin, rotten with fever, ill-fed and shivering as the air grew cooler, the troops went on, hour after hour, day after day. Their only rest at night was to lie on the sodden ground under the dripping trees, without even a blanket to cover them. Yet the monsoon which so nearly destroyed us and whose rain beat so mercilessly on our bodies did us one good turn—it stopped dead the Japanese pursuit. As the clouds closed down over the hills, even their air attacks became rare.

"On the last day of that nine hundred mile retreat I stood on the bank beside the road and watched the rear guard march into India. All of them, British, Indian, and Gurkha, were gaunt and ragged as scarecrows. Yet as they trudged behind their surviving officers in groups pitifully small, they still carried their arms and kept their ranks. . . . They might look like scarecrows, but they looked like soldiers, too." *

Throughout the remainder of 1942 and for most of 1943 there was not a large-scale land campaign on the India-Burma front, although the British sent the 14th Division probing into Arakan to capture a limited objective but were thrown back. In the meantime the Burma Road had

*Field Marshal the Viscount William Slim *Defeat into Victory*, p. 87. David McKay Co.

been cut and American bomber crews flying out of the Chinese main-land could not be supplied, nor could vital war supplies be given to the Chinese armies. But by building air bases in Assam and flying transport planes over the Himalayas to China the lifeline was kept intact. Meanwhile, work would be rushed to build a new road to China —the Ledo.

The strategy behind the decision to rush work on the Ledo Road and open the campaign in northern Burma was pressed on the British by President Roosevelt and his Chiefs of Staff. In a letter to Prime Minister Churchill in early February, 1944, the President stressed the need to build up air power in China which could be used against Japanese shipping and in raids on Japan itself. He wrote, "I have always advocated the development of China as a base for the sup-port of our Pacific advances. . . . It is mandatory that we make every effort to increase the flow of supplies into China. This can only be done by increasing the air tonnage or by opening a road through Burma. Our occupation of Myitkyina will enable us immediately to in-crease the air-lift to China by providing an intermediate air-transport base as well as by increasing the protection of the air route. . . . The continued build-up of Japanese strength in Burma requires us to under-take the most aggressive action within our power to retain the initiative and prevent them from launching an offensive that may carry them over the borders into India. . . . I most urgently hope therefore that you back to the maximum a vigorous and immediate campaign in Upper Burma." *

Churchill, on the other hand, felt that North Burma was the worst place to fight the Japanese. The country was "the most forbidding fighting country imaginable" and land advances had to be under-taken with tenuous lines of communications. He preferred "to contain the Japanese in Burma, and break into or through the great arc of islands forming the outer fringe of the Dutch East Indies . . . but we never succeeded in deflecting the Americans from their purpose." *

Against these conflicting viewpoints, one should keep in mind that all parties still believed the Japanese homeland would have to be in-vaded. The atomic bomb was not then a part of the strategic planning.

To General Slim, commanding the 14th Army, fell the task of driv-ing the Japanese back in North Burma. In the following selection, he

*Closing the Ring, pp. 561, 562. Houghton Mifflin. Copyright 1951 by Houghton Mifflin Co.

recounts his opinion of the strategy, and the story of part of the resulting campaign, dealing specifically with Stilwell's drive on Myitkyina
and Orde Wingate's Chindits operation behind the Japanese lines.

THE NORTHERN FRONT IN BURMA*

by Field Marshal The Viscount William Slim

The northern was the most isolated of the Burma
fronts. To reach it by rail—there was no road—you left
Dimapur and continued your seemingly interminable journey through the tea-garden area of Assam. As you crept
northward, it was impossible to avoid a growing feeling of
loneliness, which even the sight of the increasingly busy airfields of the Hump route, strung along the line, failed to dissipate. At last Tinsukia, the junction for the Assam oil
fields, was reached, and your train turned wearily into the
branch for Ledo. Ledo, in December 1943, seemed rather
like the end of the world. Instead, it was the start of the road
to China, the road that, if it ever were built, would replace
the one from Rangoon, so effectively closed in early 1942.

Many people at this time, Americans no less than British
doubted if the Ledo road *could* be built. They doubted if
the Chinese divisions would ever be able to drive back the
Japanese and clear the route. They doubted if the Ledo
railway would carry and maintain the troops, labour, equipment, and material required. They doubted if any road
builders could overcome the monsoon climate combined
with the extreme difficulty of the terrain. Many, even of
those who believed it possible, did not think that the Ledo
road would ever repay the expenditure in men and resources that would have to be devoted to it. Indeed, at this
time Stilwell was almost alone in his faith that, not only
could the road be built, but that it would be the most potent

*Condensed from *Defeat into Victory*, Chapter 12.

BURMA / 1944–1945

INDIA

IMPHAL

MOGAUNG

MYETKYINA

LEDO
ROAD

BLACK POOL
BLOCK
MAY 19,
1944

R. CHINDWIN

BHAMO

OLD BURMA
ROAD TO
KUNMING

R. IRRAWADDY

LASHIO

MANDALAY

IV CORPS

BURMA

XXXIII
ADVANCE
CORPS

TOUNGOO

SIAM

PEGU

RANGOON

RANGOON
LANDING
MAY 2, 1945

26 DIVISION

winning factor in the war against Japan. His vision, as he expounded it to me, was of an American-trained and -equipped Chinese force, of some thirty divisions to begin with, maintained, except for what was available in China, by the road from Ledo. This new model army under his command would drive through China to the sea and then with the American Navy strike at Japan itself. I did not hold two articles of his faith. I doubted the overwhelming war-winning value of this road, and, in any case, I believed it was starting from the wrong place. The American amphibious strategy in the Pacific of hopping from island to island would, I was sure, bring much quicker results than an overland advance across Asia with a Chinese army yet to be formed. In any case, if the road was to be really effective, its feeder railway should start from Rangoon, not Calcutta. If it had been left to me, on military grounds, I would have used the immense resources required for this road, not to build a new highway to China, but to bring forward the largest possible combat forces to destroy the Japanese army in Burma. Once that was accomplished, the old route to China would be open; over it would flow a much greater tonnage than could ever come via Ledo, and the Allied forces in Burma would be available for use elsewhere.

However, it was not for me to decide the merits or demerits of the Ledo road. The Anglo-American Combined Chiefs of Staff had told Admiral Mountbatten [1] to make the road, and so, in every way possible, even to devoting half the total transport lift and large British ground forces to the northern front, we in Fourteenth Army got down to helping Stilwell in what we knew was a tough assignment.

Before he came under my operational control, Stilwell had received orders from Admiral Mountbatten to occupy northern Burma up to the Mogaung-Myitkyina area, so as to cover the building of the road, and to increase the safety of the air route to China. The Chinese 22d and 38th Divisions had already reached Ledo from India, and their 30th Division with a three-battalion American regiment was to follow. In addition Stilwell had a Chinese light tank group,

[1] British Commander in the Far East.—Ed. note.

an irregular force of American-officered Kachin tribesmen, and I had given him the Fort Hertz detachment of a battalion of Burma Rifles with local levies. For air support he had the considerable American Northern Sector Air Force. The whole of this Chinese-American-British force was known, rather clumsily, as Northern Combat Area Command. Further, Wingate's Special Force of several brigades was to be put, mainly by air, in rear of the Japanese opposing Stilwell to cut their communications.

By February 1 the 38th Chinese Division had, after a series of small actions, occupied Thipha Ga, while a regiment of the 22d Division, moving wide on the right flank, cleared the Japanese from the Taro Valley, which lay on the east bank of the Chindwin River, separated from the Ledo road in the Hukawng Valley by a range of rugged jungle hills. This was the 22d Division's entry into the campaign, and they did well. In all these actions Stilwell had kept a close hand on the Chinese troops, steadying them when they faltered, prodding them when they hesitated, even finding their battalions for them himself when they lost them. He was one of the Allied commanders who had learned in the hard school of the 1942 retreat. His tactics were to press the Japanese frontally while the real attacks came in through the jungle from the flank, with probably a road block well behind the enemy. In this way, by a series of hooks around and behind the Japanese, he pushed forward. He also was an advocate of the sledge hammer to crack a walnut at this stage. He saw to it that if a Japanese company was to be liquidated, it was attacked by a Chinese regiment.

At the beginning of March I visited Stilwell at Thipha Ga just as he was launching up to then his biggest attack for the capture of Maingkwan, a large village and the capital of the Hukawng Valley. Besides his two Chinese divisions, he now had with him the American Long-Range Penetration Regiment. Stilwell had changed its original commander for Brigadier General Merrill, whom I had known well and liked. After him, the regiment was christened "Merrill's Marauders." Merrill was a fine, courageous leader who inspired confidence, and I congratulated myself that

I had restrained my Gurkha orderly, that day in 1942, when he would have tommy-gunned a jeepload of men wearing unfamiliar helmets. If he had, the Marauders would have had another commander, and that would have been a pity.

The fly-in of Wingate's Special [2] Force, due to commence on March 5, was intended primarily to help the American-Chinese advance, and I wanted to make sure he was completely familiar with the final arrangements.

Stilwell was always rather prickly about Wingate's force. To begin with, Mountbatten and Wingate between them had persuaded the American Chiefs of Staff to send United States troops, even if only a regiment, to the Burma front, when he himself had failed to get them. Further, he felt passionately that all American troops in the theatre should be under his direct command, and had been angered when they were allotted to Wingate. Stilwell had pressed for them to be transferred to him, and confessed quite frankly to me that he had been very surprised when Mountbatten yielded to his request. Nevertheless, he did not seem particularly grateful to the Supreme Commander and some bitterness remained. Nor did he approve of Wingate's long-range penetration methods; he preferred the short-hook tactics.

On the morning of Sunday, March 5, I circled the landing ground at Hailakandi. Below me, at the end of the wide brown air strip, was parked a great flock of squat, clumsy gliders, their square wing tips almost touching; around the edges of the field stood the more graceful Dakotas that were to lift them into the sky. Men swarmed about the aircraft, loading them, laying out towropes, leading mules,

[2] Wingate's Long-Range Penetration Force was known as the Chindits. Gen. Slim describes it as "the old cavalry raid on enemy communications which, to be effective . . . must be made in tactical coordination with a main attack elsewhere." Gen. Wavell had made Wingate commander of all guerrilla operations in Burma in early 1942. In early 1943, Wingate had conducted his first raid into Burma, penetrating some 200 miles behind Japanese lines, but according to Gen. Slim "gave little tangible return for the losses it had suffered and the resources absorbed."—Ed. note.

humping packs, and moving endlessly in dusty columns, for all the world like busy ants around captive moths.

I landed and met Wingate at his temporary headquarters near the air strip. Everything was going well. There had been no serious hitch in the assembly or preparation for the fly-in, which was due to begin at dusk that evening. For some days previously our diversionary air attacks had been almost continuous on Japanese airfields and communication centres to keep his air force occupied. Meanwhile, ostentatious air reconnaissances over the Mandalay district had been carried out in the hope of convincing the enemy that any airborne expedition would be directed against that area. The attacks on airfields were useful in keeping Japanese aircraft out of the sky, but the false reconnaissances, as far as I ever discovered, had little effect.

Just a month earlier, on February 4, Stratemeyer, the American commander of the Eastern Air Command, and I had issued a joint directive to Wingate and Cochrane, the American commander of No. 1 Air Commando. In this, Wingate's force was ordered to march and fly in to the Rail Indaw area (*Rail* Indaw to distinguish it from another Indaw not on the Mandalay-Myitkyina railway), and from there to operate under direct command of Fourteenth Army, with the objects of:

(1) Helping the advance of Stilwell's Ledo force on Myitkyina by cutting the communications of the Japanese 18th Division, harassing its rear, and preventing its reinforcement.

(2) Creating a favourable situation for the Yunnan Chinese forces to cross the Salween and enter Burma.

(3) Inflicting the greatest possible damage and confusion on the enemy in North Burma.

The tactical plan for getting the force into position behind the enemy was based on four assembly places:

"Aberdeen," 27 miles northwest of Indaw.
"Piccadilly," 40 miles northeast of Indaw.
"Broadway," 35 miles east-northeast of Indaw.
"Chowringhee," 35 miles east of Indaw.

These places were all away from roads and uninhabited. They were selected because there was enough flat ground to make the building of an air strip possible in a short time and because there was water in the immediate vicinity. They were, in fact, fancy names written on the map within striking distance of Indaw.

It was intended that in the first wave 16 Brigade should march to Aberdeen, 77 Brigade fly in two halves to Piccadilly and Broadway, and 111 Brigade land at Chowringhee. The remaining three brigades, 14, 23, and 3 West African, were to be held for the second wave, which it was expected would be required to relieve the first in two or three months.

As the afternoon wore on the atmosphere of excitement and suspense at Hailakandi grew—the old, familiar feeling of waiting to go over the top, intensified by the strangeness and magnitude of this operation. Everyone, even the mules, moved about calmly, quietly, and purposefully. Except perhaps for those patient beasts, it was, all the same, obvious that everyone realized that what was, up to this time, the biggest and most hazardous airborne operation of the war was about to begin.

During the morning the gliders had been loaded with supplies, ammunition, engineer equipment, signalling stores, and men's kits. In the late afternoon the first wave, 77 Brigade Headquarters, the leading British and Gurkha infantry, and a small detachment of American airfield engineers emplaned. Each Dakota was to take two gliders. This was a heavy load, and, as far as I know, never before had these aircraft towed more than one. There had been a clash of opinion among the airmen themselves on its practicability. Cochrane, in charge of the gliders, was confident it could be done; Old, whose Combat Cargo planes would provide the tugs, maintained it was unsound. Various airmen, British and American, took sides, and argument was heated. Eventually, after experiments, Wingate agreed with Cochrane, and then Baldwin and I accepted the double tow. Now as I watched the last preparations I was assailed by no doubts on that score. The Dakotas taxied into position. The towropes were fixed. Everyone was very quiet as the roar of engines died down and we waited for zero hour.

I was standing on the air strip with Wingate, Baldwin, and one or two more, when we saw a jeep driving furiously toward us. A couple of American airmen jumped out and confronted us with an air photograph, still wet from the developing tent. It was a picture of Piccadilly landing ground, taken two hours previously. It showed almost the whole level space, on which the gliders were to land that night, obstructed by great tree trunks. It would be impossible to put down even one glider safely. To avoid suspicion no aircraft had reconnoitered the landing grounds for some days before the fly-in, so this photo was a complete shock to us. We looked at one another in dismay.

Wingate, though obviously feeling the mounting strain, had been quiet and controlled. Now, not unnaturally perhaps, he became very moved. His immediate reaction was to declare emphatically to me that the whole plan had been betrayed—probably by the Chinese—and that it would be dangerous to go on with it. I asked if Broadway and Chowringhee, the other proposed landing places, had been photographed at the same time. I was told they had been, and that both appeared vacant and unobstructed.

Wingate was now in a very emotional state, and to avoid discussion with him before an audience, I drew him on one side. I said I did not think the Chinese had betrayed him as they certainly had no knowledge of actual landing grounds, or, as far as I knew, of the operation at all; but he reiterated that someone had betrayed the plan and that the fly-in should be cancelled. I pointed out that only one of the three landing grounds had been obstructed, and that it was the one which he had used in 1943 and of which a picture with a Dakota on it had appeared in an American magazine. We knew the Japanese were nervous of air landing and were blocking many possible landing sites in North and Central Burma; what more likely than that they should include a known one we had already used, such as Piccadilly? He replied that, even if Broadway and Chowringhee were not physically obstructed, it was most probable that Japanese troops were concealed in the surrounding jungle ready to destroy our gliders as they landed. With great feeling he said it would be "murder." I told him I doubted if these places were ambushed. Had the Japanese known of the plan I was sure they would either have ambushed or obstructed all three landing grounds. Wingate was by now calmer and much more in control of himself. After thinking for a moment, he said there would be great risk. I agreed. He paused, then looked at me. "The responsibility is yours," he said.

I knew it was. Not for the first time I felt the weight of decision crushing in on me with an almost physical pressure. The gliders, if they were to take off that night, must do so within the hour. There was no time for prolonged inquiry or discussion. On my answer would depend not only the possibility of a disaster with wide implications on the whole Burma campaign and beyond, but the lives of these splendid men, tense and waiting in and around their aircraft. At that moment I would have given a great deal if Wingate or anybody else could have relieved me of the duty of decision. But that is a burden the commander himself must bear.

I knew that if I canceled the fly-in or even postponed it, when the men were keyed to the highest pitch, there would be a terrible reaction; we would never get their morale to the same peak again. The whole plan of campaign, too, would be thrown out. I had promised Stilwell we would cut the communications of the enemy opposing him, and he was relying on our doing it. I had to consider also that one Chindit brigade had already marched into the area; we could hardly desert it. I was, in addition, very nervous that if we kept the aircraft crowded on the airfields as they were, the Japanese would discover them, with disastrous consequences. I knew at this time that a major Japanese offensive was about to break on the Assam front, and I calculated on Wingate's operation to confuse and hamper it. Above all, somehow I did not believe that the Japanese knew of our plan or that the obstruction of Piccadilly was evidence that they did. There was a risk, a grave risk, but not a certainty of disaster. "The operation will go on," I said.[8]

[8] In an account of this incident written shortly afterward, but which I did not see until after his death, Wingate reversed his role and mine. In it he stated that he used these arguments to

Wingate accepted my decision with, I think, relief. He had by now recovered from his first shock and had realized that the obstruction of one landing site need not hold all the implications he had imagined. We walked back to the group of officers and, with Baldwin's concurrence, I announced that the fly-in would proceed, adding that as Piccadilly was obviously out, it was for Wingate as the tactical commander to decide what changes should be made. He stated the case for continuing the operation clearly and calmly, and directed that the troops allotted to Piccadilly were to be diverted to Chowringhee. Although this was strictly Wingate's business and not mine, I very much doubted the wisdom of this. Chowringhee was on the east of the Irrawaddy; the railway and road to be cut were on the west. Before the troops could be effective, therefore, they had to cross the river, and I questioned if this could be done as quickly or as easily as Wingate thought. I asked Calvert, the commander of 77 Brigade, and I found him strongly against Chowringhee. Cochrane also opposed it for the very sound reason that the layout there was quite different from Piccadilly and Broadway and there was little time to rebrief pilots. Baldwin, who as commander of the Third Tactical Air Force, had the over-all responsibility for the air side of the operation, was emphatic that Chowringhee could not be used by Piccadilly air crews, and that settled it. Wingate saw the force of these opinions and accepted that the fly-in would take place as originally planned, except that the troops for Piccadilly would go to Broadway.

Cochrane collected the Piccadilly Dakota and glider pilots, whose destination was now changed, to rebrief them. Curious to see how he would break the news of the alteration and a little anxious lest so obvious a hitch at the start

urge that the fly-in should go on and that I accepted them and agreed. That is not my recollection of his first reactions, nor in accordance with my notes made nearer the time. In any case, the point is of little consequence as whether Wingate persuaded me, or I him, the responsibility for ordering the operation to continue and for all its consequences could not be his, but must be Baldwin's and mine.

might have a rather depressing effect of them, I followed to listen. Cochrane sprang on to the bonnet of a jeep. "Say, fellers," he announced, "we've got a better place to go to!"

The leading Dakota, with its two gliders trailing behind, roared down the runway just after six o'clock, only a few minutes behind scheduled time. The moment one was clear the next followed at about half-a-minute intervals. The gliders took the air first, one or two wobbling nervously before they took station behind, and a little above, the towing aircraft. More than once I feared a Dakota would overrun the strip before the gliders were up, but all took off safely and began the long climb to gain height to cross the hills. The darkening sky was full of these queer triangles of aircraft labouring slowly higher and higher into the distance. Eventually even the drone of engines faded and we were left waiting.

And an unpleasant wait it was. Sixty-one gliders had set off. The full complement for Broadway and Piccadilly had been eighty, but we had agreed that sixty was about the most we could hope to land on one strip in the hours of darkness, so the rest had been held back. I sat in the control tent, at the end of the air strip, to which all messages and signals came. At the rough table with its field telephones was Tullock, Wingate's chief staff officer, who proved himself quick, reliable, and cool in crisis, and Rome, another admirable staff officer. As the moon came up, in spite of hurricane lanterns and one electric lamp, it was almost lighter outside than within. There was a pause. Then came a report of red flares, fired from the air a few miles away. That meant a tow in distress—ominous if difficulties were beginning so soon. I took a turn outside and thought I saw a red Very light fired high up in the distance. I returned to the tent to find more rumours of gliders down or tows returning before they had crossed our lines. Not so good. Then another long wait. We looked at our watches. The leading aircraft should be over Broadway now with the gliders going in. We ought to get the first wireless message any minute. Still it did not come. Wingate prowled in and out, speaking to no one, his eyes smouldering in a pallid face. Tullock sat calmly at the phones. A garbled report over the telephone from another airfield told us that a tow pilot had seen what looked like firing on the Broadway strip. It was the time when doubts grow strongest and fears loom largest. Then, just after four o'clock in the morning, the first signal from Broadway, sent by Calvert, came in plain language, brief, mutilated, but conveying its message of disaster clearly enough—"Soya Link." The name of the most disliked article in the rations had been chosen in grim humour as the code word for failure. So the Japanese *had* ambushed Broadway! Wingate was right and I had been wrong. He gave me one long, bitter look and walked away. I had no answer for him.

Then more signals, broken, hard to decipher, but gradually making the picture clearer. Gliders had crashed, men had been killed, there were injured and dying lying where they had been dragged to the edge of the strip—but there was no enemy. There had been no ambush. A great weight lifted from me as I realized that this was going to be like every other attack, neither so good nor so bad as the first reports of excited men would have you believe. We had to recall the last flight, as Broadway was too obstructed by smashed gliders to accept them. The situation was still far from clear to us as I left the control tent after dawn, but I was confident that if only the Japanese did not locate them for the next twelve hours, the Chindits would have the strip ready for reinforcements by nightfall.

Of the sixty-one gliders dispatched only thirty-five reached Broadway. The airmen who said that one Dakota could not tow two gliders had been right. In practice the steep climb to cross the mountains, so close to the start, put too great a drag on the nylon ropes and many parted. It also caused overheating in the aircraft engines and unexpected fuel consumption, with dire results. Many gliders and a few aircraft force landed, some in our territory, nine in Japanese. There was a brisk battle near Imphal between the Chindits of a crashed glider, convinced they were behind the enemy lines and determined to sell their lives dearly, and our own troops rushing to their rescue. Gliders by chance came down near a Japanese divisional headquarters and others beside a regimental headquarters far from

Broadway. These landings confused the enemy as to our intentions and led to a general alert for gliders and parachutists through all his units.

Long afterward we discovered that it was not the Japanese who had obstructed Piccadilly but Burmese tree fellers, who had, in the course of their work, dragged teak logs out of the jungle to dry in the clearing. The firing reported at Broadway was a nervous burst from a shaken glider pilot.

Even without the enemy, that night at Broadway was tragic and macabre enough. One or two of the leading gliders, circling down to a half-seen gap in the jungle, had crashed on landing. The ground-control equipment and its crew were in a glider that failed to arrive so that, until a makeshift control could be improvised, it was impossible to time landings. Some gliders hurtled into the wrecks, others ran off the strip to smash into the trees or were somersaulted to ruin by uneven ground concealed under the grass. Twenty-three men were killed and many injured, but more than four hundred, with some stores, and Calvert, the brigade commander, landed intact. Most of the engineering equipment did not arrive, but the small party of American engineers, helped by every man who could be spared from patrolling, set to work with what tools they could muster to drag the wreckage clear and prepare the ground. Never have men worked harder, and by evening a strip was fit—but only just fit—to take a Dakota.

Next night the fly-in continued. Fifty-five Dakotas landed at Broadway and the first flights reached Chowringhee, where also there was no sign of enemy. By March 11 the whole of Calvert's 77 Brigade and half Lentaigne's 111 Brigade were at Broadway. Lentaigne's Brigade Headquarters and the other half with "Dah-force," a body of Kachins with British officers for use in raising the local tribes, were safely at Chowringhee. Between March 5 and 10 one hundred glider and almost six hundred Dakota sorties flew in nine thousand troops and eleven hundred animals. In addition, Ferguson's 16 Brigade had reached Aberdeen after its long march, so that Wingate now had nearly twelve thousand troops well placed, as he put it, "in the enemy's guts."

No sooner had these decisions been taken than Special

Force suffered a tragic loss. Wingate, flying from Imphal to his new headquarters at Lalaghat in a Mitchell bomber, crashed by night in the wild tangle of hills west of Imphal. He, and all with him, were instantly killed. The cause of the accident cannot be definitely stated. The wreckage was eventually found on the reverse side of a ridge, so it was unlikely that the aircraft had flown into the hill. The most probable explanation is that it had suddenly entered one of those local storms of extreme turbulence so frequent in the area. These were difficult to avoid at night, and once in them an aeroplane might be flung out of control or even have its wings torn off.

I was at Comilla when the signal came in that Wingate was missing. As the hours passed and no news of any sort arrived, gloom descended upon us. We could ill spare him at the start of his greatest attempt. The immediate sense of loss that struck, like a blow, even those who had differed most from him—and I was not one of these—was a measure of the impact he had made. He had stirred up everyone with whom he had come in contact. With him, contact had too often been collision, for few could meet so stark a character without being either violently attracted or repelled. To most he was either prophet or adventurer. Very few could regard him dispassionately; nor did he care to be so regarded. I once likened him to Peter the Hermit preaching his crusade. I am sure that many of the knights and princes that Peter so fiercely exhorted did not like him very much—but they went crusading all the same. The trouble was, I think, that Wingate regarded *himself* as a prophet, and that always leads to a single centredness that verges on fanaticism, with all its faults. Yet had he not done so, his leadership could not have been so dynamic, nor his personal magnetism so striking.

While all this was going on the Chindits had not slackened their activity. Ferguson's 16 Brigade from Aberdeen attempted to seize Rail Indaw by surprise, but was compelled to abandon the attempt and fall back. Exhausted by this abortive effort after their long march, there was nothing for it but to fly them out. However, Lentaigne still had three mobile brigades, considerable numbers of "stronghold" troops, and the Japanese communications both road and rail to their 18th Division were effectively cut. Meanwhile, Stilwell to the north of them had been pushing his Chinese southward.

While Stilwell struck for Myitkyina, the Chindits at Blackpool [4] had continued to block Japanese communications, and 111 Brigade with the Kachin Irregulars closed on Myitkyina. It was obvious that, as they thus approached one another, daily tactical co-ordination between Stilwell's and Lentaigne's forces was becoming urgent. On May 17 I therefore placed Special Force under Stilwell's direct orders. He now had an American brigade, five Chinese divisions, three mobile Chindit brigades, and their stronghold troops, a great superiority over the battered Japanese 18th Division, Take Force, and the odds and ends of their 56th Division pulled in from the quiet Yunnan front.

Then that front, so quiescent for two years, sprang into violent activity. On the night of May 10-11, forty thousand Chinese crossed the Salween on a two hundred mile front at three points between Hpimaw and Kunlong. Within a few days twelve Chinese divisions, seventy-two thousand men, under General Wei Li Huang, were on the west bank. The Japanese 56th Division, about twelve thousand strong, outnumbered and without air support, fought skillfully and tenaciously to hold the mountain passes against them. During May and early June the Japanese were pushed slowly back toward Lungling, but a battalion and some detachments were surrounded in Tengchung. The garrison held out with fanatical valour until September 21, when the town fell to assault and every Japanese in it died.

The battle around Lungling between the Japanese 56th Division and six Chinese divisions raged until the end of August. The Japanese Lieutenant-General Matsuyama with great skill and resolution defeated every attempt at encirclement and kept open his communications to the south. He had one stroke of luck. A Chinese plane, mistaking Tengchung for a friendly airfield, landed there with three Chinese staff officers, carrying not only complete details of the of-

---

[4] A stronghold-block established in May.—Ed. note.

fensive but the new cipher of their army. Matsuyama was, after that, the only commander in Burma who had reliable advanced information of his enemy's intentions and moves. He made good use of it. The Japanese hurried up reinforcements and then, with the bulk of their 2d Division and a regiment of their 49th, put in a fierce counterattack which for a time stopped the Chinese dead and reduced their subsequent advance to a crawl. The Chinese losses were heavy, not only from disease and privation, but because their training, armament, and leadership, which were much below those of Stilwell's troops, made them no match for the Japanese. Nor were their losses being replaced from China. Wei Li Huang had no easy task. His only real advantages were numbers and air support from American fighters and medium bombers which lost much of its value in these wild mountains.

Still, this mass, pressing in on their right flank, however slowly it moved, was a menace to the Japanese front in North Burma. Indeed, even toward the end of May their whole position there was rapidly becoming precarious. The 18th Division was beginning to crack. Stilwell's main force was closing in on Kamaing. In addition to the large Chinese force attacking Myitkyina, the Fort Hertz detachment was approaching from Sumprabum and Morrisforce was operating against the town from the east of the Irrawaddy. The fall of Myitkyina, although it no longer seemed imminent, could be only a matter of time.

A brigade of Lentaigne's Special Force held Blackpool, near Hopin, against constant attack for three weeks, cutting the enemy's main line of communication at a critical time. The Japanese concentrated most of Take Force, including a regiment of the 53d Division, against the Chindits here and bombarded them heavily with field and medium artillery. Worst of all, they established anti-aircraft guns in range of the landing ground. In spite of that, the British and American Dakota pilots, unable to land as the strip was under direct fire, continued to drop their loads, but supply was intermittent and there was no evacuation of wounded. Then the weather broke badly and, as the Japanese closed in, so did the clouds. Air supply and air support both ceased. On May 25 the Chindits, carrying their wounded, broke out of Blackpool and plodded northwest toward the Indawgyi Lake around which other columns of Lentaigne's men were collecting. The rain had made it impossible to keep earth air strips in action and there seemed little hope of getting out the increasing number of sick and wounded that were being laboriously brought in by their comrades. The R.A.F. found the answer in two Sunderland flying boats, which, as a change from submarine hunting in the Indian Ocean, flew from Colombo to this fifteen-by-five miles stretch of water in the heart of Burma. Working throughout some of the worst monsoon weather, they flew out nearly six hundred casualties.

During the first weeks of June Stilwell's Chinese had kept up their drive down the Mogaung Valley. Fighting with increasing confidence and boldness, they destroyed the Japanese who tried to bar their way at Shaduzup and Laban. Then on June 16 the Chinese 22d Division took Kamaing, and on the 20th Calvert's 77 Brigade of Lentaigne's force stormed Mogaung, just ahead of the Chinese 38th Division coming from the north. By this time, too, the great battles around Imphal had definitely turned against the Japanese. Such reinforcements as he could scrape up, Kawabe, the enemy commander in chief, was sending there to cover his withdrawal. His two northern fronts were crumbling and there was little he could do to bolster them up. He was by now plainly reduced to fighting merely a delaying campaign in North Burma.

Negotiations had been going on between Admiral Mountbatten and Generalissimo Chiang Kai-shek for Wei Li Huang's Yunnan armies to come under Southeast Asia Command when they crossed the Burma border. As seemed inevitable, however, where Chinese were concerned, there was considerable mystification about the command of these troops. To begin with, the Sino-Burmese frontier was not marked in these outlandish hills. British maps showed it in one place, the Chinese several miles farther west. In any case, whatever the line, it was likely that at times some parts of the same Chinese formation would be on each side of it—a hopeless complication. The Generalissimo kept a tight hand on these Yunnan troops, and Stilwell's control, exercised through an American mission, was, I gathered from him, pretty nebulous. Still, whether he commanded them or not, Stilwell's own force now amounted to about seven divisions and the agreement had been that when Kamaing was taken he should pass from my command. It was only logical to regard him as an army commander on the same footing as myself and place him, like me, under Eleventh Army Group, but once again Stilwell refused to serve under General Giffard. He insisted on coming directly under Admiral Mountbatten, although there was no organization at Southeast Asia Command Headquarters to deal direct with an army. When I visited Stilwell on his passing from my command he said, with his frosty twinkle, "Well, General, I've been a good subordinate to you. I've obeyed all your orders!" That was true enough, but so was my retort, "Yes, you old devil, but only because the few I did give you were the ones you wanted!"

The long-drawn-out siege of Myitkyina was a great disappointment to Stilwell, and it was at this period that he really lived up to his nickname, Vinegar Joe. He was extremely caustic about his unfortunate American commanders, accusing them of not fighting, and of killing the same Japanese over and over again in their reports. He was equally bitter against the Chindits, complaining that they did not obey his orders, had abandoned the block at Hopin unnecessarily, and had thus let strong Japanese reinforcements into the Kamaing-Myitkyina area. He asked for British parachute troops to restore the situation, but, apart from the fact that the small parachute formation available was already in the thick of the fighting at Imphal and could not have been extricated, there was no doubt he took a much too alarmist view of the position on his front. Lentaigne retaliated to the accusations hurled at him by complaining that Stilwell was demanding the impossible and that, by continually setting simultaneous tasks for all his columns, was making it impossible to give any part of his force the time essential for reorganization and evacuation of casualties without which they could not operate effectively. Relations between the two commanders became strained, and finally, at the end of May, Stilwell asked Admiral Mountbatten to withdraw Special Force. As a result, early in June, although I was no longer in command of this front, I was sent to N.C.A.C. to adjudicate between Stilwell and Lentaigne and to attempt to heal the breach.

I found Stilwell bitter and Lentaigne indignant, both obviously and very understandably suffering from prolonged strain. One of the troubles was that Stilwell, in his then mood, would not meet Lentaigne and really discuss things with him. There was too much of the Siege of Troy atmosphere, with commanders sulking in their tents. However, with me, Stilwell, after one or two outbursts, was reasonable and explained his charges against the Chindits. I had already seen Lentaigne and heard his version. Stilwell's orders on the face of it were sound enough and it was quite obvious that the Chindits had not carried out all of them. It was equally clear that in their present state of exhaustion, after the casualties they had suffered and in the rain which made movement so difficult, unless given some chance of reorganization they were physically incapable of doing so. Stilwell replied to this by pointing to his Marauders who, he said, were still operating effectively. Without belittling their efforts, I pointed out that Lentaigne's men had endured the strain of being actually behind the enemy's lines for longer periods than Merrill's and that their incidence of battle casualties, as compared with sick, was much higher. As far as his complaints against Morrisforce on the east of the river were concerned, I told him I thought it was a bit hard to reproach a few hundred men for not doing what thirty thousand had failed to do on the other bank. Finally, looking at me over the top of his glasses, he said, "What do you want me to do?" I said, "See Lentaigne, talk things over with him, give his columns a chance to get out their casualties and reorganize, and keep his force on until Myitkyina falls." He agreed, and I returned to headquarters.

I had hoped that Myitkyina would fall by the middle of June, but at the end of the month it was still apparently as far from capture as ever. It then became obvious that the remains of Special Force were not fit to continue operating throughout the monsoon. Admiral Mountbatten himself this time visited Stilwell and an arrangement was made by which two of Lentaigne's brigades that had been longest in the field should be medically examined and all unfit men flown out at once—the remainder to operate for a short time further and then follow them. The last of Special Force would remain until the 36th British Division, which was refitting at Shillong in Assam, began to come into Stilwell's command, when they, too, would be taken out.

Actually it would have been wiser to take the whole of the Chindits out then; they had shot their bolt. So, too, for that matter had the Marauders, who a little later packed in completely. Both forces, Chindits and Marauders, had been subjected to intense strain, both had unwisely been promised that their ordeal would be short, and both were asked to do more than was possible.

On the afternoon of August 3, after a siege of two and a half months, Myitkyina fell. Some days before Mizukami, the Japanese commander, had ordered what was left of the garrison to break out. He had then committed suicide. Maruyama, the original commander, had again taken over, and under his leadership the Japanese attempted to escape by night on rafts down the river. Most of them were intercepted and killed, but Maruyama himself and a couple of hundred did get away.

The capture of Myitkyina, so long delayed, marked the complete success of the first stage of Stilwell's campaign. It was also the largest seizure of enemy-held territory that had yet occurred. Throughout the operations on the northern front the Allied forces, Chinese, British, and American, had been vastly superior to the Japanese on the ground and in the air, even without including the Chinese Yunnan armies. This superiority was achieved only because the main Japanese forces were held locked in the vital Imphal battle, and any reinforcements they could rake up were fed into that furnace. The Japanese had the advantage of position and communications, but even their desperate courage and defensive skill could not hold back such a numerical preponderance. Yet, when all was said and done, the success of this northern offensive was in the main owing to the Ledo Chinese divisions—and that was Stilwell.

Behind the Japanese Lines

A dissenting opinion of "Old Vinegar Joe" Stilwell is expressed in the following selection by Major John Masters who commanded the Chindits III Brigade at the Blackpool Block. He received orders in late April to move out of the Aberdeen stronghold, where the Chindits had operated behind the Japanese lines since March, move north toward Stilwell's forces, and establish a block north of Hopin.

Masters felt that setting up these stronghold-blocks were "a waste of the Chindits' greatest asset, jungle mobility." Further, the block would bring him too close to the Jap lines where their "forward commanders" could give the Chindits a rough time. They had been in action a number of weeks and furthermore, as he says, they were primarily a raiding group, not intended for permanent defense fighting.

On May 7th, Masters chose the location of the block in a complex of ridges in view of the village of Namkwin. It was necessary to select a terrain that not only could be defended against attack, but which also provided room for an air strip for the purpose of receiving supplies and additional arms, and big enough to handle the C-47 transport planes.

Just before dusk on the 7th, Masters marched his men into the block.

"First the brigade defense platoon and Burma Rifles under Macpherson, then myself and a small command group, then the two battalions, with main Brigade Headquarters sandwiched between them. As I reached the spine of the block site, a single, long burst of light automatic fire roared in the Namkwin Chaung below, or among the dark hills beyond. Dreadful surmises flashed through my mind. We had been seen reconnoitering this morning! An entire Japanese regiment lay concealed under our feet, ready to spring the ambush! The steady advance continued. No one ever did find out who fired that burst or why; but it was a Japanese, because the fire was the extra-quick light crackle of his gun, not our Brens.

"An hour after dark the tail of the brigade entered the block. Now, barring more serious disturbance, we had the night to dig ourselves in.

"No one slept that night. Sweating, weary, we dug our trenches, we stacked our ammunition, we worked, in hundreds, to level the paddy bunds for the gliders, which I had already requested for the following night. The gliders would bring bulldozers, wire, mortar ammunition, and extra tools. On the hill, in a northward facing re-entrant, Brigade Headquarters dug in. Briggs set up his radios, and established communication with Mokso Sakan, Air Base, and Force Headquarters. III Brigade's block was in position: code name—Blackpool." *

BLACKPOOL BLOCK

by Major John Masters

The Blackpool hill looked something like a sharp-spined animal, say a boar, lying with head down, forearms and legs extended sideways, and short tail outstretched. There were other minor features and cross ridges, but that is the general outline. The area between outstretched members constituted defilade (shelter) from enemy fire, from three directions in each case. The Namkwin curved in round the animal's left forefoot and then on past its nose. Our water point was sheltered just inside that forefoot. The airstrip extended along the animal's right side, the near edge about one hundred yards away from the tips of right forefoot and right hind leg. The tail joined another hill feature, which was not part of the block. To left and straight ahead were tangled hills, split by streams and gorges and folds, all heavily forested.

To every part of the position I gave a code name. I might have used the animal simile, calling the points Neck, Right Fore, and so on; but all my men were cricket players and

*Major John Masters, *The Road Past Mandalay*, pp. 225-226. Harper & Brothers.

I named the positions as on a cricket field—Cover Point, Midwicket, Deep, etc. I wondered whether these names might displease Mr. Churchill if he ever came to hear about them. He fulminated, rightly, about soldiers who lost their lives in operations called Lollipop; if they were to die, let them die in Crusade and Armageddon. But Tommy, who knew British troops better than I did, assured me that the small, familiar names gave comfort and familiarity to the foreign field, so they stuck. . . .

While the battalions filed into the block I gave orders for the evacuation of the animals. I had seen the effects of shell-fire on the beasts, which could not be adequately protected. Nor did I have room for them in Blackpool. I kept only twenty-five, for emergency, to go out with patrols, and to help carry stores up from the strip. The rest I sent back, under Macpherson, over the hills to the Mokso Sakan base.

At first light I went round the perimeter with the battalion commanders and arranged the junction points, exact siting of reserves and headquarters, mortar defensive fire and SOS tasks, and the usual other details. The rest of the day I spent between the paddy fields, which would become the airstrip, and the block itself. I had pushed strong detachments across the paddy into the dense thickets the other side, and toward Namkwin village. The mortars began to range on their defensive tasks. On the strip, under the merciless sun, two hundred men worked stripped to the waist, with rifles slung. Now, certainly, the Japanese knew we had arrived.

One by one the paddy bunds disappeared, and early in the afternoon Chesty Jennings told me that gliders could land on the northern half. If they landed too far down they would have a roller-coaster ascent up the five-foot bank, on which we had not made much impression, to the southern half of our split-level field.

The gliders must have been waiting, ready for take-off. The first arrived in the twilight. Our mortars put down smoke bombs in front of Namkwin—they could not quite reach it—while the glider circled out over the valley. I heard the stutter and pop of small-arms fire from Namkwin, and our Vickers machine guns began firing slowly at it. The glider came on in a long, graceful approach. He picked up his line, steadied, came on. Quarter of a mile short and two or three hundred feet up, his tail flicked and he dived vertically into the ground just the other side of the Namkwin Chaung. The heavy crash reverberated across the fields and echoed back from the block. Beside me Chesty spoke urgently to the pilot of the second tow plane, even then circling high above us. "Bring him in from the hills, right-hand turn!" Chesty said. They heard and obeyed. The second glider turned over the hills, and came in faster. He landed safely, followed soon by four more. (I sent out a patrol to the crashed glider. The three men in it were dead, but none appeared to have been hit by bullets. Chesty thought that the glider had stalled. I don't know, but I shall not forget the sudden lurch in my own stomach, and the bitten-off cry I gave as the tail went up and the nose straight down.)

The tired soldiers pushed the gliders to the edge of the strip and unloaded them. Within half an hour two small bulldozers and a grader began work, and Chesty had taken over one of the gliders as control tower for the field, and began to put down the strip lights. Working parties, some with mules, began the long slow carry of wire, ammunition, and tools up into the block.

All night and all next day work continued at a frenzied pace—inside the block, digging and wiring and laying of cable, ranging mortars, cutting of fields of fire—on the paddy, the tremendous task of making the five-foot bank into a slope which a loaded C-47 could take at 50 or 60 mph in the middle of its landing run.

About four o'clock in the afternoon I went down to the strip to make the final decision. Was it ready? We walked up and down the hump. "It's not good," Chesty said, "but it ought to do." He looked at me, "How urgent is it that they should come in tonight?"

"Very urgent," I said.

The Japanese had used tanks against the White City, and I wanted field guns in, quickly. Nor had we so far received anything like enough wire, mortar ammunition, or medical supplies. Even as I spoke a shell, coming from the north, sighed lazily over the block and burst on the hills behind us. It was soon followed by another, which fell short. "Desultory shelling," an innocent might have said; but it was ranging. The Japanese were preparing to attack.

I told Chesty not to conceal the state of the strip but to make it quite clear to the air forces that I expected them to make the attempt that night.

That night they came. The lead plane circled over the valley, a dark triangle in a dark sky. Chesty pulled the switch that lit the thinly spaced rim of lights round the field. A few rifle shots went off from Namkwin out there in the valley and the droning sound of the motors came closer. Chesty talked quietly to the pilot. His headlights stabbed out above the northern jungle.

"You're high," Chesty said sharply. "Put her down."

The pilot put her down, she hit just short of the step in the middle, bounced high over it, landed out of control, swung sharply left and roared off the runway into the bushes, making a long, loud noise. After a short interval flames rose. By their light I saw men jumping out of the door, and the silhouetted black figures of Cameronians, who were on close guard that side, running to help. A few seconds later the flames went out.

Chesty called down the second plane. This one landed well, rose twenty feet into the air as she went over the hump, bounced, and taxied to a halt off the runway at the far end, where control officers and unloading parties waited.

The third plane landed smoothly, but did not stop in time. The last paddy bund ripped off its undercarriage and it slid on its nose into the bushes. The fourth landed safely. I heard rifle fire from somewhere in the block behind me; it would have to wait.

By now I had another brigade major, "Baron" Henfry, late of the Indian Cavalry, retired to Kenya, returned to battle. Geoffrey Birt, whom I urgently needed as an engineer officer, had returned to his own job. At this moment he was at the far end of the strip with a squad of sappers, waiting to unload explosives and other engineer stores from the planes. He went to examine the third plane, the one that had lost its undercarriage.

It lay dark and deserted, doors open. He stooped to have a look under the wing. From immediately behind him some-one threw a grenade. Geoffrey saw it by the strip lights, and dived flat. The grenade exploded under the wing of the plane a few feet from him. The plane caught fire. A patrol of Cameronians rushed into the scrub, Tommy guns crackling. The fifth plane came in to land. But the burning C-47 lay across the wire that linked the field lights, and all the lights went out.

The plane now landing opened up its engines with a great roar and climbed away. The crew of plane No. 4, who had just opened the doors, saw No. 3 burst into flames, heard the grenade, the clatter of Tommy guns. They felt something must be amiss, and I don't blame them. Their doors slammed shut, the engines groaned, and the plane tore off down the strip in the dark. Before it reached high speed its wing caught the only other undamaged plane, No. 2. It slewed and skidded to a halt. That made two C-47s written off and two damaged as the price of the night's work. I could think of nothing but Beatty's remark at Jutland— "I don't know what's the matter with our bloody ships today. Steer two points closer to the enemy."

Chesty said, "The strip's not that bad. They're jittery."

"Can you get the lights fixed?"

"In half an hour. But there are only two more to come in for tonight and I think we'd better send them back. By tomorrow they'll know what asses they've made of themselves, and they'll do it right."

I didn't agree with Chesty's harsh judgment on his fellow airmen. It was a difficult strip and no pilot can feel encouraged, when lumbering in low over enemy territory in a C-47 to see the plane ahead of him burst into flames on landing. He can't know that there are no casualties or, if he does, guarantee that the same will apply to his own plane. But neither we nor 14th Army could afford to lose any more C-47s, and, after confirming that the planes already down contained some stores that I regarded as vital, I told Chesty the rest of the flight could go home.

A messenger arrived, panting: "The enemy are attacking the Deep, sir. Seems like probing, Colonel Thompson says." The Deep was the tip of the boar's nose, the extreme north point of the block. I climbed back into Blackpool, joined Tommy, and listened to a desultory battle going on down the ridge below. The shooting, never very strong, died down about one o'clock in the morning, and I returned to my headquarters.

Unless I were a bloody fool or, far worse to think about, unless the Japanese had changed their tactical doctrine, the night's attack was designed to locate our strong points and machine-gun posts in the Deep sector. That, in turn, meant that the Japanese would make a serious assault on the same sector the following night. The Japanese had not learned much, though, because Tommy knew his stuff perfectly well and only Bren guns and rifles, and mortars from the central keep, had fired. The queens of the battlefield, the machine guns, had kept quiet.

Before I got to sleep John Hedley limped in, his knee heavily bandaged. I had sent him out, with a small reconnoitering patrol, to find what use the enemy were making of the road and railway. He had found out (during four hours of darkness the enemy had used neither), but he had run into a similar Japanese patrol, killed some of them, and got a grenade splinter in the knee. Doc Whyte came and said, "He'll have to go out." I swore, and John pleaded; but he had to go.

The next morning the Japanese began harassing fire with 105-mm. guns from up the valley, the guns they had ranged in the previous afternoon. I had a lump of homogenized ham and egg halfway to my mouth when I heard the distant *boom boom* in the north. I dived, map in one hand and egg in the other, for the slit trench behind me. Baron Henfry was as quick; Pat Boyle (the new Intelligence officer) a shade slower. The shells whistled with a sudden rising shriek and burst ten feet away, one behind and one in front of the trench.

I returned to my study of the map, and my breakfast. The Baron said, "I think Pat's been hit, sir." (The Baron, a wise, amusing, and extraordinarily brave man, was some fifteen years older than I and so always very punctilious to pay me all the due forms of respect.) I looked down and saw that Pat, crouched in the bottom of the trench between the Baron and me, seemed to be unconscious. Actually, a shell splinter had creased his skull, temporarily paralyzing him but not depriving him of his senses. He has recorded as the most pungent memory of his life those moments when he lay in the bottom of the trench, with more shells bursting far and near, unable to speak or move, and hearing the Baron's remark and my reply, "Oh. Is he dead?" And then the Baron: "I think so."

Until then Pat had been pretty sure he was alive, but now he had doubts. It wasn't until the Baron's saturnine face approached his that he managed to roll his eyes. Even now, he says, he can feel the welling up of joy as he heard the Baron's surprised, "No, he's alive."

Before the shelling ended we suffered several casualties in the area immediately around my headquarters, including the artillery major who had arrived only ten hours earlier, in one of the C-47s, to command the troop of field guns that would soon follow. A shell splinter in the spine killed him instantly.

After a couple of hours the shelling stopped. I had not liked it. I remembered Willy outside Deir-es-Zor—"Wait till you've really been shelled." There would be worse to come. Meanwhile, now that I knew where the Japanese had put their artillery—in the north—I could at least move headquarters and the main dressing station from their northward facing re-entrant to a more sheltered spot. This I did at once. My new command post lay high up behind the boar's left armpit.

Like a flywheel, a noisy flywheel worked by a rackety motor, the battle gathered momentum.

An hour before dusk shelling began again, on the Deep and on the sectors supporting it to left and right. After dark the assaults began with screams and yells and the Very lights shining on bared teeth, pot helmets, long bayonets— then sudden darkness and the clatter of bullets. An hour later the C-47s came. They made their last turn exactly over the spot where I calculated the Japanese officer directing the attacks would have his command post. I did not go down to the strip that night but alternated between my own and Tommy's command post, the latter on the crest of the ridge overlooking the sectors being attacked. By two o'clock the attacks faded, having lasted seven hours, almost continuously.

I got a little sleep and at daylight went down to the strip. Work was going slowly as the men's exhaustion grew on them. The guns had come in, with the gunners, and the dozers were moving them into position. Tons of stores and ammunition had come, but there were not enough men, with the battle going on and reserve companies standing to their alarm posts, to do the carrying. Everyone had been up most of the night, and now we had to carry the stores up from the strip, put down more wire, dig some positions deeper, repair others, bury the dead, patrol the jungles, protect the airstrip. I decided to remove all three-inch mortars from the battalions' control and use them as a single battery, so that I could bring the fire of all eight of them down on any sector with no delay. That meant more cable laying, more ranging. The field guns, no sooner in position, began to range on Namkwin. I sent an urgent message for sound-ranging and flash-spotting equipment so that we could find and engage the enemy artillery. The monsoon was building, the sky was seldom clear, and our fighters had not come over as frequently as earlier. Partly this was due to the demands of Stilwell, in action north of Kamaing, and to the great Imphal battle, then reaching its climax. The result was the same—the enemy artillery grew increasingly bold, and used plenty of ammunition. They were probably sited close to ammunition dumps. They were certainly not short of shells.

We buried our dead, treated our wounded. Shelling continued. Baron Henfry chose the heaviest shelling to stroll around, thumb-stick in hand, talking to the soldiers.

Tommy reported that during the night assaults some Japanese had dug in ten to twenty yards from his wire, with snipers up trees, who could look almost directly into his forward weapon pits. Over a part of his sector no one could move without being shot at. I crept up with him to the ridge crest to look. Enemy field guns began firing on some of the rear positions. King's Own snipers lurked among shattered trees, Bren guns ready, watching the tattered forest below. Single shots rang out, Bren guns stammered, leaves whispered, boughs cracked. "Got him!" Another shot.

We crept back. The forward company would have a very unpleasant day, but would suffer few casualties as long as they sat low and tight. The snipers in the trees dominated them, but from higher up the ridge we dominated the snipers. All the same it was an unpleasant development and I ought to have foreseen it. At the White City the Japanese had withdrawn a considerable distance during the day. At that distance our mortars and—above all—our aircraft could get at them. They had learned the lesson, and now were leaning up against our wire, so close that to attack them with aircraft would be very dangerous to us.

Tommy arranged to relieve his forward troops with a reserve company after dark. Meanwhile two platoons, heavily supported, went out by the Water Point and attempted to clear the Deep sector, sweeping right-handed around the block, their right on our wire.

The attempt failed, the force losing several killed, including its leader, a really brave and excellent young officer. It was a bad moment for me, rather different from the permanent knowledge that war is a bloody business, because I had emphasized to Tommy that this was an important job and he had better send his best man. He had agreed. Those words are the aching refrain of command. They beat without cease in the mind and over the heart: *Send your best man....*

That evening, with more planes coming in and the monsoon liable to break any day, I knew I had to do something drastic to complete our defensive preparations. I had to have the absolute maximum possible number of men carrying up stores from the field. Eight mortars, going fast use up sixteen hundred pounds of ammunition in a minute, and there were hundreds of Bren guns, rifles, and Tommy guns also eating it up, besides grenades; and food; and now the field guns. The Japanese had, so far, concentrated on the Deep, and they had left detachments there to harass us during the hours of daylight. Surely they would continue attacking that sector?

I decided to take the risk. I ordered the whole of the perimeter, except the Deep, to be stripped down to one section per platoon front, with no battalion reserves. The Deep, and a brigade reserve of one rifle company, I kept at full strength.

The Japanese continued their attacks—on the Deep. The actions for the next five nights defy description or reasonable analysis. At the northeast corner of the block, around the Deep, a furious battle raged from dusk till an hour or two before dawn, fought at ten yards' range with Brens, grenades, rifles, Tommy guns, two-inch and three-inch mortars and some machine guns. Three hundred yards to the left of the attacking Japanese, and in full view of them, C-47s landed with glaring headlights on the by now brilliantly lighted strip. From the hills behind, and from anywhere in the valley, they could see the aircraft being unloaded, our casualties carried into them, hundreds of men walking up and down between the strip and the block. Between the strip and the attacking Japanese I had no troops at all, though the area was thoroughly covered by machine gun and mortar emergency tasks; and the far side of the strip was only thinly protected. From my usual nightly position near the ridge top, or with the reserve company, I listened to the roar of battle from ahead and the roar of aircraft from the right. The Japanese never came anywhere but at the same place, the Deep, and head on.

The weight of this frenzied offensive fell on His Majesty's 4th Regiment of Foot, the King's Own Royal Regiment, who fought back with grim ardor. The long battle reached three crises. The climate caused the first.

Before entering the block I had thought of burning the jungles around it, partly to remove cover which the enemy could use (our own cover would, I knew, soon be removed by their shell fire), partly to ensure that the Japanese could not set fire to it at a moment opportune to them. I decided against it because a fire, once started, is not easy to control. But, on the fourth day of the Deep battle we saw movement on the ridge to the west of the block, about one thousand yards away. The ridge overlooked both the Namyung and Namkwin Chaungs, and also gave a fair view of the reverse slopes of the Deep position. We began to mortar it. After ten minutes I saw smoke rising and thickening over there. The jungle scrub had caught fire. The Japanese put it out, while we mortared them some more. Almost immediately, on the other side of the block, enemy shells or mortars set fire to the dense lantana scrub in front of the positions held by the Cameronians to protect the field guns. (This was roughly around the boar's right forefoot.)

I did not think the Japanese had done this on purpose, any more than we had in the other direction. The dryness of the air, and of the foliage, had reached their hot weather peak, and the jungle was like tinder. The heat was close, stifling, and very severe; it, more than the enemy, had caused the failure of patrols I had sent out to pinpoint and call down air strikes against the enemy artillery positions. But I had to treat this fire as part of an attack plan. I called an immediate stand-to and ordered the mortars to begin a heavy shelling with smoke bombs on and beyond the forward edge of the new fire. Smoke bombs have a fair incendiary action and I wanted to set fire to the rearward lantana, where the Japanese would be forming up if they intended to attack. Henning held a company ready to counterattack. The field guns, already half-hidden in drifting smoke, swung round to fire muzzle-burst over the positions we might have to vacate if the fire came on. Crouched on top of the ridge, looking in both directions, praying that the Japanese would not now start their daily harassing fire, Henning and I passed a taut twenty minutes.

I did not notice that the sky had darkened over. As the flames took full hold of the lantana, it began to rain.

Trembling, I returned to my headquarters and lit a cigarette. Every wonderful drop falling on my burning face and arms was like a gift from God; but every drop sparkled with new problems. The monsoon had broken. The weapon pits, in which men must lie and fight and try to rest, would fill with water. I could not now rely on the airfield, and that would delay our evacuation of casualties. One of the reasons why morale remained high was that the wounded received such prompt attention. Some badly wounded men had been on their way to hospital, in an aircraft, ten minutes after being hit. Worse, I would not be able to replenish ammunition, for we were using a great deal of it. Why the Japanese had been such incredible fools as not to shell the field and make it unusable, I did not know. Now the rains would do it for them. . . . And where in the name of God were the floater brigades? The White City had been evacuated thirteen days earlier, and 14 Brigade was supposed to come straight up here. My brigade had marched 140 route miles in fourteen days to establish this block. Surely those bloody nitwits could cover 120 route miles in thirteen days? Where the *hell* were they? Where were the West Africans?

I gave myself up to despair and anger. The enemy guns ought to have been silenced two days ago. The opportunities being missed! What use were field guns to me? They were here, inside my bastion, to support the floater brigades as they rampaged up and across the valley. The floater brigades weren't here. My men were being worked and fought into the ground while twenty bloody battalions, forty flaming columns of Chindit bullshit, sat on their arses and drank tea and wondered how we were getting on.

But soft, we are observed. A strange officer is coming to report to me. I learn that he is Major Douglas de Hochepied Larpent of the 5th Fusiliers. God knows how he got here. He just wants to fight.

(Douglas reports: *The officer in charge of the unloading party told us we must doss down on the edge of the strip and report to the Brigadier in the morning. I tried to get some sleep at the foot of a large tree. There were others sleeping nearby but I seemed to be the only one at all concerned at the prospect of being hit. It struck me as odd. At about the same time I became aware of a highly unpleasant smell which I was then too green to recognize. In the morning I found I had been sleeping in the mortuary. I was not a little relieved to get up and with the other new arrivals set out to find the Brigadier's Command Post and report to him. As we were soon to realize the situation was far from*

healthy but my chief impression of Jack was of his com-
plete confidence. He seemed to be on top of the world,
thoroughly enjoying himself and ready to cope with any-
thing. . . .)

. . . Command doth make actors of us all. Or as one might say, liars. But I recovered myself. We were holding the enemy, and would hold him. The floaters *must* arrive soon.

The second crisis came when the close-quarter fighting at the Deep reached the limit of human tolerance. I decided I must force the Japanese farther away, at any cost. First, we removed the secondary charges from the three-inch mortars and fired them with primaries only. The bombs, fired from the middle of the block, arched high and fell five or ten yards from our forward positions. Next, I called for a heavy air strike, and told the air force to use 250-pound bombs. I expected to kill twenty of my own men if they bombed accurately, forty if they didn't.

Six fighter-bombers came. Chesty, standing with a radio in a trench above the Deep, brought them down on successive east-west runs across the foot of the sector, their target being the outer limit of our wire. They raced down from the sky, one behind the other, the great bombs slipped loose and whistled, shining, down. All my mortars opened rapid fire, all the machine guns opened rapid fire. The hill quaked and heaved, the noise beat in huge waves against my eardrums, steel splinters whined and droned over the hill and far out across the valley, trees crashed and fell, raw white wounds gaping, all the leaves vanished and hung in the boiling smoke and dirt. The aircraft dived lower, firing their multiple .50-caliber machine guns. For long moments the monstrous tearing roar filled earth and sky and being.

When they flew away, no one moved for a long time, and no one fired. We went down to remove and replace our casualties. There were none.

One enemy sniper lived, and fired a few shots during the rest of the day, and the usual attack followed that night, but the following day no Japanese were within two hundred yards of our wire. I bombed them again, this time with B-25s.

The enemy began to use his heavy mortar. Its shell weighed sixty pounds (the shell of our heaviest, the three-inch, weighed ten pounds), and when it landed on a weapon pit it saved the need for burying parties. Every day Tommy and his padre moved about across the Deep sector, under sniping, speaking to the men in the trenches, pausing here and there to pick up a handful of yellow-stained earth and sprinkle it over the torn "grave," and say a short prayer.

The rain now fell steadily. The Deep sector looked like Passchendaele—blasted trees, feet and twisted hands sticking up out of the earth, bloody shirts, ammunition clips, holes half-full of water, each containing two pale, huge-eyed men, trying to keep their rifles out of the mud, and over all the heavy, sweet stench of death, from our own bodies and entrails lying unknown in the shattered ground, from Japanese corpses on the wire, or fastened, dead and rotting, in the trees. At night the rain hissed down in total darkness, the trees ran with water and, beyond the devastation, the jungle dripped and crackled.

A Japanese light machine gun chatters hysterically, and bullets clack and clap overhead. Two Very lights float up, burst in brilliant whiteness. *Click, click, click—boom, crash, boom,* three mortar bombs burst in red-yellow flashes on the wire.

The third crisis came on May 17. On that day our Lightnings (P-38s) patrolled the valley for several hours, searching for the guns which had done us so much damage. They did not find them. Toward evening the P-38s left and I went down to the water point, as I usually did, to wash, shave, and brush up for the night's battle. While I was shaving, the enemy began to shell the block with 105s and 155s. Twelve guns or more were firing. Soap all over my face, I looked across at the ridge to the west, where the enemy had once put a mortar, and saw movement there. Mortar bombs from the ridge whistled into the block. The shelling grew more urgent and I walked quickly up to my command post —I tried never to run.

The shelling concentrated on the Deep and became a violent, continuous drumfire. My stomach felt empty and I was ready to vomit. I should have relieved the King's Own.

This was more than human flesh could stand. Nothing to do now though. The attack would come in immediately after the bombardment.

The shelling increased again. For ten minutes an absolute fury fell on the Deep.

Major Heap, the second-in-command of the King's Own, tumbled in, his face streaked and bloody and working with extreme strain. "We've had it, sir," he said. "They're destroying all the posts, direct hits all the time . . . all machine guns knocked out, crews killed . . . I don't think we can hold them if . . . the men are . . ."

I didn't wait to hear what the men were. I knew. They were dead, wounded, or stunned.

I took the telephone and called Tim Brennan, commanding 26 Column of the Cameronians, and told him to bring his whole column to the ridge crest at once, with all weapons and ammunition, manhandled, ready to take over the Deep. "Yes, sir," he said pleasantly. I had time to call Henning and order him to spread out to occupy Brennan's positions as well as his own, before going quickly, my breath short, to the hill crest.

The shelling stopped as I reached it. Tim arrived. Johnny Boden, the mortar officer, arrived. *Now, now, the Japanese must come.* I told Boden to stand by with smoke and H.E. to cover the Cameronians. 26 Column arrived, at the double. Still no assault. Tim ran down the forward slope, his men behind him. I waited, crouched on the ridge top. Ordered Boden to open up with his mortars. The enemy must have this blasted slope covered by machine guns. I knew they had. They didn't fire. It was twilight, but down the slope in the smoke, I could clearly see Cameronians jumping into the waterlogged trenches, King's Own struggling out and up toward me. The Cameronian machine guns arrived, men bent double under the ninety-pound loads of barrel and tripod. Bombs burst, smoke rose in dense white clouds. I told the officer to move the machine guns again, after full dark, if he could. "Of course, sir," he said impatiently.

The men of the King's Own passed by, very slowly, to be gathered by Heap into reserve. They staggered, many were wounded, others carried wounded men, their eyes wandered, their mouths drooped open. I wanted to cry, but dared not, could only mutter, "Well done, well done," as they passed.

The minutes crawled, each one a gift more precious than the first rain. I sent wire down, and ammunition, and took two machine guns from Henning's 90 Column, and put them in trenches on the crest, ready to sweep the whole slope. Full darkness came, with rain. An hour had passed, a whole hour since the enemy bombardment ended. In our own attacks we reckoned a thirty-second delay as fatal.

With a crash of machine guns and mortars the battle began. All night the Cameronians and the Japanese 53rd Division fought it out. Our machine guns ripped them from the new positions. Twice the Japanese forced into the barbed wire with Bangalore torpedoes, and the blasting rain of the mortars wiped them out. At four a.m., when they launched their final assault to recover their bodies, we had defeated them.

The next morning, as the rain fell more heavily, our patrols found the enemy had gone altogether. They had left the Deep sector and the hills across the Namkwin. They had abandoned the mortar post on the westward ridge. They had all gone. The forest was full of blood and flesh, and mass graves, and bodies fallen into stream beds, and bomb craters, and thousands of cartridge cases.

I have no means of knowing how many casualties we inflicted during the first phase of the Blackpool battle, except a postwar Intelligence interrogation, when a Japanese officer said, "Fifty-three Division had little fighting against the Chindits except on one occasion only, when one regiment was annihilated near Hopin." This was us. A guess would be eight hundred to a thousand casualties. We suffered nearly two hundred, mostly in the King's Own.

We were now in sole ownership of the block, and all terrain for at least a mile around. I began to send urgent messages: 14 Brigade *must* get a move on; 77 Brigade now moving northward the other side of the railway valley, should come across to us. Obviously the Japanese would attack us again, and so give us a wonderful opportunity to sandwich the attackers between the block and another brigade. A decisive victory lay to hand. . . . But the rain continued to fall, and movement would soon be difficult. The battle must be fought before that happened. Then *we* would be in possession, and the Japanese line of communication totally cut, for the valley here was much narrower than at the White City, and he would have no chance of slipping even small parties past us.

If the floater brigades did not come, on the other hand, our situation would be precarious. And one particular sound I listened for above all others, for when I heard it the jig would be up—unless the floater brigades had arrived.

Meanwhile my two battalions were out on their feet, having marched hard for fourteen days, and worked and fought like maniacs for ten more, without cease. I should be surprised to learn that anyone averaged as much as five hours' sleep a day. My own figure was closer to three.

Two battalions, which had been holding the Broadway stronghold, did manage to cross the valley, and came under my command—the 2nd Battalion the King's Regiment (Liverpool) under Lieutenant Colonel Scott, and the 3rd Battalion 9th Gurkha Rifles, under Lieutenant Colonel Alec Harper. The King's did not arrive in top condition. One of their two columns ran into the enemy in the valley at night, and turned back. Mike Calvert sent them out again, but that column's morale was shaken when it finally arrived, and both were tired. The appearance of Blackpool, and the smell hanging over it, and the thin, determined ghosts who met them, cannot have reassured them. I sent the King's out at once—for they were less tired than my original two battalions—on a battalion sweep of the hills to the north, again in an effort to locate and destroy the enemy artillery. The attempt failed. The 3/9th Gurkhas I put onto the perimeter, withdrawing all the King's Own into reserve. The rain had not yet put the strip out of commission and a large daylight fly-in of C-47s, under fighter cover, evacuated all our casualties.

We heard that Merrill's Marauders had taken Myitkyina. This was most cheering news, and the brigade burst into a collective smile of joy and appreciation. *("Will this burn up the limeys!"* Stilwell wrote in his diary.) But Myitkyina was seventy miles away and the key bastion of Mogaung, between it and us, had not yet been taken. Even if the American-Chinese advance started southward from Myitkyina immediately, no one could reach us for at least two weeks. In that time enemy pressure would build up relentlessly against me. By God, those floater brigades had *got* to come, at once.

I learned that Myitkyina itself had not fallen—only the airfield. Joe Lentaigne ordered me to meet him at Shaduzup on the Ledo Road, a hundred miles due north of Blackpool, and report to General Stilwell. I handed over command to Tommy and flew out in an L-5. After an hour or so I saw the great ribbon of the Ledo Road, looking like a trench cut through the dense forest, and landed near Stilwell's headquarters.

Joe Lentaigne met me and took me to the hut allotted to him. He was in good shape and full of his usual energy, but not very happy about the relations between Stilwell, himself, and the Chindits. Old Vinegar Joe, he thought, was basically rather a volatile chap. When things were going well for him, he didn't hate everyone; when they weren't, he did. Joe saw trouble ahead.

Then he took me in to meet the general. Stilwell wasn't hating everybody that day—the Marauders' successful march to Myitkyina was the reason—but otherwise he looked just as the press photographs showed him. He asked me if I was stopping all traffic in the railway valley. I said I had stopped all traffic on the main road and railway, by shelling and by what patrols I could find, but that some enemy were certainly sidling past on the farther side, near the Namyin Chaung, and would continue to do so until the floater brigades arrived.

I asked him when Myitkyina would fall and, I think, suggested that he fly the Marauders at once from the Myitkyina strip onto my own at Blackpool, where they could take over the block and release me to attack; or, perhaps, themselves go against Mogaung. (I know that this plan was in my mind at the time, but I cannot remember whether I put it to Stilwell, or only to Joe in our private talks.) Stilwell answered my question about Myitkyina by saying, "Soon."

That was all. Joe and I saluted and went out. In his hut again we talked some more. I told him I thought the Marauders were the key to future relations between Joe Stilwell and ourselves. They were fighting infantry, they had killed a lot of Japanese, they could march, and I was certain we would get on well with each other. *("Stilwell's staff!"* Joe burst out. *"He's difficult enough, but they're impossible. There's one chap who keeps whispering in Stilwell's ear that the Chindits do nothing but march away from the enemy and drink tea, by Jove, eh, what?")* I told him that in my bad moments I shared the man's opinion, about some at least of my fellow Chindits. Joe said sharply, "Fourteen Brigade's doing its best, Jack," and I apologized. We got back to the Marauders. Stilwell was flying large numbers of Chinese into Myitkyina to capture the town itself—all we owned so far was the airstrip; couldn't the Marauders be flown to Blackpool? I would willingly put myself under their commander. Joe didn't believe Stilwell would consider it, but he'd think it over.

(It was all a waste of breath. Stilwell and his devoted staff had destroyed Galahad [code name for the Marauders] by treating them like dirt, by running them into the ground, and by breaking every promise he made them. *"I had him in my rifle sights,"* an American soldier said. *"No one woulda known it wasn't a Jap that got the son-of-a-bitch."* Merrill had suffered a heart attack. The men's morale had faded with their last physical reserves of strength. Within a week of this meeting between myself and Stilwell, the Marauder's Colonel Hunter met Stilwell outside Myitkyina and handed him a document detailing the charges against Stilwell and his staff. Two days later Hunter declared that the Marauders were no longer fit for action and must be relieved. Stilwell left Hunter in front of Myitkyina with the troops who replaced the Marauders [Galahad II], then relieved him and sent him back to the U.S.A.—by ship, by special order; so that he could not reach Washington ahead of Stilwell's own whitewashing. Stilwell and his stuffed baboons (a Marauder's phrase), having disposed of their American infantry, their best fighting force, turned their attention to us. *"Galahad is shot,"* Stilwell had noted in his diary, with understandable triumph. His next target was not hard to guess.)

Neither Joe Lentaigne nor I knew anything of this, thank God, when I returned that evening to Blackpool.

There was a letter from Barbara. She was well, my baby was well. They'd be off to Kashmir soon. Oh, yes, there'd been a terrific explosion in the middle of April, when an ammunition ship blew up in Bombay Harbor and set off other ships, and large pieces of human body sailed through windows a mile from the docks.

Damn it, I thought irritably, this is too much. But I had many men under me who had lost wives and mothers in the German bombings of 1940 and 1941. Fold the letter carefully away, write a reply on a message pad. Fold that whole world away, and passion and love, so that they couldn't be hurt; yet of course they were there, in what I felt whenever I saw a man, any man, reading a letter; for we were all human.

Three more peaceful days followed. We patrolled, and worked hard to repair the damage and prepare for more assaults. On May 22 enemy forces began to push forward from the southeast. Four artillery pieces, from the same direction, shelled the airfield. Two light planes and a C-47, which were on it, took off immediately. The third phase of the Blackpool battle began.

I sent the Cameronians out toward the enemy, to delay his advance. I debated long and anxiously whether I should send out another battalion to lie in wait on the hill feature to the south (adjoining our boar's tail), where they would be on the flank of the Japanese advance—if it continued in the direction it seemed to be taking. I decided against it, and I think I was wrong. The grim, set-teeth, bulldog struggle to hold the Deep had had its effect on me, and I was incapable of repeating the stroke (bold to the point of rashness) which had stripped the defenses of Blackpool to concentrate on the vital area. I should have done it again, trusting to my knowledge of the Japanese in battle, but there was a purposeful and professional air about this new assault which I did not like. He was pushing in my patrols and outposts; he was shelling the field; he was not coming on like a mad dog, and I did not think I could trust him to do the obvious.

I held everyone, except the slowly retreating, overpowered Cameronians, inside the block. But, oh, God, let 14 Brigade come! The greatest opportunity of the entire Chindit campaign lay there, then, before my eyes. I sent out signals which passed from urgency to frenzy. Hurry, hurry, kill yourselves, but come!

Late in the afternoon C-47s came for a daylight supply drop, escorted by P-38s. From down the valley, behind the advancing Japanese, above the intermittent pop and crackle of small-arms fire, I heard the one sound I had been expecting, and fearing, the sharp double crack of heavy anti-aircraft guns. Puffs of yellow-black smoke appeared behind one of the C-47s. They turned for home. The P-38s searched and dived, but the A.A. guns did not fire again.

With a heavy heart I sent a Most Immediate signal to Joe asking for permission to abandon the block at my discretion. The direction of the new Japanese attack would prevent night supply drops on the airfield, and, with the A.A. guns, only night drops were now possible. Night drops on the block, or on the jungle to the west, could never keep us supplied with ammunition in heavy battle. It would take too many men, too long, to find and bring in the boxes.

The prospects were grim. Had my orders been more flexible I would have moved the brigade out of the block there and then, withdrawn a short distance into the jungle, and hung about there, ready to emerge and establish a new block when 14 Brigade and the West Africans appeared. But I had no discretion, and when my request reached Joe Lentaigne he had to take it to Stilwell.

It could not have come at a worse moment, for the attacks on Myitkyina had failed, the Marauders had reported their condition, and Stilwell's misanthropy was at its strongest. He told Joe Lentaigne we were a bunch of lily-livered Limey popinjays. Joe replied hotly. Every minute of argument, accusation, and counter-accusation at Shaduzup cost my men more lives, saw the expenditure of more irreplaceable ammunition, and locked us more closely into an action which could only have one end, and from which, minute by minute, it became more difficult for me to extricate my brigade if permission eventually were granted.

I was near despair, but apparently maintained a front of unbroken optimism. (I find this hard to credit, but there are witnesses. Douglas Larpent and Desmond Whyte noticed it and wondered whether recent strain had unhinged me. The Cameronians' padre went in a kind of horrified awe to Tim Brennan and told him he'd heard me telling Johnny Boden to "drop a few bombs over the wire," with no more feeling than if I'd been asking him to lob a couple of tennis balls.) But I was not commanding a bunch of children, or starry-eyed hero worshipers. Our work had been so successful because every man knew what I was doing and why, which means that he understood tactics. All officers and men understood the situation as well as I, and the superb courage which had fought the enemy to a standstill while we had an attainable purpose now lost some of its fire. The only battle my brigade really wanted to fight at that moment was against 14 Brigade and I told all battalion commanders to see that such bitter talk stopped at once. None of us could know the circumstances of the other brigades, and we must, in the old Rifle phrase, "Look to our front."

The battle marched slowly on. Slowly the enemy forced the Cameronians back. Our field gunners fired over open sights at large masses of Japanese advancing beyond the shell-pitted airstrip. The enemy shelling set fire to the wrecked aircraft and abandoned gliders. Our Bofors light antiaircraft guns depressed their barrels and joined in.

Night fell. Shelling caused slight casualties, except that a direct hit killed many wounded men in the main dressing station. Probing attacks reached the perimeter along most of the eastern face. The enemy held the airfield. We were using ammunition at a tremendous rate. We had to.

In the morning the enemy withdrew a little from our wire and ten Zeros bombed us. The bursting bombs and the tearing roar of machine guns sounded like the end of the world, but they didn't kill many of us and the soldiers treated the raid as a half-hour of relaxation, for during it the shelling and mortaring stopped. Soon afterward they began again. The Japanese were now using, in addition to battalion guns, regimental guns, 105- and 155-mm. guns, all types of mortar, including the six-inch coal scuttle, and, of course, all types of rifle, machine gun, and grenade.

I had called for a supply drop of ammunition, particularly grenades and mortar bombs. The C-47s came in the afternoon, through rainy skies and scattered cloud. I believe they were originally escorted by P-38s, which were drawn off by Zeros. All our planes were of the Royal Air Force. It was not night, but they came in from the west, low, twisting and turning over the steaming, forested mountains. At the last they straightened and flew on a level, straight course. The boxes and crates dropped from the open doors, the parachutes opened. Hundreds of enemy rifles and machine guns glazed up at them through the irregular, drifting smoke of our mortar bombs. Then, clear as a knell, I heard from across the valley, the sharp coughing *bom-bom-bom* of heavy antiaircraft guns. Directly over me the port engine vanished from a C-47's wing; he swung down, the other engine frantically roaring. On, a wing whirled away, he hung, fell, turning like a maple seed. Another came on among the hills, only fifty feet above the jungle, twisting frantically, another crossed his bows, they were over the loads shooting out, swinging, drifting, but oh, Christ, the waste of love and life, for some fell among the Japanese, and some we could never reach, and what we did would only last a few hours. The crashed plane burned opposite the Deep, with tall orange flames and black, black smoke. I ground my teeth, and waited, and watched. My infantry were dying, too.

The Royal Air Force never did anything more gallant. I believe only four out of eight aircraft returned to base. We received, and gathered, half of one aircraft load of ammunition.

Tim Brennan brought Sergeant Donald to my command post to tell me about a successful counterattack by which he had cleared the Japanese off a small feature outside the airstrip entrance. Sergeant Donald (who got a Distinguished Conduct Medal for this action) had been wounded and as I held out a cigarette to him I saw that he was shaking violently in reaction from the close-quarter bayonet and grenade fight. He took the cigarette and said, "Thank you, sir—" and then, strongly and in a broader Scots—"Ma han's trrembling, but Ah'm no' a wee bit frightened, sirr!" Once again, I nearly burst into tears. It wasn't the responsibility, or the battle that created the strain, it was the love and pride.

The night of May 23-24 passed in some confusion. Shells kept cutting the telephone lines and I felt, at moments, that I did not have full control over my own forces. Before dawn an enormous bombardment began and in the earliest light, under incessant rain, I learned that the Japanese had got inside the perimeter, overrunning a post held by the 3/9th Gurkhas. How it had happened, no one knew. Alec Harper at once began to try to regain the position.

The telephone buzzed. It was Henning. He began to say something but after a few words the connection was suddenly changed and a young frantic voice shouted, "They're all round! I can see them! They're in everywhere, I can't hold—"

I interrupted him. "This is the brigade commander. Who's speaking?" It was that uncomfortable facility for sounding calm when I am not, for the young officer's voice changed as though by a miracle—actually, by a tremendous effort of self-control. He gave me his name and post, reported that the Japanese had broken through in such and such places, and asked for orders. I told him to prevent the enemy from moving about, and to keep his head (keep his head, by God!). He said, "Yes, sir. Thank you, sir."

The battle spread all over the eastern half of the block. Desmond Whyte reported forty-five helpless casualties in the M.D.S., all space full, and more coming. Minutes later two direct shell hits solved some of those problems with murderous thoroughness.

The 3/9th Gurkhas could not dislodge the Japanese from the hillock they occupied. From it they swept the whole of the east side with light machine guns and mortars. We blasted them with mortar bombs and at the same time tried to clear other Japanese out of the forward areas around the field gun and Bofors pits, whence the young officer had spoken to me. We failed. I ordered all troops to withdraw from that sector, the guns to be spiked and abandoned. The men withdrew, suffering few losses under smoke and high-explosive cover from mortars and machine guns.

I saw, in the middle of the block, a line of men moving very slowly across a slope fifty yards from me. They looked like Japanese and I raised my carbine. The men trudged on in the drifting mist and rain and, just in time, I saw that they were my own men. But everyone moved like that, in a kind of cosmic slow motion. The Cameronians and gunners coming out of the forward eastern sector moved like sleepwalkers, so did the Japanese wandering about among them. A Cameronian lieutenant fell head-first into a weapon pit and two Japanese soldiers five yards away leaned weakly on their rifles and laughed, slowly, while the officer struggled to his feet, slowly, and trudged up the slope. The shells fell slowly and burst with long, slow detonations, and the men collapsed slowly to the ground, blood flowing in gentle gouts into the mud.

Johnny Boden reported that he was almost out of mortar ammunition. I went to the ridge crest, the center of the block. When I was fifty feet away a coal-scuttle bomb burst on a big tree there, and killed fourteen artillerymen, just arrived and coming into reserve under Douglas Larpent. The artillery lieutenant, closest to the blast, totally vanished.

I ordered Thompson and Scott, the commanders of the King's Own and the King's respectively, to attack the Japanese-held hillock in the southeast corner of the block, meanwhile trying to group the remnants of the gunners and the somewhat disorganized Gurkhas into a new reserve. The whole eastern half of the block blazed with fire and confused movement. One more Japanese breakthrough would cut us in two.

The supporting fire for the big counterattack failed and the attack failed, in spite of Tommy Thompson's personal heroism. When he came back, a severe wound in his shoulder, near the neck, I turned away from them all and lit a cigarette.

A signal giving me discretion to leave the block was probably on its way. After what happened to the C-47s yesterday any other order was lunacy, unless the floater brigades were at this very minute preparing to attack the enemy in the rear. And they weren't. But no signal had come yet. Bombs burst round me, bullets clacked by. I was therefore bound by the original orders to hold the position to the last man and the last round. The last bullet was not quite shot. After another hour of this, it would be. The last man . . . I had plenty of men left, far too many to see killed upholding my honor and military reputation. In any case they could only court-martial me, and I would be happy to have that chance to tell what we had done. Above all, my military knowledge told me that, unless Slim and Stilwell had gone mad, the discretionary order *must* be on its way.

I decided to withdraw from the block while we still had enough ammunition to use it in the difficult task of breaking contact. This is never easy to do in daylight, between forces as large as those engaged here. And we had, at a guess, about ninety men who could not walk unaided, and another thirty or forty who could not walk at all. The mechanics of the task I knew. I had learned them on the North West Frontier. The commander thins out the forces in actual contact and, with the men so obtained, sets up a series of covering positions, one behind the other and any suitable distance apart, depending on the ground. Finally the screen in contact breaks and runs for it, covered by fire from the first layback, as the successive positions are called. When they are well clear, Layback No. 1 withdraws, covered by Layback No. 2; and so on, leapfrogging continuously. It sounds easy but it can only be carried out by troops in full control of themselves. Once you turn your backs to the enemy, strong psychological pressures urge you to keep moving, faster and faster.

I gave the orders: Henning to establish the first and strongest layback astride the water point; Harper the second and third; withdrawal along the Namkwin Chaung to the *chaung* and track junction at 227105, about four miles away; Scott and some of his battalion to go there direct and prepare the area for defense; next day, if possible, further withdrawal up the track to Pumkrawng. I sent two last radio messages, one to Force telling them that I intended to withdraw from Blackpool immediately, and by what route, the other to 30 Column at Mokso Sakan, ordering them to march at once to meet us, bringing all horses, mules, rations, and ammunition. A hundred other details I should have settled—how the wounded were to go, who was to control them, covering fire between laybacks, action in case of meeting opposition from behind—but there was no time. I had to rely on the discipline and training of my brigade.

But one matter I must decide personally—the use of animals remaining in the block. Having suffered surprisingly little at first, shells and bombs had killed many these last two days. Only three or four horses and perhaps ten mules were fit to move. It did not take me long to decide that two radio sets and a charging engine, together with the cipher chest, must have absolute priority. I think I ordered that the remaining mules should carry Vickers machine guns and ammunition, the horses severely wounded men. All animals were to be loaded to the limit of their strength. These decisions, and the hard circumstances, meant that men must carry picks and shovels, grenades, some two-inch mortars and ammunition, many wounded, and anything else necessary for our survival, in addition to their personal weapons and what rations they had left.

The orders given, men began to drift back past me almost at once—Scott and some of the King's; I went down with them, found our own barbed wire blocking the stream. Henning and I shot it away, strand by strand, with our carbines. Back up to my command post. Henning and 90 Column moving fast to the water point.

Battered, sleepwalking soldiers passed, here two fit men, here two more supporting a third with a shattered foot, then a man with a head wound, then half a dozen unwounded, each with rifle and pick or shovel. Some wore shirts and trousers, some wore one or the other, some neither. Many men had no packs, for theirs had been buried or destroyed by shellfire. Now came a group, with an officer, struggling under a three-inch mortar. These, I had specifically ordered, could be abandoned, for the barrel and base plate constituted very heavy loads, and the bombs weighed ten pounds each, but this mortar platoon was determined to hold on to at least one of its weapons, and I did not try to interfere. It rained, it stopped raining. For ten days none of us had felt any awareness of rain, or knew whether we were wet or dry, except as it affected our job, made the rifle slippery in the hand, caused the Bren-gun barrel to hiss and steam.

Men trudged on in a thickening stream down the muddy, slippery path past my command post. Shells and mortar bombs continued to burst all round. From the eastern ridge the thinning lines of our forward troops increased their fire. A soldier of the King's Own limped by, looked up at me and said, "We did our best, didn't we, sir?" I could not stop to think, to accuse myself of being unworthy of him and his like, I could only face the problems as they came, give answers, and try to keep awake.

A Cameronian lay near the ridge top, near death from many wounds. "Give me a Bren," he whispered to his lieutenant. "Leave me. I'll take a dozen wi' me."

I went to the mule lines and saw Maggy quietly eating bamboo, a red gash in her belly and her entrails hanging out of it. She seemed to be in no pain and I hugged her neck, then Briggs shot her for me. Henning reported 90 Column in position astride the water point. I looked through my binoculars at the westward ridge, which the Japanese had occupied during the first battles. If they held it now we would have a bad time, as it dominated the Namkwin for at least a mile. Mortaring from it we would have to grit our teeth and bear as we trudged past. No, I could cover it with machine guns, for a time at least. I sent a man back with a message to Alec Harper, to be sure to put strong protection on that flank of his layback.

The men passed and passed, walking, limping, hopping, supporting others, carrying them. Tim Brennan reported that he thought he could break contact when I ordered. The Japanese were not pressing their advantage, and at the moment seemed to be under shellfire from their own artillery.

A doctor spoke to me. "Will you come with me, sir?" I followed him down the path. It was clear of moving men.

306

The whole block was clear, except for a part of 25 Column. A little way down the path we came to forty or fifty ragged men, many slightly wounded, who had carried stretchers and improvised blanket litters from the main dressing station as far as this. Here they had set down their burdens, and now waited, huddled in the streaming bamboo, above and below the path. I noticed at once that none of them looked at me as I stopped among them with the doctor.

The stretchers lay in the path itself, and in each stretcher lay a soldier of 111 Brigade. The first man was quite naked and a shell had removed the entire contents of his stomach. Between his chest and pelvis there was a bloody hollow, behind it his spine. Another had no legs and no hips, his trunk ending just below the waist. A third had no left arm, shoulder, or breast, all torn away in one piece. A fourth had no face and whitish liquid was trickling out of his head into the mud. A fifth seemed to have been torn in pieces by a mad giant, and his lips bubbled gently.

Nineteen men lay there. A few were conscious. At least, their eyes moved, but without light in them.

The doctor said, "I've got another thirty on ahead, who can be saved, if we can carry them." The rain clattered so loud on the bamboo that I could hardly hear what he said. "These men have no chance. They're full of morphia. Most of them have bullet and splinter wounds beside what you can see. Not one chance at all, sir, I give you my word of honor. Look, this man's died already, and that one. None can last another two hours, at the outside."

Very well. I have two thousand lives in my hand, besides these. One small mistake, one little moment of hesitation and I will kill five times these nineteen.

I said aloud, "Very well. I don't want them to see any Japanese." I was trying to smile down into the flat white face below me, that had no belly, but there was no sign of recognition, or hearing, or feeling. Shells and bombs burst on the slope above and bullets clattered and whined overhead.

"Do you think I want to do it?" the doctor cried in helpless anger. "We've been fighting to save that man for twenty-four hours and then just now, in the M.D.S., he was hit in the same place." His voice changed. "We can't spare any more morphia."

"Give it to those whose eyes are open," I said. "Get the stretcher bearers on at once. Five minutes."

He nodded and I went back up to the ridge, for the last time. One by one, carbine shots exploded curtly behind me. I put my hands over my ears but nothing could shut out the sound.

I found Titch Hurst of the Cameronians on the ridge, and Douglas Larpent, the latter commanding the rear party. I said, "Retire in five minutes. I shall be with the first lay-back at the water point."

We looked across the shallow valley where the forward sections were engaging the Japanese with a sharp fire. The fire strengthened, under Douglas' orders. I walked down the path, looking, but the bodies had been well hidden in the bamboo and the path was quite empty. I muttered, "I'm sorry," and "Forgive me," and hurried on, and reached the water point. There, with Henning, I waited.

Soon 26 Column started coming down, some running, some walking. Up ahead I could see that the slow trail of the severely wounded had already passed the second layback. I waited, growing very tired, with Henning, until the last of 26 Column was upon us. Now was the most dangerous moment. We stared up the path, waiting for the Japanese to come on. But they did not come, and at about noon, fifty minutes after giving the first order, after seventeen days, having been defeated, I left the Blackpool block in the rain.

Last Stop Before Japan

By July 1944, the Japanese drive on Imphal and the plains of India beyond had been repulsed. The British 14th Army now gathered itself for a counterattack; their objective: push the Japanese back across the Chindwin River and burst out into Central Burma, linking up with Stilwell driving south.

Meanwhile Mountbatten hoped to launch an amphibious attack on Rangoon where, if he met with success, he could slice through the Jap communications to the north and divide their forces. He needed two or three new divisions and a sizable increase in the shipping then at his disposal. However, a series of events thwarted his plan: first, he had to postpone his attack date due to the prevailing demands for men and equipment in Europe as the German resistance continued to be stubborn through the fall of 1944; then, because the Japanese were threatening Chungking, the Chinese capital, and Kunming, the receiving base for all airborne supplies then being sent into China, Chiang Kai-shek insisted on the withdrawal of two Chinese divisions fighting in Burma under Mountbatten, recalling them to China; next, the U.S. was persuaded to shift three air transport squadrons then under Mountbatten over to help Chiang.

In spite of these frustrations at Mountbatten's command level, General Slim's 14th Army continued to push forward into Burma, while the remainder of Stilwell's forces, now under American General Sultan, fought their way south to the old Burma Road at Namkhan. These advances were won in the hardest kind of fighting in the Burmese hills and jungles under the most rugged conditions. It was this kind of attrition that Mountbatten had wanted to avoid by his Rangoon stroke.

By February 1945, Mountbatten decided to commit the 14th Army to strike directly for Rangoon. Despite Chiang's halting his Chinese troops at Mandalay, then drawing them off for his own use in China, and despite imminent monsoon weather, General Slim continued to drive forward. The Japanese fell back toward Toungoo and Rangoon. When in mid-April it looked as though the monsoon would stop the drive, Mountbatten sent his 26th Division round by sea in an amphibious landing at Rangoon. A few days later at Pegu, the 17th Division, rushing south, met the 26th Division striking north from Rangoon, and now the last escape route to the East for the Japanese was cut off.

The war in Burma was almost over. Plans were now made to invade the Malay Peninsula, but before the British could mount an attack the drive on the Japanese mainland itself reached a critical stage.

At a meeting in San Francisco in late September, 1944, certain members of the Joint Chiefs of Staff had agreed with Admiral Nimitz on the strategy for seizing the approaches to Japan itself. Prior to this meeting, arguments had been heard within the JCS for landings on Formosa and China, but these were put aside in September. It was decided that General MacArthur would invade Luzon, while Admiral Nimitz would invade the Bonin and the Ryukyu Island groups. The islands selected by Nimitz in the two groups for the assaults were: Iwo Jima in the Bonins because it would serve as an emergency landing base for crippled bombers on their way back from Japan to Saipan, and Okinawa in the Ryukyus because it would provide major air and naval facilities for the invasion of Japan itself.

The battle for Iwo Jima is told in *Combat: Pacific Theater*. While the mop-up of the last remnants of the Japs on Iwo was still progressing, invasion forces moved toward the beaches of Okinawa. D-Day would be April 1st, 1945.

The usual air strikes, mine sweeping and naval bombardment in preparation for the landings took place. In his volume, *Victory in the Pacific*, Morison describes the work of the Underwater Demolition Teams, known as the "Frogmen" whose job it was to reconnoiter the beaches, map them, and destroy obstacles placed in the way of landing craft.

"Each team proceeded to a point about 500 yards off its assigned beach in an LCVP. The landing craft then turned parallel to the reef, casting off a swimmer about every 50 yards. Each man, clad only in trunks, goggles and rubber feet, was festooned with the gear of his trade. He carried a reel of marked line knotted every 25 yards, the bitter end of which he secured to the edge of the reef. He then turned toward the beach, uncoiling the line as he swam, halting every time he felt a knot to take soundings with a small lead line; or, if the depth were one fathom or less, with his own body which was conveniently painted with black rings at 12-inch intervals. The swimmer recorded his soundings with a stylus on a sheet of sandpapered plexiglass wrapped around his left forearm. After an hour or more of reconnaissance, depending on the width of the reef, each swimmer was picked up by his LCVP, which in the meantime had been planting little colored buoys on dangerous coral heads. The method of recovering swimmers was simple and effective. A sailor held out a stiff rope to the swimmer, who grasped the 'monkey's fist' at the rope's end, while the boat was making three or four knots, and was hauled on board. Landing craft then returned to their APDs where the swimmers' data were correlated and entered on a chart. All this went on under gunfire support from destroyers and gunboats, and 'really beautiful air support,' as Commander Draper L. Kauffman USNR described it, from escort carrier planes. This kept the enemy so busy ashore that he never even fired on the underwater demolition teams." *

OKINAWA**

by Major Frank Hough

 Everybody knew that the Okinawa operation was going to be tough. But exactly how tough, and in what peculiar respects, could not be foretold with any accuracy.

 Nor could anyone foresee that this was to be in actuality the last act of the long-drawn-out and bloody drama which had been played across 3,200 miles of ocean. Before, during and immediately after the campaign, participants and military students alike regarded Okinawa rather as a rehearsal —a full-dress rehearsal and necessarily a costly one—for the grand finale to be staged on the big home islands to the north. On the basis of this preview, the ultimate prospect appeared grim indeed.

 Although Okinawa produced a few surprises and possessed certain features which differentiated it from previous Pacific actions in which the Marines had participated, it was productive of few tactical innovations of importance.

*Victory in the Pacific, pp. 120-121. Little Brown & Co.
**From The Island War. J. B. Lippincott.

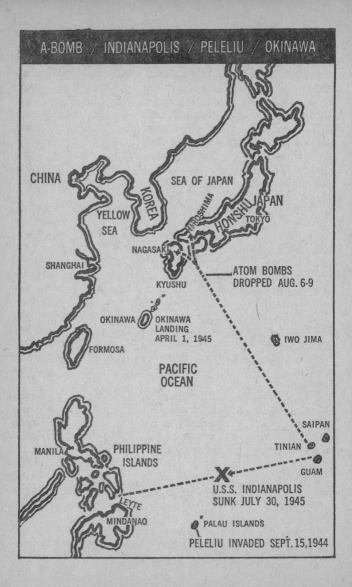

A-BOMB / INDIANAPOLIS / PELELIU / OKINAWA

CHINA

KOREA

SEA OF JAPAN

JAPAN

HONSHU

HIROSHIMA

TOKYO

YELLOW
SEA

NAGASAKI

SHANGHAI

KYUSHU

ATOM BOMBS
DROPPED AUG. 6-9

OKINAWA

OKINAWA
LANDING
APRIL 1, 1945

IWO JIMA

FORMOSA

PACIFIC
OCEAN

MANILA

PHILIPPINE
ISLANDS

SAIPAN

TINIAN

GUAM

LEYTE

MINDANAO

PALAU ISLANDS

U.S.S. INDIANAPOLIS
SUNK JULY 30, 1945

PELELIU INVADED SEPT. 15, 1944

The costly lessons of three years had been well learned; we knew the best methods of fighting the Japanese, and we had developed the weapons with which to fight them. That the fight proved protracted, bitter and bloody may be attributed to the fact that the Japanese, too, had learned much.

They fought well and skillfully on Okinawa, as they had on Peleliu and Iwo Jima, with little of the tactical blundering, the frittering away of their strength in fruitless missions, the useless dying-for-the-sake-of-dying which had marred so many of their earlier operations. That they lost in the end was due in part to a fallacy in the conception on which their defense strategy was based; this and the fact that, well as they fought, the Americans fought better.

Since the Japanese held the ground and could compel us to fight the way they wanted to fight, it might be well to examine this basic strategy at the outset. It was not, as many first assumed, an impromptu expedient forced upon the enemy. Intelligence subsequently obtained proved it to be a thoroughly studied play, worked out in detail to serve as a standard operating procedure, not only on Okinawa but on all islands within the Japanese inner-defense zone which we might attack, and presumably, in modified form, on Japan itself. Of course, all this was not known at the beginning, and Japanese behavior at the time of the landing took most of the invaders by complete surprise; very pleasant surprise at the outset, though it was to have its grim aspects later on.

This "Okinawa Defense Plan," as it was officially known, was based upon two factors U.S. troops had never encountered before: proximity to Japan proper, and reliance upon the destructive power of the newly developed Kamikaze weapons. Instead of scattering forces to attempt an all round defense of a very extensive coast line, these would be concentrated on the best defensive terrain the island afforded. There, in elaborately prepared positions arranged as a defense-in-depth, they would make the invaders come to them and fight a war of attrition, husbanding men and material against the happy day when the Kamikazes would destroy or drive off the supporting ships, thus enabling reinforcements to pour in from the near-by home islands to help with mopping up of the impudent invaders on shore. Except for the critical dependence placed upon a weapon as yet unproved, this reasoning was sound, and there is evidence to indicate that many of the defenders believed right up to the end that it was going to work.

Kamikaze tactics were something the Japanese mind could grasp—and perhaps only the Japanese mind. They constituted a logical step forward toward the goal for which Japan seemed hell bent at this period: national suicide. Kamikaze in its essence was simply large-scale organization of what had always been Japan's greatest military asset: the willingness of her men to die.

Although they boasted that every pilot was a potential Kamikaze, only a minority actually were. Had it been otherwise, the result might have been different, for there were a lot of Japanese planes over Okinawa and the offshore shipping during the campaign, often in very large flights. But most of these turned out to be ordinary bombers and fighters on routine attack missions with no more intention of crash-diving than our own people had when on similar missions.

Of the genuine Kamikazes, those who actually crash-dived their targets—or tried to—comparatively few achieved what they set out to do. Our planes intercepted many before they could attack. The accuracy and volume of our AA brought down most of them well short of their objectives. Of those who did get through to their targets, many simply missed and crashed into the sea, as a result of their own ineptness or the decrepitude of their planes, or both.

Actually, not a single major combat ship of the U.S. Navy was sunk at Okinawa, though several were damaged so seriously that they had to be withdrawn for repairs. The tremendous volume of AA fire our capital ships were capable of throwing prevented most of the attackers from getting through to the targets, and many hits were needed to sink the big ships, unless they were very lucky hits indeed. Especially during the later phases, the Kamikazes showed marked reluctance to approach these vessels at all, preferring to single out lone destroyers on patrol or outpost, or small convoys of lightly guarded auxiliaries.

314

But although it failed to influence the outcome of the Okinawa operation, or of the war itself, this sustained Kamikaze attack was a thoroughly grim business for all hands concerned. Ship and personnel losses, while absurdly small as compared with enemy claims. were nothing to be treated lightly. Yet the Navy never faltered in its support of the troops ashore.

These troops comprised the X Army (USA), commanded by Lieutenant General S. B. Buckner. The assault forces were made up of two corps: the III Amphibious Corps, Major General Roy S. Geiger, consisting of the First and Sixth Marine Divisions, both reinforced; and the XXIV (Army) Corps, Lieutenant General John R. Hodge, consisting originally of the Seventh and Ninety-sixth Infantry Divisions, both reinforced. (The Twenty-seventh and Seventy-seventh Infantry Divisions which later functioned as operational components of the XXIV Corps, were assigned initially to special missions and did not participate in the opening phases of the campaign. The Second Marine Division, which had been detached from III Amphibious Corps, was kept afloat as X Army reserve and did not participate as a division in the operations ashore.) Supporting and service troops were balanced heavily in favor of artillery, AA artillery, transport and engineers.

L-Day was set for 1 April, H-Hour for 0830. Following the conventional naval gunfire preparation and air strikes which had long since become standard operating procedure, the advance waves came in through the smoke, crossing the fringing reef in amphtracks. Beyond the line of demarcation, supporting troops bobbed about in landing craft, awaiting their turn. By 0840 the assault waves were all ashore. So far, everything had gone according to preliminary plans; from this point onward, however, practically nothing did.

Strong resistance had been anticipated; but there was no resistance, either during the landing or after the troops were safely in. Yontan Airfield, the securing of which it had been feared might require days of hard fighting, was completely overrun by 1130 of L-Day; taken almost intact, with many operational enemy planes still on the runways or in the revetments. The perimeter on which the troops dug in at nightfall embraced six thousand yards of shore line and ran inland to a depth of four thousand yards. Corps reserve and most of the tanks and artillery were safely ashore.

The Japanese defense plan was not known at this time, and all hands were inclined to regard this landing as a miracle of sorts. Had complete tactical surprise been achieved? The easy capture of the virtually undamaged airfield seemed so to indicate. The Japanese were not noted for giving away their airfields, certainly not intact airfields on islands known to be held in considerable strength. But whatever the explanation, the fact was that the troops were ashore and the supplies pouring in at a rate no one would have dared to anticipate in advance. One characteristic of American military leaders has always been their ability to adapt themselves quickly to unexpected situations; and the situation here appeared most propitious. Commanding generals and their staffs worked late into the night, amending their original plans to take advantage of it.

Actually, as subsequent intelligence proved, the Japanese command had had a very good idea of where we would attempt to land, and just about what troops we intended to put ashore. The easy fall of the airfield resulted from a slip-up on their part rather than any special acuteness on ours. They had not planned to defend it, but they had planned to destroy the planes and make the field unserviceable. For this purpose they had organized all the special and service troops in the region, together with many Okinawan conscripts, into what they designated a "Specially Established Brigade." These men proved pretty poor material: poorly organized, low in morale and so inadequately armed and equipped that they had earned the nickname within their own army as the "Bimo Butai," or poverty-stricken detachment. Under the prelanding naval bombardment, they had simply taken to their heels, in such haste that they had not paused to destroy anything and in such confusion that never thereafter were they able to function as a unit.

The region where the landing was effected lay a short

distance below the narrow Ishikawa Isthmus, roughly one third of the way up the island's long axis, which was to serve as the line of demarcation between the two operational phases contemplated in the original tactical plan. Phase I was to include seizure of all of the island south of Ishikawa by the XXIV Corps; Phase II all of the island to the north by the III Amphibious Corps. The two drives were to operate simultaneously and be mutually supporting as necessity dictated. Which phase would be completed first depended upon a number of unforeseeable factors and was a matter of no great importance.

Operation orders called for the two corps to land abreast, III on the left, XXIV on the right, each with two divisions in line. The left of the Marine sector, extreme left flank of the whole attack, was assigned to the Sixth Marine Division (less 29th Regiment which was in Corps reserve), with the First Marine Division on their right tying in with the Seventh Infantry Division, which, in turn, maintained contact with the Ninety-sixth Infantry Division, the extreme right flank of which had as part of its function acting as pivot for the southward turning movement of the XXIV Corps.

When resistance continued negligible on the second day (L + 1, or 2 April), it was decided to press the advance with all possible speed compatible with security. This led to a rapid widening of the front, necessitating movement of all division and corps reserve units into the line in order to maintain contact. So well did matters progress that the first arbitrary phase lines designated in the original plans were abandoned, and before nightfall of L + 1 permission had been given to push on beyond the line of L + 5 without pausing for further orders, should the situation warrant.

On L + 2 the First Marine Division Reconnaissance Company, pushing ahead of the 1st Marines on the III AC's extreme right reached the eastern shore. Pressing on from there, they proceeded to scout the long, narrow finger of the Katchin Peninsula, covering the entire area by nightfall without finding any enemy personnel or installations. In the center and left of the Corps area some scattered sniper fire was encountered, and rugged ground prevented these elements from completing the crossing. However, the

Sixth Division Reconnaissance Company had pushed sufficiently far ahead to scout the village of Ishikawa, on the eastern shore near the base of the isthmus.

By then the Tenth Army command had lifted all restrictions upon advances beyond the phase line L + 10. As a result, the First Marine Division secured the entire eastern shore line in its area by the end of the following day (4 April), thus reaching what had been designated originally as the L + 20 line, their final objective. In the left sector, the Sixth Marine Division reached the L + 15 line by 1250, across the base of the isthmus. Here the 4th Marines paused to reorganize while the 22nd pushed on to secure the whole of the narrow neck, moving in two columns up either shore. What the highly conservative initial plan had visualized as possibly taking nearly three weeks had been accomplished in four days. Two operational airfields (the Army had taken Kadena) were in our hands, and the island was cut cleanly in half.

For the remainder of Phase II, the activities of the First Division were confined to mopping up their area, seizing near-by offshore islands and patrolling the expanding area in the rear of the swiftly advancing Sixth Division. It was a period of rest and recuperation, though no one was quite certain what they were recuperating from. Veterans of malarial Guadalcanal, muddy Cape Gloucester and bloody Peleliu still rubbed their eyes in amazement and assured recently arrived replacements that it was never like this in the old Marine Corps. One officer summed up the feeling in a letter to a former comrade who had been transferred Stateside after Peleliu: "Peace—it's wonderful."

In the meanwhile, the Sixth Division drove on to the northward, advancing swiftly against negligible resistance. Now and again isolated riflemen or small groups sniped at them from caves or other concealment. Occasional mortar shells landed near by. In such instances the advance elements simply by-passed, leaving cleaning out of the small nests to their own reserve which, in turn, was backed up by patrols from the First Division. The enemy was considerably less of a problem than that of keeping their own supplies flowing forward in adequate quantity over a network of roads which had never been designed to handle such traffic as poured over them now.

By 8 April the Sixth Division had passed the neck of the rugged Motobu Peninsula. Captured documents and POW interrogation indicated that a force of Japanese existed somewhere in the northern portion of the island, though intelligence estimates of its strength varied. Should this force choose to make a desperate late stand—which, being Japanese, it almost certainly would—as likely a place as any would be the mountainous interior of this large headland. Air observation, though it could not be too satisfactory in terrain of this nature, tended to bear out this supposition.

The Division, therefore, paused here to regroup. Combing the rest of the island to the north was assigned to the 22nd Marines, operating a series of strong patrols rather than a solid advance. The 4th Marines deployed across the base of the peninsula to seal it off from the rest of Okinawa, and the 29th, recently rejoined from Corps reserve, moved on to Motobu in three columns.

The two flank columns made satisfactory progress, encountering no resistance more formidable than increasingly difficult terrain. The Division Reconnaissance Company, pushing hard, reached Bise, at the peninsula's western tip, on 12 April, and it soon became clear that the entire coastal perimeter was free of the enemy.

In the center, however, the story was different. The battalion (1/29) operating here met scattered resistance almost from the outset of its advance, and on the night of 9/10 April found itself involved in a sizable fire fight in the midst of as fantastic a jumble of precipitous hills, ridges, cliffs and gorges as any organized military unit was ever called upon to operate in. Here it became apparent, was the main enemy position and, being Japanese, he could be counted upon to defend it to the last. By 12 April constant probing had pretty well developed its nature and extent, but the result was not reassuring.

The defenses were of the type commonly used by the Japanese in hilly country: caves, natural and artificial, foxholes, dugouts, emplacements cunningly designed to be mutually protective with interlocking fields of fire and constructed to be proof against virtually anything but a direct hit from the artillery. As always in such a situation, the only way to oust the enemy was to go in and root him out with rifles, grenades, flame throwers. And what made this position particularly formidable was what appeared the virtual impossibility of getting in. Fifteen-hundred-foot hills, laced by cliffs and ravines barred the way for tanks. Indeed, from most directions the approaches were such as to test the skill of a professional mountain climber, even without the enemy in there shooting at him.

But here at last was an instance where no beachhead was at stake, security of which called for unremitting pressure on the enemy, regardless. Nothing threatened in the entire III Corps area, embracing about two thirds of the island. After all, this was by nature essentially an Army operation; the Division could take its time, concentrate on achieving its difficult objective at minimum cost.

More troops were brought in, and all available artillery. Naval gunfire and air strikes were called for, to no great avail in such terrain. Two battalions of the 4th Marines (the 1st and 2nd) were moved up to Suga on the west shore on 13 April, and 3/22, no longer needed for patrolling of the northern reaches of the island proper, came to Awa, to the south, in general support. 1/29 and 2/29 which had been operating generally to the north of the Japanese position, now concentrated on its eastern face. On 14 April, supported by artillery and air strikes, they assaulted from that direction, while the two battalions of the 4th together with 3/29 attacked from the west simultaneously in a pincers movement.

The action developed into a slow, deadly slugging match. Evacuation of the wounded became a major problem; bringing up supplies and ammunition was almost as difficult. On the eastern sector the terrain became so bad at length that the units operating there could advance no farther. But on the opposite side the 4th Marines, to which was attached 3/29, achieved a breakthrough in the southern portion of their sector on 17 April and, driving northward across the front of 1/29 and 2/29, overran the entire position. After that it was just a matter of mopping up isolated nests of die-hards. The peninsula and adjacent small islands were declared secured on 20 April.

The Japanese force on Motobu Peninsula was not especially formidable as regards numbers. As in all cave fighting where men are blown to bits and sealed underground, a full count of enemy killed was impossible. Subsequent intelligence indicated that this was the so-called Udo Detachment: 2nd Battalion (Colonel Udo), Second Infantry Unit, of the Forty-fourth Independent Mixed Brigade, together with reinforcing troops mustering a total strength of about 1,200. They fought stubbornly and well, however, utilizing with great skill as fine a bit of naturally defensive terrain as ever soldiers were asked to hold. The commanding officer on the scene was believed to be Major Tomio Sato, though Colonel Udo himself was known to have been there at the time of the original landing.

The 1st Battalion of the same unit, similarly reinforced, was in garrison on Ie Shima, a sizable island of about seven square miles lying three and one half miles west of Motobu and containing a large airfield. Being within practicable artillery range of each other, these positions could be made mutually supporting, and there is evidence that the Japanese planned so to utilize them at one stage of the game. As events worked out, however, they had no opportunity. On 16 April, with the Marines strongly engaged in the tumbled hills of Motobu, the Seventy-seventh Infantry Division effected a landing on the western end of Ie Shima, drove the full length of the comparatively level island against spotty resistance, and secured on the twenty-first.

During the fighting on Motobu, the 22nd Marines had gone on with their extensive patrolling of all of Okinawa lying to the north of the peninsula. It was mountainous country, inhospitable and sparsely populated in normal times, though somewhat better filled now by an influx of refugees from the south. This had not been anticipated and taxed somewhat the capacity of our Civil Affairs units, but the people proved docile and co-operative on the whole, once their Japanese-fostered terror of Americans had been assuaged.

Because of the nature of the terrain, pre-invasion plans had allowed for the possibility of the enemy making a stand in force somewhere in the region. However, the largest force encountered numbered only some two hundred, and these were believed to have escaped from Motobu. Such other soldiers as were picked up proved to be stragglers and local conscripts with no stomach for a fight. The leading patrol reached the end of the island on 13 April, and the systematic combing of the region continued until the end of the month, patrols of varying size operating from fixed bases up and down both coasts and far inland.

On 30 April, while the Sixth was resting and regrouping, orders were issued by X Army detaching the First Marine Division from the III Amphibious Corps and attaching it operationally to the XXIV Corps. For things had been going very differently in the south. The northern two thirds of Okinawa was secure; Phase II was over.

But down in the Army sector, Phase I was just beginning.

As at Peleliu and Iwo Jima, Japanese were showing signs of having become security-conscious. Papers were being destroyed to prevent their capture; diaries were disappearing from the packs of officers and soldiers; situation maps ceased to be strewn around with the lavish hand to which we had become accustomed; in short, all the various material which had proved invaluable to our Intelligence in previous operations was found in decreasing quantities on the enemy dead and in overrun bivouac areas, when it was found at all. As a result, we knew a lot less about them than we would have liked. We knew that they were on Okinawa in force, but we did not know where or how deployed. This the XXIV Corps had to find out—the hard way.

For the few days immediately following the initial landing, the experiences of the XXIV Corps paralleled those of the III Amphibious. They crossed the island without difficulty and drove southward at their leisure against nothing more serious than scattered harassing fire. On 4 April they reported "resistance stiffening." On the eighth they were advancing slowly in the face of "greatly increased resistance." On the eleventh they failed to register any gains at all and were taking a heavy pounding from the largest and best co-ordinated concentration of Japanese artillery yet encountered in the Pacific, and it took no clairvoyance to figure out that they were at least in the vicinity of the enemy's main defense position.

At this time the Corps had three divisions in line across the island: Seventh on the left, Ninety-sixth in the center, and Twenty-seventh, which had landed and been attached on 9 April after seizing some adjacent islands, on the right. They continued to operate in this formation for the remainder of the month, a stubborn slugging match in which advances were measured in yards, even feet, by which time the troops were badly in need of rest. Two minor airfields had been taken, Yonabaru on the east by the Seventh Division, and Machinato on the west by the Twenty-seventh, but there were no signs of any weakening in the fanatical resistance of the Japanese.

The first large-scale regrouping occurred on 30 April with the First Marine Division relieving the Twenty-seventh Division on the right. The Seventy-seventh, fresh from its quick conquest of Ie Shima, took over the center from the Ninety-sixth, which had encountered some exceedingly rugged going there. At this time both of the new divisions were attached to XXIV Corps, but in the case of the First Marine Division this proved only temporary. To provide more troops on the widening front, the entire western sector was assigned to III Amphibious Corps on 7 May, and the Sixth Marine Division began moving in on the right of the First the following day. Most of the Marine Artillery, which had been attached to XXIV Corps to support the drive southward, now reverted to III Amphibious control.

The next three days were spent in realigning: moving the elements of both corps forward abreast to a predetermined line of departure for a co-ordinated drive in force. The Japanese resisted with great strength, and torrential rains and the resulting mud further hampered the movement. Tanks, artillery and motor transport bogged down, and it was necessary to manhandle pack howitzers to the front lines to fire direct-support missions. Not all of the units were in position by 10 May, but the jump-off was made regardless.

The Japanese defense consisted of well-prepared positions arranged in great depth across terrain admirably suited to this purpose. They offered little in the way of novelty in the matter of construction, their outstanding features being the thoroughness with which they had been planned, the care with which they had been built, and the huge concentration of artillery which had been mustered in their support. The hard core of this resistance lay along a rough arc across the normally pleasant Okinawa hills, with their picturesque tombs which the enemy found so useful as machine gun nests: from the modern capital of Naha on the west, through ancient Shuri, to the village of Yonabaru on the east coast. It was not this main line which the soldiers and Marines faced when they jumped off on 10 May, only the outlying positions that covered it: a stretch of rough terrain some two miles in depth, packed solid with dug-in Japanese armed to the teeth.

There followed nearly two weeks of slow, bitterly contested progress. The Japanese fought with their customary tenacity; the Americans used the tactics and weapons developed through the experiences of three bloody years. As usual, every ridge and hill, every cave and pillbox, nearly every individual hole and rock had to be taken by assault. With the beachhead long since secured, the terrible urgency of most island operations was lacking. The attackers could take their time; utilize artillery, naval gunfire, and air strikes to save lives.

But the protracted struggle was terribly hard on the troops. Every effort was made to keep fresh men available—comparatively fresh, that is. The XXIV Corps, with a larger reservoir of manpower to draw on, relieved an entire division from time to time. The III Amphibious, however, had only the two Marine Divisions, the Second Marine Division having been detached from floating reserve and returned to Saipan. They solved the problem as best they could by keeping only two regiments of each Division in the lines, sometimes only one, sending the others back into reserve for a rest at as short intervals as practicable.

New place names began to find their way into the news accounts, and thence into Marine Corps lore: Dakeshi Ridge and Dakeshi Town, pocketed by the First Marine Division on 11 May; Sugar Loaf Hill, assaulted by the Sixth Marine Division on 14 May but so stubbornly defended and so fiercely counterattacked that they were able to get and retain a strong grip upon it only on the eighteenth by dint of some of the most desperate and courageous fighting in the entire war; Wana Ridge and the village of the same name, directly covering the enemy's key position at Shuri, where the First Marine Division fought from 15 to 22 May.

The Japanese dug deep into their bag of tricks and came up with a few new ones. They were conserving their manpower for once, intent on a war of attrition; nevertheless, they did not hesitate to counterattack when the tactical situation appeared to warrant, and, as at Peleliu and Iwo Jima, such operations were invariably well conceived and more or less efficiently executed. There had not been a stupid Banzai in the old-fashioned sense in the Central Pacific since Guam, and on Okinawa their ground troops enjoyed better co-ordination from the artillery and air force than had ever been achieved before. For here the Japanese had both supporting arms in formidable strength. Air attacks occurred frequently by day and sometimes almost continuously at night. Usually the main objective of these was the large fleet, necessary to supply an attack of such size, that lay continually offshore, but such strikes played a part in ground tactics, too. On 24 May they even attempted an airborne attack on Yontan Airfield in conjunction with an all-out bombing. The bulk of the attacking planes were shot down short of their objective, but one effected a belly landing within a hundred yards of the control tower and spewed forth a suicidal crew who managed to wreak considerable damage before the surprised defenders were able to liquidate them.

On several occasions they tried amphibious landings behind our lines. Alert Navy patrol craft broke up most of these en route. But on the night of 4 May during a two-day series of strongly supported counterattacks, a number of the enemy estimated between company and battalion strength contrived to get ashore in the rear of the First Marine Division, and died there. On the thirteenth and again on the fifteenth, after the Sixth Marine Division had taken over the extreme right, parties ranging from about forty to sixty men eluded the patrol craft long enough to get in, only to be eliminated with little damage to ourselves. On the east coast a similar attempt in some force was foiled by the Seventy-seventh Infantry Division.

By 22 May continuous rains and heavy traffic had made such quagmires of the inadequate roads that supply and evacuation problems stalled the drive in the center for the better part of a week.

But the sustained pounding had had its effect upon the Japanese as well. They were physically weary, their morale probably shaken by the inexorable advance which had penetrated deep into their organized defense zone. By now all of Shuri save the ancient castle was in American hands, with our line bent around it on either flank. Although we did not realize it fully at the time, this was the key to the entire situation: when it fell, so would the whole defensive position. Fully aware of this, and with the attackers in front of them too bogged down to sustain the constant heavy pressure, the Japanese seized the opportunity for an orderly withdrawal, depending upon the constantly lowering skies to veil them from aerial observation and leaving behind a strong force of die-hards to conceal their intentions and cover their retreat.

Our airmen, however, spotted the evacuation on 26 May and promptly attacked. Artillery, naval gunfire and strafing added to the enemy's discomfiture. An estimated three to four thousand were caught in this holocaust, but between the rain and mud and the suicide garrison left in the Shuri area, our ground troops were unable to pursue effectively.

Shuri Castle, strictly speaking, lay within the zone of the Seventy-seventh Division, near where its right flank tied in with the First Marine Division, but in that rugged region flanks often became mixed up. On 29 May a patrol from the 1st Battalion, 5th Marines, operating to the east of their sector, discovered the approaches unexpectedly open on this side. Receiving permission to attack, they drove westward, overcame the weakened defenders and hoisted the flag over that troublesome citadel, thus ending the most bitter and protracted fighting of the campaign.

Meanwhile, on the extreme left the Seventh Infantry Division, operating over somewhat more favorable terrain, had smashed major resistance and penetrated some distance south of Yonabaru by 24 May. Their progress now was being held up less by the enemy than by weather conditions and the necessity of maintaining contact with the center, still bogged down in front of Shuri.

On the right the Sixth Marine Division was engaged against Naha, the island capital. After some bloody fighting, they had managed to seize and hold some high ground, dominating the city from the north. Beyond here, however, they were temporarily stymied by an important natural obstacle: the Asato Gawa (river). To negotiate a crossing, the Division stole a leaf from the Japanese's own book: infiltrating under cover of darkness on the morning of 23 May, most of the 1st and 3rd Battalions, 4th Marines, got safely across and by daybreak had secured a strong bridgehead. Bridging operations were commenced immediately and completed under considerable difficulties, but the rain and the Japanese combined to curtail its usefulness for some time.

Naha was a shambles, pounded to rubble by gunfire and bombing. Under the rubble were the Japanese. Promptly the Sixth Division set about the slow, dirty work of getting them out—or sealing them in permanently. By midmorning of 28 May they had taken all the area west of a canal running north and south through the city and secured a height dominating the west, making possible a large turning movement. They reached the Kokuba River on the thirty-first, and by 1 June had taken all the land lying north of Naha Harbor and cleared the entire Division sector.

The crucial phase of the Okinawa campaign was past. It had taken an even two months of as difficult fighting as the Pacific War had produced. More hard fighting and the better part of another month would be required to ring down the bloody curtain, once and for all.

General Buckner was killed early in the afternoon of 18 June. That was the day the 8th Marines had moved into the line to contribute their freshness and full strength to the slow, weary drive. The general had not come to the front especially to watch them, but by chance he found himself near their command post, on a hill which afforded an excellent view of what was going on up forward, and he paused to watch the attack for a few minutes. By this time the Japanese artillery had been reduced close to the vanishing point. No shells had fallen in this area all morning. Now, however, by some devious quirk of destiny, a lone gun somewhere in the shrinking enemy territory let go a few random rounds. The first one felled the general, though none of the several others near him was so much as scratched. He died before they could evacuate him.

The death of General Buckner at this late date had no effect on what remained of the campaign. The end was in sight, and General Geiger, succeeding to the command, simply carried through as his late chief would have done. This was, incidentally, the first instance of a Marine officer commanding an Army unit of comparable size, though in World War I, Major General Lejeune had commanded the Army's Second Division in several major operations.

With securing of the southern shore in both sectors, organized resistance ceased on Okinawa. But owing to the broken nature of the terrain and the elaborate defenses through which the drive had penetrated, a mopping-up job of colossal proportions remained to be done on the many hundreds of the enemy inevitably overlooked.

This was accomplished simply by throwing the direction of the drive into reverse. On 25 June, with the XXIV Corps now on the right, III Amphibious on the left, the X Army started back northward through the region they had just traversed so painfully, while the reserve regiments of both Corps established a tight block along the whole length of the Naha-Yonabaru highway to prevent escape of any Japanese from the trap. The movement was regulated by predetermined phase lines, the units moving in co-ordination and keeping abreast with little difficulty.

Now there became increasingly manifest a phenomenon

which had been observed first during the closing days of the southward drive: the Japanese began to surrender; not merely individuals and small groups, but in crowds. Throughout the campaign our propagandists had labored unremittingly toward this end by means of radio, loud-speakers, printed material dropped from the air, but it had required the bald fact of demonstrated conquest to bring conviction. By 30 June when the mopping up was completed, the whole region cleared out, the III Amphibious Corps had taken a total of 4,029 military prisoners of war, including fifty-one officers; yet up until 15 June, they had taken only 322. Those taken by XXIV Corps and miscellaneous units brought the grand total to 7,401.

This unprecedented situation included some odd features. Because of the difficulty in distinguishing the Japanese from the Okinawans, many enemy soldiers sought to avoid capture by donning civilian clothes and losing themselves among the native population. Of such, eleven hundred and seventy were apprehended and identified, but it is probable that many more got away with it—for a while at least. One young Japanese lieutenant, commanding officer of a machine gun company in the Sixty-second Division, was captured hiding in a cave with his Okinawan girl friend, too warsick and lovesick to care particularly what went on. He told a number of interesting things to our Intelligence officers, and subsequently the couple was treated to a Buddhist wedding with all the trimmings, newspaper accounts of which brought many indignant letters-to-the-editor from folks back home who had never seen a Jap, let alone seen one get married.

During the Okinawa campaign, too, occurred a strange "armed truce" on a near-by island. The commander of the small Japanese garrison here, called upon to cease his hopeless, pointless holdout, asked time to consult Tokyo by radio. This done, he met several American emissaries on his beach and announced regretfully that he had been forbidden to surrender, but that he would not fire on parties of our people visiting the island for recreational purposes, provided they did not molest his people. It was never like this in the old Pacific War! By the standards of what had gone before, this was degenerating into practically civilized warfare.

Of profound importance throughout the Okinawa campaign was the work of the Tactical Air Force, X Army, under Marine Major General F. P. Mulcahy, who was succeeded in this command on 11 June, 1945 by Major General L. E. Woods. During the crucial days of the ground fighting, this force was made up predominantly of elements of the Second Marine Aircraft Wing, its staff augmented by Army and Navy officers to provide a joint operational command. The advance echelons came ashore in the wake of the assault forces and began setting up for business on 4 April. MAG 31 and MAG 33 had the fighter planes of several of their squadrons in and operating from Yontan and Kadena airfields on 7 and 9 April. MAG's 22 and 14, also fighter units, arrived in May and early June respectively, and the torpedo bombers of VMTB 232 (22 April) and VMTB 131 (29 May).

Army fighters began appearing in May and had grown to formidable proportions by the end of the ground fighting. The Army Bomber Command was set up 2 June, but did not get into full-scale operation until July, following which it gave a very vivid account of itself indeed.

The fighter planes on Okinawa performed all the missions conventional for their type: interceptor patrol, far-reaching combat patrols, bomber escort, etc., but their activity which contributed most directly to the outcome of the campaign was the flying of close-support strikes for the ground forces. The terrain and nature of the enemy defenses made this particularly important, and all possible planes were made available for this work. Rockets, bombs and strafing were all employed liberally, and napalm was used whenever the tactical situation made this practical. And a somewhat less conventional phase of air support achieved unprecedented importance in this particular operation: parachute drops of supplies to troops isolated in the more remote regions through the breakdown of the road system under the torrential rains. The torpedo bombers proved most useful at this work, too. Altogether, 612,564 pounds of food, medical supplies and ammunition were delivered in this manner, and so efficiently was the system developed that recovery was estimated at ninety-eight per cent.

The persistent, large-scale Japanese air activity over Okinawa contributed to give the TAF fighter pilots a field day. During the early stages of the operation, the enemy were sending over attack missions of three hundred or more planes, and even as mounting destruction whittled down their strength, they were able as late as 22 June to mount an attack estimated to include 150 to two hundred aircraft. As many among the attackers were suicide-bent Kamikazes, inexperienced pilots in obsolete or second-rate planes, their destruction was all the simpler. Between 7 April when the first sortie was flown and 30 June, fighters of the TAF destroyed a verified 610 enemy aircraft, killing an estimated 1,054 crewmen, with a total loss to themselves, including all air and ground units, of 77 KIA, 54 MIA and 150 WIA.

These figures do not include enemy planes damaged or destroyed on the ground, or those shot down by AA. When it is considered that the Navy (planes and guns) had destroyed 2,604 enemy aircraft and damaged 352 others within five hundred miles of Okinawa by L + 33, some idea of the magnitude of the catastrophe to Japanese airpower can be realized.

But the most important aspect, so far as the Marine Corps was concerned, was that once more the air arm had justified brilliantly the basic reason for its existence: support of the ground forces on the field of battle.

June thirtieth marked the end of mopping up on Okinawa. The last feeble flicker of Japanese military activity had fizzled and gone out. *Finis* was written to three months of sustained blood and bitterness. Now the troops could rest, those who were not among 7,283 resting already and forever in the soil they had died to conquer, or the 31,398 wounded scattered among a score of island hospitals.

A vacation from mud and blood and horror—but for how long? It occurred to few of the weary men, plodding toward their new bivouac areas or preparing to re-embark for their bases, that there was the most remote possibility that they had heard shots fired in anger for the last time.

Kamikaze

In the Okinawa campaign, the Navy fought off ten mass attacks of Kamikaze planes, or "floating chrysanthemums" as the Japanese called them; each attack numbered 45 to 355 planes. There were hundreds of smaller Kamikaze strikes, plus the more conventional sorties by dive bombers and torpedo planes.

Among the measures Admiral Turner * took to provide protection for the expeditionary forces was the radar picket screen. This was a network of radar stations fifteen to one hundred miles from shore. In the beginning a destroyer or a minesweeper patrolled day and night within an area of 5,000 yards of the station. Later, when the pickets were taking their heaviest punishment, another destroyer and additional landing craft with anti-aircraft armament helped increase the firepower of the stations.

S. E. Morison says, "Radar picket stations were the premier posts of danger in the Okinawa operation. Destroyers and other vessels assigned to this duty suffered tremendous losses, and protected other ships around Okinawa from sustaining even greater losses. By giving early warning of approaching Kamikaze attacks, vectoring out C.A.P.** to intercept, and most of all bearing the brunt of these attacks, the pickets gave the finest kind of self-sacrificing service." ***

The following selection From Morison's *Victory in the Pacific* describes two battles at picket stations off Okinawa.

*Commander of the Joint Expeditionary Force at Okinawa.
**Combat Air Patrol—a patrol of escort carrier planes was maintained over each picket daily.
****Victory in the Pacific*, p. 235. Little, Brown & Co.

THE GALLANT FIGHT
OF THE RADAR PICKETS

by Admiral S. E. Morison

Admiral Deyo's night retirement disposition,[1] still short of four heavy ships and six destroyers which had not got the word, consisted of nine battleships and cruisers steaming in circles respectively of 5,000 and 12,000 yards' diameter, with a screen of seven destroyers 4,000 yards outside. The disposition turned away towards Ie Shima. At 1753 destroyer *Leutze*, which had already been damaged off Iwo Jima, sighted a plane coming in eight miles distant and at 1800 opened fire. Within a few moments the clear evening air was spotted with black bursts from 5-inch gunfire, almost every ship was spouting red balls from her 40-mm quads, and the water was laced with spray from shorts. About twelve Kates and Oscars came in so low over the water that lookouts saw them before radar did. *Leutze* and *Newcomb* [2] bore the brunt of this attack. In quick succession one kamikaze crashed *Newcomb's* after stack, a second was splashed, and at 1806 a third, carrying a large bomb or torpedo, crashed into her, amidships, gouging deep into the bowels of the ship with a tremendous explosion that cut off all remaining sources of power and blew "both engine rooms and the after fireroom into a mass of rubble." "With intentions of polishing us off," wrote Commander I. E. McMillian, "a fourth plane raced toward *Newcomb* from the port beam and although under fire by her forward batteries came through to crash into the forward stack, spraying the entire amidships section of

[1] April 6, 1945.—Ed. note.
[2] Also a destroyer.—Ed. note.

Newcomb, which was a raging conflagration, with a fresh supply of gasoline." Flames shot up hundreds of feet, followed by a thick pall of smoke and spray which so completely covered the destroyer that sailors in nearby battleships (including the present writer) thought that she had gone down.

Destroyer *Leutze,* closing rapidly to render antiaircraft assistance to *Newcomb,* also assumed that she was sinking and swung out boats in preparation for rescue; but when close aboard she observed that McMillian's ship was still holding together. A solid mass of flame swept from bridge to No. 3 gun, but her valiant crew showed no intention of abandoning ship. Lieutenant Leon Grabowsky (Naval Academy 1941), C. O. of *Leutze,* gallantly risked his ship to help her sister, closed her weather side at 1811 (only ten minutes after the first crash), passed hose lines on board to help fight fires; and then, at 1815, a fifth plane approached, heading for *Newcomb's* bridge. One of her 5-inch guns, fired in local control, made a hit which tilted the plane just enough so that it slid athwartship and on to *Leutze's* fantail, where it exploded.

Now *Leutze* too was in trouble. A fire sprang up in the after ammunition handling room. While one of her repair parties continued fighting fires on board *Newcomb,* the other two attempted to check flooding on their own ship and jettisoned topside weights. Steering control was lost with the rudder jammed hard right. Seventeen compartments laid open to the sea by the Japanese bomb let in so much water that *Leutze* began to settle. Destroyer *Beale,* with all fire hoses streaming, now closed the disengaged side of *Newcomb;* and not until then did *Leutze* signal "Am pulling away, in serious danger of sinking." At 1842 Lieutenant Grabowsky requested Admiral Deyo's permission to jettison torpedoes and depth charges. After permission had been granted *Leutze* signaled "Believe flooding under control." Minesweeper *Defense* (Lieutenant Commander Gordon Abbott USNR), which had been slightly damaged by two kamikaze hits shortly after 1800, took *Leutze* in tow at 2005. While making her slow way to Kerama Retto *De-*

fense sent this cocky message: "Sorry to be late, have scratched a kamikaze and taken two on board. Now have destroyer in tow." She arrived off Kerama Retto and cast off her tow at 0230.

Newcomb, one of the "fightingest" destroyers in the Navy (she had led a torpedo attack in Surigao Strait), lost nothing in comparison with *Leutze;* Nelson's accolade to his sailors, "They fought as one man, and that man a hero," could well be applied to her crew. The exec., Lieutenant A. G. Capps, after being pulled out from under the tail of a crashed kamikaze, directed the local-control fire of the forward gun and then handled the firefighting; the surgeon, Lieutenant J. J. McNeil USNR, carried several severely injured men to a place of safety, operated on surgical cases in the wardroom in the midst of the uproar, and so continued all the following night; Lieutenant (jg) D. W. Owens USNR "by his personal direction and fearless leadership" quenched a magazine fire. Two out of 78 enlisted men singled out for special commendation in the Action Report may also be mentioned here: fireman Francis J. Nemeth was securing steam lines when burned to death by the spreading fires and machinist's mate Richard C. Tacey was killed trying to reach some of the black gang who were trapped by the flames. All crews of guns that could shoot fired until they were blown overboard or killed.

Newcomb had all fires under control before fleet tug *Tekesta* towed her, too, into the calm waters of Kerama Retto. One marveled at the sight of them there next morning: scorched, scarred and half wrecked, *Leutze* alongside repair ship *Egeria,* with part of a kamikaze plane still resting on her fantail; *Newcomb* with No. 2 stack gone, No. 1 leaning crazily to starboard, her entire deck abaft the superstructure buckled into the contour of a roller coaster, and her fantail about six inches above the water. *Leutze* had lost only 7 men killed or missing and 34 wounded, but *Newcomb's* casualties were 40 killed or missing and 24 wounded. Both ships had to be beached or dry-docked and there was some question whether they were worth repairing, but repaired they were.

Two destroyers fared even worse that afternoon. *Bush* (Commander R. E. Westholm), on radar picket station No. 1, and *Colhoun* (Commander G. R. Wilson), on station No. 2, were the first to be encountered by "floating chrysanthemums" flying southwest along the Nansei Shoto. The ships had been out there since April 1 and 3 respectively, with "seldom a dull moment." Advance elements of the massed air attack heckled them all through the midwatch and *Colhoun* received eleven bombing attacks, all of which missed, between 0230 and 0600 April 6. The forenoon watch was fairly quiet. Around 1500, 40 to 50 planes flew down from the north, stacked at various altitudes between 500 and 20,000 feet, and began orbiting and attacking *Bush*, while about 12 others went after *Cassin Young* (Commander J. W. Artes) at station No. 3, next to the eastward.

Bush shot down two Vals and drove off two more, a few minutes before 1500. Thirteen minutes later a Jill was sighted heading low for her. Commander Westholm promptly swung ship to bring it abeam and unmask his main battery. Fire was opened at a range of 7,000 to 8,000 yards. The plane jinked and weaved at an altitude of 10 to 35 feet above the water, and although every gun on the destroyer was firing, it kept coming and crashed between the two stacks. The bomb exploded in the forward engine room, killing every man there, and most of those in the two fire rooms. Flooding started immediately and *Bush* took a 10-degree list, but escaping steam smothered the fires and power was regained as the auxiliary diesel generator cut in. Handy-billys were used to control the flooding, the wounded were treated on the fantail or in the wardroom and although the ship had gone dead, everyone expected to save her, and all hands cheered when a C.A.P. of four planes appeared overhead.

Colhoun at 1530, learning by radio that *Bush* was in need of help, began to close at 35 knots, bringing along her C.A.P. for the short time it could remain. The chief fighter-director commander in *Eldorado,* Admiral Turner's flagship, sent out another C.A.P. which encountered so many Japanese planes en route that a general melee developed some 15 miles south of *Colhoun's* course. This C.A.P. splashed bandits right and left, but ran out of fuel and ammunition before it could help the destroyers. At 1635 *Colhoun* closed *Bush*, then dead in the water, smoking badly and apparently sinking. She signaled a support craft, *LCS-64,* to rescue the crew and tried to interpose herself between the sinking ship and a flight of about 15 Japanese planes. They approached, and one went for *Bush* at 1700. Commander Westholm ordered about 150 of his men fighting fires topside to jump overboard for self-protection, and trailed knotted lines for them to climb on board again. All his 5-inch guns that would bear were jammed in train, but his 40-mm guns opened fire and frightened one Val away.

Colhoun in the meantime was shooting everything she had at an approaching Zeke, which missed and splashed midway between the two ships. "This left one down, eleven to go," remarked Commander Wilson. Another was hit by a 5-inch shell at 4,000 yards, and its port wing caught fire. *Colhoun's* guns Nos. 1, 2 and 3 were quickly trained on a third Zeke diving at her starboard bow, and the first salvo hit him square on the nose; he splashed 50 yards abeam. Just then Wilson received a report that a fourth Zeke was about to crash his port bow. Too late he ordered full left rudder. The plane, already aflame, hit *Colhoun's* main deck, killing the gun crews of two 40-mm mounts. Its bomb exploded in the after fire room, killing everyone there and rupturing the main steamline in the forward engine room. Lieutenant (jg) John A. Kasel, the engineer officer, opened the cross-connection valve before diving for the bilge, so the after engine room had steam and a speed of 15 knots was maintained.

Colhoun was already getting her fires under control (despite loss of all handy-billys) when, at 1717, commenced the fifth attack on her within 15 minutes, by two Vals and a Zeke. The gunnery officer had the presence of mind and found the time to assign target sectors to his five-inch guns. One Val was splashed 200 yards on the port quarter. One missed *Colhoun* and was shot down by fire from *Bush* and *LCS-84.* The third plane crashed the forward fire room, where the bomb exploded, piercing both boilers, blowing a 4-by-20-foot hole below the waterline, and breaking the keel. *Colhoun* went dead in the water; all power and communications were lost. The indefatigable damage control party then applied CO_2 and foamite fire extinguisher. The gunnery officer re-established communication with guns 1, 2 and 4 of the main battery. The wounded were treated, fires brought under control; and the men had just begun to get rid of depth charges and torpedoes when at 1725 the sixth attack on *Colhoun* (and fourth on *Bush*) started.

Three planes dove on each bow and one on her quarter. All *Colhoun's* guns were now manned in local control; and it takes such strength and determination to point and train a 5-inch 38 without power, that the strong young bluejackets had to be relieved after two minutes. One Zeke was splashed 150 yards away. The other two were hit by 40-mm fire but only slightly damaged. One, a Val, caught its wing in the after stack, caromed on No. 3 gun, knocking off its gas tank which burst into flames, and then bounced off main deck into the water. There the bomb exploded, knocking a 3-foot-square hole below the water line and so deluging the after part of the ship with water that all fires were extinguished and everyone on the fantail was washed overboard. The third plane missed *Colhoun,* pulled out and started to dive on *Bush* against her 40-mm fire, the best she could now deliver. It missed the bridge, and crashed main deck between the stacks. The impact almost bisected *Bush;* only the keel held her together. Her men already overboard climbed back, the repair party threw water on the fire and almost had it under control when, at 1740, a fourth plane, a Zeke, made a weaving dive. *Colhoun's* No. 4 fired at it but missed. For the last time the 20-mm and 40-mm guns of *Bush* spoke. The kamikaze cleared her by five feet, gained altitude, did a wingover, came in again, and crashed her port side at 1745, starting a terrible fire and killing or fatally burning all the wounded in the wardroom. A handy-billy, shifted to this fire, was no better than a garden hose on such a blaze; the entire forecastle was enveloped in flames, and ready ammunition began to explode.

Still neither crew would give up its ship. *Colhoun,* with

only a bucket brigade operating, was taking water fast, but *Cassin Young* and a tug were coming in to assist. Commander Westholm counted on the fires in *Bush* above the main deck burning themselves out, as his ship was well buttoned up below; and although she could hardly fail to break in two in the heavy sea, he hoped that each half might be salvageable. Shortly before 1800 the bow began to settle. Suddenly a Hamp appeared "out of nowhere" and, evidently deciding that *Bush* was a goner, dived on *Colhoun*. Direct hits were scored on the plane at very close range. Already aflame, it hooked the pilothouse and crashed the port side. *Colhoun* was so badly damaged already that this additional hit did not make things much worse.

By that time daylight had begun to fade. Other Japanese planes were visible, but not another ship was within hailing distance. Damaged *LCS-64*, with many survivors on board, had cleared out. At 1830 a big swell rocked *Bush*. She caved in amidships, jackknifed until bow and stern sections were at a 135-degree angle, and quietly went down in a 350-fathom deep.

Commander Wilson of *Colhoun*, after consulting his exec. and heads of departments, decided to abandon ship. When *Cassin Young* closed at 1900, he begged her to search for *Bush* survivors. *LCS-84*, which also closed, commenced the arduous work of rescuing men in the rough sea. About 200 were transferred to *Cassin Young* between 2015 and 2100. *LCS-87* then came alongside and took over all who remained in *Colhoun* except a skeleton salvage crew of four officers and 17 men. Fires flared up again, and the men ran out of foamite and CO_2. When fleet tug *Pakana* arrived from Kerama Retto at 2320, *Colhoun* was listing 23 degrees and awash up to her No. 4 gun. The tug had no pumps to lend, so Commander Wilson ordered *LCS-87* to take off the skeleton crew, and, at his request, *Cassin Young* sank her by gunfire. She had lost 35 men killed or missing and 21 were wounded.

The plight of *Bush* survivors was desperate. To keep afloat they had one gig, a number of floater nets which were constantly breaking up and capsizing, and a few rubber life rafts inflated by CO_2, which were excellent—one supported 37 men. The seas were ten to twelve feet high and whitecapped. Both air and water were cold. The men had taken a beating in the successive attacks on their ship and were suffering agonies from their burns. Many could stand no more, slipped out of their life jackets and went down. The gig finally attracted the attention of *LCS-64,* which commenced rescue operations at 2130; a fleet tug from Kerama and a PC arrived shortly after. They had to work in complete darkness as Japanese planes were still about. As the rescue vessels approached survivors some became excited and tried to swim to them, and drowned from exhaustion; or when alongside were broken against the hull, or caught in the propellers. Other men died after being taken from the water. Seven officers out of 26, including Comdesdiv 98, Commander J. S. Willis, and 87 men out of 307, were lost.

The INDIANAPOLIS

The heavy cruiser *Indianapolis* had been damaged by a Kamikaze at Okinawa and in consequence had had to lay up for repairs at Mare Island in the States. Because of her chance presence on the California coast in July, she was given the task of transporting "the heart of the (atomic) bomb—a subcritical mass of Uranium 235"—to Tinian. After delivery, she was then ordered to Leyte, via Guam, to join Task Force 95. The second night out from Guam, the *Indianapolis* caught two torpedoes from a Jap lying directly in her path. She went down in 12 minutes with some 800 men awash in the sea as survivors.

"Without an escort possessing sound gear, the cruiser was dependent on radar and eyesight to detect a submarine. And she was not zigzagging when she encountered the underwater enemy. It was an overcast night and standing fleet instructions required ships to zigzag only in good visibility. Captain McVay's routing instructions directed him to zigzag "at discretion," which he did by day, but not at night. He did not appear to be disturbed that in his briefing there was a report of a submarine near his estimated position at 0800 next day, and of another 105 miles from his ship's track on 25 July. Nor was the ship 'buttoned up' above the second deck. Since these old heavy cruisers had no air conditioning, the Captain, to make sleep possible for his men in tropical waters, allowed all ventilation ducts and most of the bulkheads to remain open. The entire main deck was open, as well as all doors on the second deck, and all hatches to living spaces below." *

*S. E. Morison, *Victory in the Pacific*, p. 321.

ABANDON SHIP*

by Richard F. Newcomb

On the bridge, the watch began to settle down. Jack Orr checked his course and speed, Casey Moore strolled around the open navigation bridge and found all watch-standers on duty. The moon was appearing more often now, and was a little brighter, but at times it was difficult to make out faces on the bridge and impossible to see far out over the water. Just after midnight, the bugler of the watch, Donald F. Mack, went into the chart house to see the quartermaster, Jimmy French. French's striker, Seaman First Class William F. Emery, was also in there.

Suddenly, there was a tremendous blast forward, followed by a sheet of red-yellow flame and a giant column of water rising higher than the bridge. The ship shuddered and a few seconds later came a second blast, much nearer the bridge, much more violent, louder and more terrifying. For a split second after the second blast there was utter silence, except for the swish of water and the hum of turbines.

Nearly everyone on the bridge was thrown to the deck by the first blast, then dashed again to the deck or bulkhead by the second explosion. Within seconds, the ship roused to life in a massive reflex action. For an instant there was pandemonium, but no panic. There is always something unbelievable about your ship taking a hit. As in everyday life, things happen to the other fellow, not to you. The first reaction is one of sheer surprise, tinged with disbelief and perhaps resentment and the beginnings of anger.

---

*Condensed from *Abandon Ship,* pp. 64-101.

But—and here is where training pays off—most men snapped quickly to defense posture and began automatically to perform the tasks assigned for just such an emergency.

There was no panic on the bridge. Casey Moore raced to the splinter shield and peered forward in the murk. The bow seemed oddly down, and he could make out smoke and a few figures moving about on the deck. Orr steadied the helmsman, and the JL talker. Seaman First Class A. C. King picked himself up from a maze of wires and put his phones back on his head. The bosun's mate of the watch, Coxswain Edward H. Keyes, went mechanically to the public-address box, whistled a test pipe down it and found it dead. The blue lamp on the control panel would never glow again. King raised nobody on his phones, and Keyes told Orr, "Everything is dead on the sound system, sir."

"Go below and pass the word 'All hands topside,' " Orr shouted, drawing both consciously and subconsciously on his recent experience with the sinking destroyer in Ormoc Bay. The fatal thud of torpedoes was familiar to him now.

After his first look around, Casey Moore reacted like any good damage-control officer. He sprinted to the ladder and went below to have a look.

Captain McVay's emergency cabin was port side at the back of the house built on the navigation deck, with the door facing aft. He awoke with a start at the first blast, and it flashed through his mind that a second kamikaze had found the target.[1] The second blast threw him out of bed, and as he hit the deck it occurred to him that this was not kamikaze territory. Must be mines, or torpedoes, or internal explosion. Acrid white smoke was already seeping into his cabin, and as he went out on deck he noticed it there, too. Stark naked, he made his way around to the bridge.

"Do you have any reports?" he called to Orr.

"No, sir," the OOD replied. "I have lost all communications. I have tried to stop the engines. I don't know whether the order has ever gotten through to the engine room."

"I will send down word to get out a distress message,"

[1] The *Indianapolis* had stood duty off Okinawa.—Ed. note.

Captain McVay said. He was not alarmed. The ship had no list as yet, and this was not his first experience with battle damage. They had saved the ship before and they could do it again.

As he turned back to get his clothes, he told Orr, "See what information you can get."

McVay quickly picked up pants, shirt, and shoes and returned to the bridge, dressing as he went. As he reached the bridge, things began to happen pretty fast. For one thing, strange noises sounded from below, and strange noises on a ship usually mean trouble.

Casey Moore came back just then from his first quick look around, and reported the damage was severe.

"Most of the forward compartments are flooding fast," he said, "and there are no repair parties there. Do you want to abandon ship?"

"No," McVay replied, "our list is still slight. I think we can hold her. Go below and check again."

Moore left the bridge, but he never returned.

The whole ship was beginning to strain and groan in a way never intended.

"Have you any word from the radio room yet on whether they've gotten off a message?" the Captain asked Orr.

"No, sir, no word yet."

The ship was definitely slowing down, and the bow was low and acting queerly. It seemed to plunge head on into the seas instead of rising with them. The list was only about three degrees to starboard.

Jack Janney appeared from his cabin, on the starboard side, exactly opposite McVay's. Captain McVay sent him to the radio shack, to get the distress message out.

"Send a message saying we have been hit, give our latitude and longitude, say we are sinking rapidly and need immediate assistance," Captain McVay told him. Janney went down the ladder, never to return.

No sooner had he left the bridge than Commander Flynn came up the ladder.

"We've been badly damaged, Charlie," he said. "We're

taking water fast. The bow is down. I think we are finished. I recommend we abandon ship."

Captain McVay had been coming to the same conclusion himself. He could not see from the bridge, with flame and smoke pouring up from the foredeck, but there is a feel about a ship. She was acting most strangely, and she seemed to be almost totally without lights and power, a sure warning of mortal damage in the belly. All he needed was the opinion of a man of Joe Flynn's experience and judgment.

"Okay, pass the word to abandon ship," McVay said. Flynn left the bridge for the last time.

Not many skippers have to give the command "Abandon ship!" It is a fateful command, yet when it must be given there is no time for reflection. That time comes later, perhaps.

The captain's biggest worry was whether or not word had gotten out. Unescorted as they were, and 300 miles from the nearest land, it was vital that someone know of their plight. Not a single dispatch had been sent from the ship since she left Guam, nor had any been addressed to her, and it was another 36 hours before she was expected in Leyte. The potentialities for disaster were great, considering that the *Indianapolis* carried only two small boats.

Now that the command had been given, McVay wanted to be sure someone knew they were in trouble. None of his messengers had returned from the radio shack, so the captain decided to go himself. For all its benign look and air of tropical romance, it was not a friendly sea. Besides a probable enemy out there, who had been known to machine-gun helpless men, the ocean had its own perils. Shark, barracuda, and other strange and rapacious fish abounded, and sun and salt could be vicious enemies. Nor was there any hope of atolls or reefs, for the water here was some of the deepest in the world. It was imperative that someone know they were in serious trouble.

As McVay put his hand to the ladder leading down, the ship took a great lurch to starboard, going over to about 60 degrees. For a moment he clung to the ladder, then slid down to the signal bridge. The vessel paused for a moment in her roll, but it was obvious that McVay would never reach the radio room.

He looked to port and saw several men struggling to get to the lifelines.

"Don't go over the side unless you have a life jacket," he roared. "I think she may stay here a minute or two. Get the floater nets against the stack."

From above, Lieutenant Orr, still clinging to the splinter shield, cried, "That's the captain talking; get the floater nets."

But within thirty seconds the tired old ship rolled full 90 degrees to her starboard side. Now the bulkheads were horizontal and the decks vertical. McVay grabbed the communications deck lifelines, now above him, pulled himself up, walked across the bulkhead and pulled himself up another step to the side of the ship. There he stood for a moment, upright on her side, staring down at the vast expanse of red bottom.

He walked slowly aft, thinking she still might stay afloat. But he had gone only a few steps when the bow of the vessel began to sink. The water line advanced gently along the hull, and in a moment it washed him off. It was only twelve minutes since the first blast had ended his sleep.

Doc Haynes glanced into the warrant officers' mess as he passed and noticed a poker game. But it was nearly midnight, and he was tired. In his cabin he quickly undressed and stretched out on his bunk. He was already asleep when the impact of the first torpedo hurled him into the air and he landed on his desk. He had no sooner put his foot to the deck than the second one smacked home, directly under him. Flame swished down the passageway and singed him as he started out the door, a life jacket held in front of his face. Behind him, the room was now on fire, and forward the passageway was full of smoke and flame. The deck tilted crazily.

Haynes turned aft, hoping to get through the wardroom and onto the quarterdeck. Everywhere he turned there was fire, but he made it to the wardroom. Only a red haze illuminated it, and the heat was fierce. The doctor fell, and as his hands touched the deck they sizzled. He rose in shock and threw himself into an armchair. As he gasped for breath in this inferno, someone standing above him screamed "My God, I'm choking," and fell on him.

Haynes rose in fright, and across the wardroom someone yelled, "Open a porthole! Open a porthole!" The doctor struggled to the starboard side and reached for a port, only to find it had been blown open and was slapping against the hull. He hooked it up and leaned out, gulping in fresh air, and as he did so something kept slapping him in the face. It was a line, hanging from the deck above. Oblivious to the pain in his hands—a surgeon's hands—he grasped the line and yanked it. It held.

Scarcely knowing what he was doing, he eased himself through the porthole and pulled himself up to the main deck. The air was much better there, and he made his way across to the battle dressing station in the port hangar. He was still dressed as he had been in his bunk—pajama bottoms only. The ship was a shambles topside, and slowly Haynes' mind began developing the pictures his eyes had taken—papers and broken furniture in the water, fire-reddened decks and bulkheads, jagged metal, and an awful hole beneath his escape port. He had no time to draw conclusions yet, but in a mechanical daze turned to the scene before him in the hangar. Wounded men lay everywhere, singly and in bunches, limbs twisted, faces contorted. Some were quiet and alive, others just quiet. Chief Pharmacist's Mate Schmueck was already administering morphine in no set pattern, just to those closest and in the most violent agony.

Haynes pitched in, not as an officer but as a doctor, responding automatically to years of training. Once he collapsed across a man he was helping, and revived as the man pushed him away. For the first time he noted that his patients were beginning to slide away to starboard, and with this realization the whole picture fell into place—the gaping hole, the fire, the debris, the list, and down below those now-ominous sounds—the death rattle of a ship.

"Get some life jackets, John, we've got to get these

men ready," he told Schmueck. There was no question about it, the ship would soon sink.

Schmueck and another sailor returned with armloads of life jackets, but time was getting short. The starboard rail was already under water. They struggled as best they could, but some men shrieked and writhed in pain as they tried to get jackets around them.

"Don't touch me, don't touch me," screamed one horribly burned man, who somehow had escaped from the hell below. Escaped? He had only transferred the place of his death.

Those still able to move were given a choice. As the ship rolled on her beam, they could either drop into the water on the starboard side or scramble up to the high side. Doc Haynes and some others crawled up to port and walked out on the hull. Soon they were walking on red bottom paint, and then it was just water and thick black fuel oil in great waving blankets.

When Ensign Woolston arrived in the wardroom a few minutes after midnight for a cup of coffee after his watch, he had barely sat down at the mess table when flames from the first blast roared up the passageway and through the wardroom doors. A few seconds later, when the second fish cracked home just beneath him, the whole room burst into flame like the inside of a firecracker. Woolston instinctively rolled under the table, out the other side, and through the window into the pantry in one smooth continuous movement. As the flash flame died away, he picked himself up and returned to the wardroom. The steward's mate of the watch appeared and they began searching for a dog wrench in the reddening darkness, coughing and spitting from the smoke. Woolston felt himself slipping, growing faint from lack of air.

He shook himself and muttered out loud, "Wait a minute, Woolston, this is not the way to go."

His hand fell on the wrench, and he undogged two ports and thrust his head out into the blessed, cool air. The water was rising, even on the high side, indicating the vessel was both settling in the water and canting to starboard.

"I think I'll rest a minute," the steward's mate said, as Woolston slithered through the porthole. He may have gotten out of the wardroom later, but not one of the thirty-two stewards, steward's mates, or officers' cooks survived.

Woolston climbed to the communications deck to get a life jacket and stumbled across a crack in the deck. Glancing forward, it looked to him as if the bow was under water, at least on the starboard side, but it appeared to be still holding. Splintered wood and steel were thrown up from the main deck in several places, and flames licked up from below. As a damage-control officer, he realized that the ship was in a bad way, with fire below and the sea probably cascading into the hull from at least two holes. As he ranged back and forth on the port side, trying to find somewhere to help, he heard the word from above, "Abandon ship! Abandon ship!"

By the time Woolston reached the well deck, the list was increasing rapidly. Hands reached down to him from above, and a human chain pulled him up onto the port side of the hull. The men slithered into the water, and Woolston found another life jacket floating by him. He passed it to a steward's mate, who had none.

In Radio II, Woods [2] was no man to sit around waiting for orders that might never reach him (and never did). He sat down at a transmitter position and began sending on 500 kilocycles, the international distress frequency. Herbert J. Miner, Radio Technician Second Class, peered over Woods' shoulder and watched the antenna meter fluctuate. Woods was keying the simple SOS—three dots, three dashes, three dots—followed by the ship's position. Miner noted that the SOS was definitely going out—when that meter fluctuated it proved there was power in the antenna.

No one knew how many times it went out, but Miner told his buddies later, as they waited for rescue, that it was at least three times. In any event, Woods stuck at his key until the ship went so far over he told his men, "Get out

[2] Chief Radio Electrician L. T. Woods.—Ed. note.

of here as fast as you can." The men cleared the shack in a rush, just as the ship laid out flat on her side.

Every ship and shore station round the world is supposed to guard 500 kc. There was just a possibility—

When the *Indianapolis* departed Guam, she carried eighty-two officers (including the passenger, Captain Crouch) and 1,114 enlisted men. Around midnight on Sunday, perhaps sixty-five of the officers were in officers' country in the forward part of the ship. Most of them were asleep, but a few were still in the wardroom, or the showers, or reading in their rooms.

The two torpedoes cracking home, each carrying 1,210 pounds of high explosive, bracketed officers' country fore and aft. Well over a ton of explosive was delivered to the cruiser's tender belly within a space of 175 feet. The first hit at about Frame 7, or some twenty-eight feet back from the bow and, if she was running true to her depth setting, rammed smack into the chain locker. There is no telling exactly where she hit, but it was probably not aft of Frame 7. The two tanks for storage of high-octane aviation gas were at Frame 15. Only one was full, 3,500 gallons, but had it exploded the entire bow might have been blown off.

The second torpedo struck a telling blow. With this one shot alone, the *Indianapolis* was doomed. Besides opening a huge hole amidships, it wiped out all communications, lights, and power in the forward half of the ship, and with them went the fire mains, radio, radar, and fire control for the guns. Striking at Frame 50, directly below the bridge, the blast must certainly have opened the forward fire room to the sea, destroying any pretense of watertight integrity that the vessel might have had.

Within seconds of the two blasts, the forward half of the ship erupted into frenzied life, with men stumbling through darkened passageways, coughing and spitting from smoke and noxious fumes from dozens of sources. Some men floundered aimlessly, like beheaded chickens, others ran silently and swiftly with great purpose. Some screamed and bled, others merely bled, and some did not move at all.

On balance, officers and men did the best they could. As

the shattered bow plowed into the swells, no longer able to rise with them, the tremendous force of the sea against the exposed bulkheads was too much for man or ship. The transverse bulkhead at the chain locker leaked in a dozen places through split seams, sprung plates, and twisted doors. This alone could have been serious, but it was nothing compared to the amidships hit, which ripped the bottom open laterally—like a giant can opener. The men forward did not know the extent of the damage amidships, but they soon felt its effects. Water pouring in from starboard tipped the mighty ship to that side, and water cascading in forward pulled the bow down, as if to make it easier for her to slake a mortal thirst.

The scene on the fantail was fantastic. Within minutes it was peopled with men crawling everywhere, like flies on a piece of garbage. In the light of the intermittent moon, or flames from forward, they gathered there by instinct, droves of them, over five hundred in all. No one told them to go there, but after all instinct was invented long before thought. And once they arrived, there was no one to tell them what to do. The great bull voice of the PA system, representing the unseen presence on the bridge, was stilled. No orders, no instruction, no central direction would ever come from it again.

So they gathered and they waited. A few were wounded or burned, most of them were not, and many were naked or wore only the skivvies or shorts they had been sleeping in. Not one in a score had shoes on, or carried a knife, flashlight, or any of the dozen other items they had been instructed to have ready in case of just such an emergency. No one was figuring, even then, on abandoning ship. Some men had already gone over the side, to be sure—blown off the forecastle or driven over by panic—but they were not many. Most of the men were calm, if confused. It was inconceivable that this big ship would sink.

But as the bow slowly sank, and the stern began to rise, the feeling of impregnability gave way to a new thought. The seed of doubt matured rapidly as the list to the right developed. A few officers and leading PO's kept telling the men, "Get a life jacket, get a life jacket." Strange creakings, bangings, bubblings, and cracking sounds rose from below and the ship began to slew around, obviously out of control.

Men began to drop off the starboard lifeline, despite orders by some officers or in response to urging by others. It was all happening so quickly, and there was no word from above. Men acted individually, in response to their own natures. They were dribbling off the side now like peas from a planting machine. When the last great lurch came, there was no longer time for individual decisions. They could only get away from the ship in the best manner open to them. She was clearly going down.

Some were reluctant to go, for they feared the dark, oily void awaiting them more than the ship breaking up beneath them. By some miracle, it might stay afloat. Such things had been known to happen. Ensign Twible screamed for the men to go over the side, but no one moved. They waited until he himself went, then followed him in a rush, like sheep. Some men clung to guns, stanchions, lifelines, any projection, until it was let go or drown. Others, high in the superstructure, plotted it coolly and waited for a hole to drop through, taking no chances on getting tangled in the rigging or dropping into a swarm of debris or flailing men.

Hundreds fought their way up to the port railing, and walked or slid down the hull. Some waited too long and became fouled in the screws, as Nos. 3 and 4 rose from the water. No. 3 was still turning, a terrifying and relentless meat-grinder. In the minds of everyone was the fear of suction when the ship went down. True or not, everyone has heard that a sinking ship exerts terrible suction when it goes down, and can drag anyone near the hull down with it. So once in the water, every man struck out for safety, one thought only in mind—get away from the ship.

And the last ones off had little time, for the ship seemed anxious to go. As the head and midships, now filling rapidly, sank lower the final hundred feet or so of the giant hull raised straight up out of the water and seemed to stand there for a moment.

Hundreds of men, directly under it, watched in terror as

it hung there, fearing any moment it might topple on them. Captain McVay, now a shipwrecked sailor like the lowliest seaman, saw the screws above him and thought, "Well, this is the end of me."

But they were wrong. The *Indianapolis* waited but a moment, then slipped straight down, like a leadline, disappearing quickly and silently, without suction, without anguish. Thus ended her career of twelve years, eight months, and twenty-three days afloat—the last major vessel lost in World War II.

The time was 12:14 a.m., Monday, July 30, 1945, East Longitude date.

The nearest land was still some 250 miles away, directly south, the top end of the Palaus archipelago. Guam was 600 miles to the east, Leyte 550 miles west, and to the north there was nothing for nearly a thousand miles. The water at this point was probably 10,000 feet deep, give or take a couple of thousand.

Captain McVay was fortunate, though there were times later when he might question this. He struck out swimming, away from the menacing hulk above him. After only a few strokes, a wave of oil and water washed over his head, and he turned to look. The ship was gone.

The captain struck out again, and almost immediately ran into a crate of potatoes, late tenant of the fantail. He climbed astride this, reached out and grabbed a shattered desk floating by, and almost in the same instant saw two rafts not twenty feet away. Captain McVay quickly swam to them, and as he climbed in one he heard men calling for help.

He called back and soon Quartermaster Allard swam alongside, towing two shipmates who looked more dead than alive. Allard pushed Seaman Second Class Ralph D. Klappa toward the raft and Captain McVay reached out for him, saying, "You can make it the rest of the way."

"I can't do anything," Klappa said and started to slide. Only eighteen years old, he had been to sea just fifteen days. McVay pulled him aboard and the youngster lay in the raft, vomiting oil and salt water. Meantime Allard helped Seaman Second Class Angelo Galante, 20, over the side and then pulled himself aboard. Galante joined Klappa in retching as they lay in the raft, recovering from fright and exhaustion.

McVay and Allard lashed the rafts together and spent the night investigating their new home. They quickly discovered the rafts had fallen into the water upside down. Paddles, rations, matches, flares, and other emergency gear were all secured to the bottom. By incredible chance, they saw and heard no one else throughout the night. A man low on the water can see practically nothing, even in daylight, and particularly with a twelve-foot swell running. But at dawn they discovered another raft and floater net nearby, with five more men on it. Captain McVay directed them to come over, and soon the three rafts were lashed together with fifteen feet of line between each. This kept the party from straying but allowed enough line so the rafts wouldn't bump.

As Captain McVay surveyed his command through one eye (the other was inflamed from fuel oil and nearly closed) he thought he was seeing about him the sole survivors of the 1,196 men aboard the *Indianapolis*.

He was greatly mistaken. There were hundreds of men within a few thousand yards, all struggling for their lives, and none as well off as the captain's group. There were a number of reasons why Captain McVay could not see them, or they him.

Men left the ship in a variety of ways over a period of 12 minutes, during most of which the ship was still under way. The first off were soon left far behind, mere heads bobbing in a blanket of fuel oil, virtually undiscernible even from a ship in broad daylight. Those who stayed till the last were split into groups determined by the point at which they had left the ship, the swirling and eddying of waters around the hull, their swimming strength, and the impedimenta thrown in their way from the foundering vessel.

And hardly were they in the water than the sea began inexorably to separate them. The swimmers, nearly totally immersed, presented little surface to the wind and thus the prevailing current began carrying them to the southwest at about one knot. But those on rafts or debris felt the force of the ten-knot wind and were wafted off to the northeast at varying speeds. By daybreak, the groups were scattered over a line of several miles, on a generally southwest-northeast axis. A man with his eyes six inches above water can't see much in a moderately rough sea, even from the top of a twelve-foot swell. If his eyes are smarting from salt water and fuel oil, and partly blinded by a hot sun, he can see even less. Men on a raft have a better chance, but even on a crest you can't see into the troughs of other waves, and you may be scanning east when a head bobs up to the west, only to subside into a valley as you turn.

Monday dawned clear and the men welcomed the sun. It seemed at first to warm them spiritually after the cold night, and promise strength and help. They took heart and, as man seems to do in any circumstance, began organizing this new watery world. There was no question of over-all command, for already the groups were widely scattered. Indeed, in most cases each group knew only of its own existence and was fully occupied with its own problems. Some few small groups, finding themselves close together in the morning, did put their meager forces together. Almost from the start they fell into two large groups, and a dozen or more small, isolated clusters.

In perhaps the largest group—some three hundred men that first day—Lieutenant Commander Haynes was the senior surviving officer, and by virtue of rank, training, and force of personality he took charge. Strictly speaking, he was not the senior officer, for Commander Lipski, the gunnery officer, was there. But he was clearly dying. The flesh on his hands had been burned down to the tendons, and his eyes were burned closed. Shipmates gathered round him and tried to hold his tortured body out of the stinging sea and oil, and Doc Haynes looked on in anguish, unable to lessen his pain. From somewhere, a cork life ring appeared, and they used that for the severely injured. It knew more than one tenant. A long piece of line was formed into a large circle, and perhaps a hundred and fifty men clung around the perimeter. With only this flimsy line, they felt better. There were many other arrangements—one man clung to a toilet seat. Schecterle, just out of sick bay minus his appendix, latched onto a lard can, occasionally dipped into the contents to still the pangs, and alternately used the top as a heliograph. Plenty of ammunition cans were in evidence for a while, and the rubber-type, inflatable life belt was worn in several styles. Some put it around their middle, as indicated. Others wore it like a bandolier, lay across it side saddle, or sometimes floated—using it as a pillow. In any form, it was nearly useless, and the wise man watched for a kapok that might soon be vacated.

Off to the northwest, less than a thousand yards away at the start, was a second large group. Whatever it was at the start, by dawn Monday death had weeded it down to 120 men and perhaps eight to ten officers, senior of whom was Dick Redmayne. Now he found himself in command of three small rafts, one floater net, some 5-inch ammo cans and other flotsam. His force included one seasoned warrant officer, three or four green ensigns, and assorted enlisted men, fortunately including a couple of chiefs. Among them was Benton, whose courage would win him the Navy and Marine Corps medal.

To the northeast, capping the triangle, were the splendid isolationists: the men whose great good fortune it was to have nearly separate quarters on the rafts. Besides McVay's enclave of three rafts and nine men, the biggest single floating command fell to Ensign Rogers, a tall, rangy lad who had been to sea only two weeks. He had been aboard so briefly that though he was a junior officer of Turret IV, he still didn't know his duties or even how it worked. Only the night before, his roommate, the ever-efficient Ensign Woolston, had let him in on the open secret that a sub had been reported along their course. Rogers paid no more attention to this than anyone else. Anyway, he was busy writing a letter to his bride. It was their first anniversary (one month, that is), and he didn't want her to think he had forgotten it.

Rogers was one of the last to leave the ship, and when he hit the water he went down, down, down. He thought he would never come up, but he did and right in front of him was a raft. He grabbed a hard rope on the side and hung on as the ship reared above him, hesitated a moment, and then plunged. It was unbelievable that anything as big and safe and solid could disappear in a moment, but she did. After the final waves washed over him, Rogers climbed into the raft and met his new "shipmates," a mountain boy named Willie Hatfield, Seaman Second Class, from Salt Lick, Kentucky, and Chief Ferguson. During the night they picked up another man. Ferguson was suffering from his leg wounds, and Rogers put a tourniquet around his thigh. Throughout the night, he periodically released the pressure, fearing gangrene, and when dawn came he carefully unwrapped the bandage made of the mess-cook's pants. There was a deep cut at the knee, and four or five inches of flesh gouged out below it, besides less serious cuts on the leg and foot. "Doc" Rogers rewrapped the wound as best he could, and cut the loss of blood to a slow ooze. Figuring rapidly, he reasoned that the ship would be missed Tuesday morning, when it failed to show off Leyte for target practice. Search would start immediately and they should be found by Wednesday morning. Ferguson could last that long, he figured. Ferguson never complained.

During the night, the McVay rafters became scavengers, snatching from the sea any interesting looking objects they passed. At first light, the captain began to take stock of his possessions. His wristwatch was working fine, and he decided to keep a log, using paper and a pencil stub disgorged from various pockets and wallets. The sun gave an approximate position, and a fish line streaming in the water indicated drift. In spite of the wind, the rafts drifted west, and a few degrees south. The inventory revealed a relatively secure position. There were ten twelve-ounce cans of Spam, two large tins of malted-milk tablets, seventeen cans of biscuits, but no water. At least the food would be ample for some days to come.

Paddles were retrieved from the underside of the rafts, and one carton yielded fifty small packages of Camels. Oh boy, all the comforts of home! Well, nearly. There wasn't a lighter in the crowd, and the matches from the emergency kits were soaked. Cigarettes and no way to light them; they cast the cigarettes back into the water, removing at least that form of small torture.

They also found a first-aid kit—unneeded—and, very reassuring, a can of Very flares and an emergency signaling mirror. In the can were a small pistol for firing the flares, and twelve flares in all, four each of red, green, and white. Captain McVay began to feel better. With his little convoy stretching out over seventy-five feet of water, and his signaling devices, he was confident they would be sighted by a plane on this heavily traveled track.

Life was becoming a little grim now. The men were tired, and they ached. All soon discovered that the designer of their rafts had never had to sit on them very long. The rounded top chafed on the buttocks and soon wore them sore. Hands blistered from paddling and every cut or abrasion began to develop salt-water ulcers. There seemed no way to keep dry, even in the rafts, and the constant salt-water dousing was irritating, physically and mentally. It was uncomfortable to sit down, but if you stood up and fell, you had a new cut to contend with. Elbows were turning raw from rubbing and the skin seemed tender and sensitive all over.

For the swimmers, the battle for survival began the instant they hit the water. First it was the struggle to get their heads above the water and out of the slimy, choking oil. They sputtered and coughed, some vomited for hours, spewing out the irritating substance, and many were blinded in one eye or both. Their noses, mouths, and throats smarted from the oil, and membranes became inflamed. And always there was the chop and splash of waves. By dawn, many were already seriously exhausted, but as the sun rose and they began to see others around them, the men took heart.

As the sun rose on Monday, the sea flattened out a little and the men felt better. The kapoks were holding them high, and the worst of the oil bath was over.

As the heat rose, thirst began to bother some men, particularly those who had dehydrated themselves with retching or coughing. But there was no deliberate drinking of sea water that day. The men warned one another about that, and they all knew it was bad for you. Potatoes, canned peanuts, onions, other bits of food floated on the surface in some places, but most of the men wouldn't eat anything. They were afraid of upsetting their stomachs further, or getting even thirstier. A few ate anything that came by, and even hid a surplus in their pockets for later, but hunger was not a real problem yet.

It was some hours before they began to realize that sharks and other rapacious fish were among them. Suddenly a man screamed, his head bobbed for a moment, and he began flailing the water with his arms. Blood welled to the surface, and other men took up the cry. They beat the water with their arms and legs and shouted and screeched in an effort to scare the intruders away. At first they thought only of sharks, because everyone knew about sharks, and the telltale dorsal fin was often in evidence on the fringes of their circles. Gradually word spread from the older men that these warm equatorial waters were also host to carnivorous fish that could not be so easily seen.

The injured who survived the first few hours were weakening now, with the sun high and hot, and the sea and the oil and their wounds all conspiring to sap their strength. It was pitiful to those around them not to be able to help, but there was nowhere to put them, nothing to give them, no way to protect them. They put some in the rafts, but there their bodies were fully exposed to the cruel sun. So they put them back in the water and tried to tie them to the rafts, if they were too weak to hold on. In these last hours of agony, those who had been spared injury gave unstintingly of their strength, their food, even their life jackets to help those who could not help themselves. But in most cases it was not enough. The burned and the maimed slipped away, one by one, and by Monday night nearly all of them were gone.

The strongest and the bravest tried to stay alert, even riding herd on the group like swimming cowpunchers, bringing back the strays and holding the men together. More than one, in this way, used up the reserves that might have kept him alive in the final hours of agony. They were, in truth, laying down their lives for their friends.

For most men, the night was worse than the day. Man's spirit normally sinks at night, and during the long, dark hours they fell prey to fears forgotten by day. It was a grim band, indeed, that struggled through the first twenty-four hours in the water, and in the hours just before dawn a few men began to ask themselves why they fought on. A few, weak and dispirited, perhaps impelled by some previous purposelessness in their lives, may indeed have succumbed to the lassitude of despair. It was so easy just to slip down, to let go, to sink, and in a few moments it was all over. But the first streaks of morning light in the sky revived the great majority of them, and they prepared to meet the day of rescue. For surely help would come on Tuesday.

Tuesday was hot again, hotter than Monday, but nobody wished for night to come. Besides the fears of the dark, ships and planes couldn't see you at night. Night was a foe. But as the daylight hours passed, nothing happened. No plane passed overhead, and no ship came plowing down on them.

Almost from the first, men began discovering that life-jacket design was an art not yet mastered. The rubber life belts were the worst.

In the first place, many refused to inflate, for a variety of causes. Even if they did, they gave little support when worn around the waist, as intended. For one reason or another, perhaps because some were old or the sea water and oil affected them, many burst in a matter of hours. They were better than nothing, to be sure, but not much. The kapok jackets, of the so-called horse-collar type, gave good support, but the collars soon began to rub the men's necks and chins, increasing their suffering as the salt water and oil inflamed the irritated parts.

Thirst was more of a problem than hunger. As the sun rose higher and hotter on Monday, some men began thinking of schemes for making the sea water potable. At this stage, before dementia had set in on a large scale, and

360

their bellies began to hurt, they talked a little of "straining" the water, or "evaporating" it.

"How about it if you hold some water in your hands? Won't the sun evaporate the salt out?"

"What do you say we strain some water through this hat a couple of times? We can catch it in this handkerchief and squeeze it through again. That ought to do it."

"Knock it off, it'll still kill you," said the clearheaded around them. But pretty soon even the clearheaded had problems of their own, and they became less careful or less watchful. Then the men who could stand it no longer took first a little drink, then a bigger one, and a still bigger one. It is a horrible death, but soon over. During the last paroxysms, friends about them sought either to hold them or to escape from their wild thrashings, until at last the bodies subsided and became still. It was time then to salvage the life jacket and knife, mirror, or any other potentially useful object and let the body sink slowly out of sight.

Wednesday was a delightful day for the swimmers. It was the day they learned the *Indianapolis* had not sunk after all. She was lying just below the surface of the water, and the gedunk stand was open, featuring six flavors of ice cream, and the scuttlebutts were pouring forth pure, sweet water as usual. The first man to discover this was so delighted with the find that he urged all those around him to go down with him and slake the terrible thirst that was driving them mad. As the word passed, a sort of frenzy ran through the swimmers and in a short time many were diving like swans, using up the last resources of strength that might have saved their lives. Some men who had not yet passed fully into the world of fantasy tried to restrain them, but it was useless.

But Wednesday night was a night of terror. When darkness fell the demented men were the victims of stark fear, and every shape became an enemy.

"There's Japs on this line," someone screamed and a little knot of men would be plunged into a melee, fighting with fists, cans, cork, anything that came to hand. Now and then a knife blade flashed in the moonlight, followed by a groan and then a struggle for a life jacket whose recent owner needed it no more.

"Here comes a Jap, he's trying to kill me," a sailor shouted. "Help! help!" The frenzied men took up the shout and began swinging wildly at anyone near. Two men climbed on Doc Haynes and dragged him under. When he struggled to the top again he tried to calm the men, but it was no use. They were too far gone for reason. Those who still possessed their senses could see the toll was terrible.

Toward morning, calm slowly returned and it was obvious the men were falling into the final stupor that precedes death. Haynes moved among the pitiful survivors, trying to rouse them for one last day's fight. He lifted head after head from the water, rolled back an eyelid and, in some, detected signs of life. These men he slapped and cajoled into consciousness, trying to pull them back from the brink.

Thursday began as a day of calm—the calm of death for the swimmers. With all strength gone, all emotion spent, they seemed nearer death than life, and indeed they were. There was little talk or movement, just a quiet waiting for the end to overtake them. Hanging in their waterlogged life jackets, their mouths and noses nearly in the water, they no longer wished nor hoped for anything, not even death. The inevitable sun rose, higher and hotter, and still no complaints. They were not capable of caring any more. A few, slightly stronger than the others, looked up occasionally or even strained to listen when they thought they heard a plane. A little before noon, with the sun still mounting, a few looked up when a plane droned by, high overhead. There was a scattering of muttered curses, even a doubled fist raised weakly out of the water. The plane passed over, to the north. They had known it would.

Then, here and there, a heart fluttered. The plane seemed to pause, to turn. Some thought it was starting down. It was, it was!

"He sees us, he sees us!" someone screamed. Others joined in, and arms and legs began to splash.

"They're coming, they're coming!" "He's turning, he's turning!" "Here he comes!"

Like sleepers roused from stupor the men began to come alive, joining in the chorus one by one. Where they got the strength no one can say, but soon the ocean was kicked into a froth, and cries echoed from many throats. Some men could only croak or grunt, their gullets swollen nearly shut, and some men didn't move or utter a sound. Too late, too late.

It was almost exactly three and a half days—eighty-four hours—since the *Indianapolis* had gone down.

The big, friendly plane circled slowly and then—over the southernmost knot of men—a raft, some life jackets, and other gear spewed from the plane and fell nearby. Grateful men swam out to get the raft, careful not to overtax their strength, and when they reached it clung to the sides, too weak to climb in. Others grabbed the fresh dry life jackets to replace their waterlogged ones. Men for miles around watched as the plane slowly climbed away from them, and held their breath until they saw that she was not going away. It was comforting to have her there, even though she could do them no immediate good. As long as she stayed they knew she was helping them, telling someone by radio where to look, calling others to their aid.

The second plane, a PBM, arrived from the northeast a little after noon. She didn't stay long, but she dropped three more life rafts and then hurried on to the west, toward Leyte. Hope was getting stronger now; other planes would be coming, and ships. Another plane, a Ventura like the first, arrived a half hour later, and also from the south. The two Venturas orbited overhead and seemed to be talking, or planning, and watching. Then the first Ventura, their friend, their savior, took off southward, obviously going back to base to get more help. The second Ventura remained overhead, but it wasn't until nearly four o'clock, with the sun already starting down, that the next plane arrived. This was a big amphibian from the south, and after a look around she began to drop things, like an elephant littering the track at the circus. Out came rafts, one after another, and cartons of rations, dye marker, life jackets, casks of water. Some of the water casks split on hitting the water, some of the gear sank, and some was useless, but it was all welcome, if only as a symbol that help was on the way.

But day was definitely waning, and the men in the water began to wonder if still another night in the water, their fourth, would be required of them. To make matters worse, the sea was beginning to make up again. Toward sunset those few left in the southernmost group, the Haynes group, watched in wonder as the PBY slowly glided down as if to make a landing run. It looked like suicide, with the swells running nearly twelve feet high by this time. But the giant plane kept coming down and suddenly pancaked into a trough, took three mightly bounces in a towering spray, and came safely to rest on the water.

Strangled cheers broke through sore and swollen lips and throats as the PBY began to taxi slowly around the periphery, pausing now and then to scoop a lone swimmer into its belly. Those who now had rafts, nets, or other means of support cursed at the plane as it passed them without stopping, but it was obvious what the pilot was doing—as darkness fell he was hurrying to pick up the lone swimmers, those with nothing to cling to.

It was very nearly dark now, and just as the last light began to fade a second PBY came in from the south, low and slow. This one, bearing Army markings, quickly came down to wave-top height, knifed through the tops of several swells and cut her power, disappearing in a trough. Soon she appeared on the crest of a wave, safely landed. She seemed quite a way off from any swimmers, but maybe some could find her in the dark. Those still in the water, and there were hundreds, were alone again now, but at least they had hope, and perhaps a raft, to sustain them through the darkness.

Eight or ten miles to the north, Captain McVay and the other raft parties could see the plane activity through the afternoon. McVay was greatly cheered, not only because rescue seemed near but because the concentration of activity far south indicated there might be many more survivors than he had believed. But as the afternoon waned and the planes seemed to be working ever southward, the raft crews began to worry that they would not be seen.

Again at dusk, as he had each night, Captain McVay led the men in reciting "The Lord's Prayer." It seemed more helpful than usual this night.

But this was not to be a night like the others. About 9:30 some of the swimmers and rafters began to notice a light far to the south. At first it seemed it might be an illusion or a faint moon rising behind the clouds. As time passed, however, the light became stronger and within a half hour it seemed pretty definitely to be a searchlight, reflected off the clouds. By the time an hour had gone by, the light was unquestionably brighter, and coming closer, although still a long way off. By 11:00 they were sure—it was a ship coming at them, fast, and with all lights on.

Now that help was so near, they feared sleep more than ever and were less able to fight it, being on the outer edges of oblivion.

"I mustn't sleep, I mustn't sleep," they told themselves. Men who had not once slept in eighty hours, or so they believed, vowed they would not succumb now, with help so near, so near. But the sea was rougher Thursday night, security so close, and they were so tired—not every man kept his vow.

On the rafts to the north, the men could see the searchlights off to the south, first one, then several, and finally by dawn there was great activity. But it did not move north, or so it seemed.

For the swimmers, actual rescue in the form of help from surface vessels began shortly after midnight on Thursday, exactly four days, or ninety-six hours, from the sinking of the *Indianapolis*. By chance, the first vessel approached from the south. Had she come from the north, she might have seen the men on the rafts first—the men who could wait—and delayed long enough to cost even more lives, for with the swimmers minutes counted. But the planes on the water and the accident of approach led the ships directly to the men who needed help the most, and through the black hours from midnight to dawn the rescue vessels picked up one of the most pitiful bands of men ever to escape the sea. Men suffered from burns—sun or flame—fish bites, salt-water ulcers, inflammation of the nose and throat, acute dehydration, pneumonia, fractures, and cuts and bruises from a thousand sources. But hearts still pumped and blood still flowed and from now on it would be up to medical science.

At dawn the rescue vessels began to see what they had been doing and to realize the magnitude of the appalling tragedy before them. Command and planning took over from the frantic and haphazard methods of the dark hours. They began to take stock of how many men they had aboard, how many might still be in the sea, and how best to comb the area for the last remaining survivor. On orders now, the vessels spread out in search pattern sniffing for the living among this welter of oil, debris, and bodies.

Last to be rescued were the rafters, at the north of the group. Their most anxious moments came in the last hours of Friday morning darkness, when it seemed the ships were so near and yet would miss them. But at dawn they saw planes to the north and hope rose again. The planes were obviously on box search, and coming ever closer.

At 10:00 a.m. they saw ships, and suddenly someone shouted, "My God, ships bearing down on us! The hell with the planes, we know these guys will pick us up."

It was the end of one of the strangest, most dramatic battles of men against the sea.

Potsdam to Hiroshima

On July 26, 1945, while meeting in Germany during the Potsdam conference, President Truman and Prime Minister Churchill issued a proclamation calling for the surrender of Japan unconditionally. Nine days earlier the President had been notified that the first experimental atomic bomb explosion in New Mexico had been a success. He and the Prime Minister decided to use the bomb on Japan if their terms were not met. There was no direct reply from the Japanese Government, and on August 2nd, while President Truman was returning to Washington he issued the order to drop the bombs.

According to Churchill, "there never was a moment's discussion as to whether the atomic bomb should be used or not. To avert a vast, indefinite butchery, to bring the war to an end, to give peace to the world, to lay healing hands upon its tortured peoples by a manifestation of overwhelming power at the cost of a few explosions, seemed, after all our toils and perils, a miracle of deliverance." *

Over a million leaflets were dropped on eleven principal Japanese cities warning of bombing attacks to come. There was little effect upon the military rulers of Japan who still held full sway over the people; the die-hard militarists always managed to turn each reverse into a rationalization for eventual victory or an improvement of their strategic position. They were only too willing to commit the nation to a suicidal last stand.

Fortunately, the Emperor and certain other Japanese leaders chose to defy the militarists, but they were not able to do much until the atomic bombs were dropped. Even then, the military assessed the Hiroshima explosion as a "four ton block-buster," revising it a little later to "100 tons."

A meeting of the Japanese war cabinet was held in Tokyo on August 9. During the meeting, news of the Nagasaki bombing was reported.

*Winston Churchill, *Triumph and Tragedy*, p. 639. Houghton Mifflin.

The Japanese War Minister and his Chiefs of Staff still held out against unconditional surrender. "Finally the Emperor, who had neither constitutional nor traditional right to make a decision or even to express an opinion without Cabinet consent, took the issue in his own hands: 'To stop the war on this occasion is the only way to save the nation from destruction.... I decide this war shall be stopped.' " *

On August 10, the Japanese Government accepted the Potsdam terms. But it was too late to save the citizens of Hiroshima and Nagasaki.

THE GREAT WHITE LIGHT

by Major Gene Gurney

In the beginning, back in 1939, 1940, and 1941, the idea had been to develop a bomb as quickly as possible, and to use it. Gradually as the awesome nature of the new weapon became more apparent, some doubts were raised. The responsibility that went with the power of the bomb was great indeed, and it would trouble men forever.

President Truman assumed responsibility for the use of the atomic bomb almost as soon as he assumed the office of President of the United States. Immediately after he had taken the oath of office, Secretary of War Stimson told him of the new weapon soon to be ready for use against the enemy. A few weeks later, after the President had received a thorough technical explanation of the bomb, Stimson suggested that a committee be formed to work out just how it should be used.

Named to the Interim Committee, as it was called, were: Secretary Stimson, chairman; George L. Harrison, acting chairman in the absence of Stimson; James F. Byrnes, personal representative of the President; Undersecretary of the

*Walter Karig, *Battle Report: Victory in the Pacific,* pp. 508, 509. Rinehart & Co.

Navy Ralph A. Bard; Assistant Secretary of State William L. Clayton; and scientists Vannevar Bush, K. T. Compton, and J. B. Conant. These men were hand-picked by the Commander in Chief to deal with the most fearsome weapon ever developed by man. It was their task to recommend what was to be done with the top secret bomb which would be ready by August 1.

On June 1, after a series of conferences, the Interim Committee officially adopted a series of recommendations concerning this weapon and sent them along to the President. And with them went the blueprint of a new era of warfare.

The recommendations were:

1. The atom bomb should be used against Japan as soon as possible.

2. It should be used on a dual target—that is, a military installation or war plant surrounded by, or adjacent to, houses and other buildings most susceptible to damage.

3. It should be used without prior warning of the nature of the weapon.

The principal considerations in reaching these decisions were later disclosed by Mr. Stimson:

"As we understood it, there was a very strong possibility that the Japanese Government might determine upon resistance to the end in all areas of the Far East under its control. In such an event the Allies would be faced with the enormous task of destroying an armed force of 5,000,000 men and 5,000 suicide aircraft belonging to a race which had already amply demonstrated its ability to fight literally to the death.

"We estimated that if we should be forced to carry this task to its conclusion, the major fighting would not end until the latter part of 1946, at the earliest. I was informed that such operations might be expected to cost over a million casualties to American forces alone. Additional large losses might be expected among our Allies, and, of course, if our campaign were successful and if we could judge by previous experience, enemy casualties would be much larger than our own.

"My chief purpose was to end the war in victory with the

least possible cost in the lives of the men in the armies which I had helped to raise. In the light of the alternatives which, on a fair estimate, were open to us, I believe that no man, in our position and subject to our responsibilities, holding in his hands a weapon of such possibilities for accomplishing this purpose and saving those lives, could have failed to use it and afterwards looked his countrymen in the face."

Unaware of the momentous decisions being made in Washington, the combat crews of the 509th went through the week-long indoctrination course given to all new arrivals.[1] By the end of June they were ready to resume their flight training. First came three weeks of navigation training flights and bombing missions against Rota, Guguan, Truk, and Marcus with regular 500- or 1,000-pound bombs instead of the dummy bombs carried at Wendover. Then on July 20, training began to take the 509th to Japan. By the 29th they had made 12 strikes, each one a precision attack against a target near, but not actually in, one of the cities chosen for the atomic bomb.

A list of potential targets for the bomb had been drawn up after the Interim Committee had made its report. The Committee had pointed out the advisability of choosing a target that included a military installation plus a surrounding civilian area. The choice was further limited by the fact that the bomb's effectiveness could be measured only if it were dropped in an area still relatively undamaged. Weeks of intensive bombing by General LeMay's 21st Bomber Command had already destroyed the largest Japanese cities. Of those left, Kyoto was the largest, followed by Hiroshima, Niigata, and Kokura. This list met with the approval of General Arnold; on July 3 the Joint Chiefs of Staff ordered that there be no bombing of the four cities. Secretary Stimson, however, questioned the presence of Kyoto on the list. It was a religious and cultural center, and Stimson felt that its destruction would never be forgiven by the Japanese. With the approval of President Truman, Kyoto was removed from the list and replaced

[1] A new bombardment unit, designated the 509th Composite Group, especially organized for dropping the bomb.—Ed. note.

with Nagasaki at the suggestion of General LeMay's staff, although it was far from ideal as a target.

The four target cities were studied carefully so that the practice strikes of the 509th could be planned to give the crews as much experience as possible for the important mission they might someday have to fly. The navigation and bombing procedures used and the sharp turn away from the target were all similar to what would be the case if an atomic bomb were dropped. The bombs that were dropped were 10,000-pounders with ballistics similar to the atomic bomb.

The 509th was a highly trained outfit; its marksmanship on these training missions was impressive. But all its bombing reports and strike photos went straight to General LeMay, by-passing the usual lines of communication with higher headquarters, and so the other groups based in the Marianas wondered about the 509th. It had the very best of beautiful, new equipment, yet it didn't take part in the big fire raids on Japan. Its planes bore different markings—a black circle bisected by a black arrow. Its section of the base was full of restricted areas surrounded by barbed wire and guards, and there seemed to be numerous civilians about —the scientists and technicians who were to assemble the bomb.

If the rest of the Twentieth Air Force was in the dark about the mission of the 509th, the members of the unit didn't know much more about it. They all knew they were going to drop a special kind of bomb. Each of the men was working on his own part of the project, but security forbade discussion, even among themselves. They did not know what kind of bomb it was or how powerful it would be. They certainly hadn't seen it, because not until August 1, in one of the 509th's bomb huts where temperature and humidity could be carefully controlled, was the first bomb assembled.

The bomb lying in the air-conditioned hut on Tinian was the "Little Boy." It had never been tested, but the scientists were sure it would work. Since the 16th of July they had been sure that their second bomb, the "Fat Man," would work even better than the "Little Boy." At 5:30 a.m.

on the 16th the plutonium bomb had been exploded in the desert near Alamogordo, New Mexico, with results that exceeded the expectations of its designers.

President Truman and Secretary Stimson received the news of the successful test explosion while they were attending the Potsdam Conference. The President had agreed with the recommendations of the Interim Committee, and now he reaffirmed his earlier decision to use the powerful new weapon in the hope of saving the millions of lives that would be lost in an invasion of Japan. Japan was warned on July 26 to surrender unconditionally to avoid "inevitable and complete" destruction. Two days later the Potsdam Declaration was rejected by Premier Suzuki.

The chain of command that extended from President Truman down to the crew of the "Enola Gay" had already started to function. On July 25, General Carl A. Spaatz, commander of the United States Army Strategic Air Forces, had been given a directive which ordered the 509th Composite Group to drop the first atomic bomb as soon after August 3 as the weather would allow visual bombing. Spaatz immediately left Washington for Guam where his United States Army Strategic Air Forces headquarters had taken over the functions of the Washington headquarters of the Twentieth Air Force; he arrived there on July 29.

By August 1 it was just a matter of waiting for the 3rd, the earliest date set for the attack, and after that, for suitable bombing weather. There were now two bombs available; the scientists and technicians needed to handle them were on Tinian; the 509th had made 12 training strikes at targets in Japan; and the crew had been selected to deliver the first bomb.

Colonel Tibbets was going to lead the mission. He chose the plane and crew of Captain Robert Lewis, one of his instructors, to carry the bomb. With them would go one B-29 to measure the effect of the blast and one to carry camera equipment. In addition, three Superforts would precede Colonel Tibbets to check the weather, and there would be another Superfort waiting at Iwo Jima to take the bomb in case Tibbets' plane developed trouble.

On August 2 President Truman made his final decision

to use the bomb against Japan, and Lieutenant General Nathan Twining issued the field orders for the strike. The primary target was to be Hiroshima; the alternates were Kokura and Nagasaki. The bombing was to be visual, from 28,000 to 30,000 feet, the airspeed 200 miles per hour; the date was to be August 6.

The Superforts making the trip had their group insignia and names marked out. Tibbets later arranged to have Enola Gay, his mother's name, painted on the nose of the plane that was going to carry the bomb.

On August 4 the briefing of the crews began. At the first session they were shown pictures of the Alamogordo explosion and told that the bomb they were going to drop would have a force equal to 20,000 tons of TNT. The word "atomic" was not used to describe the bomb. Polaroid glasses were issued to all the men scheduled to go. They were given the details usual at a pre-mission briefing—take-off times, altitudes, routes, fuel loads. And they were given special instructions about avoiding clouds and keeping a critical distance from the target area after the bomb had been dropped.

The next day the Enola Gay was given a test run. Later she was taxied to a loading pit where the bomb waited. The five-ton "Little Boy" was raised by hydraulic jacks up into the forward bomb bay of the Superfort. The doors were closed and a sign posted to indicate that the plane was "cocked" and ready to go.

At midnight there was a weather briefing; the weather looked good. The crews were told of the arrangements that had been made for air-sea rescue and given final details on the procedures to be followed during the mission. Then came breakfast, and then the three weather planes took off. Take-off time for the Enola Gay was to be 2:45 a.m.

The crew started to assemble at the Enola Gay at two o'clock. Besides Colonel Tibbets there were Captain Robert A. Lewis, who was acting as copilot; Major Thomas W. Ferebee, the bombardier; Captain Theodore J. Van Kirk, the navigator; Lieutenant Jacob Beser, a radar countermeasures officer; Master Sergeant Wyatt E. Duzenbury, the flight engineer; Staff Sergeant Joe S. Stiborik, radar operator; Sergeant George R. Caron, the tail gunner; Sergeant Robert A. Schumard, the waist gunner; and Pfc. Richard H. Nelson, radio operator. Also making the trip were Navy Captain William S. Parsons, who had worked at Los Alamos and was in charge of the bomb, and his assistant, Lieutenant Morris R. Jeppson.

After Army photographers had taken their pictures of the plane, the ground crew, and the crowd gathered to see them off, one by one the men climbed into the Superfort. Tibbets appeared at the pilot's window; he waved and started the four powerful engines one after another. Slowly the Enola Gay taxied to her runway. The camera plane, piloted by Captain George W. Marquardt, and Major Charles W. Sweeney's "Great Artiste," which had been transformed into a flying laboratory, were waiting for their take-off time. The Enola Gay left the ground at 2:45 to be followed at two-minute intervals by the other two planes. The "Little Boy" was on its way to Japan.

The bomb was still not armed. There had been a series of bad take-off crashes which had made everyone worry about having the Enola Gay take off with a live bomb on board. Captain Parsons had decided to put off the final assembly of the bomb until after they were safely airborne. To make sure that he would be able to do it smoothly when the time came, he had practiced putting the explosive charge in the end of the bomb over and over again. Now, as the Enola Gay leveled out over the Pacific, Parsons and Jeppson went to work in the bomb bay. The charge was inserted and the final connections made. The bomb would now explode after it had dropped to an altitude of 1,850 feet.

At Iwo Jima the Enola Gay began a slow climb to the altitude from which the bomb was to be dropped. The decision to strike the primary or the alternate targets rested with Colonel Tibbets and was to be made on the basis of information transmitted by the weather ships flying ahead of the Enola Gay.

At 8:15 the report on Hiroshima was received: "2/10 lower and middle lower, and 2/10 at 15,000 feet." Visual bombing conditions at the primary target! The decision was quickly made. Hiroshima!

The doomed city, Japan's eighth largest, was exactly what the Interim Committee had recommended as a target for the first atomic bomb—a military installation surrounded by houses and other buildings. It was an important army transport base and contained large ordnance, food, and clothing depots. It also had a shipbuilding yard, textile mills, oil-storage facilities, electrical works, and a large railroad yard. Because Hiroshima was on the list of targets reserved for the 509th, it had received so little damage that some of its residents had come to believe they were going to be spared the fate of Tokyo and Yokohama.

As the Enola Gay flew toward Hiroshima with her deadly cargo, the crew passed the time in various ways. Some of them tried to sleep, some read, some just sat and thought about the job that lay ahead. They were all a little awed by the bomb that rode in the forward bay. It was gray and long—close to ten feet—and about a yard in diameter. It was the biggest bomb they had ever seen.

Colonel Tibbets crawled back through the tunnel from the pilot's compartment to give the men in the rear a final briefing on the bomb. He asked the tail gunner, Sergeant George Caron, if he had figured it out yet.

Caron asked, "Is it some chemist's nightmare?"

Tibbets said it had nothing to do with chemistry. Then Caron recalled something he had read about a cyclotron and asked if it was a physicist's nightmare.

To this Colonel Tibbets replied, "I guess you could call it that."

As he started to return to the pilot's compartment Caron stopped him with another question: "Are we going to split atoms?"

The colonel just smiled and went back to his flying.

As the Enola Gay neared the Japanese coast, Captain Parsons went back to take one last look at the bomb. With Jeppson he had been keeping an electronic check on it from the forward compartment. Everything seemed to be all right. The bomb run was begun 25 miles out. Each man had his goggles ready to pull over his eyes when he heard the bombing signal. When they were 12 miles from target,

Ferebee, the bombardier, took over. Below he could see Hiroshima on the delta of the Ota River.

It was 8:15 in Hiroshima when the bomb was released. The continuous tone of the signal cut off, warning the crew and those in the accompanying Superforts that the bomb was away. The Enola Gay was at 31,600 feet, traveling at 328 miles per hour. It was clear and sunny. There were no enemy aircraft visible and the flak was far below them. The men sat behind their dark goggles and waited.

The bomb, set to go off above the ground to increase the effect of its blast, exploded in less than a minute. By that time Tibbets had put the Enola Gay into a steep, tight turn—the same turn he had practiced so often—and was leaving the target behind.

Far below, the 245,000 people who had not been evacuated from Hiroshima were up and beginning a new day. There had been an air-raid alert when the weather planes had passed over, but the all-clear had sounded. War workers were either en route or had already arrived at their destinations while others were busy building firebreaks and removing valuables to safety in the country. Probably few heard the Enola Gay as it passed over Hiroshima. The Japanese jammed in the vast Bushido Arsenal or hurrying through the heart of town to their jobs had no warning of the holocaust that was to envelop them.

Suddenly a light brighter than a thousand suns filled the sky. The world's first atomic bomb had exploded. At that moment, air became fire, walls crumbled to dust, and lives flickered out by the thousands.

The explosion started hundreds of fires almost simultaneously—fires whose intense heat sucked in air from all directions, creating a fire wind which helped to spread the numerous blazes. An area measuring 4.7 square miles in the heart of the city was completely destroyed. According to Japanese figures, 71,379 residents of Hiroshima were either dead or missing as a result of the bombing; almost that many more were injured. Many of the casualties were among the personnel of the Second Army and the Chucogu Regional Army units stationed in Hiroshima.

When the bomb exploded, the Enola Gay was racing away

from Hiroshima. In spite of the bright sunlight, the flash of the explosion lit up the inside of the Superfort. The crews of the two escort planes, observing the explosion through their protective goggles, reported that the flash after the explosion was deep purple, then reddish. It reached to almost 8,000 feet. The cloud, shaped like a mushroom, was up to 20,000 feet in one minute. Then the top part broke from the stem and eventually reached 40,000 feet.

Sergeant Caron, riding in the tail of the Enola Gay, was in the best position to view the effects of the blast. He saw a flash followed by a tremendous buildup of light which grew and then faded out.

"After what seemed like an eternity," Caron reported, "I saw shock waves coming up. I reported this to the Colonel and started taking pictures. He called back and told me to keep talking. I added that the shock waves resembled a series of circles like those caused from dropping pebbles in water. Seconds later they struck the airplane and one of the pilots asked if we had been hit by flak.

"Colonel Tibbets kept asking me what was going on. Then I saw the cloud and was never so busy in my life—trying to take pictures and keep the Colonel and the rest of the crew up to date on the blast.

"By the time the cloud rose slightly into the air we were far enough away and I could see the entire city. I commented that the whole area was covered with a thick, purplish mass that looked like fluid. It looked like it was a hundred or more feet thick and flooding out over the city from the center of the blast. Then flames started breaking up through the smoke and dust. The Colonel asked me to count them. I tried but lost track. In the meantime I was still taking pictures.

"Then Colonel Tibbets turned the Enola Gay so all crewmen could see and each gave his impression over the intercom and into the wire recorder. As we headed for home, the Colonel told me to keep my eye on the 'mushroom' and tell him when it disappeared from view. The crew for the most part was quiet on the return. I just sat there and watched that cloud. Finally, I called up that I was losing sight of it. We then were 363 miles from Hiroshima."

Captain Parsons later described what he was able to see: "A few fires were visible around the edges of the smoke, but we could see nothing of the city except the dock area where buildings were falling down. The boiling dust and debris continued for several minutes, as a white cloud plumed upward from the center to 40,000 feet and an angry dust cloud spread all around the city."

The crew felt a sense of relief that the bomb had been dropped successfully after their many months of training. But it was relief tinged with awe at the unearthly flash, the shock of the distant explosion, and the sight of a city disintegrating before their eyes.

The Superfort whose single bomb had destroyed Hiroshima sped back to Tinian, 1,600 miles away. So did The Great Artiste, whose instruments had measured the blast, and the B-29 camera plane. Messages had preceded them that the bomb had been dropped successfully.

The trip back was uneventful. Captain Lewis described their landing:

"I looked at 'Ole Bull' [Colonel Tibbets] and his eyes were bloodshot and he looked awful tired. He looked like the past ten months at Wendover and Washington and New Mexico and overseas had come up and hit him all at once. I said to him, 'Bull after such a beautiful job, you'd better make a beautiful landing.' And he did."

The Enola Gay touched down at 2:58 p.m., 12 hours and 13 minutes after she had taken off on her momentous journey into the Atomic Age. Close to 200 people were waiting as the Superfort taxied to her hardstand. Among them was General Spaatz, who pinned the Distinguished Service Cross on Tibbets' flying suit.

President Truman received news of the successful dropping of the bomb as he was returning from Potsdam on board the *Augusta*. His public announcement of the bombing was released in Washington 16 hours after it happened —still August 6 in the United States because of the time difference. The President again warned the Japanese people of what was in store for them.

The men in the Marianas received their first word of the powerful new bomb that had been dropped on Japan from

378

the President's message. The 509th now became the center of attention, but the other B-29 units still had work to do. On the 7th, 131 Superforts struck at Tokokawa. The next day there was an incendiary attack on Yawata.

When no offer of surrender came from Japan, the decision was made to drop a second atomic bomb on the 9th. This time the primary target was to be Kokura in northern Kyushu, the site of a large army arsenal. Nagasaki was the secondary target. It was an industrial city covering a series of hills and valleys on the west coast of Kyushu.

"Fat Man," the plutonium bomb that had been tested at Alamogordo on July 16 and found to be more powerful than the one dropped on Hiroshima, was made ready and placed aboard the Superfort, "Bock's Car." Major Charles W. Sweeney, who had been in charge of one of the observation planes on the Hiroshima mission, was the pilot; his co-pilot was Lieutenant Frederick Olivi; the bombardier was Captain Kermit K. Beahan; and Captain James F. Van Pelt, Jr., was the navigator. Lieutenant Commander Frederick Ashworth was in charge of the bomb, which this time had to be armed before the plane took off.

Sweeney's regular B-29, The Great Artiste, which had been filled with instruments, accompanied Bock's Car as an observation plane and was flown by Captain Frederick Bock, who usually flew Bock's Car. This switch of planes between Sweeney and Bock led to confusion in stories about the dropping of the second atomic bomb. For years afterward there were accounts of the mission that had The Great Artiste carrying the bomb to Nagasaki.

Once more, in the early hours of an August morning, Superforts were prepared for take-off. Two observation planes went with Bock's Car; two weather planes were sent ahead to check bombing conditions at Kokura and at Nagasaki. A spare B-29 would be waiting at Iwo Jima in case Bock's Car couldn't make it all the way with the bomb.

The strike force got safely off at 3:49 a.m., much to the relief of the scientists, who feared a crash with the armed bomb would destroy half of Tinian. At 9 a.m. the report received from the Kokura weather plane indicated visual bombing conditions over the primary target. With orders that called for a visual drop, Sweeney headed for Kokura.

But by the time Bock's Car arrived over the target, the weather had closed in and visual bombing was impossible. In his report Major Sweeney described what happened:

"The navigator made landfall perfectly. We passed over the primary target, but for some reason it was obscured by smoke. There was no flak. We took another run almost from the I.P. Again smoke hid the target. 'Look harder,' I said to the bombardier, but it was no use. Then I asked Commander Ashworth to come up for a little conference.

"We took a third run with no success. I had another conference with the Commander. We had now been fifty minutes over the target and wanted to drop our bomb in the ocean. Our gas was getting low. Six hundred gallons were trapped in one of the tanks.

"We decided to head for Nagasaki, the secondary target."

The report received from the Nagasaki weather plane at 9:19 had been "ceiling and visibility unlimited," but when Bock's Car reached there the target had a 8/10 cloud cover. Because of their fuel shortage Sweeney and Ashworth had decided to make one run and drop the bomb by radar if they had to. Commander Ashworth took the responsibility for the change in procedure.

The big ship was on instruments for 90 per cent of the bomb run. At the last moment Captain Beahan, the bombardier, called out, "I can see it, I can see the target!"

He took over and made a visual release of the bomb. It was 10:58 Nagasaki time. As the thundering Superfort turned in a tight arc and sped south, the city vanished in a sky-searing flash of light.

Nagasaki had had an air-raid alert at 7:45 a.m.; the all-clear had sounded at 8:30. When Bock's Car was sighted, the raid signal was given again but few people bothered to go to the shelters. If they had, the loss figures would have been less than the estimated 35,000 killed, 5,000 missing, and 60,000 injured.

The Nagasaki bomb's blast effect seemed greater than that at Hiroshima because of the difference in topography and the type of bomb used. The area totally destroyed was an oval 2.3 miles long and 1.9 miles wide; every building in it was destroyed, with severe damage extending in an irregular pattern beyond that. Over 68 per cent of Nagasaki's industrial area was destroyed.

The men in Bock's Car had donned their polaroid glasses before the bomb was dropped, but they were nearly blinded by the flash. Sergeant Raymond C. Gallagher, the assistant flight engineer, told of a tremendous white flash such as he had never seen before; this was followed by a black cloud which billowed up like a balloon.

The tail gunner, Staff Sergeant Albert T. Dehart, saw what looked like a big red ball coming up at him. On the ground was a big black cloud and out of it came a huge white cloud.

The shock of the explosion was felt by those in the strike plane. "The turbulence of the blast," said Major Sweeney, "was greater than that at Hiroshima. Even though we were prepared for what happened, it was unbelievable. Seven or eight miles from the city shock waves as visible as ripples on a pond overtook our plane, and concussion waves twice thumped against the plane, jolting it roughly.

"The underside of the great clouds over Nagasaki was amber-tinted, as though reflecting the conflagration at least six miles below. Beneath the top cloud mass, white in color, there gradually climbed a turbulent pillar of black smoke and dust which emitted a second fireball less vivid than the first. It rose as solid as a stump, its base dark purple, with a reddish hue in the center that paled to brown near the top."

The last look they got at Nagasaki showed a thick cone of dust covering half the city. On its rim near the harbor great fires were raging.

Aboard Bock's Car there was serious debate as to whether to bail out over an air-sea rescue craft in the Pacific or to try to reach Okinawa's Yontan airfield on their shrinking fuel supply. The decision was to make a run for Okinawa. As Bock's Car, practically dry of gasoline, descended to land at Okinawa, Sergeant Dehart, the tail gunner, saw smoke from Nagasaki 385 miles away.

The Emperor's Role

The question that continues to plague the world is whether dropping the bomb was an "immoral act." Could a more humane way have been found to settle the war without the atomic weapons. The obvious alternative—the invasion of Japan itself—is an equally chilling possibility. Admiral S. E. Morison describes what it could have been like:

"It was the Emperor who cut governmental red tape and made the great decision. This required courage. The Army chiefs and Admiral Toyoda were not greatly moved by the atomic explosions. They argued that the two bombs were probably all that the United States had; and if more were made we would not dare use them when invading Japan; that there was a fair chance of defeating the invasion by massed kamikaze attacks, and that in any event national honor demanded a last battle on Japanese soil. All the fighting hitherto had been little more than peripheral skirmishes; the way to victory was to "lure" the Americans ashore and "annihilate" them, as had been done by the original kamikaze "divine wind" to the hordes of Kublai Khan in A.D. 1281. Such had been the propaganda line given to the Japanese people to explain the series of defeats; they had no idea that Japan was really beaten.* Nothing less than an assertion of the Imperial will could have overcome these arguments and objections.

*Shigemitsu, *Japan and Her Destiny,* p. 334. An intelligent and patriotic French banker, M. Jacques Bardac, who was interned at Peiping through the entire war and cut off from all news and propaganda except Japanese, told me that it was so well done as to convince him up to the very last that Japan was winning. The older Japanese on Oahu, who could not understand English, believed even after the end of the war that Japan had won, and scores of them assembled one day on Aiea Heights to see the victorious Imperial Fleet enter Pearl Harbor. War Research Lab. Univ. of Hawaii, Report No. 8 of 1 Mar., 1946; Y. Kimura, "Rumor among the Japanese," *Social Process in Hawaii,* XI (1947), pp. 84-92.

"On the Allied side it has been argued that the maritime blockade, virtually complete by mid-August, would have strangled Japanese economy and that the B-29s and naval gunfire ships would have destroyed her principal cities and forced a surrender before long, without the aid of the atomic bombs, or of invasion. Fleet Admirals King and Leahy lent their distinguished advocacy to this view. Whether or not they were correct, not even time can tell. But of some facts one can be certain. The stepped-up B-29 bombings and naval bombardments, had they been continued after 15 August, would have cost the Japanese loss and suffering far, far greater than those inflicted by the two atomic bombs. And the probable effects of the projected invasions of Kyushu and Honshu in the fall and winter of 1945-1946, and of a desperate place-to-place defense of Japan, stagger the imagination. It is simply not true that Japan had no military capability left in mid-August. Although 2,550 kamikaze planes had been expended, there were 5,350 of them still left, together with as many more ready for orthodox use, and some 7,000 under repair or in storage; and 5,000 young men were training for the Kamikaze Corps. The plan was to disperse all aircraft on small grass strips in Kyushu, Shikoku and western Honshu, and in underground hangars and caves, and conserve them for kamikaze crashes on the Allied amphibious forces invading the home islands. Considering the number of planes, pilots and of potential targets, all within a short distance of principal airfields, it requires little imagination to depict the horrible losses that would have been inflicted on the invading forces, even before they got ashore. After accepting these losses there would have been protracted battles on Japanese soil, which would have cost each side very many more lives, and created a bitterness which even time could hardly have healed. Japan had plenty of ammunition left; the U.S. Army after the war found thousands of tons holed up in Hokkaido alone. And, as Russia would have been a full partner in this final campaign, there is a fair chance that Japan would have been divided like Germany and Korea, if not delivered completely to the mercy of the Communists.

"We must also point out that even after two atomic bombs had been dropped, the Potsdam Declaration clarified, the guards' insurrection defeated and the Emperor's will made known, it was touch and go whether the Japanese actually would surrender. Hirohito had to send members of the Imperial family to the principal Army commands to ensure compliance. His younger brother Prince Takamatsu was just in time to make the Atsugi airfield available for the first occupation forces on 26 August, and to keep the kamikaze boys grounded. They were boasting that they would crash the *Missouri* when she entered Tokyo Bay. If these elements had had their way, the war would have been resumed with the Allies feeling that the Japanese were hopelessly treacherous, and with a savagery on both sides that is painful to contemplate.

"When these facts and events of the Japanese surrender are known and weighed, it will become evident that the atomic bomb was the keystone of a very fragile arch." *

*From *Victory in the Pacific*, pp. 351-354.